Artifacts

Artifacts

How We Think and Write about Found Objects

Crystal B. Lake

Johns Hopkins University Press, Baltimore

© 2020 Johns Hopkins University Press
All rights reserved. Published 2020
Printed in the United States of America on acid-free paper
9 8 7 6 5 4 3 2 1

Johns Hopkins University Press
2715 North Charles Street
Baltimore, Maryland 21218-4363
www.press.jhu.edu

Library of Congress Cataloging-in-Publication Data

Names: Lake, Crystal B., author.
Title: Artifacts : how we think and write about found objects / Crystal B.
    Lake.
Description: Baltimore : Johns Hopkins University Press, 2020. | Includes
    bibliographical references and index.
Identifiers: LCCN 2019017729 | ISBN 9781421436494 (hardcover : alk.
    paper) | ISBN 1421436493 (hardcover : alk. paper) | ISBN 9781421436500
    (paperback : alk. paper) | ISBN 1421436507 (paperback : alk. paper) | ISBN
    9781421436517 (electronic) | ISBN 1421436515 (electronic)
Subjects: LCSH: Antiquities—Collectors and collecting—History—18th
    century. | Archaeology—Political aspects—History—18th century. |
    Antiquarians—18th century.
Classification: LCC CC100 .L34 2020 | DDC 930.1—dc23
LC record available at https://lccn.loc.gov/2019017729

A catalog record for this book is available from the British Library.

All illustrations are courtesy of Special Collections and Rare Books, University of Missouri Libraries.

Special discounts are available for bulk purchases of this book. For more information, please contact Special Sales at specialsales@press.jhu.edu.

Johns Hopkins University Press uses environmentally friendly book materials, including recycled text paper that is composed of at least 30 percent post-consumer waste, whenever possible.

Contents

Illustrations

Acknowledgments

Although I didn't know it at the time, I began writing *Artifacts* as a doctoral student in 2003. This book would not exist without Devoney Looser and Noah Heringman, who have supported me and my work for more than fifteen years now. The best parts of this book will always be theirs.

I have taken what has felt like an unusually long time to finish writing my first book. I'm grateful for the many, many people who have indulged my antiquarian foibles while reminding me about the things that matter most. Marilyn Francus first introduced me to eighteenth-century England, and I'm thankful for the opportunities we've had ever since to find each other there again. At the University of Missouri–Columbia, Jason Arthur, Nicky Beer, Leigh Dillard, Michael Kardos, Karen Laird, Elizabeth Langemak, Catherine Pierce, Angela Rehbein, and Zak Watson—as well as Samuel Cohen, Andrew Hoberek, and *the* George Justice—inspired me to be a better thinker, reader, writer, and friend. When I was a postdoctoral fellow at the Georgia Institute of Technology, Aaron Santesso asked me a lot of important questions, and James Mulholland helped me to find the right answers.

Artifacts would not have been possible to complete without the advocacy of our faculty union at Wright State University. I've also benefited from the kindnesses of my brilliant colleagues in the Department of English Language and Literatures. I thank Barry Milligan for reading and responding to parts of my manuscript. I thank Lars Söderlund for the Latour Summer Seminar and so much more. I'm also grateful to Deb Crusan, Christopher DeWeese, Erin Flanagan, Hope Jennings, Lynette Jones, Carol Mejia LaPerle, Annette Oxindine, Alpana Sharma, and Kelli Zaytoun for letting me think along with them over the years.

In the wilds of Ohio, David Brewer, Sandra Macpherson, Roxann Wheeler, and Greg Anderson generously read parts of my manuscript and helped me to see better ways forward. In the field at large, I've learned a lot from conversations with Rebecca Barr, Andrew Burkett, Timothy Campbell, Al Coppola, Helen Deutsch, Joe Drury, Michael Gavin, Eric Gidal, Anne Greenfield, Collin Jennings, Steve Karian, Heather Keenleyside, Jess Keiser, Jonathan Kramnick, Jayne Lewis, Jack Lynch, Tina Lupton, Ruth Mack, Robert Markley, Adam Potkay, Matthew Reeve, Courtney Weiss Smith, Rivka Swenson,

Helen Thompson, Mark Vareschi, Roger Whitson, and Claude Willan, and more. Joseph Roach encouraged me when I needed it most.

While writing this book, I have been consistently dazzled by the work of Brad Pasanek and Sean Silver. I'm more indebted than I can say to both of them for the time and care that they've given to me and my work. Chloe Wigston Smith read the entire manuscript of *Artifacts*, and everyone should be so lucky to have her as a reader. I'm thankful that Catherine Goldstead and Johns Hopkins University Press were willing to dig in the dirt with me—and that David Goehring's copyediting has prevented me from making a complete mess out of things.

Research for *Artifacts* has been supported by fellowships from the Lewis Walpole Library, the Yale Center for British Art, and Chawton House. I'm grateful to their archivists and curators—as well as to those in the Pforzheimer Collection at the New York Public Library, the Huntington Library, the Newberry Library, the British Library, the British Museum, and the Society of Antiquaries of London—for helping me to dig things up. Earlier versions of this book have been previously published. Part of chapter 2 appeared as "Ten Thousand Gimcracks: Artifacts and Materialism's Political History at Don Saltero's" in *Word & Image* in 2017 (vol. 33, no. 3: 267–278), and part of chapter 4 appeared as "Bloody Records: Manuscripts and Politics in The Castle of Otranto" in *Modern Philology* in 2013 (vol. 11, no. 4: 489–512).

As I was writing about old and broken things, Benjamin Kahan put me back together when I fell apart, Michele Wilson taught me how to tell new stories, and Sarah Tindal Kareem rambled right along with me. My parents, too, have been there through all of it. To Mom and Frank: thank you, for everything. To Soren and Marcela: thank you for believing me *almost* every time that I said something was invented in the eighteenth century. To Adrian: there's more of you in this book than you will ever know. If I have sometimes seemed like I was lost in the past, please know that you—more than anyone else—have inspired me to hold on to the things that shouldn't be lost or forgotten and to speculate about all of the amazing things that are still to come.

Lastly, to Dr. Strombeck: I could not have written this book without you. We have figured it all out, together, and in every way.

Things Speaking for Themselves

In the brittle winter of 1649—a few weeks before the execution of Charles I —John Aubrey glimpsed a series of large stones on the horizon as he galloped along on a hunt. Squinting at the stones through the frosty fog, Aubrey fancied that they marked a mythical battlefield where, once upon a time, giants might have hurled huge rocks in a war "against the gods" (*Monumenta* 1.18). After the hounds led the hunting party straight into the stones' midst, Aubrey dismounted and told the others to go on without him. Few before Aubrey had paid much attention to those stones, but they would preoccupy him for the rest of his life. The site that captured Aubrey's imagination on that cold January day in 1649 is now called Avebury and is known to be the largest prehistoric stone circle still extant in Britain.

Aubrey was one of the first people to see Avebury for what it really was: not a myth and not a natural phenomenon but an ancient stone henge that was worth studying as well as preserving. Despite Aubrey's realizations, most of the stones at Avebury had disappeared by the nineteenth century. The locals had long been cracking and hauling the big rocks away for building projects in the nearby villages even before Aubrey got there, and in the seventeenth century iconoclasts saw the stones as convenient fodder for the symbolic destruction of pre-Christian monuments. Today, Aubrey's drawings and descriptions of Avebury remain as records of the stone henge as it was once.

Aubrey visited Avebury repeatedly throughout his lifetime, and he discussed the site with his colleagues in the Royal Society after it was founded in 1660. Charles II heard about Aubrey's interest in the site and, having hidden in Stonehenge to escape the Battle of Worcester, Charles wanted to see this other stone henge for himself. In 1663, Aubrey personally guided Charles II through "Aubury," as it was then propitiously named. Aubrey politely declined the king's suggestion that he should dig under the stones to look for human remains, but he did agree to write a treatise about England's mysterious henges. The result, Aubrey's *Monumenta Britannica* (c.1665–1693), is now commonly credited as the first work of archaeology.[1]

Aubrey's *Monumenta* was not the first work to be written about England's mysterious stone henges, but it was the first to make the case for dating their construction to pre-Roman Britain, based on painstaking and comparative fieldwork. Previously, Inigo Jones had published his own ideas about England's henges; Aubrey's *Monumenta* showed that Jones's claims were primarily speculations.[2] Jones had focused his research on Stonehenge, and in his own treatise, Jones provided images of the henge to prove his case that it was a temple that had been built in the relatively recent past by the Britons' Roman colonizers. Jones's illustrations rendered Stonehenge as a perfect, proportional hexagon: proof positive that it had been designed by Romans. After he saw Avebury, Aubrey trekked to Stonehenge himself on multiple occasions with Jones's images in hand. As he walked around the stones, Aubrey tried and failed—and tried and failed again—to make the stones he saw right in front of him fit into Jones's Vitruvian geometry. In the end, Aubrey rejected not only Jones's findings but also his methods. Others before Aubrey had suspected that the stone henges were older than Jones thought, but it was the way Aubrey studied the henges that became especially important. Aubrey declared that Jones had not "dealt fairly" with the "thing itself"; instead, Jones had "framed the monument to his own hypothesis" (*Monumenta* 1.19–20). By sketching drawings in person and on-site over the course of repeated visits to both Stonehenge and Avebury, Aubrey had also drawn more accurate conclusions.

Aubrey described his new and improved method for studying the past in strikingly simple terms: old objects should be allowed to "speak" or "give evidence for themselves" (*Monumenta* 1.32). For Aubrey, it was necessary to let objects like stone henges reveal their own histories because they were "so exceeding old, that no books do reach them" (*Monumenta* 1.25–26). Since no texts existed describing the original designs, purposes, or construction for the henges, Aubrey admitted that he was "groping in the dark" when he speculated that the Druids must have built them (*Monumenta* 1.25). Aubrey was convinced, however, that he was right about how old the henges were, because he had "writ" his history of them "upon the spot, from the monuments themselves" (*Monumenta* 1.26). Aubrey would tinker with the passages defending his method of studying the stones, but his phrasing remained much the same. In the "deluge" of written "Historie," the "memorie of these British Monuments" had "utterly perished" (*Monumenta* 1.32). The historical method that Aubrey briefly sketched out in his *Monumenta*—a deference to the curious way that old objects have of speaking or giving evidence for themselves when examined up close and in person—informed his life's work, which included investigating not only England's mysterious henges but also historical objects of all kinds.

Although today's scholars often cast Aubrey in the role of the first archaeologist in order to emphasize the fieldwork he incorporated into his historical research, Aubrey's contemporaries would have described him as an antiquary.[3] Aubrey's declaration that things like stone henges could and should be allowed to "speak" or "give evidence for themselves" distilled the essence of antiquarianism: a method for studying the past that premised claims about history on the evidence offered by primary sources and physical remains. Antiquaries like Aubrey, however, were frequently castigated by their contemporaries for the zeal with which they pursued the discovery, preservation, and study of old stuff. In a now-classic essay first published in 1950, Arnold Momigliano aimed to redress the long-standing reputation of antiquaries as "muddle-headed" enthusiasts for any and every object that seemed like it might be left over from the past (297). Momigliano argued that the "whole modern method of historical research" was "founded on the distinction" that antiquaries first made between primary and secondary sources (286).[4] Antiquaries like Aubrey, in other words, fundamentally shaped the discipline of history by establishing the analysis of archival and material sources as one of its cornerstones.

Following Momigliano's lead, scholars have continued to reevaluate the research conducted by early antiquaries. Rosemary Sweet, for example, argues that early antiquaries "should not be regarded as the eighteenth-century equivalent of stamp collectors or devotees of Civil War re-enactments" (xiv). Rather, they should be recognized for the important parts they played in "that explosion of print and ideas, that thirst for knowledge and understanding which some have called the British Enlightenment" (xiv). Noah Heringman similarly finds that early antiquaries collaborated with their contemporaries in making new discoveries and developing new methodologies that "supported an unprecedented range of new and emerging disciplines" from the seventeenth until the mid-nineteenth centuries; importantly, as Heringman shows, antiquaries worked on subjects that today intrigue not only humanists but also scientists (2). Likewise, art historians have recovered the effects that antiquarianism had on aesthetics, artistic techniques, and collecting practices, while literary historians have assessed its influence on the ways that poets, novelists, and nonfiction writers represented the past.[5]

These recent accounts affirm that early antiquaries helped to establish the interest that researchers working in a variety of disciplines now take in material cultures. Revisionist histories of antiquarianism have, however, focused on recovering the characters of individual antiquaries, the rigors of antiquarianism as a methodology, and the ideological implications of its rise in popularity at the expense of consigning most of the objects that early antiquaries discovered back to the dust.[6] We have remembered the big ruins tourists flocked to see, the sentimental tokens that people kept close to their hearts, and the one-of-a-kind items that collectors cherished or museums enshrined.[7] We have also rediscovered the commodities and fashions that were prized in a nation of shopkeepers.[8] But we've forgotten about most of the old, dirty, rusty, moldy, and broken items—the small bits and bobs whose origins or backstories were unknown and whose worth or meaning was not self-evident—that once called out to so many people.

The most common but now least considered of the objects that antiquarianism popularized were the objects that people could hold—or imagine holding—in their hands: old coins, manuscripts, weapons, and grave goods.[9] These four types of objects serve as the basis for the case studies that follow in this book, because beginning in the seventeenth century they seemed suddenly to be everywhere, just waiting to be discovered and given a chance to "speak" or "give evidence" for themselves. They could be found buried not only under stone henges, as Charles II suspected when he toured Avebury with Aubrey, but also in city ditches and country gardens. They could be discovered moldering in between the walls of abbeys and castles or gathering dust in its cottage cellars and manor attics. Lots of coins, manuscripts, weapons, and grave goods turned out to have been hiding in plain sight all along because they had previously been stuffed into *Wunderkammern* (cabinets of curiosities) and official repositories.

I designate many of the old objects that began piling up in the seventeenth century as artifacts instead of antiquities for several reasons, one of which is to emphasize the sheer quantity of small, nameless historical things that people once discovered, displayed, described, and debated with unprecedented fervor. I also use the term "artifacts" as a way of keeping in the foreground the influence that antiquaries have had on the modern disciplines of historical study that prioritize research on material cultures. Additionally, I borrow the term from the second of two polemical treatises on the nature of matter that were published together as a set in 1644 in order to underscore these objects' materiality. Sir Kenelm Digby's *Two Treatises [on] the Nature [of] Bodies [and] Mans Soule* marked the first time that "artefactes" appeared in print for an English readership. Written while the English Civil Wars raged, Digby's treatises offered his readers what we might today recognize as "a theory of things"—one that also conveniently justified a sovereign's absolutist power.[10] Digby was a natural philosopher as well as a courtier; his alchemical experiments were as well known to his readers as his loyalties to the Stuart kings. Digby used the word "artefactes" to group together under one term the "works and arts of men": all the things that people created and controlled according to their will (411). As Digby explained, a sovereign's power was conceptually akin to the power that people had over their "artefactes." A monarch created and controlled "an army," a "commonwealth," and "a good life" in the same way that an individual created and controlled their "house" or their "garden," according to Digby (411). Many of his contemporaries, however, saw things differently, maintaining that polities as well as objects were more inherently unruly and freer to act according to wills of their own than Digby allowed.[11]

Although Digby's "artefactes"—a house, a garden, an army, a commonwealth, and a good life—are not antiquities, the context in which he grouped these items together under one term draws our attention back to the materiality of the old objects that piled up in the "long eighteenth century" and the competing ideologies that their materiality sustained.[12] The execution of Charles I in 1649 and the exhumation of his body in 1813 loosely bookend this study, because it became imperative for old objects to start speaking and giving evidence for themselves in the midst of the seventeenth-century crises of state. Wary that philosophers, scientists, and historians could be as biased as politicians, people turned to objects in the hopes that they would yield immutable facts and thereby resolve the deep ideological conflicts that had erupted in English culture.[13] Antiquaries maintained that antiquities could convey unbiased information about the past and, especially, about the history of the English government. By testifying for themselves, antiquities seemed like they were capable of resolving the conflicts over the nature and history of England's government that people themselves could not resolve.

The word "artifacts," therefore, retains a connection between the coins, manuscripts, weapons, and grave goods that antiquaries prized and the political urgency that characterized the first blush of antiquarian activity in the seventeenth century. Throughout the long eighteenth century, an artifact could vindicate or undercut a range of political claims, from those that asserted a sovereign's divine right to those that pleaded for radical democracy, because it could also corroborate competing theories of matter. Artifacts, in other words, confounded as much as they confirmed when it came to the histories as well as the ideologies they were called upon to produce. In academic discourses today, the word "artifacts" primarily conjures either the fragments that archaeologists discover and reassemble—that is, the primary sources that historians locate and interpret—or the items that curators find and evaluate. Contemporary archaeologists, historians, and curators alike speak authoritatively for the artifacts that failed to speak for themselves in the ways that Aubrey once believed they could.[14] Outside of the contexts in which archaeologists, historians, and curators work, the word "artifact" often serves as a catchall synonym for "object," usually designating an individual object as either an entirely unknown entity or as a representative specimen of a larger category of similar things. The history of artifacts suggests, however, that the old things that experts speak for should not always be described as artifacts—and not everything is an artifact.

Collectively, the writers who depicted old coins, manuscripts, weapons, and grave goods in a variety of genres throughout the long eighteenth century allow us to refine our definition of the artifact as follows. An artifact is a fragment, but one that remains sufficiently intact to support reconstructions of the object's full shape and history; however, although reasonable interpretations of the object's meaning or significance appear to be achievable based on those reconstructions, never enough of an artifact persists for either the reconstructions or the resulting interpretations of the object to be conclusive.[15] An intact object can be described as an artifact if it appears to be a piece of something that was previously whole or part of a sequence that was previously closed. However, objects—whether broken or intact—that can be readily restored to their original shapes or histories are not artifacts; neither should we describe as artifacts those objects that can be readily disassociated from their original shapes or histories. In order for an object to be an artifact, that which is missing from the object must exceed the perceptual capabilities of its immediate observers while that which persists must continue to be available for observation. Interpretations of artifacts, therefore, always require a degree of speculation about the artifact's earlier states and its various networks of relationships; those speculations will also be grounded, but supported only imperfectly, by the object itself.

In other words, although an artifact is a fragment, enough of the object remains for the artifact to appear as if it is capable of speaking and giving evidence for itself, but not enough of the object remains for it to do so definitively. We should reserve the term artifact, therefore, for naming those objects that either have a troubling tendency to keep changing their story or to stop talking at the very moments when we need them to say more. Artifacts should be understood as conglomerate objects composed of both solids as well as empty spaces that exist in a state of flux. They disintegrate and parts go missing that we imagine could be found or reconstructed. Artifacts' dynamic materiality allows them to be plotted simultaneously in various temporal moments. When we encounter an artifact in the present, we are aware of its previous existence and the prospect of its continued endurance. Imagine a graph that charts objects as they physically change over time. The horizontal axis of this imagined chart represents the object's physical body. The terminus on the left marks the point at which the object exists as a complete object; the terminus on the right marks the point at which the object has vanished. The vertical axis represents the object as it exists in time, extending downward to the object's point of origin and upward toward its future. An artifact lurks in the middle of the chart, caught in the medias res of change.[16]

Artifacts' material and temporal plasticity enabled them to enter into a variety of networks, and from their position in the middle of the chart artifacts could slip into other categories of objects that were popular throughout the long eighteenth century, including wonders, curiosities, souvenirs, and antiquities. For example, wonders were remarkable for their singularity; standing "at the limit" of "objective order," wonders constituted "a distinct ontological category," as Lorraine Daston and Katherine Park explain (13–14).[17] Stuffed with items like "coral, automata, unicorn horns, South American feather-work, coconut shell goblets, fossils, *antique coins*, turned ivory, monsters animal and human, Turkish weaponry, and polyhedral crystals," the *Wunderkammer* exemplified sheer physical heterogeneity (266, emphasis added). Wonders are almost off the artifact-plotting chart, hovering near the far-left terminus that marks an object's completeness. From such a position, wonders resist attempts to move them along the chart's temporal axis. As a distinct ontological category, wonders are transcendent.

Daston and Park's list of the contents that filled a typical *Wunderkammer* shows that artifacts like "antique coins" could join wonders' ranks. As wonders, antiquities—even fragmented ones—would have been appreciated for their materiality. Unlike wonders, however, artifacts' states of fragmentation register their status as objects that change over time. Artifacts have a propensity, as a result, to edge closer to the vertical (temporal) axis on the chart, where their similarities to other, more familiar, objects become more apparent. Accordingly, artifacts could also provoke a very different kind of response than wonders did throughout the period. Daston and Park argue that the wonders left their spectators "dumbstruck" as they gazed at the *Wun-*

derkammer's collection of so many "exceptional," "anomalous," and "bizarre" objects (273). Wonders, in other words, were associated with the experience of wonder: a "spectrum of emotional tones or valences, including fear, reverence, pleasure, approbation, and bewilderment" (Daston and Park 16). In contrast, artifacts engaged individuals in acts of reasoned, discursive speculation about the object's provenance and its history as well as its relevance for the present.

Many of the objects in a *Wunderkammer* were also labeled "curiosities," and artifacts were implicated in the distinctions that emerged between wonders and curiosities throughout the long eighteenth century, accordingly. When applied to wonders, the label "curiosity" acknowledged either a wondrous object's "meticulous workmanship" or its "lack of function," Daston and Park explain (273). "Curiosity" could also designate an object that "excite[d] a desire to know about the object in all its odd particularity," and in this sense, the objects in a *Wunderkammer* were not curiosities (Daston and Park 274). Eager to exploit wonders' stupefying effects, powerful individuals as well as institutions maintained a vested interest in sublimating those objects that sparked a "desire to know" throughout the medieval and early modern periods (Daston and Park 331). Daston and Park find that partly as a consequence of the "political, religious, and aesthetic abuses" of wonders, curiosities superseded wonders as objects of intrigue during the Enlightenment (331). According to Barbara Benedict, curiosities were soon, however, mobilized in the service of disciplining "subjective identity" in the modern state (*Curiosity* 248). Between 1660 and 1820, a thriving marketplace of commodities as well as texts transformed curious objects into "mediated representations" (*Curiosity* 245). These mediated representations of curiosities inculcated a "habit" of "sequestering objects from social use, revaluing them, and reordering them in the collector's private space" (*Curiosity* 248).[18] "Mental accumulations" of curiosities, Benedict finds, allowed individuals to indulge and control their "desire to know" and thereby construct differences between the self and other, especially with regard to the categories of gender and class (*Curiosity* 248).

Like curiosities, artifacts "excite[d] a desire to know" during the long eighteenth century, but they also retained the material heft that had previously landed them spots on the shelves of *Wunderkammern*. Because artifacts could be more fragmented and familiar than wonders, they were more likely to prompt individuals to ponder the purposes artifacts could serve in different time periods. Yet although artifacts could be unmoored from wonders' material and temporal transcendence, a part or parts of the artifact still persisted as concrete substance. As a result, artifacts were not as easily rendered into "mediated representations" and "sequestered" into "mental accumulations" as curiosities were; neither were artifacts as readily assimilated into the ideological services of modernity. Interpretations of artifacts turned primarily to old-fashioned political contexts in search of explanatory paradigms for establishing the object's significance, and artifacts were infrequently personalized throughout the long eighteenth century.

While wonders held steady as solid objects on the left-hand side of our imagined artifact-plotting chart, and curiosities disintegrated into the ideological constructs of modernity on the right-hand side, souvenirs emerged to join curiosities as objects that also dissolved into imagined, immaterial entities. Susan Stewart has famously expounded on souvenirs as tokens of private intimacies that were subsumed by personal narratives. Her account of the souvenir takes its cue from Horace Walpole, who first introduced "souvenirs" into English in 1775. Writing to Lady Ossory in November of that year, Walpole added a postscript in which he acknowledged a note he had just received from Lady Ossory thanking him for a cup he had given her from his own collection as a token of their friendship. Lady Ossory need not have thanked him for the gift, Walpole said. "[I]f my *souvenirs* were marked with cups," he continued, "there would be many more than milestones from hence to Ampthill" (*Correspondence* 32.278). Walpole here uses "souvenir" as a synonym for memory, and the cup itself functions metonymically for the many old memories that he and Lady Ossory share—as many memories as there are miles that separate them.[19]

The slippage between object, memory, and distance in Walpole's postscript leads Stewart to conclude that the owner of a souvenir ultimately jettisons the object's "materiality" in order to produce its "meaning" (140). The narrative that the souvenir supports is relevant "only to the possessor of the object," and the object, like the cup Walpole gave to Lady Ossory, becomes entirely incidental to the "narrative of interiority" that the souvenir "miniaturize[s]" (Stewart 135–136). As mediated representations and mental accumulations through which the modern state constructed as well as disciplined subjective identities, curiosities could swing between the categories of the transcendent and the timely relative to the chart's temporal axis. Stewart suggests that by offering individuals opportunities to ground some of the objects in their mental collections in times and spaces that were relative as well as relevant to the souvenir's possessor, souvenirs assuaged the cognitive dissonance that Benedict recognizes curiosities' oscillations often produced.[20] Souvenirs, then, joined curiosities on the right-hand side of the chart, where the objects' meanings became detached from the objects themselves. When the matter that persisted in an artifact was especially fragile or when vacancies in an artifact's fragmented body were substantial enough for narratives that negated the object's matter altogether to develop, an artifact could be nudged into the territories of the chart occupied by curiosities as well as souvenirs. That which distinguished artifacts from curiosities, however, also frequently distinguished artifacts from souvenirs; although artifacts were fragments, the matter that remained proved difficult to disregard.

The recalcitrant nature of artifacts' materiality also helps us to identify the relationships between artifacts and antiquities. Antiquities functioned similarly to curiosities and, especially, souvenirs in the period—but they continued to be appreciated for the physicality that made them appropriate objects for display in *Wunderkammern*. Like both curiosities and souvenirs, antiquities' materiality was translated into meaning; like souvenirs, specifically, antiquities manifested a desire to establish a definitive time and space for the object. Unlike curiosities and souvenirs, however, antiquities' meanings were grounded in the objects' materiality which, in turn, also meant that antiquities' meanings were isolated in specific places and times that appeared to be objectively, rather than subjectively, determined. As Leon Rosenstein explains in his *Antiques: The History of an Idea*, an antique is an "object of rarity and beauty that, by means of its associated provenance and its agedness as recognized by means of its style and material endurance, has the capacity to generate and preserve for us the image of a world now past" (14).

Rosenstein's emphasis on the antique's "rarity," "beauty," and "endurance" helps us to place antiquities on the left-hand side of the chart near wonders. However, the importance Rosenstein also places on the antique's "provenance" and "agedness" indicates how antiquities could diverge from wonders once they were plotted, much as souvenirs were, at specific points along the chart's temporal axis. Throughout the long eighteenth century, "antiquity"— not antique—was the noun used most frequently to refer to the kind of object that Rosenstein describes, but the definitions of "antiquity," "antique" (as an adjective), and "to antiquate" all suggest that antiquities were classified primarily based on the identification of their "provenance" and "agedness." In Samuel Johnson's *Dictionary* (1755), an "antiquity" was a "remain of ancient times; an ancient rarity"; "antique" was an adjective describing something "ancient; old; not modern"; to "antiquate" something was to "put [it] out of use" or to "make [it] obsolete" (1.146). Such usages indicate that antiquities were objects that yielded certainties about their temporal geneses and that could therefore be assessed in terms of what they revealed about either their individual makers or the particular historical moments and cultures in which the objects originated. However, just as that which persisted in the artifact could thwart the object's dissolution into a curiosity or a souvenir, that which was missing from the artifact could halt its ability to coalesce into an antiquity.

Although artifacts could veer into the conceptual territory occupied by wonders, curiosities, souvenirs, and antiquities throughout the long eighteenth century, I do not mean to suggest that artifacts should be classified solely based on how they are perceived or represented. The artifact's material qualities partly determine the degrees to which it can be apprehended as a complete or fragile object and the timelines for which it can be considered to be relevant. In this regard, the definition of the artifact that I have proposed reflects Bruno Latour's influential assertion that nonhuman objects have agency. Latour points out that our everyday grammar acknowledges objects as "things that do things": "kettles 'boil' water, knives 'cut' meat, baskets 'hold' provisions, hammers 'hit' nails on the head, rails 'keep' kids from falling, locks 'close' rooms against uninvited visitors, soap 'takes' the dirt away, schedules 'list' class sessions, prize tags 'help' people calculating, and so on" (*Reassembling* 71). Objects, Latour insists, are not entities that we construct out of thin air or control by the sheer force of our will, but this does not mean that we should say objects do things for us or without us. Rather, Latour simply asks us to recognize that objects have the ability to instigate, redirect, and impede what we do.

I began this study of artifacts with Latour's imperative to "follow the actors" —all the actors—in mind, hopeful that artifacts could be caught in the act of doing things. The methodology that Latour outlines in *Reassembling the Social* seemed like the right one for studying artifacts, not least because early antiquaries appear to have shared Latour's conviction that objects have agency when they asserted that old objects could speak or give evidence for themselves.[21] Latour reports that it isn't easy, however, to follow the actors. A researcher using actor-network-theory (ANT) must "trudg[e] like an ant" through a morass of data and testimony provided by a variety of actors, human and nonhuman alike, in order to find "even the tiniest connection" between objects, events, systems, and ideas (*Reassembling* 25). That researcher has to work "agonizingly slow[ly]" (*Reassembling* 25) and has to accept being "constantly interrupted, interfered with, disrupted, and dislocated" (*Reassembling* 25). And that researcher has to become accustomed to "costly and painful translations" while trying to discover what objects-as-actors have actually done.

Early in antiquarianism's history, Francis Bacon described antiquarianism as a research method that similarly required "an exact and scrupulous diligence" so that "observations" could be derived "*out of* monuments, names, words, proverbs, traditions, private records and evidences, fragments of stories, [and] passages of books" (Book II, sec. 2:3, 90). In order to derive observations "*out of*" old and disparate objects, antiquaries undertook their research in the manner that Latour encourages actor-network-theorists to undertake theirs. Antiquaries began with the premise that artifacts could communicate matters of fact that no living person could know for themselves. They trekked to sites; they laboriously gathered and documented their materials; they collated their sources and compared their findings—all in order to arrive at the truth-in-objects. Antiquaries regularly reported on the ways that such research was arduous, slow going, and collaborative.

What I discovered by following the actors was that artifacts did do things in the long eighteenth century, but they rarely did what they were supposed to do: act as the agents of facts. As reports about new discoveries and interpretations of artifacts issued forth from Grub Street, many of the old objects that were discovered turned out to be unreliable narrators. When readers dug deeper into the texts that reported what a coin, manuscript, weapon, or grave good had supposedly said or evinced for itself, they almost always came up with some dirt—something that revealed that the object had not really spoken for itself; rather, it had been spoken for. Nevertheless, I find that the facility many of those old objects had for producing competing narratives about the past and thereby supporting competing political agendas was a consequence of their materiality, which is what made them artifacts.

I develop these claims by beginning with a chapter that revisits the contexts in which Aubrey attested that the stones at Avebury could speak for themselves and that he could hear what it was that they had said. I show that artifacts were first called upon in the seventeenth century to give evidence primarily about the history of kings, parliaments, and people as well as about the philosophical principles regarding matter and causality that might help to settle the nature of England's government; after the Glorious Revolution of 1688, artifacts continued to testify about those same controversial topics.[22] In particular, coins, manuscripts, weapons, and grave goods preserved old conflicts over both political history and philosophy. Consequently, I suggest that throughout the long eighteenth century, artifacts were "vibrant"—a term

borrowed from Jane Bennett, whose work has extended the findings of Latour into the field now commonly described as the new materialisms—but
not in the ways we might expect.[23] Artifacts' vibrancy did not inhere in their
ability to convey matters of fact and thereby to authorize specific political
histories or related theories of matter. Rather, artifacts' vibrancy inhered in
their propensity to occasion ongoing disputes over how to interpret what it
was, exactly, that they revealed about the past and the nature of government.

The next chapter follows the "gimcracks" that made their way from Don
Saltero's coffeehouse into the period's popular periodicals in order to more
closely examine artifacts' actions and affordances in the long eighteenth century. Don Saltero's was one of England's most famed public museums. Tourists flocked to see for themselves the artifacts that were everywhere on display
as well as to catch a sighting of the famous literati who were Saltero's regular
customers. Descriptions of the coffeehouse's collection appeared regularly in
the press. These show that Don Saltero's artifacts were encountered as lively
actors insofar as deep suspicions emerged about the authenticity of the artifacts' competing performances of political histories and philosophies at the
coffeehouse—what Joseph Roach describes as a "city of the dead." Writers
like Joseph Addison, I argue, recognized that the artifacts' suspicious performances also revealed their affordances. Projects like *The Spectator* (1711–1712)
took up artifacts as objects worth representing and adapted the artifact as a
model for the genre and materiality of periodical texts themselves. Texts that
were modeled after artifacts proved to be especially adept at keeping their
readers engaged by encouraging them to suspect, critique, and supplement
what they read.

The chapter on Don Saltero's gimcracks establishes a template for succeed-
ing chapters, each of which follows one kind of popularly collected artifact
in the long eighteenth century, beginning with coins and then moving on to
manuscripts, weapons, and grave goods. Each chapter opens by recovering
the artifacts' popular histories, including the historical, political, and philosophical disputes that the artifacts were called upon to settle. Each chapter
then proceeds to assess how writers represented the artifacts in question and
how the artifacts can be seen to have shaped the form as well as the function of literary texts. The chapters are arranged in a relatively chronological
order. Coins attracted a lot of attention early in the period; the grave goods
of monarchs attracted it later. Artifacts, however, notably resist order. They
hop-skip, dally, or return repeatedly to the same spot in time; they dredge
up historical minutiae and philosophical impasses; they coalesce and dis-

integrate. Artifacts' resistance to order, however, brings to light aspects of eighteenth-century English culture that might otherwise go overlooked. For example, artifacts show that the seventeenth century's crises over sovereignty remained unresolved for far longer than we generally assume. Likewise, artifacts challenge our sense of the Enlightenment's commitments to the hallmarks of modernity. Finally, artifacts register recursive, contradictory shifts in themes, tastes, genres, and styles in the period's literary history.

The chapter on coins begins with the history of numismatics. Coins and medals (the two terms were often used interchangeably) were the first artifacts to be popularly collected in the period. Late in the seventeenth century, John Evelyn declared coins to be the most "vocal" artifacts. He felt that they were more permanent than other kinds of artifacts and less likely to be fakes; he also felt that they could directly commune with their collectors' memories, minds, and hearts: face-to-face, as it were. Many, however, started to suspect that coins had been vested with too much power. Coins could mint icons out of villains. They could depict falsehoods as monumental truths— and the falsehoods they impressed could be all the more convincing because coins and medals seemed able to speak so intimately to their interlocutors. In the same way that periodical writers transformed their doubts about Saltero's artifacts into opportunities to imagine how their own texts could benefit from engaging with artifacts, writers like John Dryden, Joseph Addison, and Charles Johnstone also experimented with styles that were stamped by the coins that they distrusted.

I continue to explore the history of questioning artifacts' authenticity in the next chapter, on medieval manuscripts. The recovery of medieval manuscripts became especially urgent and especially suspicious during the seventeenth-century crises of state as competing factions staked their rights to govern on the legal precedents preserved by documentary evidence. By the eighteenth century, many were eager to contain manuscripts' unsettling vibrancies by relegating them to the archives, where only specialists needed to trek to squabble over historical minutiae. This chapter recounts the history of one such archive, the Cottonian Library. When a fire in the library in 1731 singed copies of the Magna Carta, a flurry of preservationist work raised the suspicions that characterized seventeenth-century manuscript recovery efforts once again. I proceed to reconsider Horace Walpole's *The Castle of Otranto* (1764) as a response to those suspicions. *The Castle of Otranto* shows how writers like Walpole could present their fictions as found manuscripts in order to encourage their readers to call into question the political motives of historical claims that purported to be based on the authority of primary sources.

Like coins and manuscripts, weapons kept the political conflicts of the recent past close to the surface in the long eighteenth century, but they also show how artifacts could lead their interpreters into a longer *durée*. Reverberating with Thomas Hobbes's famous claim that the state of nature is a state of war, old weapons incited debates about the relationships among government, human nature, and technological determinisms. This chapter follows the period's tourists into the armories of the Tower of London, where hundreds of thousands of weapons could be seen hanging on the walls and from the ceilings, arranged into sculptural installations, and set on top of effigies of England's monarchs. I focus on two individuals, Ned Ward and Samuel Molyneux, who reported feeling discomfited by such a spectacle. I also consider how Jonathan Swift and Tobias Smollett, two writers who were familiar with the Tower's armories, represented weapons in their texts and imagined their own texts as weapons. Weapons inspired Swift and Smollett to reconsider their aesthetic commitments to imitation and invention and to interrogate philosophies that would vest objects—be they sharpened swords or barbed polemics—with the power to shape the public sphere.

The final chapter returns to the problem of sovereign bodies by scrutinizing four exhumations of kings' graves that occurred between 1775 and 1813. Although official accounts of the exhumations depicted the kings' bodies as dead matter, the public eagerly looked for signs that the sovereign's body was still vital. Meanwhile, Romantic revolutionaries embraced vitalism as a force for democratic change, and conservatives like Edmund Burke embraced vitalism as a force for continuity and tradition. I find that the exhumations inspired a change of heart for Percy Bysshe Shelley and George Gordon, Lord Byron, two poets who had previously celebrated vitalism as a force for democracy. With the 1813 exhumation of Charles I in mind, Shelley and Byron struggled with how to represent a king's body. Both writers realized that if all matter was lively, then a tyrant sovereign's body was lively, too. Byron's "Windsor Poetics" (1813) exemplifies the difficulties that the exhumation of a king introduced into vitalism's politics, while Shelley's "Ozymandias" (1818) and his "Defense of Poetry" (1821) suggest that he reimagined poetic texts as artifacts that were livelier than the artifacts themselves.

Shelley's claim that poetry was livelier than the artifacts it depicted leads to an afterword that considers how the actor-network-theory that Latour outlines in his *Reassembling the Social* translates into an "artifact" network theory. An artifact network theory considers artifacts to be actors insofar as their fragmented states compel representations that swerve between facts and fictions. Although artifacts falter when called upon to act as the agents of matters of fact, they thrive at inviting people to complete them by producing a range of interpretations that attempt to explain what it is that the object really means and how, specifically, it communicates its meaning. That an artifact's material remnants might be as notable as its immaterial vacancies, and that it might be situated in multiple temporalities, help to explain why attempts to reconstruct artifacts' shape and establish the origins and the trajectories of their influence in order to settle their meanings came to be as enticing as they were controversial. Artifacts, in short, were objects whose states of fragmentation allowed them to enter into the categories of fact and art but also prevented them from settling into either category for good. As such, artifacts thrived in textual networks where they could be discursively interpreted and debated, but they eventually receded from the networks where objects were valued as either obstinate things or constructed entities.[24]

The realization that artifacts' materiality spurred the production of texts also leads me to identify commonalities in the texts that surfaced around artifacts. These texts consistently tended to do several things. They encoded networks of referential allusions that made it difficult to classify them as either fiction or nonfiction. They demonstrated a commitment to mimesis, imitation, or unity while they also questioned the viability of such commitments. They presented themselves as the unwilled effect of objects that appeared to be prior or external to the texts themselves. They exhibited affective ruptures over the text's failure to fully depict what it aimed to represent. And they shared an interest in historical, political, and philosophical topics. These are the elements, I conclude, of an artifactual form. The writings that developed around artifacts throughout the long eighteenth century drew attention to the artifact as an incomplete, imperfect object. Writers also, however, seized on the opportunities that artifacts provided for interjecting their own texts into the networks that the artifacts themselves traversed. Artifacts enticed people to turn their observations about what remained in the objects into speculations about what was missing; the authors who wrote about artifacts engaged their readers in similar modes of fact finding and guessing. Like artifacts, however, the meanings of the texts that referred to and were inspired by artifacts engendered interpretations that could always be called into question.

Recognizing that artifacts' partial materiality produced interpretations that also seemed partial (in the other sense of the word) allows us to see more clearly why so many of the old odds and sods that piled up in the long eighteenth century eventually receded from our critical purview. Artifacts were objects that seemed capable of speaking and giving evidence for themselves, but few could agree about what they said and evinced. As the debates about what all those artifacts really said or evinced got louder and louder, the objects themselves were often drowned out; some were left to languish in history's junk drawer; others were tossed away. Many artifacts are preserved today only by the texts that attempted to interpret them. Contemporary readers who are versed in cultural histories of England in the long eighteenth century may be surprised, therefore, to discover just how much crumbly bric-a-brac was found, exhibited, and debated throughout the period. Artifacts complicate our sense of the commitments to the ancients as well as the moderns that are commonly taken as the quintessence of the Enlightenment. As the Enlightenment appeared to announce a decisive break with the past, ancient history famously emerged as a mythical point of origin for a newly "polite and commercial people," in William Blackstone's iconic phrasing (*Commentaries* 3.326).[25] The overwhelming popularity of domestic coins, manuscripts, weapons, and grave goods from the relatively recent past suggests, however, that English history continued to incite controversy.

Focusing on artifacts also recontextualizes some of the period's most canonical texts. Representations of artifacts frequently refer not only to real stuff that once circulated through popular culture but also to historical events, public figures, and controversies that were au courant. Artifacts facilitated reflections about the relationships between what was timely and what had already passed. Many of the allusions that artifacts helped writers to make are so specific that they have hitherto escaped critical notice, and attending to them often clarifies a work's particular ideological investments. Additionally, artifacts frequently reveal the presence of nonfictional elements in fictional texts and the fictional qualities of works that have previously been classified as nonfiction. The antiquaries who first prioritized the study of artifacts did so before science, philosophy, history, and literature became isolated into specialized disciplines of study. The history of artifacts, therefore, illustrates both necessity and the benefits of using interdisciplinary methods and resources in our contemporary research and thinking about objects.

In this way, artifacts reintroduce literary history and the methods of literary study into not only historical studies of material culture but also theoretical writing on objects. Following the precedent set by Latour in *We Have Never Been Modern*, contemporary writers who theorize the nature of objects often announce their departure from the intellectual traditions commonly associated with the long eighteenth century: in particular, the privileging of mind over matter taken to epitomize Enlightenment philosophy.[26] Recent work in eighteenth-century studies has shown that writers in the period were less invested in this dualism than Latour suggests.[27] The history of artifacts confirms the findings of those recent scholars. Not only were artifacts things that were understood to be capable of doing things, even when subsumed into the Enlightenment's mechanisms; they also preserved vestiges of pre-Enlightenment materialisms for an ostensibly Enlightened present.[28] The philosophical and political claims that individuals premised on the hard evidence supposedly offered by artifacts were repeatedly undermined throughout the long eighteenth century by the objects themselves. Artifacts' states of fragmentation meant that they could authorize as well as contradict vitalists' and the mechanists' theories of matter—and the political investments such theories of matter also belied.[29] Individuals, whether they maintained that artifacts were things that could do things or they were not, could appear oblivious to their own fallibilities as the interpreters of nonhuman objects. At worst, they could be accused of having conveniently touted or denied artifacts' agencies in an attempt to conceal their own personal biases and polemical agendas.

Although the history of artifacts suggests that long-standing political or philosophical problems cannot be resolved by listening to what artifacts say or evince for themselves, that history does confirm that artifacts are things that do things. In the end, I agree with Aubrey that artifacts can, in their way, speak and give evidence for themselves, but we must recognize that artifacts never tell us the whole story. The history of artifacts is therefore not only a literary history but also a history of suspicion and critique. Writers who engage with artifacts lead us to believe that there's something about what they have written that, if we could only discover it—by, for example, tracing allusions back to their sources, determining the author's motives, reconstructing contexts, or discovering for ourselves the very objects the work represents—then we would be able to say what the text means and why it matters. Artifacts' power, therefore, inheres in their ability to get people to try to complete their stories for them—and to keep us digging for more.

PART ONE

TERMS AND CONTEXTS

CHAPTER ONE

Leaving Room to Guess

John Aubrey articulated the crux of antiquarianism when he declared that old objects, such as the stones at Avebury, could "speak" or "give evidence for themselves." Today, antiquarianism is a musty term. If used at all, it is a carefully chosen word for summing up the pastime of collecting old stuff just because it is old. Yet, as Arnold Momigliano established in 1950, the "whole modern method of historical research" was "founded on the distinction" that antiquaries like Aubrey first made between primary sources that could speak for themselves and the secondary sources that spoke for them (286). Antiquaries would have used the word "antiquities" to classify the primary sources that they studied, but this chapter will continue to make the case that "artifacts" is the right word for describing quantities of small, broken objects that captured not only the antiquaries' but also the public's imagination in the long eighteenth century.

The Oxford English Dictionary credits Sir Kenelm Digby with coining the term "artefactes" in 1644 in his *Two Treatises [on] the Nature of Bodies [and] Mans Soule.*[1] Digby's two treatises articulate a science and philosophy of matter. Digby's definition of "artefactes" (as the "works and arts of men") serves to demarcate a fundamental difference that he believes exists between thoughts and objects (411). For Digby, "a good life," "a commonwealth," "an army," "a house," and "a garden" are "all artefactes": things that people first imagine and then create (411). Digby goes on to nest artifacts as gears in a clockwork universe where matter will always be subject to the control of something more ephemeral, like human "understanding" (411). Readers might readily see how Digby's logic applies to the houses or gardens that they design and build, but an "army," a "commonwealth," and a "good life" are markedly more difficult for casual readers to envision making on their own. Digby's listing of "artefactes" belies the political implications of his theories of matter. In the same way that a house or a garden are the "works and arts of men," an army and a commonwealth are the "works and arts" of a sovereign. "A good life" constitutes the whole and, in Digby's schema, is governed by the spirit of God.

Digby's philosophy of matter was also, therefore, a philosophy of government, and Digby was well known for his loyalty to both Charles I and Charles II. His philosophy was famously, however, more inconstant than his political allegiances.[2] Although Digby subjected matter to the government of the understanding, a sovereign, and God, he also concluded that spirit itself was best conceptualized as a kind of substance. Moreover, Digby maintained that matter moved by itself and often in unpredictable ways. "[E]xceedingly little bodies" floated everywhere, he explained. Even our memories were tiny particles that we absorbed from external objects, some of which we had seen or touched ourselves and some of which we had never seen or touched at all. In Digby's writings, spirit proved to be so material and matter proved to be so spirited that it is hard to go back and say what those "artefactes" were really made of, who made them, and who controlled them—or if they could even be controlled at all.

For antiquaries like Aubrey, letting coins, manuscripts, weapons, and grave goods speak or give evidence for themselves entailed resisting polemical theories of matter. Artifacts were not—or should not be understood as—objects "made or modified by human workmanship." Although antiquaries were eager to distance themselves from the political motives that philosophies like Digby's belied, they were not always successful at doing so. This chapter situates the artifacts that antiquaries prized at the nexus of the competing scientific, philosophical, and political ideas that circulated in seventeenth-century England. The satires that were written about antiquaries, I suggest, reveal both the antiquaries' investments in a range of discourses as well as the political stakes of their object-oriented research. I also make the case that Aubrey's *Miscellanies* (1696), a text often sidelined as a whimsical study of occult phenomena, was a more thoughtful engagement with the political implications of antiquarianism than we have previously realized.

The satires and Aubrey's work lead me to consider more carefully the relationships between debates about matter and debates about the nature of government that occurred throughout the long eighteenth century. Whether encountered as mechanistic or vitalistic matter, artifacts were "vibrant," in Jane Bennett's phrasing, but they were not vibrant in the way that they were supposed to be: as agents of facts. They were vibrant because their states of fragmentation afforded competing interpretations of their significance. I conclude by considering artifacts in relation to Carlo Ginzburg's clues and Rita Felski's work on the hermeneutics of suspicion. Artifacts, this chapter shows, were called upon but failed to settle political or philosophical conflicts. The fragmented bits and bobs that antiquaries studied not only registered these political and philosophical conflicts; they also continued to preserve those conflicts in a state of contentious stasis throughout the long eighteenth century.

Political Bric-a-Brac

Momigliano explains that antiquarianism crystallized as a method for studying the past in the seventeenth century when "political and religious disputations" reached a fever pitch in Europe. These disputations meant that "[b]ias was easily scented everywhere," including in the work of historians. Although Momigliano focuses on the culture of distrust that swept across Europe, England too was caught up in "political and religious disputations" of its own. The execution of Charles I in 1649 marked the rapid coordination of revolutions that were political, secular, scientific, and literary: a quickening of a new historical consciousness in which the past was brought to bear on the present. In the previous century, the dissolution of the monasteries had infused the British antiquities market with an unprecedented number of historical objects, while it left just as many to languish as the detritus of an old-world order, awaiting rediscovery. Antiquaries in England joined their European counterparts in attempting to solve the problem of perceived bias by bypassing secondary sources and going straight to "statements by eyewitnesses, or documents, and other material remains" of the past (Momigliano 286).

Momigliano finds that historians came to accept the antiquaries' key idea: that original sources were more reliable than secondhand sources. By 1950, therefore, Momigliano considered antiquarianism to have been subsumed by the professional historians who consulted original sources, including material remains, as a matter of course. Momigliano downplays the complaints leveled at antiquaries throughout the seventeenth and eighteenth centuries. He admits that some of the antiquaries' contemporaries thought that their resistance to consulting secondary sources, including especially "literary" texts, bordered on the "pathological" (302). Relatedly, he notes that on occasion, some early antiquaries developed "many fantastic theories" by interpreting the material evidence they gathered and considered as if it were in a vacuum (306). Momigliano brushes aside most of these complaints, though. The facts that could be gleaned from eyewitness statements, archival papers, and especially material remains did not yield conventional accounts of the past because they were not supposed to. Instead of using the sources they gathered to explain the past or arranging their evidence into chronological narratives of history, antiquaries preferred simply to present what they had found, letting it speak for itself.

Momigliano suggests that what few challenges the antiquaries faced merely resulted from their attempts to reform how the past was studied. However, the satires that have dogged antiquarianism since it was first presented as a new method for history suggest otherwise. The static of the seventeenth century's "religious and political disputations" continued to crackle in this satirical tradition for more than two centuries; as a response to polemic, antiquarianism was, of course, also polemical. We can see in the satires that the problem was not just that antiquaries contravened historiographical conventions. The problem was also their artifacts, which endured as the disquieting remnants of political controversies.

In 1628, John Earle offered one of the first and most damning character sketches of a stereotypical antiquary in his *Micro-Cosmographie*. An antiquary, as Earle defines him, has an "unnaturall disease" that means he "loves all things" that are "mouldy and worme-eaten" (36). "[B]eggars coozen" the antiquary by charging extravagant prices for these "musty things which they have rak't from dunghills" (36). An antiquary is a fetishist. He prizes those things that have been raked out from dunghills as if they were "precious Reliques," and he brings so many of those "rotten and stinking" things home that even his own "Maw" thinks of him as an "enemy" (36). According to Earle, an antiquary has more portraits of Caesar than his own monarchs, Queen Elizabeth or King James I, combined. These old pictures hang, "decorated with the Antique work of cob-webs," in his library, which is also stuffed with "more Spider volumes than Authors." The antiquary relishes thumbing through his "Moth-eaten" pages, and he looks with reverence on his "Roman coins," the "rust of old monuments," broken statues, and his collection of "bones extraordinary" (36–38). He does not fear old age or death because he looks forward to his body dissolving until it becomes one with the same stuff of the past that he idealizes.

Earle's sketch quickly settled into a satirical refrain.[3] Samuel Butler described an antiquary as "an old frippery-Philosopher, that has so strange a natural Affection to worm-eaten Speculation that it is apparent he has a Worm in his Skull" (76). In Thomas Shadwell's oft-staged *The Virtuoso* (1676), Nicholas Gimcrack putters about as "the most speculative Gentleman in the whole World," giving a "Tongue" to "inanimate" things and "break[ing] his brains about the nature of Magots [*sic*]" (8–9). In Ned Ward's the *London Spy* (1703), an antiquary "has as many *Maggots* in his *Noddle* as there are *Mice* in an old *Barn*" (9). He amasses his objects with the "same abundance of Whims" that characterize his scientific research as a member of the Royal Society. Out of his "Trinkets," the antiquary conjures "Ridiculous Romances" (10). He shows off his stock of items to unsuspecting customers in a coffeehouse, including "the Tooth-picker of *Epicurus*," a "Nail drawn out of the *Ark*" that when placed in water, will "Swim like a Feather," and "one of *Judas's* Thirty-Pence" (9–10). Every time the antiquary sees Judas's thirty-pence, he is "ready to hang himself" (10). In 1729 Alexander Pope named the antiquary Thomas Hearne "Wormius" in *The Dunciad* (1729). Pope considers Hearne to be a dunce, of course: a myopic, eccentric pedant who worms his way through dusty detritus, "preserv[ing] the dullness of the past" (Pope 5.189–190).

In 1751, George II granted the Society of Antiquaries in London a royal charter, but the satires hardly abated. Samuel Foote said that he wrote his popular *Taste* (1752) specifically in order to mock those "*Goths* in Science, who had prostituted the useful Study of Antiquity to trifling superficial Purposes" (ix). Foote was still irate twenty years later when he thought about the antiquaries' "unpardonable frauds" (ix). Act III of *The Nabob* (1772) begins at a meeting of the Society of Antiquaries. Its members catalogue their recent acquisitions: "the toe of the slipper of Cardinal Pandulpho, with which he kick'd the breech of King John at Swinstead Abbey," a "pair of nut-crackers presented by Henry the Eighth to Anna Bullen [*sic*] on the eve of their nuptials," the "cape of Queen Elizabeth's riding-hood," a "cork-screw presented by Sir John Falstaff to Harry the Fifth, with a tobacco-stopper of sir Walter Raleigh's made of the stern of the ship in which he first compassed the globe," "a curious collection of all the tickets of Islington Turnpike," and a "wooden medal of Shakespeare made from the mulberry tree he planted himself" (42–43). Horace Walpole did not always agree with Foote, but *The Nabob* reportedly inspired him to resign his membership from the Society. Sitting among his own unparalleled collection of antiquities at Strawberry Hill, Walpole declared that the members of the Society were a bunch of "boobies" (*Correspondence* 1.384), universally ridiculed as the "midwives of superannuated miscarriages" (*Correspondence* 2.250).

By the end of the eighteenth century, the antiquaries acknowledged with good if sour humor their long-standing reputations as the butts of common jokes. The antiquary Francis Grose penned a satire in 1792 from the perspective of a beleaguered wife married to a newly inaugurated member of the "Society of Anti-queer-ones" (*Olio* 48). Her husband had once enjoyed the "rational pursuit" of looking for "wheat-ears" or "gathering mushrooms" during their summer travels (*Olio* 48). Now, though, he scans the landscape for "large bumps of earth, or ragged stones set up on end"; he even "talks of digging them up" to look for bones (*Olio* 48). He has replaced the tasteful decor of their home with a crowded, haphazard arrangement of "absurd nick-nacks [*sic*]": "broken pans, brazen lamps, copper chizzels, bell metal, milk-pots, and a parcel of outlandish halfpence, eat up with canker," as well as "strange books," some "as big as a table, full of prints of tombs" and "men in armor" (*Olio* 48–49). Peeping out from all the clutter, his wife worries that their home has become a mausoleum. She confesses that if her husband's "mind does not take a speedy turn, to more agreeable objects," she will leave him because she cannot continue to "live like an undertaker's wife, surrounded by every thing that can remind one of mortality" (*Olio* 49). By the time Sir Walter Scott published *The Antiquary* in 1816, its titular character—Jonathan Oldbuck—was a confirmed type.

Certain patterns can be detected in these satires. Although the satires ridicule antiquaries for their eagerness to collect seemingly any and every old thing, the antiquities that they itemize remain fairly consistent for almost two centuries. Coins, manuscripts, weapons, and grave goods constitute a critical mass in the satirical lists of antiquaries' bric-a-brac. The satires were accurate in this regard. For example, the index compiled in 1809 for the first fifteen issues of *Archaeologia,* the Society of Antiquaries' official journal, features five pages of entries for "coins and medals," and another five pages of entries for "arms and armour"—far more than the average entry of only several lines. Manuscripts and the contents of kings' tombs are a little more difficult to quantify, but the index consistently belies the Society's interest in "letters," "papers," "charters," "treaties," "warrants," and "writs," while it features substantial entries grouped under the various kings of England (not to mention entries for objects like "bones" and "coffins") that point toward the study of royal funerary practices and burial sites (*Index to the First Fifteen Volumes of Archaeologia*).

With their refrain of the rust, mold, and dust that covered such objects, these satires also foreground the close relationships that existed between antiquaries and the natural historians who would later come to be known as scientists. Both dug in the dirt together, hoping to make new discoveries. The Society of Antiquaries would be founded as a sister organization to the Royal Society later in the eighteenth century, and many individuals were members of both.[4] Additionally, the vermin that crawl over the antiquaries' putrefying objects evoke the philosophical questions that the "new science" raised throughout the long eighteenth century. The coins, manuscripts, weapons, and grave goods in the hands of antiquaries were metal, paper, and bones in the hands of the period's scientists and its philosophers. Whereas scientists subjected the materials that intrigued artifacts to experimentation, philosophers used them to consider the relationships between body and spirit as well as between objects and the mind. There is, for example, the cultural preeminence of paper or parchment as a metaphor for mind. Coins likewise figured both the malleability of an impressionable mind as well as the durability of a strong, moral character. Weapons summoned speculations about intentionality and the state of nature while, along with grave goods, they inevitably raised questions about the nature of the mortal, decaying body and the everlasting soul.[5]

As Butler jabbed in his satire, an antiquary was an "old frippery Philosopher." The satirists all agree that the antiquaries were infected by the kinds of artifacts that they studied. Their brains were as broken as their things. "Worm[s]" crawled from the objects into the antiquaries' "skulls," and so an antiquary was "the most speculative Gentleman in the whole World." The artifacts caused a certain kind of madness that, in turn, produced wild interpretations of the objects—rank fictions about what they were and what they meant. Antiquaries were easily "coozened"; they imagined that "inanimate things" had tongues; they had an "affection to [*sic*] worm-eaten Speculation"; they collected an "abundance of Whims" and things that really had "no being but in Fancy"; out of their "trinkets," they conjured "ridiculous romances." The satires are at their most vicious when they pivot from lists of artifacts to attacks on the antiquaries' states of mind and the irrational conclusions produced by their object-oriented studies.

A logical hiccup happens here. If the antiquaries were madmen who only collected junk out of which they conjured "ridiculous romances," then what was the big deal? A closer look at Aubrey's antiquarian activities shows that a great deal was at stake in the historical, scientific, and philosophical study of old "knickknacks." Like the antiquaries in the satires, Aubrey did not arrange the evidence things gave for themselves into the orders prescribed by the conventional genres of history. Aubrey managed to see just one of his projects through to publication during his lifetime, and that only right before he died in 1696: a work titled simply, *Miscellanies*.[6] Critics have dismissed Aubrey's *Miscellanies* as a very different kind of project from his serious, antiquarian pursuits. They should not. The *Miscellanies* is more similar to Aubrey's archaeological research than it might at first seem, and it helps explain why the satirists kept attacking antiquaries. Aubrey's *Miscellanies* reveals that as well-intentioned as antiquaries may have been, and as important as their method of letting objects speak or give evidence for themselves has turned out to be, the objects they listened to had controversial things to say.

The *Miscellanies* examines a range of hair-raising mysteries such as "lucky and unlucky" days, "omens," "apparitions," "visions in a Beryl or Crystal," "converse with Angels and Spirits," "prophecies," and "transportation by an invisible Power." Aubrey expected that these topics might raise not only the hairs on a reader's neck but also an eyebrow. The "matter" of such a "collection," he confessed, was technically "beyond human reach" (*Miscellanies* vi). Documenting matters "beyond human reach" entailed consulting a variety of matter. The *Miscellanies* draws on print and manuscript sources as well as Aubrey's own experiences in order to establish records of supernatural events. These sources all zero in on objects that appear to act on their own. As they did in his more orthodox antiquarian research, the objects in Aubrey's *Miscellanies* give evidence of events that cannot be perfectly authenticated or explained by the eyewitness testimony of a single individual.

Aubrey does not interpret the phenomena he records. He briefly suggests that the objects he studies gesture to the existence of an "Invisible World, which knows what we do, or incline to," but he does not draw larger conclusions about the nature of this "Invisible World." In the dedication to the *Miscellanies*, Aubrey simply and preemptively concluded that we remain "miserably in the dark" when it comes to understanding how or why objects appear to act on their own. Aubrey's resistance to explaining the phenomena he observed led many of his readers to dismiss the *Miscellanies* as the stuff of old-fashioned superstition. A closer look at the objects in the *Miscellanies* suggests that there was something else about the things themselves that was just as disturbing as the interest Aubrey seemed to take in the supernatural. For Aubrey, objects not only whispered about an "Invisible World" that was "beyond human reach"; they also whispered about the secret histories of the state.

The very first topic addressed by *Miscellanies*, "day-fatalities," illustrates how Aubrey's objects produced spooky political histories. "Day fatalities," according to Aubrey, are unusually unlucky days on which "remarkable accidents" in history seem always to happen. Such a historical arrangement of days marks the *Miscellanies* as an experiment in historiography. Day fatalities do not fit easily into eschatological or chronological orders, but Aubrey still seems to sense that there is a logic at work in the events that he records. November third—Aubrey's own birthday—was especially and unfortunately fatal. Several famous men died on that date. In 1099, a catastrophic flood occurred. Another such flood occurred in 1645, one that wiped out Aubrey's personal fortune. On the third of November in 1640, Parliament would convene on the eve of the Civil War, making it a day "direfully fatal to England, in its peace, its wealth, its religion, its gentry, its nobility; nay, its King." Cromwell's victories at Dunbar and Worcester both occurred on the third of November; so too, however, did Cromwell's death (*Miscellanies* 11).

Aubrey's section on "day-fatalities" starts with his own private history of accidents, moves forward and backward in time, but then settles into a record of the remarkable historical events bearing down on the state in Aubrey's own lifetime. Throughout the *Miscellanies*, the political crises of the seventeenth century—those "disputations" in Momigliano's tepid phrasing—haunt Aubrey. Although Aubrey personally witnessed many of the events he records in the *Miscellanies* or had direct reports from his correspondents about what had happened, the objects that knocked about during the tumultuous years between the Civil War and the Glorious Revolution seem to have seen and known more than he did. By the time readers get to the *Miscellanies'* section on "omens," the objects seem to have seen and known more than anyone. Aubrey records, for example, how a "drop of blood" from a "strange bird" spoiled Gianlorenzo Bernini's bust of King Charles I early in his reign. No amount of scrubbing could get the blood spot out (*Miscellanies* 38). Likewise, at Nottingham, "King Charles I did set up his standard upon the top of the tower there," but "the first night, the wind blew it so, that it hung down almost horizontal" (*Miscellanies* 38). Similarly, on the day the "Long Parliament began" in 1641, "the Sceptre fell out of the figure of King Charles in wood" at an estate in Dorset. Finally, at Charles's trial "the head" of his "staff did fall off" (*Miscellanies* 39).

Charles I's reign isn't the only one omened by objects that topple at untimely moments. Right before Charles II's death, the "iron crowns of the white tower" snagged two birds to their death (*Miscellanies* 41). At James II's coronation, which Aubrey himself attended, the Peers "almost kissed" the crown right "off [James's] head," and it "totter'd extreamly [*sic*]" as James made his way to Westminster. Meanwhile, a "puff of wind" almost blew away the canopy of gold cloth that was carried over James II, a gust whisked the flag bearing James II's arms into the Thames, and the fleur-de-lis on the top of his scepter fell off (*Miscellanies* 41–42). In 1688, the "Iron Crown upon the council house" in Salisbury collapsed (*Miscellanies* 42). When James II arrived in Ireland to try to reclaim his crown the following year, the gentleman carrying his mace "stumbled without any rub in his way," and one of the "little crowns upon the crown" of the mace got "stuck fast between two stones in the street" (*Miscellanies* 46).

While the seventeenth-century state fractures, the objects that litter Aubrey's *Miscellanies* also tarnish, tremble, and break. The objects simultaneously register and respond to historical events. Sometimes, they appear to presage those events, and in so doing, they also appear to play some part, however mysterious, in causing those events to occur. By resisting the narrative orders of eschatology or chronology that characterized conventional histories, Aubrey likewise resisted ready-made polemical readings of objects' actions. The objects in the *Miscellanies* do not take sides in the seventeenth century's revolutions. Charles I's fate seems writ in stone, blood, and wood, yet still somehow provoked by hasty, hubristic standard bearing. Cromwell's death occurs on the same day of the month as some of his most important victories. Charles II is restored under a sky both auspicious and ominous. The coronation of James II trips into a slapstick of accidents: as unsteady in concluding the reign of the Stuarts as it is in commencing the Glorious Revolution.[7]

Many of the sources to which Aubrey refers in the *Miscellanies* were those supplied by his fellow antiquaries. There's only one coin in *Miscellanies*—an "Antique Coin" first seen in a dream locked away in a glass desk but found years later in London in waking life—but there are plenty of weapons and manuscripts. They all portend political "trouble" (*Miscellanies* 51). For example, Aubrey includes the story of Edward Seymour, who was walking with his wife in his picture gallery when both of them saw "a Hand with a bloody Sword come out of the Wall"; Seymour was beheaded shortly thereafter (*Miscellanies* 60). Aubrey also describes how "in the time of the Civil Wars" one Lancelot Morehouse "rescued a sheet of Parchment in Quarto, delicately Writ, from a Taylor's Sheers" (*Miscellanies* 94). The parchment "was a Prophecy concerning England in Latin Hexameters" (*Miscellanies* 94). Aubrey himself saw it in 1649 and attested that it "pointed at our late Troubles" (*Miscellanies* 94). By the time of the *Miscellanies* publication, it was lost "among other good papers" (*Miscellanies* 94). Although Aubrey would not dig under stone henges for the bones of the deceased, as Charles II once suggested he should, the *Miscellanies* does address the curious powers of corpses. Aubrey describes the common practice of healing tumors by laying a corpse's hand on the malignity: "'Tis certain, the Touch of a dead Hand, hath wrought Wonderful Effects" (*Miscellanies* 91). By far, however, the most controversial aspect of the *Miscellanies* was the persistent interest Aubrey took in examples of the living being haunted by the dead, who bumped into things, seeking redress for betrayals.

Later editions of the *Miscellanies* included excerpts from the materials Aubrey had prepared for his antiquarian history of Surrey. These materials suggest that Aubrey realized that the objects knocking about in the *Miscellanies* would one day be the antiquities that antiquarians would study. When historical events receded so far into the past as to be unremembered in the present by any individual, objects alone would remain as witnesses to what had once happened. Because antiquities outlived us, they were—like the occult phenomena that Aubrey describes in the *Miscellanies*—"beyond human reach." In Aubrey's description of antiquarian research, we catch a glimpse of the superstitious flair that purportedly made the *Miscellanies'* Enlightened readers so suspicious. Aubrey defined antiquities using Francis Bacon's phrasing: "Antiquities" were *"tanquam Tabulata Naufragii"*—like the detritus from a shipwreck—scattered on the shores of history. Aubrey reports that he searched for those old treasures in the shipwreck of time as if under a spell: "[T]he retrieving of these forgotten Things from Oblivion in some sort resembles that of a Conjurer, who make those walk and appear that have lain in their Graves many Hundreds of Years" (*Miscellanies* [1714], 24). Antiquaries dug like necromancers through time's wrecked ghost ship in order to gossip with the dead, but the objects also worked a magic of their own. They disappeared and reemerged at will; they captivated some individuals, but not others. Antiquities, as Bacon once said, had mysteriously "escap'd the Teeth of Time" to live through the "Revolution of so many years" (*Miscellanies* [1714], 23).[8]

However, like the objects that knocked around in Aubrey's *Miscellanies*, antiquities stoked suspicions because of the earthly histories they invoked, too. Aubrey indicated as much when he updated Bacon's language for defining an antiquity. Aubrey agreed that antiquities had "escap'd the Teeth of Time" as well as the "Revolution of so many years," but he added two more critical details: antiquities had also survived "the Revolution" of "Governments" and the "Hands of mistaken Zeal" (*Miscellanies* [1714], 38). Aubrey remembered the objects that had witnessed the ceremonial pomp of the Stuarts, the solemn rites of the Interregnum, and the oaths of the Glorious Revolution. He also remembered the iconoclasms, the suspected forgeries, and the symbolic totems of regime change: how revolutions acted not only through but also on objects. The encounters that antiquities brokered between the cosmic and the local, the dead and the living, the past and the present aroused what Aubrey described as a "kind of oestrum" that he experienced when in the presence of old things: that sense of being "incite[d]" "into an activity" with real "vehemen[ce], passion, or frenzy (*Miscellanies* [1714], 24)."[9] This was a feeling provoked by the dizzying glimpses of gods and ghosts that objects afforded. Antiquities, however, also plainly attested to mere mortals' capacity for vehemence, passion, and frenzy. They raised not only the gauzy specters of an "Invisible World" but also the bloody specters of the worldly state.

What's Really the Matter with Artifacts?

As Ernst Kantorowicz explained in his now-classic study, *The King's Two Bodies: A Study in Medieval Political Theology* (1957), medieval political philosophy endowed the king with two bodies: a body natural and a body politic. Although the king's natural body suffered and died like all human bodies, the body politic of the monarchy persisted as a transcendent spiritual entity vested with the divine right to rule.[10] Throughout the Middle Ages, objects conveyed this "political theology." Coins, for example, featured the faces of individual monarchs on their obverse and symbols of their virtues and rights to rule on their reverse. Manuscripts depicted kings as doubled-figures, at once human and Christ-like. The weapons wielded by kings were not personal possessions, but rather implements of the state. Even when the king's natural body had died and been buried, his body politic persisted as a "fiction of endless continuity" (Kantorowicz 291).

As long as antiquaries dug up old coins, manuscripts, weapons, and grave goods, they were inevitably going to dig up controversy. It was not just that the king's two bodies symbolically inhered in these four types of artifacts. These were the artifacts through which revolutions wrenched the king's two bodies asunder. Antiquarian activity throughout the period suggests that the extent of the monarch's, parliament's, and people's rights were both established and contested through these four types of objects more than any other. Each artifact might verify a sovereign's absolute right to rule. Each might also call into question the existence of such a right.

Coins, for example, were commonly given as tokens of the "royal touch," thus serving as evidence of the king's divinely ordained ability to cure diseases and, by extension, a king's inherently benevolent relationship to his subjects. Coins could also, however, be exposed as counterfeit propaganda, or they could exemplify the perils of idolatry and the vanity of tyrannical despots. Coins could validate a monarch's authority to establish and guarantee the most basic aspects of a social system. Or they could epitomize the virtues of social systems left to run on their own, without the intervention of an individual head of the state. Ordered chronologically, coins could authenticate hereditary lines of succession. Coins could also, however, show that succession had been disrupted, either rightly or wrongly. The other three types of artifacts were similarly vexed and vexing. Medieval manuscripts were used to establish the exclusive rights that England's old sovereigns enjoyed. But they were also used to assert the rights of Parliament and the people to check those powers. Like coins, manuscripts could also be fakes and exposed as propaganda. Meanwhile, weapons were implicated in arguments over the states of nature. They could illustrate the necessity of subjecting to the power of an absolutist sovereign; or they could speak to the righteousness of resisting such arbitrary power. Finally, the bones of kings could perform wonders as secular relics, or they could putrefy and dissolve into dust like all mortal bodies.

The very matter of these artifacts—not just their shapes or their symbolic and historical functions—entangled them in the political melees of the seventeenth century. John Rogers's *The Matter of Revolution* documents how disputes over England's government in the seventeenth century were conducted by way of scientific and philosophical investigations into the nature of matter.[11] Rogers describes the years between 1649 and 1652 as an acute "Vitalist Moment" during which a wide range of writers and thinkers wondered whether matter was imbued with the "power of reason and self-motion" (1). The notion that matter might move on its own or think for itself was controversial, and not just because it brimmed with the unorthodox implication that God could be extracted from the equation of the universe's logic. Debates about whether matter acted with free will were also debates about a sovereign's power, a parliament's prerogatives, and the rights of people. Theories about matter were theories about government.

Rogers finds that two competing theories of matter emerged in the seventeenth century that corresponded to two competing theories of government. On one side were the vitalists, who believed either that body and spirit were "inseperabl[e]" or that all matter was capable of moving and, perhaps, even thinking for itself (Rogers 1). The vitalists' theory that matter could move or think for itself was "charged with the momentum of revolutionary fervor," according to Rogers. Vitalism, in other words, established a "theoretical justification for the more collective mode of political agency and the more inclusive vision of political organization that were among the unquestionable products of the English Revolution" (Rogers 14). The mechanists opposed the vitalists. Mechanists "were more likely to embrace a vision of matter internally devoid of soul, cast about by external or immaterial spirits and overseen by a providential God" (Rogers 12). Mechanism tendered a "determinist" model of "agency and organization" (Rogers 5) that conveniently "offered scientific proof for the necessity and inevitability of a political process of conquest and domination" (Rogers 8). Mechanists, in other words, doubted that matter could move or think for itself. This meant that mechanists were usually royalists who sympathized with Charles I.[12] When Charles II was restored to the throne in 1660, he became a patron of the mechanists, who gathered under the auspices of the Royal Society.

Rogers concludes that the royalists' mechanism would go on to win the day, dominating both the science and the political philosophy of eighteenth-century England. The Glorious Revolution in 1688 heralded that a compromise had been reached not only among kings, parliaments, and the people but also between the vitalists and the mechanists. Isaac Newton's idea of a mechanical cosmos designed and put into motion by a deity vindicated hierarchical organizations of earthly governments. John Locke's idea of reason as a governing principle of morality promised to keep the mechanism in working order.[13] On the one hand, then, the terms of the Glorious Revolution accommodated mechanists' vision of matter by affirming that a sovereign deity had delegated control to a sovereign who existed as a veritable neutron in the atom of the nation-state. On the other hand, the terms of the Glorious Revolution accommodated the vitalists by implicitly acknowledging that the machine of government could break and that reasoning individuals were entitled to return the state to order and to enjoy the liberty it ensured. Newton's science and Locke's liberalism were therefore the means by which the problem of the king's two bodies was finally put to rest.[14]

Such, at least, is the standard story we often tell about the beginning of the long eighteenth century and the English Enlightenment.[15] Yet the compromises of 1688 did not avert future violent clashes in or over England's government.[16] The specters of power-hungry tyrants and bloodthirsty revolutionaries alike continued to darken the doorways of the salons and coffeehouses, where a newly polite and commercial public gathered to talk and shop in the 1700s. Coins, manuscripts, weapons, and grave goods kept England's recent history of regicide, republicanism, restoration, and tenuous compromise close to the surface while they also dredged up its gothic, medieval, and prehistoric pasts. More generally, these artifacts exposed the ways in which the political allegiances, between the royalists and the mechanists on one side and the revolutionaries and vitalists on the other, were neither so dogmatic nor so quickly resolved as they appeared to be.

William Somner's reflections in 1640 on his study of the antiquities of Canterbury illustrate how artifacts exposed instabilities in the links between theories of matter and the political doctrines that those theories were used to authorize. For Somner, studying objects from the past led him to ponder, as it did for Aubrey, the categories of the living and the dead. Somner begins his *Antiquities of Canterbury* (1640) with a discourse on immortality. "[S]ome ancient Philosophers," he writes, have suggested "that all men, for the most part, have a naturall desire to [*sic*] Immortality" (*Antiquities* i). According to Somner, immortality has primarily been understood as genealogy since the time of the ancients and under the sway of their "divers [*sic*] good Arguments" (*Antiquities* i). As he explains it, the dead "in some sort may be thought yet alive" if their "Progeny is living" (*Antiquities* i). Somner here invokes what would become the vitalists' and the mechanists' favorite enigma: Is there something immaterial that somehow lives beyond matter or not? And if so, is it—or is it not—responsible for the actions that matter takes?

Somner sided with the royalists. After the regicide, he published an elegy for Charles I in which he briefly illustrates the links between his political allegiances and his philosophical convictions. In *The Insecuritie of Princes* (1648/1649), Somner imagines that kings are fixed, massy entities in a divinely ordered cosmos that tilts inexorably toward divinely ordained ends. He contrasts this vision with the republicans' "sensual, Epicurean" theory of matter (*Insecuritie* 5). According to Somner, the republicans pursued the body of the state and the head of the king in the same way that they consumed other objects right in front of them: with a shortsighted gusto for the taste and touch of things. He depicts Cromwell's men guzzling bowls of wine, stuffing "their bellies," and luxuriating in "beds of down" (*Insecuritie* 5). Somner rejects their politics and their fervor for physicality when he concludes his elegy by taking comfort in a future state of "true hearts-ease" that only God can deliver after the regicide. Somner's "hearts-ease" is produced by something immaterial, "Such as no eye hath seen, ear heard, nor can / Conceived be by heart of mortall man" (*Insecuritie* 6). Somner trusts that such a spirit will right the course of political history.

Somner also recognizes that the republicans had adopted for themselves a term that the royalists had previously used to characterize how matter functioned: "NECESSITIE" (*Insecuritie* 4). For the royalists, "necessity" described a world that was ordered and controlled: a world in which the actions that matter could take—and the effects it could produce—were constrained by either a divine force or the laws of nature. The republicans, however, used "necessity" to describe the actions that matter might take of its own accord and the effects that, they claimed, would inevitably ensue. Somner snorted: "Necessity? O Heaven's! curs'd be that need" (*Insecuritie* 4). Noting that the revolutionaries' political and philosophical dissent resulted in a murderous regicide, Somner quips that their "bad beginnings to worse ends are ty'd [*sic*]" (*Insecuritie* 3). If the republicans would describe their theory of matter using the royalists' mechanistic idea of "necessity," then so be it. Somner shows that while the royalists used mechanism to position the king as an absolute authority in a wind-up universe, the revolutionaries used it to justify revolution as an inevitability. The turn Somner takes toward an immaterial spirit likewise suggests that the royalists had appropriated the revolutionaries' vitalism, using it to imagine the king's body as a unique entity and one thereby entitled to rule with absolute authority.

As Somner indicates, vitalists and mechanists not only argued with one another; they also argued among themselves. Vitalists disagreed about whether matter's capacity for self-movement or thought was a tangible property of matter itself or evidence that something more ineffable and immaterial, like spirit, directed matter's motions. They likewise debated if such a spirit might exist within matter, might somehow be produced by matter's internal operations or superadded to matter by an entity outside of matter itself. Meanwhile, the mechanists disagreed about how matter's courses of motion were established: Did an external force set matter into a predetermined sequence of motion only once and once upon a time, or did it intervene constantly to control how matter behaved? Some mechanists imagined that this external force was a deity; others maintained that it was simply nature.

When it came to understanding the matter of antiquities eight years before the execution of Charles I, Somner's faith in an immaterial spirit that controlled matter's actions over time wavered. He appears to have been less convinced that a spirit or deity could be perfectly conceived of as something that existed outside of matter itself and counted upon to constrain matter's actions. Somner's faith wavered because he could not align his belief in an immaterial spirit that set objects into motion or constantly directed their movements with his way of imagining antiquities as material objects that conveyed history into the present. In the presence of antiquities, Somner disagrees with the ancients, despite their "divers, good Arguments." Immortality is not best understood genealogically as the transfer of spirit from parents to their living descendants. Instead, he argues that true immortality is a quality of mind and not the biological body because it depends upon the *"Remembrance of things past*, and *Foresight of things to come"* (Somner, *Antiquities* ii). The minds of mere mortals cannot remember a past that came before their bodies; nor can our eyes see beyond the grave. For Somner, then, "things past" can only be known by past things.

He names the things from the past "memorable things" and defines them as physical objects: "undoubted Records and Monuments" (Somner, *Antiquities* ii–iii). These objects remember for us that which we cannot remember for ourselves. Specifically, they preserve *"historicall events,"* which Somner further glosses as the "series of *chances* and *alterations"* that produced "the present times and places" from "such or such a beginning" (*Antiquities* iii, emphasis added). By examining "memorable things" or "undoubted Records and Monuments," an individual *"may probably* foresee what will happen in time to come" based on what the objects remembered about what had happened before (*Antiquities* iii, emphasis added). This, Somner concludes, is the nature of "true immortality." Ready-to-hand, memorable things make the immaterial past materially present for our direct, sensory apprehension as well as our cognitive reasoning, but they are also very nearly thinking things themselves, full of memories that we do not and cannot have for ourselves.[17]

Somner's "memorable things" are poised to accommodate both mechanistic and vitalist theories of matter. On the one hand, the objects preserved a history of "alterations": changes wrought by something outside of the object itself. On the other hand, they also preserved a history of "chances": unusual, unexpected swerves in the cosmic system, perhaps even swerves produced by the objects themselves. By arguing that "memorable things" revealed the a priori causes of present effects and thus could be used to predict future events, Somner seems to imagine antiquities as mechanistic entities. But he also says that an individual "may probably" predict the future based on the study of antiquities. Such hesitancy constrains the objects' ostensibly mechanical functions. Somner's use of "may probably" also throws into relief his use of "such or such" to characterize the causal origin of the past preserved by antiquities, too. The conjunction "or" in "such *or* such," accommodates the viability of two contradictory chains of events (rather than the more definitive "such *and* such").

Somner knew that theories of matter were political not only because they belied philosophical convictions about how government should be organized in the abstract but also because they were used to establish the present organization of the English government as the necessary effect of how government had previously been organized. Somner himself, for example, justifies his research on the antiquities of Canterbury by first explaining that he was from Canterbury himself: physically proximate to his objects of study. He moves quickly, however, to point out that Canterbury was one of England's "ancientest [*sic*] cities" (*Antiquities* iii). Likewise, Somner describes Canterbury as a site where the conquering Romans had left the original Britons to "enjoy their ancient Laws, Liberties, and Form of Government, as though they had not been conquered" (*Antiquities* iii). Somner imagines antiquities as waypoints for accessing a more original because more temporally distant political history.

Both royalists and republicans vindicated their arguments for how the English government should be structured in the present by insisting that historical precedents functioned, or ought to function, causally. Either the current structures of state had been legitimately determined by earlier forms of government, or the current structures were anomalies that needed to be brought back into alignment with historical forms of government. As waypoints to the past, coins, manuscripts, weapons, and grave goods were key objects for substantiating claims about how the state had once been organized; older and then still older specimens of these artifacts were hotly sought after, accordingly. However, when embedded in moments of genesis or plotted alongside earlier and earlier formations of the state, artifacts also made manifest the need for the political histories that theories of matter inspired to reckon with chronology: to account for not only where but *when* causality occurred, and to name which causes produced which effects and in what order.[18] As a consequence of the need to impose structures of causality onto the "Historical events" that "memorable things" preserved and presaged, it becomes increasingly difficult for Somner to maintain that memorable things were "*undoubted* Records and Monuments." Instead, they only "probably" offered to the present a history of "such or such a beginning."[19]

As objects that preserved a history of chances as well as alterations, artifacts proved to be available equally to those royalists and those revolutionaries who were eager to reconstruct the origins of government and its aftereffects in the service of their present cause. The history of the Society of Antiquaries that Richard Gough prepared in 1770 hints at how competing political factions used artifacts in support of their arguments about the past and present organization of the state. According to Gough, a group of like-minded antiquaries began collaborating shortly after Henry VIII's dissolution of England's monasteries in order to rescue the manuscripts and other antiquities that were being dispersed. Despite their efforts, the antiquaries' petition to Elizabeth I for a charter and a public place to meet went nowhere. Gough never explains why Elizabeth I refused the antiquaries' petition, but he suggests that they continued to meet happily as a society that was formal in spirit if not in name—that is, until 1603, when James I ascended the throne and "thought fit to dissolve" their fledgling club. In Gough's words, James I dissolved the antiquaries' informal society because he was "alarmed for the arcana of his Government" ("Introduction" xv).

James I couldn't exactly "dissolve" a society that wasn't official, but the antiquaries decided to stop meeting together in public because, according to Gough, they "fear[ed] being prosecuted as a treasonable cabal" ("Introduction" xv). Gough needs us to read between the lines, but the implication is clear: James I believed that antiquaries' research endangered his claim to the throne as well as the terms on which he planned to rule.[20] Hearne published some of the research that these early antiquaries had compiled in an anthology titled *A Collection of Curious Discourses* (1720). A cursory look into these "curious discourses" shows that the early antiquaries overwhelmingly discoursed about the "Origin of the Laws of England" (Hearne, *Curious* iii). Gough goes on to describe the antiquaries' activities during the second half of the seventeenth century with guarded brevity, reporting simply that they continued to meet privately "through all the impediments and horrors of civil war," doing what they could to stop the "sweeping havock [*sic*]" that the iconoclasms of the crisis wreaked on England's ancient "Monuments" and "Records" ("Introduction" xxii). Gough's institutional history here is intentionally understated. Throughout the seventeenth century, research on antiquities reached new controversial heights as original sources were found and used to counter the arguments of John Cowell, Thomas Hobbes, and Robert Filmer, on the one side, and Edward Coke, Algernon Sidney, and John Locke, on the other.[21]

The satires also register the political power that artifacts wielded. Earle casts doubt on antiquaries' loyalties when he points out that they neglect to collect the portraits of their own sovereigns in favor of idolizing images of Caesar. Ward's description of the antiquary who "is ready to hang himself" every time he looks upon the "Thirty-pence" of Judas in his collection associates antiquarianism with seditious treason.[22] Hearne made an easy target for

Pope because he was well known as a Jacobite non-juror. By foregrounding images of waste, putrefaction, dust, and rust, the satires signal the artifacts' relationships to the categories of the microscopic and the chemical, thereby implicating them in the polemics of the philosophical debates about matter that were ongoing throughout the seventeenth century. With their facility for mysterious regeneration and transformation, the worms or maggots that crawl over the artifacts invoke the question of matter's capacity for autonomous action.[23] Shadwell's antiquaries give their "inanimate things" a "Tongue." Ward's antiquary has a "Tooth-picker of *Epicurus*" and a nail that floats like a feather. As Foote's antiquaries quickly demonstrate, however, it was hard to know which side the antiquaries and their artifacts were on. In *The Nabob*, the very same artifact—that "toe of the slipper of Cardinal Pandulpho, with which he kick'd the breech of King John at Swinstead Abbey"—inspires one antiquary to swoon in a reverie as he declares it to be "a most noble remain," while another antiquary scoffs that it "proves the Pontiff's insolent abuse of his power" (Foote, *Nabob* 42).

Physically fragmented and rife with gaps in what could be known about their origins or histories, artifacts could speak to vitalists as well as mechanists and supply republicans as well as royalists with historical evidence.[24] The difficulties that artifacts introduced into both political philosophy and history did not, however, discourage people from looking for or continuing to interpret artifacts. Such difficulties, in fact, appear to have heightened the appeal of artifacts.[25] Whether one concluded that matter moved according to its own will, was moved by an immaterial spirit, or was set into motion by an external entity, artifacts still appeared to function as causal agents themselves when encountered in the immediate present. Vitalist and mechanistic theories of matter alike imbued artifacts with the power to act—by granting them the ability to affect the minds and senses of the people with whom they came into contact and to relay the past, however imperfectly, into the present—even if one speculated that such power was the effect of spirit or something prior and external to the object itself. Similarly, royalists and republicans both imbued artifacts with the power to convey England's history of political conflict into the Enlightened present.[26] Returning to Aubrey's *Miscellanies*, we might ask how we should understand the matter of the artifacts that knocked about during the seventeenth-century crises of state. Were they vital or mechanical? And did they teeter and break in the service of kings or revolutionaries? What was equally intriguing and frustrating, therefore, about artifacts that could supposedly speak and give evidence for themselves was that they would talk to anyone and give evidence for almost anything.

Digging Up Suspicion and Critique

In her recent *Vibrant Matter: A Political Ecology of Things*, Jane Bennett listens, like Aubrey once did, to the call of things. *Vibrant Matter* begins with Bennett stumbling upon a "large men's black plastic work glove," a "dense mat of oak pollen," an "unblemished dead rat," a "white plastic bottle cap," and a "smooth stick of wood" stuck in a storm-drain grate outside of a coffee shop in Baltimore: a modern-day scene of shipwreck that Bacon and Aubrey might have also found intriguing (4). As Bennett stops to look at the wreck, the objects seem to "shimmer and spark" (5). What she first took for "dead stuff" transforms into "live presence" (5). Bennett describes feeling "provoked," "repelled," and "struck" by the objects that "call" out to her, although she can't "quite understand what [they are] saying" (4).

This scene introduces *Vibrant Matter's* overall argument, which is both philosophical and political. We are accustomed to the idea that we are alive whereas objects are dead, and that living is defined by our ability to feel, to think, and consciously to choose how we act. *Vibrant Matter* challenges this presumption by exploring objects' "vibrancy": the ability of all material bodies, not just those we would describe as organic or conscious, to act on their own. As Bennett explains, "*artifacts*, metals, berries, electricity, stem cells, and worms" have power (n.2, 123, emphasis added). They can not only "block the will of humans"; they can also "act as quasi agents or forces with trajectories, propensities, or tendencies of their own" (viii).

Bennett hopes that by convincing her readers to think of matter, all matter, as vibrant, she will also inspire them to engage more thoughtfully and empathetically—and therefore more sustainably—with the world around them. Although Bennett frames her project primarily as an ecological one, she remains acutely aware of "vibrant" matter's implications for a politics of equality, broadly conceived. "[A]n animal, plant, mineral, or artifact," she writes, has the power "to catalyze a public" (107). Once we recognize that, "we might then see how to devise more effective (experimental) tactics for enhancing or weakening that public" (107). In other words, Bennett believes that appreciating matter's vibrancy will lead us to discover new means for resisting abuses of political power and inspire us to more equally distribute political rights to a range of human as well as nonhuman entities.[27]

Vibrant Matter stands as a representative example of "the new material-isms."[28] There are important differences among the approaches of recent critics to the study of objects, but object-oriented ontologists, speculative realists, and thing theorists alike all share an interest in the qualities objects possess that we cannot perceive and the ways that objects act on their own, without us. Likewise, they all remain attuned to the political implications of their philosophical consideration of objects as things that humans can neither fully know nor completely control. Bruno Latour's work looms large in the new materialisms—including his characterization of the long eighteenth century as the moment when our thinking about objects started to go awry in *We Have Never Been Modern*. After Newton, after Locke, and after the Glorious Revolution, the so-called moderns privileged mind over matter, according to Latour. Arbitrary as well as unequal divisions were drawn between nature and culture, bodies and minds, things and people when the Enlightenment declared its commitments to empirical science and liberal humanism. In England's secular laboratories as well as its philosophical salons, objects became the dead, mute stuff of a clockwork universe, governed by mechanical laws discovered through orchestrated experimentation or conscious reasoning.

Artifacts, however, were never modern to begin with. Although studies of artifacts in the long eighteenth century took their cues from the then-new sciences and philosophies, artifacts dredged up the past, which included dredging up old thing theories.[29] Moreover, royalists and revolutionaries agreed that artifacts had information that no single, perceiving individual in the present could have. Both were also eager to grant artifacts the power to exert influence on the moderns' sociopolitical systems. When Bennett looks into the storm grate, she glimpses this history of artifacts. Physically fragmented, artifacts invited people in the long eighteenth century to imagine them in their more completed states, just as Bennett imagines the mate or the hand for the plastic work glove, the bottle for the bottle cap, the oaks for the pollen, the nest for the rat, the tree for the stick. Coming from another time or place, artifacts also asked people to imagine their backstories, just as Bennett wonders where the glove, pollen, rat, bottle cap, and stick came from and how they got to the storm grate. And when Bennett is moved to make philosophical and then political claims based on what she encounters in that storm grate, she is also keeping company with the long eighteenth century and its artifacts.

If we go back to stay with the artifacts for a little longer than Bennett lingers at the storm grate, we will find that difficulties arise when one aims, as the new materialists do, to make the case that objects like artifacts have the power to confirm or enact a given philosophical principle or a specific political agenda. As incomplete objects with missing backstories, artifacts could substantiate as well as controvert seemingly any philosophical or political position. At best, artifacts exposed how a deference to their agency made it possible for human subjects to disavow political or moral culpability. At worst, they exposed how a deference to their agency made it possible for individuals to disguise their own polemical motives as the will of things.

Extolling the pleasures of his antiquarian research, Aubrey mused on how the old objects that he liked to study were compelling because they "[kept] the Eye from being lost, and [left] us Room to guess" (*Miscellanies* [1714], 24). The matter that persisted in the artifact—that which could be empirically known about the object—grounded historians', scientists', and philosophers' claims. Yet artifacts were still shipwrecked in time. Some guessing was necessary in order to reconstruct what they used to look like, where they came from, and where they had been. While interpretations of an artifact could always be based on what remained of the object, they could also always be called into question based on the room that was left for guessing. Artifacts were akin, therefore, to the "clues" that famously concerned the historian Carlo Ginzburg. Ginzburg considers how the "trivial" details of a painting— like "earlobes, fingernails, shapes of fingers and toes"—became important in the nineteenth century as a means for identifying the artist of paintings that had either been mistakenly attributed to someone else or whose authorship was unknown (97). Examining these small clues, which were available for immediate and direct sensory perception, promised to reveal something bigger than the clues themselves and also distinctly different in nature from them. Clues traffic between what Ginzburg calls the "evidential paradigm" and the "conjectural paradigm." Both are Gordian knots of contradictions. The clue, a lone piece of evidence, remains an entity unto itself; the knowledge it conveys is specific; the clue is therefore always imperfectly translated into a conjecture.

Ginzburg recognizes that evidential and conjectural paradigms are related to modes of narrative, or what he characterizes as "venatic deduction" and "divination." By "venatic deduction," Ginzburg links the clue to archetypal hunters, tracing the tracks of their prey (104). The hunter first "decipher[s]" a material sign—a broken twig, for example—by recognizing it as a twig that was broken by an animal passing through rather than a twig that had simply broken or been broken in a storm (104). The hunter next "reads" the broken twig, assembling it along with other clues, such as a hoofprint in the mud, in order to recreate a historical narrative of the path traveled by the animal (104). The hunter's "venatic deduction" becomes "divination": a narrative about the future path on which the animal is likely to be found. Venatic deduction and divination are structurally similar, according to Ginzburg. "[H]istorical knowledge," like future prognostications, "is indirect, presumptive, conjectural" (106). Both move from a small, material clue to a theoretical proposition, and do so by way of narrative.

Evidential and conjectural paradigms are the moderns' versions of venatic deductions and divinations. Ginzburg argues that "two decisive historical milestones" shaped these processes: "the inventions of writing and printing" (107). The invention of writing codified venatic deductions and divinations. The invention of printing and, more specifically, the "literature of the imagination" ensured that "the conjectural paradigm enjoyed new and unexpected success" (115). By the late eighteenth century, "access to specific experiences," of the kind that might involve using the clues of tracks to stalk your prey, "was mediated by means of the printed page" (115). Individuals found their evidence in the texts that they read and proceeded to engage in the pleasures of conjecture. For Ginzburg, this was a restaging of venatic deduction and divination not least because texts made the "specific experiences" of history, which the modern reader could not have had for themselves, available as clues out of which they could deduct the past as well as divine the present and the future.

Ginzburg's formulation draws our attention to artifacts as objects enmeshed in networks, where texts circulated in print cultures that were increasingly frenetic for fictions throughout the long eighteenth century. John Leland was convinced that the invention of printing inspired people to begin hunting for artifacts. In the preface to his *Itinerary*, Leland remarks that after the invention of the printing press "[a] great many Countries then began to look with some Curiosity into their Antiquities, to explain what the first Writers had related of them, and to draw up Descriptions of each both according to their ancient and modern State" (1.v).[30] Leland understood that artifacts were not only supplements to written history but also opportunities to write and publish the as-yet-unwritten histories that artifacts alone could disclose. As Miguel Tamen might put it, artifacts were well suited to use printed texts to find a "society of friends" eager to reconstruct them and to tell their stories (4). In part, this was an inevitable consequence of the artifact's fragmentations. The room they leave for guessing invites, even requires, imaginative completion of their shapes and speculative restorations of their pasts. However, artifacts acquired not only a society of friends but also a society of enemies. When historians and politicians reached further back into "time immemorial" to identify the precedents that both settled and unsettled England's government, they pulled up artifacts that were battered and broken by crises in and over government.[31] No single individual could tell the whole story of the past or the state or be trusted to tell it without bias.

Artifacts became important objects of study because they were vested with the power to establish historical facts that could be used to justify, reform, or overthrow present political conditions. Artifacts became popular objects of study because they roused at least as many controversies as they were called upon to soothe. As evidentiary clues in conjectural paradigms, mediated and remediated through print cultures, artifacts revealed histories of intrigues, conspiracies, machinations, and treacheries that were readily suspected of being fictions. Factors specific to the booming print cultures of the long eighteenth century—such as the vigor with which politics entered the public sphere in the forms of satire, propaganda, and news, the myths about old forms of government that various factions deployed, revised, or downright invented, and the rise of realist fiction and popular, sentimental history— helped artifacts to acquire societies of both friends and enemies who were eager to debate their interpretations of the artifacts' significance in discursive, textual networks.

Artifacts have an important part to play, therefore, in the history of suspicious reading and critique.[32] With Ginzburg's work on clues and Paul Ricoeur's phrase, the "hermeneutics of suspicion," in mind, Rita Felski argues that suspicious reading distrusts what a text actually says and presumes— ominously, warily—that the "real meaning" of a text is hidden or obscured and that it can be dug out, as if it were an object. Suspicious readers "are convinced that things are not what they seem"; they look for clues to "decode and decipher" in order to produce interpretations of texts that "push beyond the obvious" and "draw out what is unseen or unsaid" (Felski 38). Felski classifies the interpretations produced by suspicious readings as critique and notes that critics who practice critique tend to adopt one of two positions relative to their suspicious textual objects of study. They either "dig down" or "stand back." A critic who digs down is "like a valiant archaeologist" who "excavates" the "rocky and resistant terrain" of a text "in order to retrieve, after arduous effort" a "repressed or otherwise obscured" meaning (Felski 53). A critic who stands back also "stands over" a text, "looking down with a puzzled or ironic gaze"; the critic "detach[es]" from the text, questioning the text's tendency to appear "natural" or neutral. A critic who stands back rejects the "excavation schema" of those who dig down, but Felski finds that such a critic does not "entirely supplant" such a schema (70). Whether digging down or standing back, a critic presumes that the text being studied is "always already guilty" of the "crime" of meaning something other than what it says.

Felski proposes that instead of reading texts suspiciously and critiquing them, we should handle literary texts as if *they* were artifacts. Felski urges us, for example, to embrace the "curatorial role of the humanities—preserving and caring for the vulnerable *artifacts* of the past" (183, emphasis added). She also encourages us to acknowledge how the "busy life of the literary *artifact* refutes our efforts to box it into a moment of origin, to lock it up in a temporal container" (160, emphasis added). Felski continues, explaining that literary works are "social *artifacts*" (176, emphasis added), which means that although they bear traces of the specific cultural and historical contexts in which they were first produced, these contexts do not fully determine their meanings. In reorienting her readers to the literary text as an artifact, Felski invokes the work of Latour, arguing that critique privileges the agency of human critics over that of their textual objects of study. Felski encourages her readers to see that "[l]iterary texts can be usefully thought of as *nonuhuman actors*": things that have the power to "modify states of affairs," "participa[te] in chains of events," and "shape outcomes and influence actions" (154).

To imagine literary texts as artifacts in this way is also to engage with the history of artifacts. The chapters that follow suggest that the hermeneutics of suspicion and the practices of critique share a literal and not just a figurative relationship to the history of artifacts. Artifacts promised that there really was something materially present outside of and before texts—an object that knew more than its interpreters and that could guarantee the terms of its interpretation. When artifacts turned out to be capable of producing competing interpretations, the artifacts were still imagined to be there, speaking and giving evidence for themselves, if only their listeners could hear what it was that the artifacts were really trying to say. And still, the listener had to guess once again. All the while, reports of artifacts' soliloquies sounded uncannily like ideologues' ventriloquisms. Much of what follows in this book, therefore, charts the anguish and frustration that many experienced when they realized that artifacts—be they material or textual—failed to act as the reliable agents of their own meanings in the long eighteenth century. But artifacts also showed writers that there were benefits to be had if they could keep their readers not only digging for artifacts but also digging into texts.

CHAPTER TWO

Ten Thousand Gimcracks

Throughout most of the eighteenth century, Don Saltero's coffeehouse stood as a rowdy one-stop shop for drinks, meals, haircuts, and dentistry. Don Saltero's was also one of London's most famous tourist attractions: a must-see "knackatory" where, reportedly, more than ten thousand artifacts were on display, including old coins, manuscripts, weapons, and grave goods.[1] Its original owner, James Salter, had been the servant of Sir Hans Sloane (who would later bequeath a trove of items that became the founding collection of the British Museum). Allegedly, Salter was bitten by the collecting bug after Sloane gave him two hundred leftovers from his own famed cabinet. Salter set these items up in a coffeehouse on Lawrence Street in 1695. He moved his booming business and growing collection to Danvers Street and then, in 1717, to its final destination on Cheyne Walk.[2] Salter died around 1728, but his daughter and her husband continued to run the coffeehouse, while people continued to donate more items to the collection. Two copycat ventures popped up to compete for Saltero's customers, but tourists still thronged to Saltero's to see the artifacts on display and to gawk at the celebrated literati who had made Saltero's their regular haunt.[3] In 1799 the entire collection was auctioned off for the pitiful sum of £50.8s, and Don Saltero's became just another seedy tavern in Chelsea. Yet even in the nineteenth century, tourists still stopped by to peer through its windows and reminisce about the coffeehouse as it had once been.[4]

In its heyday, a visit to Don Saltero's rivaled a visit to the British Museum. James Granger, the author of the *Biographical History of England* (1769)—and famous for stuffing his own books with extra stuff—followed a meeting of the Society of Antiquaries on Thursday, May 10, 1771, with a tour of the "noble collection of curiosities in the British Museum" on Friday and an outing to Don Saltero's on Saturday (Malcolm 304). The tourist William Hutton found his experience at Don Saltero's to be far superior, in fact, to his experience at the British Museum. At the British Museum, the guide refused to explain any of the objects to Hutton, shamed him into silence when he asked a simple question, and "hackneyed" him through all the rooms "with violence" (192).

Hutton, who had skipped his breakfast, trekked through the rain, and spent more than he could afford to cross a visit to the British Museum off his bucket list, "came away completely disappointed" (193). He had only been allowed to spend thirty minutes in the museum. At Don Saltero's, Hutton had been allowed to take his time looking at the collection, and he especially enjoyed the catalogue "explaining every article in the collection" that Salter provided for his customers (198).[5] "The history and the object must go together," Hutton concluded, because "[i]f one is wanting, the other is of little value" (191). Hutton felt that Don Saltero's objects and their histories went together and that, as a result, both became more valuable.

Hutton seems, however, to have been the only person in the eighteenth century to feel this way. This chapter recovers and contextualizes representations of Don Saltero's artifacts that appeared throughout the period especially in popular periodicals. I argue that these representations show that the artifacts at Don Saltero's were encountered as actants: things that, as Bruno Latour pithily puts it, "do things" (*Reassembling* 71). That Salter's visitors experienced its artifacts as actors or "actants," suggests that Latour's influential account of the Enlightenment's ostensible subjugation of objects to the will of the liberal humanist subject is in need of some revision. Descriptions of Saltero's, in other words, offer a representative example that complicates the characterization of the Enlightenment that prevails in the new materialisms; the artifacts at Saltero's were not readily purified in part because they preserved the vestiges of pre-Enlightenment materialisms.

As actants, the artifacts at Don Saltero's came to be suspected of being actors who reenacted over and over again old debates about matter and politics. Working with Joseph Roach's notion of the cities of the dead, I examine how the artifacts at Don Saltero's performed philosophies as well as histories that were contradictory, repeatedly staging a "doomed search for originals," in Roach's phrasing (3). I pay particular attention to how the artifacts at Saltero's performed competing theories of matter—and the competing ideas about sovereignty those theories belied—that were discussed in chapter 1. The relics on display in Don Saltero's coffeehouse, I show, proved especially suspicious because they became a means through which the new corpuscular science appeared to validate a doctrine of divine right. I go on to suggest that the artifacts' feats and flops of performances drew writers' attention to the artifacts' affordances. By provoking competing interpretations of history, politics, and philosophy, artifacts lead their societies of friends as well as enemies into the marketplace for texts. Popular periodicals, like *The Spectator*, recorded the controversies that surrounded the interpretations of artifacts. They also appeared to register writers' recognition that they could enhance readers' interests by incorporating aspects of the artifacts themselves into their texts.

Artifacts in the Cities of the Dead

When Don Saltero's artifacts came to mind, ideas about the nature of matter seemed to come with them. In *Some New and Accurate Observations . . . of the Coast of Guinea* (1725), for example, James Houstoun describes all the "rarities" that he has collected in his travels.[6] He intends to donate most of the haul to "*Don Saltero Curioso, at Chelsea*" when he returns to England (38). Houstoun regrets that he will not, however, be able to count his recently deceased pet chameleon as one of the gifts he will make to Don Saltero's. Houstoun explains that the loss of this specimen is especially poignant because the chameleon "afforded [him] Matter of Speculation . . . by evidently demonstrating to [him] the Sympathy between the Soul and the Body" (38). Body and soul, or matter and spirit, seemed inextricable for Houstoun, as he watched his chameleon's colors change in response to external stimuli as well as to the chameleon's evident pleasures and irritations. He was sorry that Saltero's customers would not have the same opportunity to indulge in speculating about the relationships between spirit and matter that the chameleon afforded.

John Hunter—who was a benefactor of Don Saltero's and also the anatomist who would later inspire the vitalists' debates of the early nineteenth century—moved rapidly from thanking a correspondent for the specimens of a heron's legs that he had received, to wishing he could have a live heron of his own, to asking when he could expect his order of hedgehogs, to promising to find "some Don Saltero's" to exchange with his correspondent in return. Immediately after promising to find some Don Saltero's for his friend, Hunter pivots to consider the nature of matter (4.89). Like Houstoun musing on his chameleon, Hunter's theory of matter is occasioned by a consideration of color. "My proof of the non-existence of matter is in colours," Hunter explains (4.89). Because all colors are "mixture[s]" of other colors, they must logically be understood as compounds of nothingness. Hunter concludes, therefore, that there is nothing "immutable in matter" and "no such thing as permanency in one species of matter" (4.89).

In the midst of arranging an exchange of object-specimens, Hunter declares that matter does not really exist. As he considers an object-specimen that no longer exists, Houstoun marvels at the ways in which matter and spirit appear to be fundamentally entangled. Neither Hunter nor Houstoun linger long with the questions of substance and causality that were urgently considered in the context of seventeenth-century science and politics; both, however, register the sense that things are vibrant. Chameleons, herons, hedgehogs—dead or alive—are vibrant as they loiter just outside the door of Don Saltero's coffeehouse, suspended in modes of transformation. Their colors change. Their elements mix and combine. They disintegrate and yet still proliferate.

When Richard Steele visited Don Saltero's, he also registered the vibrancy of the objects that had made it into the coffeehouse's collection. Steele's satirical description of Don Saltero's in *The Tatler* No. 34 (June 28, 1709) remains the most extensive and by far the most well-known account of the collection.[7] On a mild June day in 1709, *The Tatler*'s "Isaac Bickerstaff" (the nom de plume Steele borrowed from Swift) struck out for a ramble. He required frequent "fresh air" to soothe his "spare and hective constitution," and a daily jaunt of "of a mile or two" did just the trick (Bond, *Tatler* 1.251). This daily jaunt had the added benefit of offering a spectating tattler the opportunity to "know the world" by observing and then reporting on "the Nature of the People, their Soil, their Government, their Inclinations, and their Passions," like a traveler perambulating in strange lands (Bond, *Tatler* 1.251). Steele made it only as far as Chelsea that day in June, but he found at Don Saltero's more than enough material to mull over.

As soon as Steele walks into Don Saltero's, where all the *"Literati* sit in Council,"* he seems to sense the ways in which the seventeenth-century debates about matter had not settled easily into a truce (Bond, *Tatler* 1.252). Steele does not experience the objects in Saltero's collection as dead matter. Nor does he experience Saltero's coffeehouse as a rational, well-ordered microcosm. Steele reports, for example, that the "ten thousand gimcracks round the room, and on the seiling [*sic*]" arrested his attention by "divert[ing]" his "eye" (Bond, *Tatler* 1.252). In Steele's grammar, Saltero's artifacts take action and redirect his gaze away from the celebrated writers in the room to themselves. Likewise, Salter's own constitution appears to Steele to have been contagiously infected by the artifacts. Salter's "genius" had also been his "misfortune," Steele muses. Salter's faculties had been "dissipated" by paying "attention to too many things at once" (Bond, *Tatler* 1.253). Steele's emphasis on the gimcracks that possess the power to divert his eye and to "dissipate" Salter's "faculties"—even as both men may be said to have willfully looked for the objects—shows how artifacts like those at Saltero's could still be imagined to exert control over the body and the mind, even in a clockwork universe.

Many accounts of Don Saltero's suggest that the coffeehouse was always on the verge of descending into pandemonium, as if its variety of gimcracks was matched by a variety of behaviors. While Salter's regulars sauntered in to order the usual and peruse the papers, others came in for haircuts, tooth extractions, and revelry. Salter was not only a businessman and a collector; he was also a barber, a dentist, and—by all accounts—a fine fiddle player. Things could get out of hand at the coffeehouse. In 1736, throngs of people gathered at Don Saltero's to celebrate the marriage of the Prince of Wales. They spilled out onto the street as a mob late that night, shouting "huzzas" and shooting their guns (MacMichael 111). Saltero's was one of the alleged meeting places of Harriet Errington and Captain Buckley, two notorious lovers who were tried and convicted for adultery in 1785 (*Trial* 35). The brewer Felix Calvert shot himself at Saltero's in the middle of a spring afternoon in 1802 (*Annual Register* 502). Robert Squirrell staged his experimental inoculation of two young girls against scrophula at Don Saltero's; one girl survived (45). Clients at Don Saltero's could also marvel at the repurposed steam engine on the premises. Where previously it had supplied all of Piccadilly with water, now it steamed Don Saltero's meat. The colloquial phrase, "cat's paw," apparently "took its origin" at Don Saltero's because the coffeehouse's resident pet monkey had learned to grab the paw of the resident pet cat and use it as a proxy for stealing chestnuts roasting on the fire so that the monkey could escape unsinged (Pulleyn 303).

The theatrics at Don Saltero's suggest that it was what Roach describes as a "city of the dead": a public site characterized by the "magnetic forces of commerce and pleasure" that "suck the willing and the unwilling alike" into their orbits (28). In particular, the artifacts on display at Saltero's embodied the ways in which cities of the dead teem with performances that attempt to reenact histories that have either unintentionally been forgotten or willfully erased. While we often imagine performances as "quotations"—repetitions that refer to, stand in for, or restore something that precedes the performances themselves—cities of the dead expose performances as "inventions" (Roach 33). Performance is always a "doomed search for originals," Roach writes (3). In inventing rather than quoting history and memory, performance flirts with failure. But even as they flirt with failure, performances in cities of the dead become even more lively; "[m]emory reveals itself as imagination," and the pleasures of the imagination proliferate (Roach 29). The city of the dead begins to take on a life of its own, generating more performances as well as texts that record and interpret them.

Amid all the hubbub, Saltero's artifacts were also performers. Like a traditional *Wunderkammer*, Don Saltero's featured a panoply of seemingly rare and singular things. Based on the unpaginated catalogues that Salter prepared for his customers, there were many natural history specimens on display in the coffeehouse, as both Houstoun's and Hutton's brief mentions of the collection indicate. Salter actually had a "camelion" (item no. 92) in his collection already, although he may well have welcomed receiving another specimen. The hedgehogs and herons that Hutton discusses could have fit easily somewhere in between Salter's "large Porcupine" (item no. 64) and his "Ostrich's Leg" (item no. 74).[8] The antiquities on display, however, are what mark Don Saltero's as a city of the dead. These included the relics as well as the coins, manuscripts, weapons, and grave goods that are the subjects of the following chapters.

Such artifacts were supposed to perform history, but they often borrowed their lines from the other things on display at Saltero's, like the natural history specimens of strange creatures, fossils, flora, and fauna.[9] At Saltero's, in other words, scientific and philosophical examinations of matter collided with new developments in historiography. As Barbara Shapiro explains, the scientific revolution went hand in hand with the rise of antiquarianism. "[C]hanges in conceptions of evidence and proof" that attended work in the natural sciences "brought historical thought into closer contact" with the kind of fact-based, evidence-driven research practiced by members of the Royal Society (Shapiro, *Probability and Certainty* 119). As a result, deep affinities emerged between "natural history," which included studies of geology, botany, astronomy, biology, physics, and history. Both historians and natural historians came to share in the conviction that "history—any kind of history—consisted of an accurate report of past and present facts and events" (Shapiro, *Probability and Certainty* 126).

Shapiro finds that two kinds of historiography jostled for preeminence in the course of the Enlightenment: perfect history, which was "characterized by explanations and causal analysis" that could "provide guidance for future policy makers and actors," and imperfect history, which "limit[ed] itself to topics where visible remains and documentary evidence were available" (*Probability and Certainty* 130–135). Perfect history initially tended to share more with literature than science. Perfect histories took the form of well-written biographies of historical worthies or narratives of momentous events. The goal was to deliver moral maxims by making the relationships between causes and effects visible as well as memorable. In contrast, imperfect histories took the form of reports, description, lists. The goal was simply to present historical evidence—documents and material remains—as if they were scientific specimens.

Imperfect historians won the day, according to Shapiro, but they also remained devoted to recovering the civil, legal, and political institutions of the past that had preoccupied perfect historians. The "causal analysis" that had been a central feature of perfect history, therefore, persisted as a feature of the new scientifically minded historiography. Such investments in causality continued to stoke anxiety in the new historiography because they threatened to reintroduce bias into claims about the past. Antiquaries made frequent visits to Don Saltero's, where they expected that the artifacts would perform facts about the past.[10] Not even artifacts, however, could ensure the viability of causal claims that extended into the mists of time. While the antiquaries came to Saltero's in order to discover the truths about the past that only the artifacts could know, Saltero's other customers found themselves plunged into a cacophonous city of the dead where artifacts played dubious parts in their performances.

Old Relics, New Sciences

Invested with the causal agency to convey facts, artifacts acquired the agency to preserve political histories that many preferred to forget and the philosophical disagreements that they thought had been resolved. When Steele reports that the gimcracks at Don Saltero's arrested his attention and dissipated Salter's, he registers a sense of unease at the authority that scientific and historical objects had in the eighteenth century as the means by which causes and effects could be known. In Steele's description, such unease becomes especially acute around the artifacts at Don Saltero's that veered between the categories of the antique and the relic. These items threaten not only to preserve a history of superstition for the present but also to do so under the guise of performing as evidence of natural, scientifically proven phenomena. When Steele turns his attention from Salter's dissipation to items in the collection, he takes particular issue with the things that he claims threaten to "deceive religious persons" and "inspire heterodox opinions" (Bond, *Tatler* 1.254). It is not entirely clear from the early catalogue which specific artifacts Steele has in mind, but the first fourteen entries introduce Don Saltero's as a veritable reliquary: "The model of our Blessed Saviour's Selpuchre in Jerusalem" (item no. 1), "Painted Ribbands from Jerusalem, with the Pillar to which our Saviour was tied when scourged, with a Motto on each" (item no. 2), a "Box of Relicks from Jerusalem" (item no. 3), a "Piece of a Saint's Bone, in Nun's Work" (item no. 4), and so on—culminating in "A Coffin of State for a Fryar's Bones" (item no. 14).[11]

The charge that artifact enthusiasts were covert Catholics was common enough, and the conviction that they thought magically about their objects was latent in these charges.[12] The champions of the new empirical sciences, however, also frequently flirted with the magical powers of things. A belief in the relic as an object capable of acting as the agent of miraculous cures was not so far from a belief in matter's capacity for instantiating a long chain of effects, however predictable and rational, on the body, on the mind, and on history. Robert Boyle's investigations into medicinal amulets offer a representative example of the affinities that could be detected between the spirited relic and corpuscular matter.[13] Boyle's principle (that matter in motion caused a chain of correlated effects as particles physically collided with one another) finds its most obvious expression in the oral ingestion of medicine. For Boyle, however, the principle by which ingestion worked applied to all bodily encounters with external objects. Boyle observed, for example, that our skin is "perforated with a great multitude . . . of little outlets and inlets" (*Works* 5.102). "[I]t is not very difficult to conceive," Boyle writes, how tiny particles from external objects can enter the body through the pores of the skin and then travel through a "multitude of capillary vessels" with "blood" and "other juices" to other parts of the body, including the brain (*Works* 5.102–103).

For Boyle, then, one need not eat or drink medicinal cures for them to work. Boyle marshals several examples in support of his case. He describes a man with whom he once shared a house, a "learned and judicious person," who found that his stomach pain was ameliorated by "handling the tooth of a true hippopotamus" (*Works* 5.104). Likewise, Boyle himself confesses that the cramps in his own feet were relieved by wearing a "ring" made from a "true elk's hoof" on one of his fingers (*Works* 5.104). Boyle takes another case study to heart. When visiting a physician in London, he noticed "a fine new-fashioned clock" in the parlor. The physician, eager to convince Boyle that he is not so "rich and vain" as to collect "so dear a rarity," explained that the clock was a gift from a "courtier" (*Works* 5.105). The physician had cured a tumor in the neck of the courtier's daughter by having her place the hand of a recently deceased corpse on her throat "till she either complained or confessed, that she felt the coldness of it penetrate to the innermost parts of her tumor"

(*Works* 5.105). They attempted this remedy daily, "whilst the body continued without smelling," and her tumor was cured (*Works* 5.105).

Boyle takes one more case as evidence of his philosophical principle that external objects travel into and through the body. Having been the victim of continuing, and often violent, nosebleeds, Boyle had his sister procure a rare specimen from Ireland of "some true moss of a dead man's scull [*sic*]" (*Works* 5.106). Boyle plans to place this moss directly in his nostrils, but instead decides to experiment with simply holding the "moss" in his hand. "[T]o the wonder of the by-standers," his nose bleeding immediately stopped (*Works* 5.106). The external objects that Boyle identifies here—the tooth of a hippopotamus, the "true" elk's hoof, the corpse's hand, and the "moss of a dead man's scull"—all bear traces of the history of the relic. All would have found a welcome home at Don Saltero's next to its relics. The relics trouble Steele scientifically and philosophically, but they also trouble him politically.

The relics on display at Don Saltero's brought not only a history of Catholic superstition but also a history of political conflict into uncomfortable proximity to the body and the present. For Steele and his contemporaries, a theory of matter that vested the tooth of a hippopotamus, the "true" elk's hoof, the corpse's hand, and the "moss of a dead man's scull" with the same kind of power once enjoyed by relics went hand in hand with the question of divine right. William Beckett examined the links between relic worship and divine right—rationally explaining away both by recourse to the new historiography—in his *Free and Impartial Enquiry into the Antiquity and Efficacy of Touching for the Cure of the King's Evil* (1722). Beckett's *Free and Impartial Enquiry* is two essays. The first, as the title suggests, is a history of the popular belief that the king could cure scrofula simply by touching the afflicted. The second is "A Dissertation Concerning the Ancient Method Made Use for the Curing Diseases by Charms, Amulets, &c." Both essays curate collections of archival sources in order to assess the history of how kings were once thought so divine as to be able to cure diseases. By setting the history of the king's touch alongside the history of charms and amulets, Beckett believed he would show his readers that the fact of the matter is, neither kings nor charms cure diseases. Not even the new corpuscular science could explain the phenomenon of the royal touch for Beckett. Instead, he concludes that a sick person's imagination effected the cure.

Beckett excavates the first record of the "royal touch" in an extended case study that mirrors Boyle's example of the woman whose neck tumors were cured by the hand of a corpse. According to Beckett, eighty years after Edward the Confessor's death, the historian William of Malmsbury reported that a woman, plagued with neck tumors, had once sought Edward's healing ability after she dreamed that he could cure her. She went to Edward and found him at his "Devotions" (8). He "dip'd his fingers in Water, and dabbel'd the Woman's neck, and he had no sooner taken away his Hand, but she found herself better, the loathsome Scabb dissolv'd so that *Worms* and purulent Matter bursting out together" (8–9).

Beckett has no truck with this or similar reports, however. Comparing and contrasting a tour de force of historical sources, Beckett concludes that the cures effected by kings as well as amulets were merely placebo effects. Beckett also concludes that the "king's touch" was a rank form of propaganda. "[S]ome have plac'd the Efficacy of the *Touch* in the *Hereditary Right of Succession*," he writes (26). According to Beckett, England's monarchs took advantage of the confluences between relic worship and superstitious attachments to amulets or "charms," and none more than Henry VIII. As Beckett explains, Henry VIII needed to "strengthen his Title to the Crown, which he knew was at best but precarious" (50–51). He introduced gold into the ceremony of the royal touch as a way of translating the Catholic rite and relic into secular alchemy. Meanwhile, Beckett asserts that the old historians had been just as guilty of misleading the nation as its kings. He includes a range of historical, archival sources in an appendix to his *Free and Impartial Inquiry*. Detecting bias repeatedly in these sources, Beckett says that they prove "how the Original, the Progress, and the Supports" of the "*divine Gift of Healing*, were nothing more than Impositions on the People" designed to bolster spurious claims for the authority of sovereigns (53).

Beckett called the legitimacy of the royal touch into question by doubting both the physical objects and the archival material sources that had been offered as proof of its power—but he still envisioned truth itself as a durable, material thing. Falsehood is a material thing, too, but less durable in his view. Falsehood "sculks [*sic*] under the Supterfuge [*sic*] . . . till the inquisitive Mind dislodges it from all its Securities, and exposes it with its feeble Supports, till it entirely vanishes and appears no more" (54). Like an artifact, "Truth" "may for some Time suffer and lie concealed," but underneath falsehood, the truth persists with "inherent and unalterable Marks and Characters" (54). When brought to the surface, truth "displays it self with fresh Beauties to an inquisitive Person and charms the Passions of the Discover" (54). Even as Beckett interrogated the matter of the relic and the royal touch, then, his own method of assembling a collection of archival sources in order to dig out the truth preserved a structural relationship between objects and effects that his treatises were designed to call into question.

In his 1699 treatise, *An Exposition of the Thirty-Nine Articles of the Church of England*, Gilbert Burnet had also recounted the history of worshipping relics in England. He shows how Beckett's conflation of truth with matter could circle back around to reinvest the relic or the amulet with the power to persuade. Burnet entertains the possibility that perhaps, at one point in the past, the bodies of saints *may* have engendered miracles, but the continued call for the objects to function outside of their original contexts threatened to degenerate into idolatry. Burnet described relic worship as a "novelty" that began in the fourth century, a period characterized by intense religious persecution, which produced a surge of superstitious thinking (*Exposition* 244). Conveniently, new discoveries of catacombs had been made previously, late in the third century. Suddenly, a lot of new relics were to be had, and just in time (*Exposition* 244).[14] "Bones and Relicks grew to encrease and multiply, so that [the Saints] had more Bones and Limbs than God and Nature had given them" (*Exposition* 245). According to Burnet, St. Jerome solved this problem by appealing to the nature of miracles, finding no issue with the idea that the same knuckle could be in two places at once or that magic could hop-skip from thumb to thumb or thumb to tibula; such is the nature of miracles. For Burnet, however, a duplicate relic "very much shakes the Credit of the Miracles wrought by them; since we have no reason to think that God would support such Impostures with Miracles" (*Exposition* 245).

Burnet confessed, though, that the fact of relics' falsehood didn't stop them from being powerful objects. The "World" became "fill[ed] with many Volumes of Legends, many more lying yet in the Manuscripts in many Churches, than have been published," thanks to the narrative vignettes produced by those who believed relics and the sovereigns who were eager to appropriate them for their own purposes (*Exposition* 245). Moreover, Burnet admitted, even "though these things are too palpably False to be put upon us now, in Ages of more Light . . . the same Trade is still carried on, where the same Ignorance and the same Superstition does still continue" (*Exposition* 246). Whereas Boyle offers a secular, scientific account of how objects can cause "miraculous" effects by virtue of their corpuscular interaction with the body, Burnet reminds us that the public continued to believe that more miraculous forces might still be at work. Boyle's secular and Burnet's historical accounts of the relic contextualize the artifacts' performances at Don Saltero's. On the one hand, the artifacts performed and preserved a genealogy that the Reformation had ostensibly eradicated, speaking powerfully to the legacies of England's past even when the artifacts in question were not necessarily identified first and foremost as antiquities. On the other hand, the artifacts also performed the ongoing debates about scientific materialisms, embodying questions over matter's nature and its agential capacities. Steele's complaint about those artifacts that "calculated to deceive religious persons" and "introduce heterodox opinions" splits the difference between Boyle's and Burnet's account of relics' seemingly miraculous, curative effects, and it does so with some noted grammatical ambiguity regarding the causal source of those religious calculations and heterodox introductions.

An Accumulative Virtuoso and an Accumulative Traitor

The artifacts at Don Saltero's that, as Steele put it, threatened to "deceive religious persons" and "inspire heterodox opinions" remained tangled up in old philosophies as well as old politics while the new sciences and historiography did little to set them straight. The cornucopia of artifacts associated with English monarchs was similarly vibrant. These included a "Wooden Shoe put under the Speaker's Chair in K. James the IId's Time" (item no. 15), "Henry the VIIIth's Coat of Mail" (item no. 38), "Queen Elizabeth's Stirrup" (item no. 39), "K William the IIId's Coronation Sword" (item no. 46), "K. Charles I. and his Sons, in a tri-form Picture" (item no. 48), and "A Piece of the Royal Oak" (item no. 265). Although Steele never takes explicit issue with these items, his essay's conclusion suggests that they are as troubling as those of Salter's would-be relics. Steele concludes his description of Don Saltero's by inviting his readers to look up and around the coffeehouse in which they currently sit, reading *The Tatler*, to observe the politicians Steele assumes are also there gathered. "[H]alf [of these] politicians," Steele declares, are like Salter: "of the class of tooth-drawers" (Bond, *Tatler* 1.252).

By chastising politicians as "tooth-drawers," Steele means to condemn the tendency of the British government to redress conflicts between two factions by simply extracting one of them. Which half of the government, though, does Steele have in mind as belonging to the class of tooth-drawers: the Whigs or the Tories? The Whigs appear at first blush to be the irreverent dentists in Steele's description. They had ousted the Tories Robert Harley and Henry Bolingbroke in 1708. Yet Steele was himself an avowed Whig, having voiced clear support just two months previously for the ousting in an allegory published in *The Tatler* No. 4.

The attempted Jacobite Rebellion of 1708 may have meant that Steele had the Tories and not the Whigs in mind as the tooth-drawers. This event, of course, had made Britain's seventeenth-century history of regicide, restoration, and compromise surface once again. Viscerally, the execution of Charles I must have struck Steele's readers as an instance of extracting the part to cure the whole, and a tooth of Charles I would even be taken from his grave in 1813. Throughout the eighteenth century, the Jacobites' persistence in endeavoring to overthrow the compromises of the Glorious Revolution could have been read as a series of attempts to extract a Protestant monarch from the throne. Steele's allusion to politicians as tooth extractors, therefore, handily expresses a general antipathy to faction qua faction: the turbulent ministerial conflicts in which the Whigs and Tories alike jostled for power defined against and within England's history of regicide and revolution.

Other anecdotal accounts of Don Saltero's illustrate the propensity of its artifacts to perform ambivalent, even diametrically opposed, political histories. For example, Lewis Theobald, the playwright and eminent editor of Shakespeare in the 1700s, included an account of Don Saltero's in his periodical, *The Censor* No. 21 (1715). When the narrator arrives at Saltero's, he asks to see, specifically, an "Antiquity." A female guide directs him to a "*sword*" from the "*Battle of Hochsted* [sic]" (1.149–50). Chagrined by this mistake, the narrator speculates that if he had asked to see "something Modern," the guide would likely have shown him "a *Splinter* of the *Pillar* of *Salt* into which *Lot's* Wife was turn'd, a Piece of the *Ruins* of Old *Troy*, or *Diana's* Temple *Ephesus*" (1.150). A sword from the Battle of Höchstädt, fought only a decade earlier, becomes an antiquity; antiquities, like pieces of the Temple of Diana, constructed in the fourth century BC, become modern objects. Such confusion of shape-shifting, time-bending objects (and the objects' confusion) leads the *Censor's* narrator to conclude that Don Saltero's "is furnish'd with such Variety of Objects for Speculation" that the collection is "sure to content *every* Disposition and Capacity in their several ways" (1.151, emphasis added).

The narrator insists, nevertheless, on reading the artifacts through the lens of Hobbes's brute mechanism. Saltero's detritus of artifacts proves that "Man," who has "all the Products of the Creation at his Service, aims his Arrows chiefly against Man; runs him down with Fraud and Artifice, hunts him into the Toils of Perplexity, and triumphs in his Ruin" (1.154). Despite the *Censor's* recognition that the objects appear to perform history or philosophy or politics for the pleasure of any spectator, readers can detect a conviction that the artifacts mechanically reenact a government in which nature necessitates subjection to a sovereign.

Other anecdotes suggest that a completely different political history lurked in Saltero's dark corners. According to the antiquary Thomas Pennant, who as a young boy went with his father to the coffeehouse to view an object his father had donated—item 102, "A Root of a Tree in the Shape of a Hog"—none other than Richard Cromwell was one of Salter's regular customers in the early eighteenth century (13). A later account of this fact published in John Fisher Murray's *Environs of London* (1842) delighted in imagining Cromwell himself as an artifact among Saltero's other artifacts. *Environs* recommends a historical, imaginative trek to Salter's establishment, now several decades gone: "If it were for nothing else than to muse upon the various fate of sublunary things, it were worth while to take a turn in the coffeehouse where an ex-Protector of an extinct Commonwealth was accustomed to resort: to see, or reveal by imagination, the man who had wielded supreme power settling a tavern score; or, instead of deciding upon the destinies of nations, criticising [*sic*] the beer, or approving the tobacco." (14)

The "fate of sublunary things" grinds onward at Saltero's, and Cromwell himself disintegrates into an object subject to forces he cannot control. Murray goes on, for example, to "imagine how many curious spirits must have thronged Don Saltero's to catch a glimpse of the placid son of a fearful father; the fool and coward who stole away from his palace with 'the lives and fortunes of the people of England' in his pocket; or, if you will, the truly wise man, who was content to be obscurely happy, rather than miserably great" (14).

It is not clear, however, that Salter's original customers, those who may have flocked to see Cromwell ensconced among the artifacts, drew the same conclusions as the readers of the *Censor* or *Environs* who were happy to have their mechanist philosophies and, perhaps, their royalist sympathies, confirmed by the artifacts on display. For example, the edition of the *Catalogue* produced at Saltero's in 1795 hints that the monarchical memorabilia as well as the relics—which had previously been grouped together in respective sets—had been regrouped by object type: a rearrangement that suggests a purposeful dismantling of their assemblages as covert manifestations of royal sympathies. An item like King Henry VIII's coat of mail, for example, was moved into a collection of weapons rather than displayed along with Queen Elizabeth's stirrup and coronation paraphernalia.

More items from the Commonwealth appear to have been added to the collection as well over the years. These included copies of the "broad seal of the Commonwealth of England, 1651" (item no. 19 in Glass Case No. IV and item no. 16 in Glass Case No. V), a "plaister" and "gilt" copy of the reverse of Cromwell's medal (item no. 54 in Glass Case No. I, now notably beside one of the displaced relics: the painted ribbon with the motto used to tie Christ to the cross), and a "Print of the dead warrant for beheading King Charles the First" (item no. item 206 on the Wainscot), among others.[15] Perhaps Richard Cromwell donated some of these or similar items to Don Saltero's. In any event, it seems unlikely that Cromwell's son would have made Salter's establishment a regular haunt if its artifacts consistently and mechanically performed royalist dogmas.

There is evidence that Salter himself was not only aware of his artifacts' volatility but understood that it enhanced the popular appeal of his collection. Two advertisements attributed to Salter revel in the collection's ambiguities. The first of these appears in *The British Apollo* No. 102 (1708). In its regular question-and-answer feature, the *Apollo* contains an address signed "J.S." that begins: "I am by Trade a Coffee-man, a Punch-maker, a Barber, a Tooth-drawer, a Fidler, a Gimcrack Collector, a Game-keeper, and, as you may perceive a Grubstreet-Dabler" (*British Apollo*, not paginated). The address goes on to ask the *Apollo* to decide if Salter can be called a "Vertuoso [*sic*]" and admitted with Sloane's blessing into the Royal Society. Salter defends his case for being admitted to the Royal Society and deemed a respectable virtuoso with an analogy. "There was once an Accumulative Traytor," he writes, and so he "fanc[ies] himself an Accumulative Vertuoso."

Here, Salter invokes a legal context for his claim to be a virtuoso. An "accumulative traytor" refers to the impeachment of Charles I's chief counselor, Thomas Wentworth. The Parliament convicted Wentworth of "accumulative treason." The Wentworth case was an exercise in creative legal reasoning. Wentworth had committed a crime against Charles I by taking action to support Charles I's cause. Such action, the conviction maintained, had been treasonous because it had the opposite effect from what was intended: Wentworth had alienated the king from his subjects. Additionally, the Parliament concluded that no single act of Wentworth's was in and of itself an act of outright treason, but taken together, discrete and disparate actions that Wentworth had taken had "accumulated" to amount to the same. Wentworth was found guilty and executed in 1640.[16]

Salter's invocation of this episode in history does not, however, result in an easily identifiable political affiliation with either royalists or revolutionaries. Thus, the *Apollo* responds by associatively emphasizing Salter's political as well as his philosophical mutability. "An Accumulative *Vertuoso!*" the *Apollo* (not paginated) declares, and continues:

> Why you are an accumulative one, in the most Superior Superlative Degree. . . . First, your Dealings in Contemplative *Coffee*, whose adult Property reduces the Body to a Philosophical Consistency. Then Speculative *Punch*, which after *fiat mixio*, leads you into the *Arcana* of Sympathies, and their Wonderful Effects. By *Barbing* you bring Rude Matters into Form, and Obvious to Perspection [*sic*]. Your *Drawing Teeth* gives demonstration of the *Axiom*, That *Pain* which is *Great must be short*, by twitching them out. Your *Fidling* shews the Harmony of Science. A *Gimcrack Collector* is a Vertuoso's true Badge. Your *Game-keeping* instructs you in the Loco-motive Faculty; and a *Grubstreet-Dabler*, is of the Conclusion of the matter.

In this formulation, Salter's nature as an "accumulative one" means his body is of a porous "philosophical consistency," which makes it possible for Salter to absorb the "effects" of the individuals and objects—no matter their individual differences—with which he comes into contact. Likewise, terms such as "property," "speculative," "matter," "form," "perspection [*sic*]," "science," and "faculty" signal the *Apollo's* awareness that Salter's political allusion has philosophical implications. Readers may infer that any and every object is as liable to influence Salter as is any and every politician. The *Apollo* doesn't name Salter a virtuoso or admit him to the Royal Society. Instead, Salter is deemed a "*Grubstreet-Dabler*."

Similarly, the poetic advertisement for Don Saltero's that was published in *Mist's Weekly Journal* (1723) announces that Salter has for "[f]ifty years" "stroll'd, with maggots in [his] pate"; now, after having served as "[a] Scraper, Vertuoso-Projector [*sic*], / Tooth-Drawer, Trimmer," he has "at last" become "a Gimcrack Whim Collector" (quoted in MacMichael 110). At his establishment, "Monsters of sorts" are to be seen: "Strange things in nature as they grew so; some relicks," and even "fragments of the famed Bob Crusoe" (quoted in MacMichael 110). As the early twentieth-century commentator Reginald Blunt noticed, almost all the professions attributed to Salter here are puns. A scraper refers, on the one hand, to Salter's offer to "gratis" shave his paying customers, but on the other hand, it also references his prowess as fiddler (46). Similarly, a virtuoso denotes Salter's collecting habits as well as "one who forms schemes or designs," such as a curious and profitable coffeehouse (47). As Blunt writes, "this last brings at once to ask, what was a 'Trimmer?'" (48). His answer: a trimmer was a barber, but as Samuel Johnson's definition attests, it was also a slang term for an individual who "altered his political views in order to balance parties" (48).

Artifacts' Affordances

Representations of Don Saltero's suggest that the artifacts were vibrant—but not always in ways that should have been celebrated. The artifacts that were like relics in the collection threatened to convey old, outmoded theories of matter and divine right into the Enlightened present. But even the new sciences meant that those artifacts could still be imagined working invisibly, mysteriously on the bodies as well as the political sympathies and antipathies of Saltero's customers. The demands of the new, imperfect historiography further enlivened the effects of Don Saltero's artifacts. Histories based on the hard evidence offered by objects promised to redress the suspicions of historians' political biases by making the political conflicts of the past available for empirical evaluation. In his *Essay on the Manner of Writing History* (1746), for example, Peter Whalley embraced the antiquaries' deference to the authority of objects. Whalley observed that biased historians "must" depict the "objects" that affirm their political principles "in all the Glare of Light," while they must also depict those objects that do *not affirm* their political principles "in the darkest Colours" (15). "The *Eye of Party*," he said, could be "pleased only with *black* or *white*" (15). Whalley was optimistic, though, that the new historian's "Mind" had transcended the limitations of the biased eye. The mind of an imperfect historian "resemble[d] a pure and polished Mirrour, which represents all Objects in the same Form, Colour, and Dimensions, which naturally belong to the Things themselves" (19–20).

Joseph Addison agreed. Whereas poets could "borrow" "materials from outward objects, and join them together at their own pleasure," historians—like natural philosophers and scientists—were "obliged" to "describe visible objects of a real existence" (Bond, *Spectator* 3.574). Both Addison and Whalley imagined that a history based on objects was a nonpartisan history, but that did not mean that they imagined that such a history demurred from describing partisanship. Whalley thought that the "collisions" of conflicting histories could "hardly fail of striking out the Truth" (13). Addison said that the best historians "set before our Eyes the Divisions, Cabals, and Jealousies of Great Men" in order to "lead [their readers] into the several actions and events" of the past, "unfolding" history "step by step" and by "just degrees" (Bond, *Spectator* 3.10). Readers of these histories—rife with all their gore and complexity—would be left in "pleasing suspense" while the past would "[break] upon them insensibly" (Bond, *Spectator* 3.10). This affective state bought readers "time" to decide for themselves which "Parties" were in the right and the wrong (Bond, *Spectator* 3.10).

Addison recognized that describing history in all its minute complexity entailed an expansion of narrative. He also realized that for all the benefits and pleasures readers enjoyed as they were suspended in a narrative of history's oscillating, unspooling networks, the close links between past causes and present effects could disintegrate in the process. Or, as Steele put it in his description of Salter's mental state, paying "attention to too many things at once" threatened to introduce states of dissipation. Whalley also feared that the truth could "easily be lost in the Croud" (13). Addison recognized that the historiography he advocated for threatened to make history more "art" than "veracity" (Bond, *Spectator* 3.10). While imperfect histories aspired to lead their readers straight into the collisions of historical political conflicts so that they could "strik[e] out" the truth (Whalley 13), the artifacts at Don Saltero's preserved those conflicts in a state of ongoing action—the effects of the past remained perennially in flux, its causes difficult to settle. Consequently, Saltero's artifacts were quick to flit between the spotlight and the shadows and catch the eye of not only "*Party*," as Whalley feared, but *any Party*.

According to Jonathan Lamb, the antiquarian impulse of the eighteenth century—the desire to represent unmediated history by virtue of direct encounters with its objects—has traditionally been linked with fiction's rising interest in participating in "Cartesian skepticism" and "Lockean sensationism"; imperfect history and formal realism share a commitment to precise, empirical descriptions of objects as they really exist and as they are really perceived. Yet Lamb argues that such a rendering of the rise of realist fiction, which has been ascendant since Ian Watt first assessed the "rise" of the novel, neglects to consider the role that the seventeenth-century political crisis played in shaping how individuals understood the relationships between objects and imaginative fictions. For Lamb, the execution of Charles I was an unprecedented "narrative event" (*Things* 156). It established the sovereign not as the narrator of the nation but as a Hobbesian figure in a narrative "naturalized by the fiction of the original contract," set into motion by formal realism's commitment to constructing rather than representing experience (*Things* 156).

In other words, after the events of 1649, "no one was under any illusion about the power of imagination to supply, under the right conditions, the historical evidence that would justify [a political] rupture" (Lamb, *Things* 156). As Lamb writes (*Things* 159),

> So, rather than supposing the formal realism of the novel to be a celebration of the real experience of individuals rendered in probable pictures that reflected the common sense of things, it is more useful to view it as part of what Hume calls the propensity to fiction. In which case, what is represented is not a picture of reality achieved by the bringing home of objects in all their concrete particularity, so much as the power of imagination itself to create the materialities and propel the continuities upon which the sense of identity or nationality is founded, those selves and communities that are productive of events which we call solid and real.

For Victoria Kahn, whose work Lamb draws on, these "new politics" should be read as "part of the history of poetics" (*Wayward* 15). In turn, the poetics of the early modern state, according to Kahn, were both imitative and imaginative in the service of "creat[ing] new artifacts" (*Wayward* 15).

Touting himself as a "Grubstreet dabbler," Salter appears to have understood that there were pleasures as well as profits to be had in reveling in his artifacts' "poetics and propensity to fiction." The artifacts' composite qualities or mixed states ensured that they would appeal to the political sensibilities of any party who walked through Salter's door and back into a past characterized by political turmoil and disagreement. Salter appears to have appreciated not only the political but also the aesthetic benefits conferred by objects that were part fact and part art, part history and part fiction. Mark Akenside, famous not least for celebrating flights of fancy in his *Pleasures of the Imagination* (1744), took satirical aim at Salter in his poem, "The Virtuoso" (1737). Akenside depicts Salter as a "subtile wight" who "delight[s]" in "[u]ncommon thing[s], and rare were his delight" (244). A "spright ycleped Phantasy" stands among Salter's collection of "[t]hings ancient, curious, value-worth, and rare"—which include medals and mummies, dissected animals and "Indian feathers," "[a]ir-pumps and prisms" (245). "Phantasy" has a "wild look" and wears a robe of many colors and flowers in her hair; she holds a chameleon in her arms, and she changes shape. She shape-shifts from "monarch" to "mendicant," "statesman to monk," "lord to swain," "papal father" and "scribbling dunce" (245). She fills Salter's brain until he "will for a dreadful giant take a mill, / Or a grand palace in a hogstie [*sic*] find" (245).

In Akenside's poem, Phantasy transforms from a monarch to a statesman to a scribbler, and Salter transforms from a collector into Don Quixote. Salter's coffeehouse was called Don Saltero's for just this reason. While Saltero tilted at windmills and scribbled on Grub Street, the "literati"—some of whom Steele noted were Salter's most regular celebrity customers— introduced the coffeehouse to their readers, further strengthening the relationships between artifacts and texts.[17] Don Saltero's makes brief but notable appearances, for example, in Sarah Fielding's *David Simple* (1744) (2.315), Tobias Smollett's *Peregrine Pickle* (1751) (2.139), and Frances Burney's *Evelina* (1779) (2.105–114), among many, many other literary works.[18] The influence of Saltero's artifacts can likewise be discovered in the poems, plays, novels, and essays in the long eighteenth century that took up artifacts as topoi. The literary lives of artifacts suggest that the desire for artifacts to perform as agents of content was as powerful as the frustration over their propensity to perform for the pleasure of any historian, philosopher, or politician—and that taken together, this desire and frustration proved to be, as Salter knew, aesthetically provocative.

In the chapters that follow, artifacts will show up especially in works that engage with the periodical boom market of the 1700s.[19] Antiquaries frequently published their imperfect histories of found objects in magazines and newspapers—and the word "magazine" denoted a "storehouse" and was used as a synonym for "museum," which was used as a synonym for a published magazine in turn.[20] Antiquaries also exchanged their writings in short print runs circulated among a select group of club-like readers or publicized their research piecemeal before revising and assembling their finished work later into collections and anthologies. Literary works taken up in the ensuing chapters, like Dryden's *The Medall* (1682), were designed to be circulated as pamphlets and then recited from memory; other texts, such as Johnstone's *Chrysal* (1760–1762) and Horace Walpole's *The Castle of Otranto*, made references to the celebrity newsmakers of the day. Some texts, including "Addison on the History of a Shilling" (1710), saw their first publication in a periodical. Others, like Smollett's *Sir Launcelot Greaves* (1760), were issued serially. Polemical verses, like Byron's "Windsor Poetics," were well suited for coterie circulation. Artifacts, in short, were swept up in the media "event" that Clifford Siskin and William Warner describe as one of the defining features of the English Enlightenment (26–32).

Returning to the work of Roach with which this chapter began, we can see why artifacts might have seemed to be especially well suited for representation in periodical publications. Roach's idea of performance draws directly on the work of Steele and Addison. As performances of memory in the cities of the dead pursue historical points of origin only to get lost, come back, and then try to go back to the beginning all over again, they produce "tattling" and "spectating" (Roach 30). Steele and Addison's reports on everyday experiences in venues like *The Tatler* and *The Spectator*, which make extensive use of gossip (tattling) and first-hand observation (spectating), reenact in order to preserve performances, including the bodies that perform and the spaces in which their performances occur (Roach 26). Spectating and tattling complement by contrast the "doomed search for originals" that lends performances their qualities of immediacy (Roach 3). Texts enter from stage left and stage right to stand in as the means of preserving the action of the performative moment, which constantly threatens to dissipate or be forgotten—just like the origins that such performances attempt and always fail to recover (Roach 26).

Roach finds that periodical print cultures emerged in the midst of a zeal for theatricalities in the cities of the dead, but Barbara Shapiro shows that they also emerged in the midst of the period's dedication to the Enlightenment's "culture of the fact" (*Culture* 86–87).[21] Periodicals included reports on historical, political, and legal matters alongside reviews, advertisements, and letters that referred to real things, events, and people—all of which emphasized the periodical as a timely, necessary, and dependable textual project. Michael G. Ketcham describes this as the periodical's quality of transparency.[22] The matters of fact that stuffed periodicals, however, occupied the same bounded page space as fictions, poems, and essays. Artifacts found a particularly welcome home *in* such textual venues while they also demonstrated *for* those venues the aesthetic benefits that could be derived by comingling the factual and the fanciful.

Artifacts and *The Spectator* might both be said to anticipate the aesthetic category that Sianne Ngai identifies as the "interesting." For Ngai, the aesthetic category of the interesting—notably, a category that predominates in criticism that's written "in the spirit of science, history, or art"—pits "wonder" against "reason" and vice versa. The qualities of wonder and reason that characterize interesting objects repel one another, like two magnets, and the objects' interpreters double down on explaining away the "feeling-based judgments" incited by the objects' wondrous qualities and proceed to erect elaborate "concept-based explanations" that emphasize the interpreters' reasonability (128–129). As Ngai further explains, the interesting object exists in a constant state of "conceptual indeterminacy," and it has a "special relationship to evidence." Interesting objects call for subjective judgments to take the form of objective explanations; these ostensibly objective explanations, in turn, always refer to something outside of the interesting object itself (120). Almost "anything can presumably count as evidence" when it comes to explaining what it is about the interesting object that makes it, well, interesting —but "no particular kind of evidence will ever seem especially or finally convincing," according to Ngai (120).

Ngai finds that the wanton pursuit of evidence outside of the interesting object works "to foster and prolong dialogue, to circulate information, and to bind subjects together" (234). The interesting aesthetic object proves to be particularly ripe, therefore, for pricking at the interests and interestedness of its spectators and interpreters who protest too much in their acts of judgment. Ngai allows that there may be something inherent in the interesting object itself that propagates a "relay between pleasure and cognition": the allure of the interesting is the distinctive if somehow yet indescribable way it invites us to engage in ongoing acts of recasting our feelings as forensics. This constant bid for relay also establishes the interesting as a mode of retrospection as well as projection, and the interesting's "temporal orientation" is therefore at once in the past and in the future; within this "extended time frame," we return to the interesting object over and over again in order to "verify to ourselves that it is still interesting and thus potentially to find it interesting again" (133).

Artifacts' materiality made them interesting. They called out for interpretations—for readings, we might say—that supplemented their states of fragmentation with discursive explications. Many of these discursive explications, inevitably, circulated as texts in the long eighteenth century. These texts suggest that artifacts should be reconsidered not for their failures to disclose matters of fact or convincing interpretations, but for their affordances. James J. Gibson first used the term "affordance" to characterize how physical features of the environment facilitate the behaviors of animals. Affordance describes how shapes, textures, locations, and substances—qualities that are "objective, real, and physical"—make certain actions in a particular place and time possible (125). Recently, both Rita Felski and Caroline Levine have adapted the term "affordances" for literary studies. For Felski, considering the affordances of literary texts is one way of avoiding standing back or digging down to critique a work of literature. For Levine, affordance is a way of describing literary form itself; she argues that literary form is analogous to the kinds of objects that have been studied by art historians, anthropologists, psychologists, and historians of science for their affordances. While a doorknob "affords not only hardness and durability, but also turning, pushing, and pulling," a sonnet affords the representation of a "single idea or experience" (6). In contrast, a "triple-decker novel affords elaborate processes of character development in multiplot social contexts" (6). Form's possibilities as well as its limitations prove to be durable over time, but they can also be expanded by an "imaginative user" (6). In the same way that someone might use a doorknob to hang up their towel, a writer or a reader may use a sonnet or a triple-decker novel in unexpected ways.

Although the concept of affordance accommodates a variety of creative uses, such uses remain delimited by the object or form in question. You can do a lot with a doorknob, but you can't use it to pen a sonnet or type out a triple-decker novel. I have previously suggested that artifacts' materiality afforded multiple and competing interpretations. Addison, who was no stranger to artifacts and antiquaries, casts the terms of *The Spectator* in ways that suggest artifacts like those at Saltero's also afforded opportunities for conceptualizing not only the content of periodical texts but also their investments in genre and materiality. Artifacts' "imaginative users" could borrow from the objects a range of representational strategies for spectating and tattling that were particularly versatile and materially mobile. Artifacts like those on display at Saltero's afforded ways of reporting on matters of fact while also indulging in flights of fancy—without losing sight of a work's overall coherence of form or alienating reading customers.

Addison begins *The Spectator*, for example, by anticipating that his readers already come to the periodical with an established taste for history. They will want to know the "particulars" of its narrator's personal past (Bond, *Spectator* 1.4). The first two essays are therefore designed to "gratify this Curiosity," but Addison never supplies the longed-for particulars. Instead, he treats the reader to an allegory of his youthful reputation as a "judge" and his subsequent reputation as a silent spectator (Bond, *Spectator* 1.4). The former seems true enough, but the latter is curious for Mr. Spectator, who is nothing if not loquacious, at least in print. Addison hammers, though, on his in-person persona's reputation as a man so silent he might be mistaken for a ghost—even as he spins out his monologues in page after page of *The Spectator*. Additionally, Mr. Spectator has "enjoyed" "[o]bscurity" "for many years;" he is anxious of being addressed and "[s]tared at," even as he appears to court and ruminate on his status as a visible object of rising celebrity (Bond, *Spectator* 1.9).

Like an artifact, Mr. Spectator promises to convey particulars but never quite manages to give his readers a true and complete history of all the facts.

Like an artifact, Mr. Spectator could be anywhere, hiding in plain sight, waiting to be discovered. And like an artifact, Mr. Spectator circulates among people, places, and time. Mr. Spectator tells his readers that he's gone on the grand tour, of course, and traveled a little farther than most tourists. Driven by his "insatiable Thirst after Knowledge," he went all the way to Egypt to see the "Antiquities" and he even personally "Measure[d]" a "Pyramid" (Bond, *Spectator* 1.5). Surely, Mr. Spectator brought home a souvenir artifact or two from his tour because, as Mr. Spectator goes on to explain, he likes being in the presence of antiquities. In a well-known essay from *The Spectator*, Addison describes taking a walk among the old tombs at Westminster Abbey (Bond, *Spectator* 1.101). While others experience a feeling of "Terror" among the tombs, Mr. Spectator adopts a longer historical perspective that allows him to find both pleasure and benefit amid such a morbid heap of "six hundred years" of history (Bond, *Spectator* 1.103). With both "Sorrow and Astonishment," Mr. Spectator thinks about how the "Little Competitions, Factions, and Debates of Mankind" become even smaller and more meaningless when we consider the vastness of history (Bond, *Spectator* 1.104).

Despite his preference here for history writ long and large, Mr. Spectator joins Salter's artifacts to witness the daily minutia of eighteenth-century London. Mr. Spectator tells us, then, that he spends his days "thrusting [his] Head into a Round of Politicians at Will's," "smoak[ing] a Pipe at Child's," discussing "Politicks" at "St. James's," and popping in at the "Grecian," and the "Coca Tree" (Bond, *Spectator* 1.6–7). Mr. Spectator hears a lot of political gossip in these coffeehouses, but he insists that he maintains a stance of "exact Neutrality between the Whigs and the Tories" (Bond, *Spectator* 1.9). Such a stance ironically threatened to make him—as many of Mr. Spectator's correspondents charged—appear even more factious. Steele will find himself declaring, after a contentious political engagement with his readers, that Mr. Spectator adopts the "shortest way to impartiality"; the "dispute[s]" he reports on are "not about persons and parties, but about things and causes" (Bond, *Spectator* 3.405).

Mr. Spectator's conviction that the "shortest way to impartiality" is through "things and causes" means that he is as intrigued by the minute and particular sciences of the Royal Society as he is by the scraps of everyday news he reports. Natural philosophers, he marvels, have shown that "every green leaf swarm[s] with Millions of Animals," and "we are filled with a pleasing Astonishment, to see so many Worlds hanging one above the other" (Bond, *Spectator* 3.575). This passage parallels not only Mr. Spectator's penchant for observing the particulars of everyday life but also one in which he once again returns to a scene of history. Taking yet another walk among some ruins, Mr. Spectator confesses that the detritus of the past leads him to indulge in bouts of superstitious thinking. He is inclined in such scenes to agree with "those who believe that all the Regions of Nature swarm with Spirits; and that we have Multitudes of Spectators on all our Actions, when think our selves most alone" (Bond, *Spectator* 1.69–70). Mr. Spectator can look at the tombs in Westminster with "Sorrow and Astonishment"—but without terror or bias—because he scales down disquieting events by scaling up his sense of time. He manages the potentially disquieting glimpse of so many swarming worlds of inhuman creatures and specters of ghostly historical spectators by scaling time back down again to the immediacy of a temporal moment experienced perennially in the present. When he thinks of all those ghosts that might be watching him, he says that he is "wonderfully pleased to think that [he] is *always engaged* with such an innumerable Society" (Bond, *Spectator* 1.70, emphasis added).

Mr. Spectator, therefore, shares several qualities with artifacts. He is embodied and speculative. He is situated in the immediacy of the present and vested with historical perspective. He is familiar yet still anonymous. And he claims to be politically neutral. Mr. Spectator translates these qualities into a narrative persona that is embedded and omniscient as well as descriptive, timely, and timeless: a narrative persona uniquely well suited for scaling up and down inside categories of size, quantity, and duration. But Mr. Spectator knows that in scaling up and down in this way—by making some matter so small and other matter more numerous, or by making time so long and other time indistinguishably immanent—his readers might lose sight of *The Spectator*. Addison needed to ensure that *The Spectator* would not turn out to be just another dusty, dubious gimcrack telling the same old suspicious stories.

Artifacts also, therefore, afforded a means by which Addison could see how grounding a text in fragments facilitated flights of fancy that kept the imagination from getting lost in particulars or generals—or mired in political deadlock. The problem in Akenside's send-up of Salter in "The Virtuoso," for example, is that Phantasy stands, petting her chameleon and tattling her fictions, *in between* the virtuoso and his things. As Akenside described it, the "idea train" of the imagination "preserves/intire [*sic*]" the "mysteries" and "dark oblivion" of all "the various forms of being to present" (*Pleasures* 83). Therefore, the "aim of mimic art" is to make "permanent" the objects that we can only apprehend in constrained times and places—but such art must maintain a tendril, however tenuous, to real objects themselves. Corrupted by Phantasy's many-colored arts, the virtuoso has lost his through line to the things themselves. Mr. Spectator does not make the same mistake. A "noble writer," Addison says, is "able to receive lively Ideas from outward Objects" and "to retain them long" while also discovering associations between those outward objects, other words, other ideas, and other objects—the better to make "something more perfect in Matter" without, however, ever eclipsing the matter entirely (Bond, *Spectator* 3.568).

Addison's theory of the imagination, therefore, travels archaeologically between subatomic depths and airy prospects, moving upward from the body to the sky and downward from the body to the microcosms of plants and dirt. Mr. Spectator must keep his eye all the while on "growth" and the promise of "perfection," but he must also always keep his eye on something more substantive. Addison admits that the imagination can encounter difficulty moving upward and downward, expanding and contracting. He remains convinced that "[n]othing is more pleasant to the Fancy than to enlarge it self by Degrees" (Bond, *Spectator* 3.575). It is a "speculation" that may seem "ridiculous," but that is "founded on no less than the *Evidence* of a Demonstration" (Bond, *Spectator* 3.575, emphasis added). The turn to "evidence" here is telling because it leads Addison on to introduce a quick clarification into his theory of the imagination. The "Understanding," he writes, "indeed, opens up an infinite Space on every side of us," but the imagination can be thwarted by such vast prospects. "Our Reason," Addison continues, "can pursue a Particle of Matter through an infinite variety of Divisions, but the Fancy soon loses sight of it" (Bond, *Spectator* 3.576). The imagination, he concludes, needs and "wants to be filled with Matter of a more sensible Bulk" (Bond, *Spectator* 3.576).

The fragmented "sensible bulk" of artifacts offered a model for theorizing the imagination as a faculty both tethered and loosened to real objects and historical matters of fact.[23] Like an imaginative user who hangs her clothes from a doorknob, however, Addison points to the ways that artifacts' affordances could be multiplied. *The Spectator* invites us to recognize—in a way similar to Salter's embrace of being called a "Grubstreet dabbler" and as Don Quixote does—how useful the artifact was as a means of conceptualizing not only *The Spectator*'s content or purpose but also its materiality. Mr. Spectator himself is self-styled as not quite human, but not quite object. He admits that he lives "rather as a Spectator of Mankind, than as one of the Species" (Bond, *Spectator* 1.8). The first issue of *The Spectator* notably ends with the claim that a character like Mr. Spectator can only "Print [its] self out" (Bond, *Spectator* 1.9).

In one essay for *The Spectator*, No. 105 (1711), Steele takes up the question of the periodical's material form pointedly and directly. He bemoans that "[w]ritings" sent out into the world as "loose Tracts and single Pieces," like *The Tatler* and *The Spectator*, are subject to more disadvantages than works published as whole "Volume[s]." "Thoughts," printed "in distinct Sheets" and "Piece-meal," must immediately interest their readers; their "Matter must lie close together" (Bond, *Spectator* 1.438). Even though sometimes the nature of the medium demands that periodical publications be "made up of broken Hints and irregular Sketches," readers expect each "Sheet" to be a "kind of Treatise" that "make[s] out in Thought what it wants in Bulk" (Bond, *Spectator* 1.438). "Piece-meal" and made up of "broken Hints and irregular Sketches," *The Spectator's* bulk was admittedly wanting. But one of Mr. Spectator's favorite rhetorical tricks is to turn things on their head, and so Steele concludes that if "the Philosophers and great Men of Antiquity" had had recourse to the "Art of Printing," they would have certainly joined *The Spectator's* ranks, "dealing out their Lectures to the Publick" (Bond, *Spectator* 2.225).[24] Like Mr. Spectator, the writers of antiquity would have "obtruded upon the Publick," appeared "in every Assembly," and been "exposed upon every Table" (Bond, *Spectator* 2.225). As a fragment always supplementing material substance with "Thought," *The Spectator* is free to enter speculatively as well as historically into the company of the ancients, its timely weekly meditations promising to bulk up by adding up to timeless truths, eventually.[25]

Relatedly, Addison frequently takes up the question of memory and preservation in *The Spectator*: "I shall endeavor to enliven Morality with Wit, and to temper Wit with Morality," Mr. Spectator declares, so that readers "may, if possible, both Ways find their Account in the Speculation of the Day. And to that End that their Virtue and Discretion may not be short, transient, intermitting Starts of Thought, I have resolved to refresh their Memories from Day to Day, till I have recovered them out of that desperate State of Vice and Folly into which the Age is fallen" (Bond, *Spectator* 1.54). Mr. Spectator prioritizes his firsthand reporting on particulars, however, without ever taking full recourse in a perfect omniscience definable by first causes—recognizing, perhaps, that having the final say on first causes would mean that *The Spectator* need not print another word. *The Spectator* pieces together pages that do not quite constitute a whole volume and histories that can never fully be tallied up.

And readers ate it up. The "many letters" Mr. Spectator receives from his correspondents confirmed Steele's conviction in the viability of the form that he and Addison had adopted for their writing, and "[b]esides," he smirks: the "Bookseller tells" him that the "Demand" for *The Spectator* "encreases [*sic*] daily" (Bond, *Spectator* 2.226). Both Steele and Addison also knew that another way to increase the bulk of *The Spectator* was to invite their readers to supply what was missing. Addison appears to have been surprised by the enthusiasm his readers had for engaging with Mr. Spectator's fictional persona. Purporting to be overwhelmed by letters from *The Spectator's* fans that critiqued the latest fashions, shared salacious gossip, and pleaded for a particular political "party," Mr. Spectator declares that he will not publish all those letters. He will, however, use them (Bond, *Spectator* 1.66):

> I shall therefore acquaint my Reader, that if he has started any Hint which he is not able to pursue, if he has met with any surprising story which he does not know how to tell, if he has discovered any Epidemical Vice which has escaped my Observation, or has heard of any uncommon Virtue which he would desire to publish; in short, if he has any Materials that can furnish out an innocent Diversion, I shall promise him my best Assistance in the working of them up for a publick Entertainment.

The Spectator, in other words, encouraged its readers to collect fragments from their own everyday experiences, while Mr. Spectator promised that he was the one who could piece them all together into ideas as well as morals that were unbounded by the specific conditions of their origins. Addison describes this as *The Spectator's* "formal" as well as its "material" benefit.

In Addison's breathless elucidation of *The Spectator's* material benefits, he explains that his periodical profitably employs rag collectors, paper makers, and printers. "[S]o many Hands [are] employ'd in every Step" of the periodical's publication process that the venture is sure to "provid[e] Bread for a Multitude" in the local economy. In the presence and presentism of Addison's rendering of *The Spectator's* contributions to the liberal economy of the eighteenth century, it can be easy to miss the claim he also makes about *The Spectator's* future "material" benefit. Mr. Spectator winks that some will undoubtedly use his papers for lighting their pipes, wrapping their spices and pies, or stuffing their fashions. He goes on to humblebrag that maybe even, one day, *The Spectator* will be "raised from a Dung-hill" and transformed into "the most valuable piece of Furniture in a Prince's Cabinet" (Bond, *Spectator*

3.381). In short, Addison imagines *The Spectator* as just the kind of artifact that was on display in Don Saltero's coffeehouse.

Deidre Lynch finds that "eighteenth-century novelists" were particularly "enthusiastic" about the "portability" of not just their books as bound volumes but also their words, plots, characters, and digressions, which could "be conveyed from book to book" like so many "collectibles" ("Novels" 136). By provoking debate and fomenting suspicions, artifacts afforded the production of texts that aspired to share in the artifacts' interesting materialities. Such texts also seized opportunities to deploy a variety of nonfictional as well as fictional tropes and literary techniques in order to intrigue their readerships. These tropes and techniques were well suited for publication in popular periodicals, but Lynch reminds us that they were also well suited for writers who worked in other genres and mediums. Although the artifacts at Don Saltero's performed dubiously their roles as the agents of historical, political, and philosophical certainties, they succeeded in engaging their spectators and transforming them into tattlers. Artifacts like those at Don Saltero's coffeehouse proved to be the most vibrant, in the end, when they didn't prove much at all.

PART TWO

CASE STUDIES

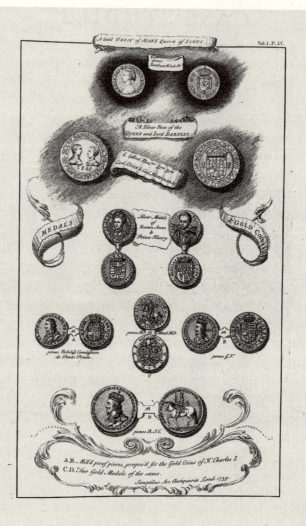

A Gold COIN of MARY Queen of SCOTS.

penes Jacobum West Ar.

A Silver Piece of the QUEEN and Lord DARNLEY.

C. Collect. Harmonum Dmm Dmm Com. Oxon & Com Montrosum.

MEDALS

Silver Medals of Queen Anne & Prince Henry.

& GOLD Coins

penes Nobilifs Comitifsam de Ponte Fracto.

penes Rdo M Leoland MD.

penes G.V.

penes R.J.C.

A.B. Mill'd proof pieces, propos'd for the Gold Coins of K. Charles I.
C.D. Two Gold Medals of the same.
Sumptibus &c. Antiquaria Lond. 1739.

CHAPTER THREE

Coins: The Most Vocal Monuments

Old coins and medals were the most popular artifacts in England during the long eighteenth century.[1] Because they were small and existed in vast quantities, coins were the most affordable and available artifacts that could be collected. They were considered to be the most reliable evidence of what had really happened in the past because they were durable and, usually, their inscriptions meant that they were both identifiable and datable. Coins depicted the people, rituals, battles, maps, buildings, fashions, gods, and symbols that were long gone; their inscriptions preserved histories of poetry and aphorisms. Likewise, coins were compelling because they were portable and personal. They featured the faces of the dead, and they could be held in the hand or kept secretly in a pocket.

For the period's scientists and philosophers, coins provided models for scaling theories of matter up from individual bodies to the body politic and down from external objects to their component elements. As small antiquities, coins glossed investigations into matter's microscopic properties and served as vehicles for imagining how matter interacted with the senses and entered into the body. As pieces of metal, coins complemented analyses of matter's force and permanence: the ways in which matter was durable and the chains of causes and effects it was capable of producing. As objects that could easily circulate, coins could exemplify matter's networks of association and influence; they offered a way of imagining how individual entities affected larger systems, and vice versa. Taken together, coins' size, substance, and movability presented opportunities for conceptualizing not only the relationships among external objects, the body, and the mind but also the relationships between governments and polities in the past as well as in the present.

Coins just as frequently exposed the limitations of using objects to explain or prove intangible ideas: about the mind, about invisible phenomena, about the past, and about political histories as well as principles.[2] Their diminutiveness threatened to render their influence dangerously insidious. Their metal threatened to be malleable and fake. The networks constituted by their circulation threatened to be capricious or corrupt. When prodded and scratched for their true histories, coins could attest to the ways competing political factions often recast their political motives as the mechanical or the vital effects of objects. Coins could be especially adept as agents of factious propaganda. When coins proved incapable of holding up to the bite of suspicion, however, they became supple in the service of critique.

This chapter begins with John Evelyn's *Numismata* (1697), in which Evelyn argued that coins were both the most reliable antiquities and also the most affecting. I track Evelyn's ideas about coins, intimacy, mind, and memory as they also appear in eighteenth-century philosophical discourses where coins' facility for influence coincides with a wariness about their facility for falsehood. John Dryden's *The Medall* offers an important backstory to Evelyn's treatise in this regard. Dryden knew that politicians manipulated coins' materiality for their own purposes. He exposed coins as objects capable of being more duplicitous and malleable than they seemed to be. Like the periodical writers who responded to the questionable performances of the gimcracks at Don Saltero's in chapter 2, Dryden experimented with adapting coins' shape and substance for his own satirical, poetic ends. Following an examination of Dryden, I return to the writer Joseph Addison. In his *Dialogues upon the Usefulness of Medals* (1726), Addison seized—as Dryden had done—an opportunity to base stylistic experimentation on the materiality of coins, but he did so to reimagine coins as agents of aesthetic sensibilities that could transcend the limits of corruptible bodies and problematic histories. Charles Johnstone's wildly popular it-narrative *Chrysal* is a text, I conclude, that recoins Addison's aesthetics into narrative in order to encourage readers to revel in coins' story-telling affordances—but to prioritize reading texts over artifacts if they want to know the truth about political history.

Minting Memories

In his *Numismata* (1697), John Evelyn asserted the value of old coins. According to Evelyn, coins and medals were easy to collect because there were a lot of them to be had, and they were cheap (1). More importantly, however, they were beautiful—like little pieces of art, according to Evelyn, and especially handy to use as illustrations for the ancient texts one might also collect. Most importantly, however, Evelyn argued that medals were the most durable and the most "Vocal Monuments" (1). He revised Aubrey's claim that antiquities like stone henges could speak for themselves. "Enormous" monuments seemed to Evelyn to be "mute and dead, without any Soul" (1). They lacked inscriptions, "Character," as Evelyn put it. They couldn't "tell us by whom, or to what end they were erected" (1). Such was also the case with "*Marbles, Statues, Trophies, &c*" (2). Even "*Books*" paled in comparison to medals, Evelyn claimed, because their paper matter made them especially vulnerable to decay (71).

"Nothing in all this Tract of Time" had proven more lasting than coins, Evelyn declared. And so coins were more loquacious, too, than the stones that Aubrey claimed could speak for themselves (2). Coins, those "small pieces of Metal . . . seem to have broken and worn out the very Teeth of Time, that devours and tears in pieces all things else" (2). For Evelyn, medals' physical bodies, including their substance, shape, size, and design, made them vibrant. Their small size and shape were enlivened by virtue of a contrast with their elemental heft and aesthetic force. Moreover, the coin-artifact appeared, literally, to speak its truths through its prominent visual depiction of faces and its inclusion of textual snippets or inscriptions—all stamped in metal.

The "vocal" nature of medals' small but heavy matter went hand in hand with their power to inspire the imagination: to cut not only through the teeth of time, but to transgress the limits of the body and whisper directly to the memories of their collectors. With these powers of coins in mind, Evelyn celebrates how medals were once used by the ancients: as lively surrogates of the dead.[3] Medals not only reminded people of the "brave and glorious Persons they represented"; they could also stand in for the dearly departed (68). People considered their medals "as yet alive," according to Evelyn (68). They believed that the eyes looking out from the faces on the medals "observ[ed] their Actions" (68). People were "charm'd" by the "Conversation" they had with their medals, according to Evelyn, and "they carried" their coins everywhere, through all their "Triumphs" and "to their very Funerals and Graves" (68).[4] As Evelyn here suggests, medals fortified moral character by memorializing personal attachments and translating private memories into vibrant, ongoing actions.

Evelyn argued that medals were especially powerful agents of history in the seventeenth century for two reasons. They had survived for remarkably long periods of time, and they were physically well suited for conveying memorable historical content to the mind through the body. Evelyn's interest in the combined force of medals' historical and affective power owes a degree of debt to older epistemes in which coins were bound up in metaphors for memory and mind, as his invocation of the ancients' numismatic practices implies. As Mary Caruthers explains, classical and then medieval descriptions of memory often supplied the mind with the figurative matter of coins.

According to Caruthers, the twelfth-century writer Hugh of St. Victor popularized the image of the mind as a "money-pouch" and compared the process
of making a memory to that of stamping a coin (45). Not only could coinage
account for the act of making a memory and then, subsequently, yield representations of the mind as a bank; these metaphors also described the retrieval
of memories as a cashing out (or in) on an individual's mnemonic currency
(Caruthers 116).[5]

Representations of the mind as a bank of coined memories made coins
especially useful as mnemonic devices for the study of history throughout the
long eighteenth century. If you had a mind for history, you needed a cabinet
of coins. Having a collection of medals to see and to touch made it possible for
the amateur and professional historian alike to store and then retrieve facts
as if such details were so many coins in a cabinet. By remembering the visual
features of the coins arranged into chronological and geographical orders in
a cabinet, one could more quickly and easily associate historical names and
events with the medals that depicted them and then cognitively put them
back into the right orders. Richard Grey began his popular guide to memorization, *Memoria Technica* (1730), by claiming that it "is a general Complaint
amongst Men of Reading . . . that they find themselves not able to *Retain* what
they read with any Certainty or Exactness. And in no part of Literature is
there greater Room for this Complaint than in *History*" (iii). Although Grey
goes on to promote his own phonetic, metrical schema for memorizing historical facts, he takes note of "the great Help to Memory" old coins provided.

The numismatist David Jennings similarly declared in his *Introduction to
the Knowledge of Medals* (1764) that "being conversant with" a "Cabinet of
Medals" will "fix historical facts and circumstances upon the memory with
more ease" (56).[6] That coins and their various visual forms could serve as
powerful memoria technica in the field of historical study was further exemplified by their prominence of place as material objects in everyday life. Maria
Edgeworth reports that it was common to use medals as instructive deco-
rations in nurseries in order to support children's study of history (2.419).
Guidebooks for juvenile science experiments included "directions for obtain-
ing an exact Representation or Picture of any Coin or Medal" by making
wax, paste, or paper copies of coins. Henry Baker's *Of Microscopes* (1785) explains that the practice of making coin molds allowed everyone to "be fur-
nished with a noble Collection" of coins. They could arrange these "in Books,
in orderly Series"; the "Usefulness" of this, he says, no one doubts (2.441). In
1800 there appeared a pocketbook for children titled *A Concise Epitome of the*

History of England, composed almost entirely of small, numismatic images based on the designs of the acclaimed medalist, Jean Dassier.

As this last example of the popular, mnemonic uses to which coins were put suggests, the shape and size of a coin came to be as important as its three-dimensional body. Although this formal malleability of the coin proved Evelyn's point, it also threatened to unseat the coin's status as a guarantor of facts. Still, the period's histories supplied plenty of images that copied or mimicked old coins' designs for the express purpose of aiding the reader's memory. The most conspicuous of these is James Granger's *Biographical History of England* (1769).[7] Granger originally intended this publication to be a "Methodical Catalogue of British Heads"—a series of portraits of England's historical luminaries—but he extended the project to include short biographical anecdotes, and the work soon grew to four, and later six, volumes (ii). The *Catalogue of Engraved British Portraits* (1769–1774) was sold separately to supplement the biographical sketches. Granger's portraits were often copies of medals or based on engravings of coins, and he cites the work of numismatists as his inspiration for the whole. Granger celebrates the coin as a "visible representation of past events," and "a kind of *speaking chronicle*" that translates "into civil story" (1.12). His portraits emphasized the face and head, and they were frequently accompanied by "arms, mottoes, and devices" so that they "convey[ed] much the same kind of instruction as the reverses of medals" (1.12).

The whole, Granger declared, had been designed for "transmitting" and "perpetuating the memory" of England's most important historical figures. He promised that his coin-like portraits would provide a "wonderful service" for those who were engaged with "reading histories" and would have "a surprising effect upon the memory" (1.12). Granger concluded that his work would "happily convey, and that in a manner almost insensible, real and useful instruction. For such a collection will delight the eye, recreate the mind, impress the imagination, fix the memory, and thereby yield no small assistance to the judgment" (1.12). But Granger also worried about his project's relationship to numismatics and, especially, those "almost insensible" effects it could have, whereby the memory and the judgment would be fixed "in a manner almost insensible" as the eye was delighted, the mind recreated, and the imagination impressed. "[C]ollections of engraved portraits," he confessed, "have lain under the same prejudices [as] ancient coins" (1.15). At best, both have sometimes been suspected of being "little more than empty amusements"; at worst, they have been suspected of nurturing idolatry. Granger assures his readers that his intentions are rooted in contemporary theories of mind rather than in "superstition" (1.15).

Evelyn's suggestion that coins' matter afforded not only historical knowledge but also affective allure proved, as Granger indicates here, to be risky. Coins continued throughout the long eighteenth century to be prized as vehicles of unbiased information about the past and as mnemonic devices for remembering historical facts. But, once they were vested with the power to translate history into personal memory and morality, coins also accrued the dangerous power to mint falsehoods as if they were solid truths. The matter of the coin itself—its prominent placement of the head and the face, its small, durable, metallic body—meant that the facts to which it testified seemed more immediate and influential because more sensual and more verifiable, and more memorable because solidly based on something that could be held in the hand, looked at eye to eye.

For Evelyn, privileging the matter of the medal as a direct conduit of historical facts and moral feelings was a means of expressing his royalist sympathies. These sympathies came to the fore in the vitriol with which he described coin clippers and counterfeiters in his *Numismata*. During the fall of Charles I, the rise of Cromwell, the fall of Cromwell, the restoration of Charles II, and so on, nearly every coin in the nation had seemingly been filed and clipped around the edges or melted down and subject to recoinage.[8] Evelyn suggested that clippers and counterfeiters struck at the king's very body. "Effigies and Images of the Prince" that appeared on coins, he explained, should not be "look'd upon as merely stamp'd for Ornament or Honour, or to proclaim and set forth Titles only, where or when they Reign, but as publick Vouchers of the real and intrinsic Value of the Species and Matter according to the constant and general Estimation of the World . . . so as he that either diminishes it or sophisticates it, does as much as in him lies, make the King as great a Cheat and Imposter as himself" (224). Not surprisingly, Evelyn is suspiciously brief and sometimes silent in the parts of his treatise that deal with coinage during the reign of Cromwell.[9] Evelyn's political investments were clear, however, even from the beginning of his treatise. As he explained, the ancients did not limit medals' capacity to influence the minds of their owners by preserving memories of the past by conceiving them as objects of "bare and transitory entertainment of the Eye only" or as tokens of personal, sentimental attachments. Rather, the ancients felt that medals "had a secret and powerful Influence, even towards the advancement of the best of Governments, by their continual representations of great and virtuous Examples; So as in that point Art became a piece of State" (69).

It was difficult, however, to determine which government coins served by circulating their "secret and powerful Influence." As Neil Guthrie meticulously documents, coins in particular functioned as tokens of Jacobite sympathies throughout the eighteenth century.[10] In his study of the royal touch, Marc Bloch argued that the "exiled Stuarts were still wonder-working figures," and their touchpieces, medals "struck for the distribution on the days of the royal touch" and "preserved by the common people as amulets," were prime collectibles (396). More frequently, "common money" that could "still be found and collected from the reign of Charles I," was sought after—proxy touchpieces, "endowed with a special kind of dignity by the fact that they bore Charles I's effigy" (396).[11] One of the first acts of the Parliament in the wake of Charles I's execution was to requisition the coins of Charles I, melt them to mint new ones reflecting the change of regime, and commission commemorative medals as well as new official seals for the government.[12] These Interregnum medals were known and collected in the eighteenth century.[13] They were engraved elaborately by George Vertue, the official engraver for the Society of Antiquaries, and published in his *Medals, Coins, Great-Seals, Impressions from the Elaborate Works of Thomas Simon* (1753).[14]

Brad Pasanek shows that coins continued to be used prominently as metaphors of mind throughout the eighteenth century, but their "ductility"—both material and ideological—constantly threatened to undermine their "durability," and so much depended on their durability (53). In the opening to his *Essay concerning Human Understanding* (1689), Locke tellingly uses a coin metaphor to characterize the antithesis of his argument. Locke's adversarial interlocutors have argued that "certain innate principles" and "primary notions" are "stamped upon the mind of man" before birth (48).[15] Locke goes on, of course, to assert that the mind is stamped with ideas, but he argues that ideas are impressed through the senses and minted in the seat of reason rather than formed a priori.[16] The mind, in other words, is not like a coin when we are born. Rather, the mind takes in information from our sensory encounters with external objects. We learn to use our reason to parse this information so we stamp or coin the malleable matter of the mind into our ideas and our character.

In declaring that the mind is not like a medal pre-stamped with ideas, Locke appropriates the old coin metaphors of mind and memory by characterizing our ideas themselves as being made up of so many small coins of memory. Saying that ideas are "innate," according to Locke, is like saying that a "Man hath 100 *l.* sterling in his Pocket" while denying that his "100 *l.* sterling" is made up of "either Penny, Shilling, Crown, or any other coin, out of which the Sum is to be made up" (96). In the section immediately following Locke's description of innate ideas as currency without coins, he turns to consider the foibles of our memory. For Locke, memory is the most immediate source of our misconception that ideas are innate in the first place: "If there be any innate ideas," he explains, "they must be lodg'd in the memory; and from thence must be brought into view by Remembrance" (96). In other words, if an individual operated under the mistaken assumption that she had one hundred pounds sterling but couldn't immediately find the pennies, shillings, and crowns in her pocket, she should *remember* (although she may have forgotten) that her sterling ideas had, in fact, once been materially present in the past like so many pennies in her pocket.

The history of how we had come to have an idea in the first place could fall easily out of our memories, like so much loose change through a ripped seam. As Locke's twist on the coin metaphor for mind suggests, the memory's facility for tricking our senses maintained an uneasy relationship to the affordances of objects, like a coin, to convey accurate information to our bodies, minds, and hearts. If the memory could simulate our encounters with things and, in so doing, also falsify that encounter, then how were we to depend on something like a coin to guarantee the transmission of a past we could not remember for ourselves? Coins could also, then, be used as metaphors for especially insidious types of false knowledge. Robert Boyle uses the coin as a figure for false knowledge when he says in his *Free Enquiry into the Vulgarly Received Notion of Nature* (1686) that he is "wont to judge of opinions, as of coins: I consider much less, in any one that I am to receive, whose inscription it bears, than what metal it is made of . . . [I]f I find it counterfeit, neither the prince's image or inscription, nor its date (how ancient soever [*sic*]), nor the multitude of hands through which it has passed unsuspected will engage me to receive it" (5).[17] Boyle's analogy, like Locke's metaphor, still finds purchase in the substance of the coin, however—even as he disavows the coin's visible features of image and text. In this way, Boyle also unexpectedly agrees with Hobbes, who similarly insisted that coins' ultimate value inhered only in their metal.[18]

It was difficult, then, to disassemble the matter of the coin itself from its content, not least because medals' matter was both durable and ductile. The effect was one in which the past itself became celebrated for its materiality. Lord Bolingbroke famously and influentially claimed that the "true use of history" was to offer "examples" to the "senses" as well as the "understanding" in order to "train us up to private and public virtue" (14–15). According to Bolingbroke, history's examples were compelling because they appealed, like coins, directly to our senses before moving on to offer fodder for our "understanding" (16). Bolingbroke argued that the "force of examples" from a past we had never personally experienced was powerful because they could be as tangible as our private memories (16). Bolingbroke supported his claim in ways that speak to Locke's coin metaphor not of mind, but of memory. Our memories, according to Bolingbroke, can recreate experiences that are no longer "immediate," or directly "under our sight" with perfect similitude (16). History as a kind of collective memory harnesses our individual memories' ability to present our own pasts to us as if they were materially present again. In so doing, history inculcates a "useful" "habit" of "imitating" remembered experiences (16). Bolingbroke maintained that by feeling once again exactly the way something had felt before—even if we had not felt it ourselves—we would learn how to become virtuous. Good choices, our own and others', could be repeated; bad ones, emended.

Bolingbroke, not surprisingly, shared Evelyn's appreciation for the numismatic practices of the ancients not least because he shared his royalist loyalties. He admired the Romans' propensity to populate their domestic spaces with "images of their ancestors" (17). These were constant material reminders that seemed like they "transferred by the magic of example," the "virtues" of previous generations" to the present (17–18). But Bolingbroke also understood that his way of imagining the past as just these sorts of memorable, material objects meant that "history, true *or false*, speaks to our passions always" (13, emphasis added). He worried about those historians who wrote "wild," "fantastical" histories in order "to prop up a system" (7). In terms similar to Bolingbroke's, James Beattie also celebrated the force of examples in his *Dissertations Moral and Critical* (1783).[19] Advocating both for the "remembrance" of "history" and the exercise of the faculty for "recollection," Beattie maintained that memory ought to bring "past actions, thoughts, and purposes" into an individual's view, such that those that inspired virtue could be found "right," and those that did not, could be "condemned and rectified"; this practice was "indispensably requisite to moral improvement" (1.39).

Like Bolingbroke, Beattie believed that "[r]eligious, political, and moral doctrines, when enforced by facts . . . lose their abstract nature, and become, as it were, objects of sense; and so engage attention, are easily understood, make a deep impression upon the mind, and produce a durable remembrance" (1.15). Beattie goes on, therefore, to demand that "those whose business is to instruct mankind" pay strict regard to this phenomenon, because "if our attention is engaged by matters of importance," such as "historical facts," then "our Memory will be stored with matters of importance" (1.15–16). But "if we are captivated by trifles only, we shall remember only trifles" (1.16). Lord Kames agreed in his *Introduction to the Art of Thinking* (1761), arguing (69) that "[h]e who indulges the thirst of ambition, the stubbornness of pride, the savageness of conquest, the shame of deceit, the misery of avarice, and the bitterness of prodigality, must for ever be an enemy to memory. The past . . . is, to the virtuous only, a constant source of enjoyment. What satisfaction, in looking back with approbation? What uneasiness, in looking back with shame and remorse?"

Concerns over false histories and trifling memories continued to gloss the coin's appearance as a historical guarantor and as a metaphor of mind in various discourses throughout the long eighteenth century. As both a mnemonic for history and as a metaphor of mind, the coin exposed the ways in which encounters with the past could be enhanced as well as compromised by the relays between facts and affects that artifacts incited. This problem doubled back on the metaphorical tropes of the coin, and counterfeit or corrupt coins inspired anxiety not only in obviously economic contexts, but also in the contexts of cognition, memory, and character. If Boyle and Hobbes were certain that they could arrive at the truth of a coin by digging in to its metal, others were less sure. Coins' capacity for duplicity troubled epistemological models, whether scientific, historical, or purely philosophical, that emphasized matter's agency and appealed to its ontological certainty. Counterfeit or corrupt coins especially threatened to set the histories that were based upon them to totter on falsehoods and, concordantly, the virtues they promised to preserve and disseminate, on unsound material principles.

Small, Fake, and Two-Faced

In the *The Medall* (1682), John Dryden vented his suspicions that the problem with coins was that corrupt politicians took advantage of their material affordances—even as he inclined to side, like Evelyn and Bolingbroke, on the side of monarchs. After a grand jury refused, in November of 1681, to indict the Earl of Shaftesbury for treason based on his participation in the Popish Plot against Charles II, the Earl's admirers commissioned a medal to celebrate the occasion. They distributed copies to Whig sympathizers in London. Dryden's *Absalom and Achitophel* (1681) had already demonstrated that the Popish Plot proved to be a gold mine for satirical poetry, and so he again turned his attention to Shaftesbury's politics and, this time, also his medal.[20] Dryden illustrates how Evelyn's vision of the coin as a historical fact and as vibrant agent of moral virtue conflicted with coins' more questionable capacity to act on behalf of partisan politicians. In *The Medall*, Dryden also revels in the vibrant materiality of coins, and he imagines his own poem as a kind of coin. Yet he does so in order to expose the shortcomings of histories as well as philosophies that would grant artifacts like coins the agency to establish political facts and principles. Dryden insists that his readers and his political opponents recognize that deep philosophical contradictions emerge when the influence artifacts exert on their publics is understood to be determined by their physical properties.

Dryden's "Epistle to the Whigs," which prefaced *The Medall*, gets to the point in short order by addressing the size of Shaftesbury's coin: "For to whom can I dedicate this Poem, with so much Justice as to you [the Whigs who supported Shaftesbury]?" Dryden rhetorically asks. "'Tis the representation of your own Heroe [*sic*]: 'tis the Picture drawn at length, which you prize and admire so much in little" (38). Dryden juxtaposes his poetic prowess against the Whigs' jingoistic numismatics. Where their coin is "little," Dryden's poetry has "length"; behind the "inch" of their medal, Dryden can "detect" "gross Fallacies" (38–39). Dryden's emphasis on the discursive "length" of his poem in contrast to the "little" form of the coin launches the first volley in *The Medall's* political purpose: to expose how the Whigs' theory of matter licenses them to release propagandistic materials into the body politic. *The Medall* goes on, for example, to describe the coin as a representative example of the Whigs' preference for trite wit over substance: they "shorten'st all dispute" and "Power is [their] essence" (45). "Wit" is their "attribute," and they "leap'st o'er all Eternal truths" (46).

Dryden finds that the Whigs' penchant for short forms makes their choice of the medal as propaganda an apt one. However, Dryden observes that the transference of rhetorical brevity onto and into the medal is also, ironically, out of step with the Whigs' professed political convictions. In *The Medall*, he promises, readers will find "None of [the medal's] Ornaments are wanting; neither the Landscape of the Tower, nor the Rising Sun; nor the Anno Domini of [the Whigs'] New Sovereign's Coronation" (38). Slyly here, Dryden recognizes that although the medal's appropriation of sovereign iconography appears to perform as a parliamentary government's ornamental understudy, the medal nevertheless belies the ways the Whigs would invest it with an agency that exploits radical vitalisms in order to exceed the limits imposed by the medal's small size. For Dryden, Shaftesbury's medal exposes the Whigs' grander ambitions, which exist on a dynastic scale that not only stands at odds with the matter of a small coin but also hearkens to the ideologies the Whigs would assign to their opponents, the royalists.

Consequently, the poem extends the temporality encoded in Shaftesbury's medal. For example, Dryden notes that although Shaftesbury's coin is small, the time it took to design and engrave was long. Shaftesbury reportedly spent "[f]ive daies [*sic*]" sitting for the artist to design the image of his profile that appeared on the medal: "[f]our more than God to finish *Adam* took," Dryden quips (43). In the "Epistle to the Whigs," the detail of the time Shaftesbury spent modeling for George Bower's design surfaces as well. "[T]he Lineaments [of Shaftesbury's character]" contained in *The Medall* "are true," Dryden declares, "though [Shaftesbury] sate not five times to me, as he did to B[ower]" (38). For Dryden, this fact serves as more than just a jab at Shaftesbury's presumed vanity; he continues to excavate the temporal secrets behind the medal's small matter. The medal's singular iconographic representation of Shaftesbury's face obfuscates the long mechanical trajectory of the villainous character it depicts.

As Dryden describes it, Shaftesbury's character has historically shuffled through many and various types: from the "Martial-Hero" swept "by the Winds, to War," to a "Rebel" even before he was a "Man," to a "Vermin" in Cromwell's "Ear," to a political sellout who "[barters] his venal Wit for Sums of Gold" and now finally, Shaftesbury has reached his apotheosis as a man who would assume the idolatrous position of "Saint" and king (9). The medal erases Shaftesbury's multitudinous past selves, "for Hypocritick Zeal / Allows no Sins but those it can conceal" (44). Although the coin's small matter is appropriately coeval with the Whigs' quick and propagandistic rhetorical style, its form proves to be a perverse performance that obfuscates the real scale and time behind its design. Its small size hides a surprising quantity of transgressions, each of which Dryden finds to be morally bankrupt.

The trope of the counterfeit coin, therefore, also floats throughout *The Medall*. Although minted as a commemorative token and not as a species of currency, Shaftesbury's medal nevertheless functioned in a marketplace of exchange in ways that Dryden suggests were at uncomfortable odds with its real value as a piece of metal. On the one hand, as Dryden describes in the

"Epistle to the Whigs," the price of Shaftesbury's medal exceeds its essential worth. Bower has "made a good Market" for the coin (38). Most of the medals were "bought up already," and "the value of the remainder enhanc'd" that no one could afford to purchase the few that remained on the market (38). On the other hand, the coin itself was a specious fiction: both a presentation of Shaftesbury's character that Dryden found false and a hypocritical expression of Shaftesbury's real political pretensions to assume a king-like position of power he did not deserve in a monarchical system he presumed to despise. Dryden uses quick metaphors to characterize Shaftesbury and his cronies as economic swindlers. When the Whigs commissioned their medal, they "wor[e]" their "Modesty" "to rags": the same base substance that constituted the essential form of the paper banknote. Likewise, Dryden asks by what "right" do the Whigs assume to "license of traducing the Executive Power [of Charles II], with which [they] own he is invested"—a cunning comment on the implied usurpation of what Hobbes identified as the most powerful right of a monarch: to determine the value of money (38).

In the poem, Dryden makes the charge of counterfeit explicit, as "Villain and Wit exact a double price" (44). Such counterfeit "doubling" initially yokes the medal's material features to its ideology. "Never did Art so well with Nature strive," Dryden sarcastically pronounces, because the image on the coin is "[s]o like [Shaftesbury]; so golden to the sight, / So base within, so counterfeit and light" (43). At the same time, however, the medal's corruptions troublingly exceed the bounds of its material form. The medal's "light" and "base" matter allow it to circulate prolifically and profitably. Therefore, "plenty makes us poor" (47), and London itself emerges in the poem as "too bounteous," monstrous in its commercial excesses (48). Like the counterfeit Popish Plot satirized by Dryden in *Absalom and Achitophel*, the medal works to inspire treasonous "Rebellion . . . Which, though not Actual, yet all Eyes may see / 'Tis working, in th' immediate Pow'r to be" (49). Thus, Shaftesbury's false medal trades perfectly in fictions. The medal's worth is entirely speculative, but the medium in which it tenders its fictions remains thoroughly material. For Dryden, this leads directly to a comparison between the act of executing the king and melting down or clipping coins so as to alter their value. The London mob, characterized by its dubious economic practices, also "rise[s] *Cyclops*-like" from "pretended Grievances" to "deal" "in humane Flesh" and "Chop up a Minister, at every meal: / Perhaps not wholly to melt down the King; / But clip his regal Rights within the Ring" (49–50).

The medal's counterfeit performances operate not only as a function of the unreliable value of its metal but also as a function of its two-sided quality. Dryden, for example, observes that Shaftesbury and his supporters "pretend . . . zeal for the Publick good" in order to express their parliamentarian convictions, while they also profess a "due veneration for the person of the King" (39). Dryden argues that such speech, spoken out of both sides of the mouth, proves especially valuable for fomenting dissent: "That it is necessary for men in your circumstances to pretend both, is granted you; for without them there could be no ground to raise a Faction" (39). Consequently, the mob to which they would appeal is a similarly fickle, flip-flopping entity in *The Medall*; "Crowds err not," the Whigs would maintain, yet Dryden recognizes that crowds "to both extremes . . . run; / To kill the Father, and recall the Son" (46). The mob's religious convictions prove volatile as well. Their "Worship" now is "onely true," "but for the time; 'tis hard to know / How long we please it shall continue so. / This side today, and that to morrow [*sic*] burns" (46). Here, the medal works as a reliable monument, but in a perverse way; it manifests its subject and purpose—factious mayhem among the polity—with absolute precision.

That Shaftesbury's medal performs as an artifact whose size, metal, and double-sidedness make it an apt material monument to the Whigs' beliefs and practices—beliefs and practices that Dryden finds essentially short-sighted, worthless, and duplicitous—proves both tantalizing and frustrating for Dryden throughout the poem. In many ways, Shaftesbury's medal was a perfect artifact: a form of "unity" that Dryden considered in his *Essay of Dramatic Poesie* (1668). For Dryden, the medal's material properties made it an unfortunately unified monument to Shaftesbury's politics. At the same time, however, Dryden insists that the medal's matter appears unable to contain the Whigs' political ideologies or their effects, even as it embodies their essential, small, corrupt, and hypocritical nature. In this way, Dryden recognizes the medal as a dubious agent, an actor as prolifically vocal as Evelyn's numismatic specimens, but he attempts to wrench the medal's performances away from the matter of the object itself and back into Dryden's more reliable, and textual, satire.

Dryden's anxiety about the medal's ability to serve as a vocal, causal agent appears especially profoundly in *The Medall*'s frequent, apprehensive representations of the coin as an object that transgresses physical limits in order to influence the minds of those who come into contact with it. Dryden appears well aware of the popular assumption that informs part of Evelyn's numismatics: that the features of the face depicted on a coin should align with essential moral traits, linking the coin to mind and memory. Both the "Epistle to the Whigs" and the opening of the poem linger, for example, over the "lineaments" of the portrait of Shaftesbury's face. The poem itself pauses when Dryden encounters the difficulty of constructing a static, visual image of such a movable character as Shaftesbury: "cou'd the Style that copy'd every grace . . . cou'd it have form'd his ever-changing Will, / The various Piece had tir'd the Graver's Skill" (43–44).

Attempts to align the image of Shaftesbury's profile with the essence of his changeable nature calls into question one of Evelyn's central claims for the value of numismatic study: that coins and medals preserve and inspire virtue by fixing the faces of virtuous figures permanently in metallic forms. Dryden both recognizes and is appalled by such perversion of the coin's face value, as is evident in his suggestions throughout the "Epistle to the Whigs" and *The Medall* that Shaftesbury and his supporters secretly subscribe to the kind of idolatry that characterizes, ironically, the absolutist's philosophy of divine right. Dryden speculates, for example, that Shaftesbury's friends will turn the medal into "Thumb-Rings" upon his death, "as if there were virtue in his Bones to preserve [them] against Monarchy" (39), an invocation of the kind of relic-worshipping culture that characterized the magical thinking of royalist imperatives like "the king's touch."

Throughout *The Medall*, therefore, Dryden emphasizes Shaftesbury's medal as an object designed to breach the boundaries of the body, especially through the mouth and hands. Taking his cue from the coin as a vocal monument that coincides with the Whigs' penchant for short jingles designed to inflame the London mob, Dryden first characterizes Shaftesbury's medal's incitement to rebellion as a spur to the "hot-mouth'd horse" that "takes the Bit between his teeth and fl[ies] / To the next headlong steep of Anarchy" (46). This image of the wild horse's hot mouth, its teeth clenched on its metallic bit, takes monstrous advantage of the orality of the coin: its prominent depiction of the head, its presumption to vocality, and the practice of tasting coins to test their authenticity by comparing them to apples and turnips. Soon after this, Dryden alludes to the anecdote in Lucillius describing the Roman who laughed only once in his lifetime: at an ass chewing on a thistle. Even this reluctant giggler, Dryden claims, would laugh now "to see a Jury" sympathetic to the Whigs "chaw" on the "prickles of an unpalatable Law" (47). The associative invocations of the mouth arrive, finally, at a grotesque metaphor of disease; Shaftesbury's allies "Leech-like, [live] on bloud [*sic*]" sucked from a "fester'd sore" (47), and a "pox'd Nation" feels the metallic "*Mercury*" of the Whigs' "Venom" "in their Brains" (51).

The Medall imagines the body politic much like Dryden's opponents do: as porous and vulnerable to cognitive corruption through its material contact with vital matter like Shaftesbury's medal. The medal's effects reflect both Boyle's theory of things (that matter acts through secret proto-osmosis on the discrete parts of the body) and Hobbes's theory of the nation-state (as an interconnected mechanical body). Dryden shows that such theories of matter and government, however promising they may have been for the royalist agendas with which he sympathized, also made it possible for Shaftesbury's medal to act disproportionately on the body politic. Part of the issue for Dryden is Shaftesbury's and the Whigs' apparently willful misunderstanding of matter's causal agency, which they put to hypocritical use in minting Shaftesbury's medal in the first place. Shaftesbury, for example, "preaches to the Crowd, that Pow'r is lent, / But not convey'd to Kingly Government; / That Claimes successive bear no binding force; / That Coronation Oaths are things of course" (45). The Whigs would insist that royalism's rituals are arbitrary "things of course" while, at the same time, exploiting things, like a medal, as agents: an "Idol" that "seem'd so much alive" (43).

The Medall reveals how easily theories of matter could be confused when their principles were reduced and applied by "analogical contact" to the debates between royalists and revolutionaries (Rogers 2). Dryden appears aware, for example, of the coeval relationship between the medal's form and the Whigs' economically motivated politics: their desire to replace "the sovereign's control over currency and trade" with the "autonomous laws of the market" (Rogers 22). For Dryden, the kinds of vitalisms that appealed to radical revolutionaries, however, resembled ways of thinking about the king's divine body that they supposedly rejected. If vitalism imagined a democratic narrative of free will alongside free trade, extending agency out not only to everyone but also to everything, then it also threatened to make humans the puppets of arbitrary, material circumstances and economic environments by assigning to objects a kind of mystical, powerful force over which people would be powerless.

Moreover, as Dryden implies, such a worldview of animate objects proved convenient for Whig politicians who were as eager to foment dissent as they were to disavow their own agency in the resulting social upheaval. Such an implication allows Dryden to trade in the Whigs' terms, coyly suggesting that their vitalisms make for an easy exchange rate in the philosophical market where the public's subjection to the will of objects can be recast as subjection to the arbitrary forms of authoritarianism that the Whigs supposedly reject. In other words, we might expect Dryden, as a royalist sympathizer, to disavow the agency of Shaftesbury's medal. But Dryden imagines the Whigs' medal as a mechanical, unified object in which both its political significance and causal agency are commensurate with its form. The medal's matter appears to be at one with its essential ideological nature: small, double-sided, and counterfeit. These qualities, in turn, also characterize the nature of its agency. Shaftesbury's medal will work on the body politic for a delimited time, Dryden insists. Yet the political ideology it engenders will inevitably introduce contradictions that cannot be sustained and will eventually be proven counterfeit. This is a neat Aristotelian trick, for Dryden will let Shaftesbury and his supporters have their vitalisms after all, but he will insist that the causalities of their objects match their objects' physical state.

The tantalizing if frustrating unity that joins Shaftesbury's medal's form to its agency is tossed by *The Medall* into the wishing well of royalism. There, Shaftesbury's medal may, in fact, become a mere artifact: a bit piece of history, out of joint with time. But by linking the coin-artifact's agency to its form, and by appropriating that form for satirical, poetic purpose, Dryden's poem succeeded perhaps too well. Dryden's concluding nod to a historicity outside of matter failed, in the end, to secure his poem's status as a meaningful artifact. In his assessment of *The Medall*, Samuel Johnson claimed that because "the superstructure cannot extend beyond the foundation, a single character or incident cannot furnish as many ideas as a series of events or multiplicity of agents" (*Lives* 1.349); in many ways, this was exactly the point that *The Medall* was trying to make. Johnson goes on to suggest, however, that Dryden's poem had fallen under the weight of its commitment to exposing philosophical contradiction. Dryden's *The Medall*, "since time has left it to itself, is not much read, nor perhaps generally understood," Johnson confesses (*Lives* 1.349). When Dryden insisted that Shaftesbury's medal's agency be understood in terms of the coin-artifact's matter, he inevitably mired his own poetic accomplishment in the medal's base substance.

Numismatic Fictions

Dryden's poem calls into question the historical value of ancient coins by pointing out the political exigencies of Shaftesbury's medal. In the *Dialogues upon the Usefulness of Ancient Medals*, Joseph Addison takes up *The Medall*'s anxieties alongside Evelyn's certainties. Likely composed around 1702 but published posthumously in 1726, Addison's treatise repeats many of the same sentiments as Evelyn's *Numismata*.[21] Addison's nod to *The Medall* has received less attention. His "Eugenius" in the *Dialogues* invokes the figure of Sir William Davenport in Dryden's *Essay on Dramatic Poesie*; so too, does the character "Philander" bear a notable phonological resemblance to Neander, the figure who represents Dryden himself in the *Essay on Dramatic Poesie*.

These references to Dryden, however, do not trade easily with either Addison's admiration for Dryden or the *Dialogues'* celebration of numismatic study. Addison's plea for the value of numismatics begins with Evelyn, not Dryden. Like Evelyn, Addison takes pleasure in looking directly at the "[f]aces of all the great persons of antiquity" and "compar[ing]" their physical features with their "characters" in order to "try if we can [to] find out in his looks and features either the haughty, cruel, or merciful temper that discovers it self [*sic*] in the history of his actions" (13–14). Likewise, Addison agrees with Evelyn that medals stand in where other textual records may be wanting and when architectural or sculptural monuments have been lost. Addison's Eugenius notes "the great help to memory one finds in Medals" (21). By "consider[ing] in what part of the cabinet [a medal representing an emperor] lies; and by running over in their thoughts such a particular drawer," even an amateur historian will be able to "give you an account of all the remarkable parts" of history from memory (22). Eugenius makes this observation, however, not the *Dialogues'* protagonist, Philander. Philander agrees, but he confesses that it is not a "use" he had previously "thought upon" (23). Philander glosses over the mnemonic "use" of coin collecting, quickly moving to discuss the numismatist's ability to recognize the faces of sculptures based on his memory of the faces on coins. Indicating the *Dialogues'* commitment to art over history, Philander's turn here signals Addison's appropriation of the political and philosophical anxieties raised by Dryden. The *Dialogues* insists on the aesthetic value of old coins, eclipsing in the process their function as material agents of historical facts.

When Philander must encounter the doubtful politics of medals that, like Shaftesbury's coin in Dryden's hands, represent questionable politicians as heroes, the polite nature of his numismatics becomes especially clear. "Had we no other histories of the *Roman* Emperors, but those we find on their money," Philander admits, "we should take them for the most virtuous race of Princes that mankind were every blessed with: whereas, if we look into their lives, they appear many of them such monsters of lust and cruelty, as are almost a reproach to human nature" (151). This kind of "flattery," however, is set a notch above the more modern practice of using coins to satirize political enemies. Coins and medals "of a modern make are often charged with Irony and Satyr," he writes, and "[o]ur Kings no sooner fall out, but their mints make war upon one another, and their malice appears on their Medals" (151).

Philander's invective against satire spills over into his literary criticism as well. He finds that classical satire castigates a character only in order to "illustrate a precept or passage" rather than "to abuse him" (49). English satirists, however, "show a kind of malice" and craft a "whole Poem on purpose to abuse the person" (50). This kind of satire is a function of faction, engendering a hermeneutics that depends on excavating a "somebody," in Catherine Gallagher's terms, from a specific historical network.[22] This kind of explicit referentiality threatens to make the nation-state a historical entity at the expense of cultivating its imagined aesthetic transcendence. In his attempt to explain why contemporary British culture falls short of the model for minting medals established by Rome, Philander claims that "where Statesmen are ruled by a spirit of faction and interest, they can have no . . . concern for the figure [they] will make among posterity" (147). More than any other genre, Philander declares, "Satyr is more difficult to be understood by those that are not of the same Age with it. . . . Love-verses and Heroics deal win Images that are ever fixed and settled in the nature of things, but a thousand ideas enter into Satyr, that are . . . changeable and unsteady" (141–142).

Addison's numismatics, therefore, depend on casting the coin as a monument to permanence, but the coin should be pristine and scoured of rust. In other words, for Addison, the coin's agency ought to be disentangled from its matter and, finally, reassembled in a presentist collection where it can be interpreted within a classical textual canon that elides or exceeds historical contexts. Benedict finds that for Addison, "coins' morality lies in their materiality, their defeat of time" ("Moral in the Material" 82). Yet this is only part of the story. As David Alvarez notes, Addison is more concerned with coins' visuality. The difference is important, for Addison appears aware that Dryden had already severed the links among objects' physical shapes, their histories, and their agencies. This can especially be seen in the ways that Addison's treatise, despite its lip service to Evelyn's tenets, decries those antiquaries who followed in Evelyn's wake, privileging the coin as a physical object rather than as an aesthetic signifier of moral virtue.

Cynthio, Philander's polite antagonist, launches the first volley in the *Dialogues'* critique of coins' matter. His critique engages directly antiquarian methodologies for numismatic studies. Cynthio begins the treatise with a complaint against "several unprofitable parts of learning," those modern scholars who, like the popular image of antiquaries, prefer erudition to common sense (10). After condemning such a "set or two of *Virtuoso's*," Cynthio directs his satirical aim "upon the Medallists" (10). "These gentlemen, says he, value themselves upon being critics in Rust" (10). They are hoarders of useless objects and, just as problematically, useless details; they debate the cut of a Roman toga, count their money in sesterces instead of in pounds, and privilege brass over gold. Cynthio's debasement of numismatists is met with polite disagreement by Philander who, nevertheless, condemns a subtype of the medalist in similar terms to Steele's critique of Don Saltero; any science might be taken to ridiculous extremes, he admits. The astute critic naturally subjects the myopic pedant who would count sunspots or devote his time to studying "Spiders, Lobsters, and Cockle-shells" to "raillery" (11). Coins and medals, however, do have their merits for Philander; and the third companion, Eugenius, polite and eager to please, splits the difference between his two friends. While Eugenius acknowledges that many numismatists go too far, he suggests that since Philander is himself a collector of coins and medals, there must be something redeeming in numismatics.

Philander's defense follows, interspersed with objections from his companions and his responses. Like the antiquaries that Cynthio critiques, Philander appreciates coins as three-dimensional, material objects. When Eugenius, inspired by Philander's defense of coin collecting, proposes an assembled collection featuring a "Roman wardrobe," an arsenal of weapons, and a room featuring ancient religious monuments—in short "a magazine for all sorts of antiquities" that would allow individuals to immerse themselves in rooms populated by artifacts and "show a man in an afternoon more than he could learn out of books in a twelve-month"—Philander demurs from the proposal (18–19). "[Y]ou find on Medals every thing that you could meet with in your magazine of antiquities," he insists (19). Moreover, he points out that such a "magazine" of antiquities would have to be verified and authorized based on the representations of antiquities that were to be found on medals in the first place.

Yet Philander's characterization of coins as objects that remediate other antiquities signals a curious retreat from the matter of the coin as an artifact. In the end, he agrees with Cynthio that the antiquaries Eugenius is eager to join are "critics in rust" (13). Philander's defense of numismatics depends upon reclaiming the criticism, not the rust. "The intrinsic value of an old coin," he says, "does not consist in its metal but its erudition" (13). Philander returns to this point toward the end of the *Dialogues* when he declares that "[o]ne may understand all the learned part of [numismatic] science, without knowing whether there were Coins of iron or lead . . . and if a man is well acquainted with the Device of a Medal, I do not see what necessity there is of being able to tell whether the Medal it self be of copper or . . . brass" (13, 145). Philander admits that some kinds of rust "are extremely beautiful," and that rust can "preserve a Coin better than the best artificial varnish," but he demurs from a "learned dissertation on the nature of Rust"; instead he explains that a "skillful Medallist knows very well how to deal with [it]" by cleaning the coin and excavating "out of its rubbish" the medal's beautiful images (24).

This sentiment was profound enough in the *Dialogues* to inspire Alexander Pope's accompanying prefatory poem to make a fierce jab at rust-loving antiquaries: "With sharpen'd sight, pale Antiquaries pore" over their coins. They "value" "th' Inscription," but they "adore" the "Rust" (6). They "[scheme]" to acquire their specimens, and they can "taste no pleasure" in a coin that's been "scour'd" (6). Pope slyly blends the practice of tasting coins to determine their authenticity with the philosophical implications of coins' atomistic abilities to act on the individual body and the body politic, an image exploited by Dryden and taken up directly by Addison in the *Dialogues*.[23] As Pope recognizes, Addison implies that appreciating coins for their materiality fails to result in satisfying interpretations; Pope concludes his poem with a swipe at the antiquary who "neglects his Bride" and "sighs for an Otho" instead. For Pope, the antiquary's relationship to the coin as matter is a fundamentally vain and solipsistic one, rooted in the body and the self; when coins are "touch'd" by Addison's "hand," however, they "shine" with the "glories" of the classical past. Within the context of Philander's celebration of numismatics, Pope's subsequent turn to the "Gods" and "godlike Heroes" that "rise to view" in Addison's treatise conveys the *Dialogues'* concern with form over matter—a point made visible by Pope's recapitulation of Addison's plea that England emulate Rome in the practice of minting medals to commemorate great men. Pope imagines that the roster of British heroes would include Bacon and Newton alongside the unexpectedly "British" hero, Plato. Plato's place in the panoply of great "British" heroes here, where his "looks agree" with Newton's and Bacon's, illustrates Addison's interest in disentangling the coin's agency from its historicity and its materiality (7).

In Philander's defense of numismatics, he critiques those antiquaries who excavate small, local details from a single coin specimen. Whereas Dryden insists that the facts and effects of a coin must match its physical shape, Addison claims that antiquaries pick up pieces of historical data but fail to recognize the narrative arc effected by the coin's aesthetic properties. Although Philander himself happily lists the discrete facts of everyday life in Rome that might be verified by coins, he derives more pleasure—as Pope's prefatory poem knows—from viewing allegorical figures on coins rather than real historical individuals, and then linking the former to their representations in ancient poetry. This practice of comparing allegorical figures to their representations in classical poetry constitutes the bulk of the *Dialogues,* which goes on to examine a series of coins in a collection alongside excerpts from their literary counterparts: the *Dialogues* resembles an anthology of poetry more than it resembles a history. For Philander, "the old Poets" must "step in to the assistance of the Medallist" (30). The antiquary fails as the kind of literary critic Addison believes a numismatist ought to be because the antiquary "never thinks of the beauty of [an author's] thought or language" (32).

Popular endorsements of numismatics after Addison followed his lead. Pinkerton's *Essay on Medals* (1784)—a representative antiquarian treatise on coins—begins with the observation that "[t]he amusement arising from medals is so common and universal, that we meet with few people who have not formed a little collection of some kind or other" (1). He remains suspicious, however, of antiquaries' coin-collecting activities. Pinkerton begins with a jab at Evelyn's style ("very uncouth and unintelligible") and moves quickly to sneer that he will "not attempt" to explain the "ineffable delight which the sheer antiquary takes in any rusty commodity, and defaced medals in particular"; instead, Pinkerton "leave[s]" such an explanation to "any author who may, in future times, think of writing a much-wanted treatise on the diseases of the human mind" (33–34).

Numismatists, Pinkerton argues, should "treat all the parts" of their study "with coolness and candour, as matters of the merest indifference, and certainly of no necessity or importance" (xx). Pinkerton's treatise inevitably finds that the real value of numismatic study—the "principal and most legitimate source of pleasure" to be found in the "science"—rests in the appreciation of coins' and medals' "workmanship" (31). Although Pinkerton takes issue with Addison's preference for Latin rather than Greek poets, he takes up Addison's rallying call for England to mint medals like the ancients. Notably, however, Pinkerton insists that historical events ought not to be commemorated. Instead, he proposes a series of coins featuring allegorical representations of

"Liberty," "Fortitude," "Agriculture," and "Commerce" on their reverses coupled with jingoistic mottoes written in English (223–224).

Once bound in their beautiful textual networks, coin-artifacts can witness political history but only as mnemonic chronology; coins should be treasured for their ability to transmit ideology by virtue of their aesthetic function as agents of the polite, rather than the politic, arts. This can be seen in the ways Addison limits his focus to those coins produced in the classical past. More timely, modern medals—such as Shaftesbury's, which by the time Addison wrote, did constitute a record of history—are conveniently missing from Addison's treatise, brushed aside into the heap of the satirical mode and mired in impossibly specific contexts. The *Dialogues* is, perhaps, conspicuously silent on this point of numismatic history given Addison's familiarity with Dryden and his interest in reviving the English mint to produce commemorative medals in the service of a nationalist agenda.

Dryden glimpsed the ways Addison's emphasis on the usefulness of coins as agents of aesthetics could be structurally recast so as to resemble a theory of matter that could be used to bolster a claim for divine right insofar as the medal might act powerfully and directly on the minds of the individuals with whom it came into contact. Addison appears to have recognized the inverse. For Addison, the theories of matter on which divine right might be premised could be transferred from the body of a sovereign to the idea of history. A past seen dimly through the glimmering expanse of time could thereby become the secret engine of an aesthetic sensibility that transforms a factious public into a polite and commercial people. In other words, Addison's *Dialogues* illustrates the other side of Dryden's conceptual coin by attempting to eschew the problem of the relationships between the coin's matter and its agencies—as well as its histories and its politics—by recourse to a logic of substitution.

This logic of substitution entails replacing coins' contradictory performances of political history with their performance of myth. The beginning of the third dialogue in Addison's treatise illustrates as much when Cynthio admits that he has been so persuaded by Philander's endorsements of numismatic study that he dreams of coins. He has "had nothing but figures and inscriptions before [his] eyes" all night long (144). Cynthio's dream occurs after the narrator has briefly interrupted the *Dialogues* to remark on Cicero's invocation of Plato's representation of "the Plane-tree," which "did not draw its nourishment from the fountain than ran by it and watered its roots, but from the richness of the style that describes it" (143–144). In Cynthio's dream-scape, the coin-artifacts are not objects. They are images and texts. When Cynthio describes his dream, Philander retorts with a truism, remarking that "they say it is a sure sign a man loves money, when he is used to find it in his dreams" (144).

Here, Roland Barthes's characterization of "classic humanism" and its my-thologies can be applied to explain the function of Philander's truism. Barthes invites us to recognize the ways in which Philander's numismatics "[postu-late] that in scratching the history of men a little," "one very quickly reaches the solid rock of a universal human nature" (101). Addison's preference for form means, in Barthes's phrasing, that "history evaporates" until "only the letter remains" (116). For Barthes, a mythological form in particular evacu-ates its "concept," a term that connotes the kind of rusty historical contexts, content, and facts that Addison suggests antiquaries following in Evelyn's footsteps problematically privileged. Barthes recounts how the concept of mythological form "reconstitutes a chain of causes and effects, motives and intentions" (117).

Addison appears to have understood this philosophical nicety as thor-oughly as Dryden. By advocating for the aesthetic agency of a rust-free coin, indeed even insisting on the preeminence of readings of coins that prized their pristine visual representations of the allegorical figures of mythological poetry, Addison does exactly what Barthes's *Mythologies* might expect him to do: "[I]n passing from the meaning to the form, the image loses some knowledge: the better to receive the knowledge in the concept" (Barthes 117). The knowledge of the coin's mythological concept is the knowledge of its form, not its historical content. In Barthes's phrasing, this process is "a para-doxical permutation in the reading operations, an abnormal regression from meaning to form, from the linguistic sign to the mythical signifier" (116). On the one hand, this "abnormal regression" erases content, and once "History" is "remove[d]" from conceptualizations of forms, there's conveniently "noth-ing more to be said" about them; "any comment about them becomes purely tautological" (101). On the other hand, the function of myth eclipses a mate-rial conceptualization of the relationships between form and concept, such that "there is no regular ratio between the volume of the signified and that of the signifier," an observation couched in Barthes's reading in the equally telling metaphorical terms of "poverty" and "richness," as well as size and quantity (118).

In ways strikingly similar to Dryden's own tautology, therefore, Addison's investments in coins' mythologies mean that he also understands the coin-artifact's historicity ultimately in terms of its futures. "[Coins] are a kind of Present that those who are actually in Being make over to such as lie hid within the depths of Futurity," Philander writes (161). Scouring the rust of the coin, in such a scenario, is akin to removing the specific ideologies—themselves a thorny case of flip-flopping substitutions—that the coin collects as it circulates over time; the medal's essence, for Addison, is its mythical ability to act in the first place. The specific content of the panegyrics or the satires it soliloquizes does not—or at least, should not—matter. In short, Addison's appeal to the classical past and the future conveniently skips the middle, but both temporalities present a kind of immediacy of affect and a body of facts that threaten to compromise Addison's aesthetics by introducing too much content, or in Barthes's terminology, too many concepts. Suggestively, for example, in Addison's own experiment with an it-narrative, the short "Addison on the History of a Shilling," the object-protagonist participates briefly in state politics by being used to raise an army against Charles I, but afterward remains—thanks to its good luck—hidden, "undiscovered and useless," under a wall "during the usurpation of Cromwell" (185). Conveniently, the shilling cannot offer any insight into the facts of this moment in British history as a result.

The logic of substitution, in which the coin maintains its status as an agent but of which historical facts no one seems either able to settle or, for Addison, no one really *needs* to settle, became the defining feature of the period's relationship to many of its artifacts, especially its coins and medals. Despite Addison's plea for form, the artifact's vexed materiality still mattered because it afforded the logics of substitution and the resulting mythologies on which Addison's defense of numismatics depended; the coin's polyvocality remained its selling point. David Jennings begins his foray into numismatics' defense with the unexpected claim that "besides a thousand little impertinences, as Addison calls them," coins and medals were "very gratifying" to collect because they offered beguiling glimpses "of the most celebrated Ladies of antiquity" (54). In his *Britannia Romana* (1724), John Pointer takes a more serious tack and, lifting key phrases from *The Dialogues*, recapitulates Addison's plea for a literary history of coins, quipping that there is such a "great Affinity between Coins and Poems" that "*Est Pictura loquens, mutum Pictura Poema: Estque Numisma loquens, mutumque Numisma Poema*" ("A speaking painting, a silent picture-poem: a speaking coin, a silent coin-poem." That is: In the same way that a painting speaks and is like a silent painting-poem, so too does a coin speak and is like a silent coin-poem.) (6).

However, Pointer's treatise elides the difficulties of the coin's accurate representation of history, especially that of individual rulers, by collapsing the poetic past and present into a conflation of object and place. *Britannia Romana* is a hybrid numismatic map: a catalogue of Roman coins organized around the sites in Britain where they have been recently found. Not unlike Addison, Pointer concludes that the archaeological record that coins write proves that before the Romans "took their last Farewell of our Renown'd and Warlike Ancestors, the bold Britains," they had "[beat] them into Civility, Learning, and good Manners: So that we their Successors may be bold to say, we are now become the most civiliz'd Nation in the World" (20). Yet even as he insists that coins and medals are the most stable of material signifiers, Pointer cautions his readers against believing that "all that is thus recorded [by] them is true" (5).

The chronological arrangement of coins assembled into a collection, coupled with Dryden and Addison's tautological emphasis on the medals' future value, encased coin-artifacts in temporalities or chronotopes that invited them to perform prolifically as narratives.[24] Fiction writers eagerly speculated about the histories that coins might tell about the present for the future. Featuring a guinea as its narrator, Charles Johnstone's popular *Chrysal* offers one example of the ways in which the coin-artifact's capacity for narrative functioned symptomatically as a consequence, on the one hand, of its own fraught history as a piece of history and, on the other hand, of the fraught theories of matter that made the coin into a piece of art as well as a piece of state.[25] As a narrative device, Chrysal presumes to act as a faithful record of history, but it does not exert influence on its sociopolitical networks. Moreover, Chrysal makes unmediated contact with the minds and memories of the individuals it encounters, but does not sway their moral character.

Although *Chrysal*'s status as a political satire has been readily recognized, its status as an early example of historical fiction has gone unremarked. The first two volumes, published in 1760, narrate events from the previous decade and revolve primarily around characters and events associated with the onset of the Seven Years' War. Many of the characters in *Chrysal* were deceased by the time of its publication. Chrysal directly describes its narrative as a historical narrative, a description bound up in Chrysal's materialist explanation of its unusual ability to act as an object-narrator. The best parts of *Chrysal* read as salacious gossip about the debauched bon ton, leading its modern editor, Kevin Bourque, to compare it to a contemporary celebrity tabloid, but *Chrysal* also works in the vein of Charles Gildon's *The Golden Spy* (1709), providing insight into the secret lives of military officials, politicians, and their proxy agents—a facet of the work that indicates not only its status as political satire but also as a precursor to Sir Walter Scott's "big bow wow" historical fiction. *Chrysal's* twin commitments to politics and history are coeval with its use of the coin as a narrator and bound up in the materialist philosophy that explains Chrysal's unusual narrative capacity.

Chrysal engages with theories of matter almost as quickly as it engages with its historical and political contexts. Following the dedication to William Pitt the Elder, the first chapter directs readers who want an explanation for the mysterious circumstances that would give rise to a speaking, knowing coin to "see all the modern hypothetical philosophy" (1.21, 1.24). Johnstone alludes to George Berkeley and John Locke, but he refers specifically to Robert Clayton's *Essay on Spirit* (1751). Ridiculed after its publication, Clayton's *Essay* argued that all matter was imbued with a spirit that acted as matter's causal force, determining its motions and effects. These spirits, however, were organized hierarchically—some having more agency than others—and all of them were subject to the sovereignty of God.[26] Tellingly, Chrysal picks up Clayton's recourse to political metaphors when explaining its own theory of matter as a "system of *government*" in which there exists a variety of "*ministerial* spirits" acting in and on all bodies (1.21, emphasis added). Although Chrysal spends most of the novel as a guinea, it begins as a piece of gold imbued with the spirit of gold. But once it is a guinea, it is difficult to imagine Johnstone's readers not chuckling at the unlucky synergy of a coin-narrator stamped with the visage of George II but governed by a minister, especially given *Chrysal's* fawning dedication to Pitt.

In ways that might have pleased Addison, Chrysal claims to possess a "knowledge" that is "very different from men" insofar as it "know[s] all things *intuitively*, without the trouble, delay, and errors of *discourse* or reasoning" (1.71). Chrysal's knowledge is historical, but such knowledge does not necessarily derive from its status as an object from the past. In fact, Chrysal's knowledge works the other way, such that it begins on "the present face of things" and proceeds to take in "a retrospect to the whole series of their existence, from its first beginning: the *concatenation* between cause and effect being so plain to [its] eyes, that let [it] but see any one event of the life of man, and [it will] immediately know every particular that preceded it" (1.71). Chrysal's historical consciousness, aided by its ability to travel directly to the mind of any individual it physically touches, is therefore also highly "particular," an implicit function of its size and material nature that inflects the form of its narrative (1.71). As Chrysal circulates, its narrative collects a panoply of characters and incidents. As Chrysal accrues a quantity of historical data, the type of causal history Chrysal knows intuitively and illustrates again and again proves to be a typology of vices: greed, corruption, deception, and hypocrisy.

Chrysal interrupts its narrative early on to respond directly to the reader incredulous at "the depravity of human nature" she has read about so far (1.120). Objects like Chrysal, the narrator affirms, "see things as they really are" (1.120). The cold comfort that Chrysal can offer in the face of such stark empiricism is that the "vices" it has witnessed need not be understood as the vices of a particular nation, like England, but are instead "the weeds which, in every age and clime, have always, and always will, overrun the human heart" (1.120). The narrator goes on to claim that vices, in fact, may be not only necessary insofar as negative exemplars have their uses, but also may have their "beauty" (1.120).

This is a mythical knowledge of human nature, use, and even beauty that is far different from that which Addison would have his medals possess and transmit, but Chrysal's tautology here is not quite coeval with what Dryden assigns to Shaftesbury's medal, since the epistemological certainty engendered by Chrysal's material form does not precisely define Chrysal's causality. Chrysal can intuitively deduce cause and effect, but Chrysal maintains that it cannot cause effects. This limitation extends as well to the nature of Chrysal's historical and political knowledge. Although "some" may surmise that objects like Chrysal possess the "power of *foresight*," the matter is not settled (1.71). Chrysal can predict "natural" extensions of "cause and effect," and trace effects back to their original causes, but Chrysal refuses to engage in speculation or prophesy and "confine[s] [its] narrative to matters already past" (1.71).

Chrysal's ability to encounter and narrate vice and its origins is profound. The sheer quantity of moral transgressions Chrysal witnesses is so overwhelming that one soon wonders if the history of vice that Chrysal knows best might function as an effect of *its* essential nature as coin imbued with the spirit of gold. Chrysal's claims that it does not act as a causal agent of the corruptions it witnesses can appear, therefore, disingenuous. To read *Chrysal* this way is to read against the claims made by the object and the text itself. Both purport to act as moral agents by virtue of providing negative and shocking exemplars of social and, especially, political behavior. However, to read Chrysal as an agent of corruption is also to re-align its status as an object and a textual gambit. Just as the coin's comprehensive knowledge of vice might be said to derive from its capacity to cause vice, so too might the it-narrative's penchant for detecting political hypocrisies derive from its status as one text among many in a literary marketplace that trades fast and loose in propaganda.

Chrysal exemplifies the ways in which coins repeatedly failed throughout the long eighteenth century to do what they were supposed to do: convey historical facts into the minds, memories, and hearts of their interlocutors. Coins, many realized, could preserve histories that might best be forgotten. Additionally, coins' capacity for relaying information, which was premised on the material stability of their metallic substrate, came into inevitable conflict with that same matter's vulnerability. Coins proved to be more ductile and malleable than they at first seemed—subject to rust, clipping, and counterfeiting. Coins' fallibilities called into question their capacity to act reliably as the agents of not only historical facts but of personal as well as political virtues. Although coins failed to act as reliable agents of history, character, or the state, they ironically succeeded at enticing interpretation, debate, and critique. Coins thereby became revalued in the literary marketplace as vehicles for documenting deception and corruption: as fictions of the state that monumentalized the state's fictions.

CHAPTER FOUR

Manuscripts: Burnt to a Crust

In October of 1731, the *Gentleman's Magazine* recorded the month's most notable "casualties," as it did every month. That month, a body was found "on the Road betwixt Bath and Bristol" with its limbs cut off and the skin "stript off" the face, and a blacksmith accidentally shot his estranged wife while purportedly attempting a marital reconciliation ("Preferments, Marriages, and Casualties" 451). A blasé sixty-seven-word description of a fire in which no one died appeared as one of the month's casualties. The notice taken of the fire is easy to miss because, next to the murders, it hardly seems remarkable. With an impartial tone, the *Magazine* informs its readers that flames broke out in Richard Bentley (the younger's) house, that Bentley lived next door to the Westminster School, that Bentley's house was home to the king's and Cotton's libraries, and that most of the printed books and part of the manuscripts were destroyed. The *Magazine* mentions the fact that the manuscripts that Richard Bentley (the elder) had collected for his Greek Testament were lost, and that they were valued at two thousand pounds. This is all the information readers are given before the casualty report clips along to the month's more gruesome losses.

That fire is now known as the Ashburnham House fire. It was, as Andrew Prescott puts it, "perhaps the greatest bibliographical disaster of modern times" (391). The Ashburnham House fire destroyed nearly 25 percent of the roughly 950 volumes of medieval manuscripts that Sir Robert Cotton and his fellow antiquaries had rescued from dispersed monastic libraries in the sixteenth and seventeenth centuries. Statistics and numbers, however, don't adequately quantify the damage. The figure of 25 percent accounts only for those manuscripts that were "burnt to a proverbial crust"—not those that were rendered partly illegible (Keynes 116). *Beowulf* remains the most famous victim of the fire, and the missing words on the charred edges of the manuscript continue to trouble readings of the poem today.[1] Moreover, non-standardized cataloguing practices both before and after the fire have made it difficult to know what was even in Cotton's library in the first place. Cotton's manuscript collection is famous for holding many one-of-a-kind manuscripts.

The fact that we cannot know for sure what was lost is one of the fire's most poignant consequences.

The *Gentleman's Magazine* suggests, however, that the fire was but one of any number of random casualties in October of 1731: a minor catastrophe in a collection of miscellaneous dross that mattered only to a few eccentric antiquaries. This chapter shows that this was not the case. Cotton's Library, in particular, was well known as an archive that was assembled in the midst of the seventeenth-century's crises of state; its manuscripts were regularly consulted as legal precedents vested with the authority to determine the nature of England's government. By the eighteenth century, antiquaries claimed that they merely preserved manuscripts for their own sake, but they could not shake the reputations they had previously acquired for meddling with their sources on politicians' behalf. Consequently, manuscripts were not as readily assimilated into the Enlightenment's cultures of fact as we have assumed; often accused of being factional fictions, old manuscripts could trouble as much as they could strengthen appeals to historical precedent that used documentary evidence to make the case for or against revolution. A writer like Horace Walpole found it perspicacious to embrace manuscripts as dubious agents of facts: the better, ironically, to preserve the force of their political influence.

Like coins, manuscripts proved to be vulnerable objects—not only to fire, but also to misinterpretations, willful misreading, and outright fakery. Chapter 3 explored how writers variously borrowed the material properties of coin-artifacts for their own aesthetic and ideological purposes. Artifacts offered opportunities for thinking about the causal relationships between physical objects and immaterial ideas and relatedly, the relationships between past events and present conditions. Coins were compelling as supposed material guarantors of truth; they were confounding when they seemed to spin out fictions instead. As objects that were both compelling and confounding, artifacts afforded ways of situating literary texts between objects and ideas. Timely references to real things, events, and people, as well as speculations on probable causes and effects, created ideal conditions for inviting readers to engage with a text. Writers adapted, therefore, the artifact's material as well as its conceptual qualities; they took advantage, for example, of the coin-artifact's small, movable, two-sided, and metallic qualities—as well as its incompleteness, and its temporal suspension—in order to position their own texts as agents alongside artifacts in historical, philosophical, political, and literary networks.

One goal of this chapter, therefore, is to explore at more length how artifacts afforded aesthetic provocations to read suspiciously. To accomplish this goal I examine how Horace Walpole used manuscript-artifacts in *The Castle of Otranto*. Walpole's Gothic experiment invites a reassessment of the relationships between romance and realism in the long eighteenth century. It has been commonplace to read the found manuscript trope as one of the means by which realist or proto-realist fictions established their plausibility.[2] The trope of the found manuscript looks differently, however, once we realize that not only were there, in fact, a lot of old manuscripts still to be found in the long eighteenth century but also that the manuscripts that had already been found were frequently disparaged as rank fictions.[3] In considering the ways in which fictional texts borrowed their quality of factuality from paper, we have neglected to consider how profoundly suspicions characterized representations and interpretations of manuscripts in the period. For Walpole, the only way out of the problem of manuscripts' reliability as artifacts was through; that is, rather than try to prove that manuscripts were reliable documents, Walpole proceeded as if they were not. He embraced manuscripts as objects that were rife with romantic fictions. Manuscripts offered for Walpole, therefore, a way of thinking about the historical and political uses to which the fictions that lingered and flourished in artifacts' gaps could be put.

Political Archives and Archival Politics

Sir Robert Cotton began his manuscript collecting at a tender age under the tutelage of the antiquary William Camden. Early antiquaries like Camden devoted themselves to the study of the English antiquities that had been left behind in the preference for classical antiquities that characterized the Renaissance. To this end, early antiquaries collected materials indiscriminately: anything and everything that might shed some light on the so-called dark ages of England's past. Camden, famously, scoured England for archival materials that he used to write his *Britannia* (1586): a sweeping county-by-county history of England and Ireland since the Roman conquest. Medieval manuscripts were not only key documents for reconstructing English history; they were also in dire need of rescue. Early antiquaries worked throughout the reign of Elizabeth to stop the flood of manuscripts let loose by Henry VIII's dissolution of the monasteries. As monastic libraries were dispersed, medieval manuscripts were increasingly used in a variety of ingenious, if troubling, ways. They made great stoppers for wine vats, stuffing for candlesticks, wrappers for butter, covers for new books, toilet paper, and kindling. As Aubrey lamented, the "manuscripts flew about like butterflies" as England's abbeys became the property of the state or privately owned warehouses and factories (*Brief Lives* 15). The work of the earliest antiquaries was therefore timely and urgent, and no one tried to rescue medieval manuscripts with as much tenacity or enthusiasm as Cotton. According to C. J. Wright, between 1585 and 1631 Cotton gathered what is "arguably the most important collection of manuscripts ever assembled in Britain by a private individual" (i).

On the surface, Cotton's enthusiasm for collecting was merely a righteous attempt to rescue England's past for posterity. Below the surface, however, Cotton and his fellow antiquaries were motivated to discover historical documents that could be used to challenge the Stuart kings, who increasingly asserted their divine rights. Herbert Butterfield describes the opposition to the Stuart monarchy as the "view that the law, the constitution, and the liberties of England had existed from time immemorial so that they only needed to be recovered by antiquarian enquiry and to be reasserted where they had been forgotten" (18–19). For many, the model of divinely ordained, absolutist sovereignty that the Stuarts touted was an imported notion that had wrongly superseded more original forms of Old English government. Opponents to James I and then Charles I declared, with growing conviction, that the early kings of England had been elected, and that they had ruled jointly with the blessings of a parliament that they were pleased to consult, and that this more original and therefore more perfect form of government should be reinstated.

The antiquaries' recovery of medieval manuscript materials that fluttered about like butterflies proved useful for Elizabeth and initially pleased James I. For a time, Cotton enjoyed basking in James I's favor. Cotton had consulted materials in his library to help James I with his heraldry. Once Cotton was known to be interested in old legal documents, however, he found himself quickly ostracized from the court. As opposition to Charles I grew apace, "[Cotton's] manuscript collection drew scholars, common lawyers, and members of Parliament to his house to pore over them in search of material for polemics against Charles I's absolutist rule" (Turner 64). These scholars, lawyers, and MPs descended on Cotton's manuscript collection to look specifically for earlier and earlier copies of state documents. Consequently, Cotton filled his own collection with manuscripts such as Old English charters. In 1628, Cotton himself publicly proclaimed his personal opposition to the idea of a free monarchy in a treatise titled *The Dangers Wherein the Kingdom Now Standeth*. Cotton advised the young Charles I to turn away from his father's ideas about kingship and go back to an earlier model of government: one in which kings had willingly shared their power with parliaments.[4]

About this time, Cotton also suddenly acquired two copies of the Magna

Carta. Both predated Henry III, and one bore the seal of King John. These discoveries were explosive, and they were timely because they provided lawyers and politicians opposed to Charles I with even earlier precedents for their legal arguments. Moreover, the language of King John's charter suggested that it was a reinstatement of an even older rule of law. Cotton's copies of the Magna Carta were also rescued documents. They seemed magically to have been discovered, just in the nick of time. One was rumored to have been discovered by Cotton himself when he realized that his tailor planned to use the Magna Carta as filling for Cotton's new ruffled collar. The other was accidentally discovered among some random papers at Dover.[5] Shortly after acquiring these manuscripts, Cotton found himself accused of stealing minor state papers, and Charles I confiscated his library. The manuscripts, including those copies of the Magna Carta, remained in Cotton's home, but they were locked up as the property of the king, who ordered them to be guarded and dutifully catalogued. Rumor has it that Cotton, disgraced and forbidden from entering that most cherished room in his house and examining his favorite manuscripts, soon died from a broken heart.

According to Richard T. Vann, the drive to find, preserve, and interpret ancient laws and statutes that questioned the rights of the king continued throughout the seventeenth century (270). Hugh A. MacDougall calls these celebrations of the rights established by legal documents and medieval chronicles "Gothic enthusiasm" (73). Manuscript evidence was increasingly used to "emphasize . . . liberties" as "an inheritance from Gothic ancestors of outstanding virtue" (74). Medieval documents were also used, however, to the opposite effect: to document royal lineages and to establish a historical precedent for the king's rights.[6] Both Vann and MacDougal demonstrate that it was not unusual for conceptual gymnastics to be performed when interpreting medieval manuscripts. Domestic manuscripts provided the fodder for both legitimate theories and imaginative "myths" about the ancient Britons and their forms of government—for both royalists and revolutionaries. J. G. A. Pocock claims that "to the typical educated Englishman [of the seventeenth century], it seems certain, a vitally important characteristic of the constitution was its antiquity, and to trace it in a very remote past was essential in order to establish it in the present" (*Ancient Constitution* 46). The pursuit of documentary proof for institutions that had existed since time immemorial was, inevitably, a fraught affair. The effect was one in which archives grew but few certainties could be pinned, in the end, on the actual documents they contained.

Cotton's own collection of manuscripts was haphazardly cared for throughout the Civil War and Restoration by his descendants in just such conditions. Cotton's family added to the collection, and various antiquaries and lawyers still came to the house to peruse the materials, although with less urgency and diligence. In 1700, Cotton's son and grandson asked the state to take responsibility for the preservation and upkeep of the collection, and so an Act of Parliament made the library official state property. The *Act for the Better Settling and Preserving the Library . . . Called Cotton-House . . . for the Benefit of the Publick* (1701) only obliquely mentions the political value of the collection.

The *Act* begins by noting that Cotton "collect[ed] and purchas[ed] the most useful Manuscripts, Written Books, Papers, Parchments, Records and other Memorials" at great personal expense (1). A sense of potential economic loss pervades the *Act*. It renders null and void any sales of the manuscripts, and the bulk of the *Act* is devoted to parsing the Cotton family's inheritance. Very briefly and almost grudgingly, the *Act* admitted that the library was "of great use and service for the knowledge and preservation of our constitution both in Church and State" (1). The brief oath it contains for future keepers of the library asks the librarian to swear that "he will not willingly or wittingly permit . . . any of the said Books, Papers, Parchments, Records, or other particulars . . . to be given away, aliened, disposed, or otherwise Imbezeled. So help me God" (51). These are the only gestures the *Act* makes to the political nature of Cotton's collection. No specific manuscripts, including those two copies of the Magna Carta, are named or described.

Although the *Act* said that the library was a national treasure, little was actually done to preserve Cotton's collection. Other government reports suggest that the collection was not, in fact, even considered to be of much monetary worth. In 1706 the House of Lords petitioned the Queen to renovate the Cotton house because the room that housed the manuscripts "threatened at any moment to fall down" (Miller, *Noble Cabinet* 32). Christopher Wren was consulted about the renovations. He felt that the library needed to be "purged of much useless trash" (quoted in Miller, *Noble Cabinet* 32). In 1707, another report described the Cotton house as now "ruinous" and admitted that "very little hath been done . . . to make the said Library useful to the Publick" (quoted in Miller, *Noble Cabinet* 33). It would be another *fifteen years* before anything more would be done. In 1722, the collection was removed from the decrepit Cotton house to a rented house in Essex. It was moved again in 1730 because the rent at Essex had been raised to a sum that the Board of Works was unwilling to pay. This is when the library was moved to Ashburnham House, where it had hardly been established before it caught on fire in 1731.

The Ashburnham House fire occasioned a brief flurry of preservationist work in the collection and a government report on the damage. Beginning on November 1, a team of antiquaries began to assess and repair what damage they could. They hung those manuscripts that had been soaked by the water engines out on clotheslines to dry. These manuscripts were comparatively easy to restore. Those that had suffered damage by the fire itself were in a far worse condition. The fire had melted the animal fat used to make medieval vellum, and the manuscripts had shriveled up into hardened "lumps" that were surrounded by a congealed, "glutinous," burnt substance. Some of these damaged specimens were not restored and can still be viewed at the British library today. Andrew Prescott describes them as "irradiated armadillos." The sticky crusts had to be pulled off by hand, and the manuscripts were then soaked in water and hung out to dry. Re-collating the damaged manuscripts often proved to be an impossible task. Prescott estimates that the antiquaries spent only about three months working on the damaged manuscripts; although their work was in many ways laudable, it was also admittedly shoddy—even by eighteenth-century standards of preservation.

The antiquaries did, however, transcribe as well as create a facsimile engraving of one of the copies of the Magna Carta; "Words or Parts of Words" of one copy had been "eaten out," and the seal of King John had melted. One antiquary, John Pine, worked quickly to engrave a facsimile copy that compiled and cross-referenced the damaged document against the unsinged one. Written on the back of the copy was a description of the fire and a promise that this copy "agreed exactly with the . . . Originals."[7] Pine's engraving was reproduced by William Blackstone in his *Great Charter and Charter of the Forest* (1759). Blackstone—himself not one usually reluctant to offer commentary—declared that it was neither "in his present intentions, nor (he fears) within the reach of his abilities to give a full and explanatory comment on the matters contained in these charters" (ii).

In a report on the Cotton collection prepared in 1756, the antiquaries Matthew Maty and Henry Rimius noted the "carelessness" of the rescue efforts (Hopper vii-ix). At the time of the fire, Richard Bentley (the elder) had said that the fire itself was "the Nemesis of Cotton's Ghost [come] to punish the Neglect in taking due Care of his noble Gift to the Publick" (quoted in Keynes 114). "Neglected" and "careless" seem like apt words for describing the treatment of the Cotton library after the fire as well. The manuscripts were moved to Westminster House, where they "languished" for another twenty years until they became part of the British Museum in 1753. When the trustees of the British Museum visited the Cotton Library in 1754, they beheld a sad sight: the organization of the library had continued in a state of chaos since the fire. Loose leaves and damaged manuscripts had been stuffed into press drawers where they had become covered in dust and mold. The keeper of the library, Dr. Casley, was senile and nearly blind, and his wife had gotten into the habit of giving out scraps of Cotton's manuscripts as souvenirs to those who infrequently stopped by to tour the collection. Although some of the souvenirs were returned later, little work was done to restore the manuscripts even after they were moved to the newly established British Museum. The cost, "three shillings for every dozen sheets," was just too expensive. It would be another fifty years before serious cataloguing and restoration work began in earnest (Prescott 404).

Although the point is rarely made, the British Museum—where the Cotton library ended up—was primarily a collection of manuscripts. Established from the collections of Sloane, Cotton, and Robert Harley, two of the museum's three main departments were devoted to printed books and manuscripts. The third was reserved for curiosities. The director of the museum bore the title of "Principal Librarian," a title that remained until the end of the nineteenth century (McKitterick 41). Only Sloane's collection contained significant amounts of materials that were non-textual. The rules for examining the museum's archival holdings were even stricter than the restrictive rules for general admission. In order to gain general admission, one had to provide one's name, "condition," address, and the time one planned to call. Initially, only ten tickets were available for every hour in which the museum was open—which meant that around sixty to seventy-five tourists could visit on a given day. The waiting list could number in the thousands. The wait for a ticket could be as long as three months. Getting into the reading room to peruse the documents was even more difficult because it required a personal recommendation.[8]

By the eighteenth century, then, old manuscripts had real difficulty speaking for themselves partly because they had once said too much, and not enough about political history. Anyone who hoped to go into the archives to find the documents that could speak reliably about even the recent past found that the problem had only been compounded since antiquaries like Cotton first began building their archives. The crises of the seventeenth century had produced a lot more paper: letters, news, legal documents, and propaganda. A sympathizer with the revolutionary cause, the historian John Rushworth said that "[s]ome" of the papers left over from the seventeenth century contained the "Truth," but many did not. "Speeches" that "were never spoken," "Declarations" that "were never passed," descriptions of "Battels which were never fought" and so on and so on had all been published (Rushworth, "Preface," not paginated). Rushworth nevertheless argued that the collection of documentary evidence he was now publishing constituted a "bare Narrative of matter of Fact" and was designed "to separate Truth from Falshood [*sic*]" and "things real from things fictitious and Imaginary" ("Preface," not paginated). From the opposite political side, however, John Nalson could say exactly the same thing in his own so-called *Impartial Collection* (1682–1683) of documents from the same time period. "History without Truth, or with a Mixture of Falsehood, degenerates into Romance," he declared (1.i).[9]

Pocock argued that "famous antiquaries were treated as authorities of recognized political wisdom" (*Ancient Constitution* 46–47), but Cotton's fate and that of his library show that being famous in the political climate of seventeenth-century England had its downsides. Rosemary Sweet explains that eighteenth-century antiquaries were eager to beat a retreat from the polemics that had attended the research conducted by antiquaries on manuscripts in the seventeenth century. They returned to writing local histories, as Camden once had. "Topographical and local antiquities," Sweet explains, were "certainly more easily pursued independent of . . . ideological imperatives" (194).[10] This "independence" and localism also shaped their manuscript investigations, which in turn became increasingly descriptive and mired in complicated debates about dating, provenance, and previous scholarship.

William Nicolson's *The English Historical Library* (1696), one of the earliest attempts to catalogue and describe all the manuscript material extant in England, offers a representative example of the antiquaries' attempts to distance themselves and their archival research from suspicion. *The English Historical Library* is little more than a long, dry list of descriptions of archival repositories that pauses on occasion to nitpick with previous scholarship. Just as Addison did for coins in the *Dialogues*, Nicolson celebrates the aesthetic merits of manuscripts. England's manuscripts will be "justly reckon'd to excel, in Age and Beauty, whatever the choicest Archives abroad can produce of the like Sort" (iv). The thrust of Nicolson's *Library* is a complaint that England's and Ireland's archives had remained largely unorganized, un-catalogued, and in a state of continuing deterioration. "Nothing," Nicolson wrote, "wanted a more speedy Care and Attendance than the Deplorable Condition of our public Records; many whereof (through the Supine, and long continu'd, Negligence of their Respective Keepers) were in a Useless and Confus'd State, and others expos'd to the last Injuries of the Weather" (iii). The conditions of the nation's archives were, in short, "Grievances" that sorely needed to be "redress'd" (iv).

Others were less certain that action was called for. While documentary evidence had come increasingly to be accepted as the foundational basis for history, manuscript-artifacts continued to be foxed with suspicion.[11] In 1727, William Warburton railed against the "State of *English* History," what with its "unnatural Fondness for any abortive Manuscript, that pretends but to relate to *English* Affairs" (*Enquiry* 1.63). He goes on with naked vitriol: "Every Monkish Tale, and Lye, and Miracle, and Ballad, are rescued from their Dust and Worms . . . For of all those Writings given us by the *Learned Oxford Antiquary*, there is not one that is not a Disgrace to Letters; most of them are so to common Sense, and some even to human Nature" (1.63–64). Warburton is castigating Hearne—a favorite target among antiquaries because his Jacobite sympathies were well known. For Warburton, polemics still stalk the archive. More importantly, the kinds of materials that have made their way into the archive not only actively preserve but also propagate the worst kinds of fictions: medieval romances, here conceived not only as literary genres but a misguided political philosophy taken for actual history.

The antiquary Richard Gough would come to regret the ways in which antiquaries' studies of manuscript-artifacts had become overburdened by their pretensions to dry-as-dust factuality in the antiquaries' attempts to escape the charges that they were either motivated by faction or easily gullible to being duped by the same. "The French," he clucked, "handled [their manuscript-artifacts] with the same ease as romances" (*Anecdotes* vi). The English, however, had "trodden only in mazes overgrown with thorns" (*Anecdotes* vi). Some of their work was "incorrect," the rest of it was full of "futile etymologies, verbose disquisitions, crowds of epitaphs, lifts of landholders, and such farrago" (*Anecdotes* xviii). All of it had been "thrown together without method, unanimated by reflections, and delivered in the most uncouth and horrid style" (*Anecdotes* xviii). The study of manuscripts had plunged the whole "study of antiquities into disgrace with the generality, and disgust[ed] the most candid curiosity" (*Anecdotes* xviii-xix). Warburton was outraged that manuscripts continued to fuel romances. Gough was sorry to see that they had been reduced to ash.

Walpole in the Archives

From its outset, Horace Walpole's *The Castle of Otranto* engages with the history of recovering manuscripts. The first edition begins with a faux editorial preface that represents the text as an authentic archival find:

The following work was found in the library of an ancient catholic [*sic*] family in the north of England. It was printed in Naples, in the black letter, in the year 1529. How much sooner it was written does not appear. . . . If the story was written near the time when it is supposed to have happened, it must have been [between 1095 and 1243]. There is no other circumstance in the work that can lead us to guess at the period in which the scene is laid: the names of the actors are evidently fictitious, and probably disguised on purpose. . . . The beauty of the diction, and the zeal of the author concur to make me think that the date of the composition was little antecedent to that of the impression (iii–iv).

This preface establishes a plausible history for the text through a careful manipulation of the kinds of practices—including the use of material evidence, historical contexts, and empiricist rhetoric—that defined eighteenth-century antiquaries' research on primary archival sources.[12] Readers are drily informed that the book was found in an old private library, and they may infer that it is a recent discovery. William Marshal, the book's pseudonymous finder, editor, and translator, implies that he has inspected the physical object itself, enough to consider its typeface and deduce its original place and date of publication from its front matter.

Based on further examinations of the text's content and form, Marshal suggests that although the work was originally published in 1529 in Naples, the story predates its publication by as much as four hundred years. Marshal supports this assessment by historically contextualizing the text he's found: he alludes to religious reforms, changes in governance, and the state of letters during the period he argues the work was originally written (iii–iv). Readers are led to believe, though never explicitly told, that Marshal is a diligent antiquary who has gone so far as to undertake a comparative search for archival precedents. How else could he be sure that the original author fictionalized names (iii), making it impossible to correlate the text to historical documents in order to identify the real people the work ostensibly describes?

These kinds of speculations create a rhetorical facade of empiricism around the scaffold of the manuscript as an artifact. However, as the introduction goes on, that scaffolding appears increasingly unable to withstand scrutiny as it totters on a set of contradictory and subjective judgments about the ultimate uses and aesthetic merits of a supposedly found medieval text. Contradictions pile up, and the editorial preface transforms from faux scholarship to sly satire as Marshal becomes increasingly unreliable and his archival find an increasingly questionable historical resource.

For example, Marshal undermines his credibility when he tries to parse the relationship between fiction and fact in the text that he's found. He claims that because the story blatantly represents impossible supernatural events, it must have been ideologically designed to cultivate the superstitious beliefs of readers, to "enslave a hundred vulgar minds" (iv). For Marshal, this means that the text functioned as Catholic propaganda. This reading is reasonable enough, but Marshal goes on to claim that any story written between the eleventh and thirteenth centuries would require an author to be "faithful to the *manners* of the times" (v). Such a claim destabilizes Marshal's initial ideological interpretation and makes the "artful priest" not so much a propagandist as an impartial recorder of his own cultural norms and mores. Confronted with these competing interpretations of the realist author / artful indoctrinator, Marshal admits that "his solution of the author's motives is . . . mere conjecture" (vi).

And so William Marshal turns to recommend the text to the public by focusing on the literary pleasures it can offer its readers. For example, Marshal analyzes the characters, claiming that though they believe in impossible supernatural events, the author and contemporary readers need not be so gullible. Despite being the products of an irrational medieval belief system, the characters counterintuitively act in perfectly realistic and natural ways that will, Marshal promises, mechanically elicit the sympathy of eighteenth-century readers (v-vi). Likewise, Marshal celebrates the work's "language," "conduct," and "style" (vi-vii). These kinds of affective and formal qualities become Marshal's focus, an ironic twist given not only the preface's early intimation that the found text is of primarily historical value but also the general cultural antipathy—including Walpole's—toward antiquaries' aesthetic sensibilities.[13] Despite, however, emphasizing the beauty of the work's form, Marshal also admits that he is, in fact, "prejudiced" when it comes to his analysis of the work's literary value and that "more impartial readers may not be so much struck with the beauties of this piece as [he] was" (vi).

The overall effect of the editorial preface is to make it impossible to feel confident about the antiquarian editor's interpretations and, inevitably, the validity and relevance of his archival "find." The preface calls into question the reliability of historical texts and the individuals like Marshal who would rescue them, and it solves the problems of history and empiricism that such unreliability invokes by treating found manuscript-artifacts as pleasing fictions. The editorial preface mires *The Castle of Otranto* in questions of intent and reception: it speculates on the historical circumstances that conditioned the original composition of the story as well as the current use value of historical texts that contradict contemporary norms and mores. The preface epitomizes problems of attribution, provenance, and relevance: Who wrote what and when, where did texts come from, why were they written, how do we know, what bearing do they have on history, and what use are they for contemporary readers? The preface concludes not with answers to these questions, but with two seemingly incompatible requests: that contemporary readers ferret out the hypothetical, original medieval manuscript on which the story is based, and that they use the manuscript they may find to make the story even more entertaining (viii).

Given his call for readers to seek out an actual medieval document, we might have expected Marshal to validate his found text in some more meaningful way here. Perhaps its form will suggest that the "darkest of ages" is not so dark; perhaps its ineffective moral will help establish a time period in which superstition began to wane; perhaps it will encourage readers to reflect on eighteenth-century civility in contrast to ancient barbarity; perhaps the "real" history it fictionalizes will clear up a historian's confusion. No such apology occurs for finding, editing, translating, and publishing the story. Marshal's ultimate conclusion—that the found text is just a form of literary entertainment—might seem commonplace for readers accustomed to the shock value of Gothic novels or for readers accustomed to thinking of Walpole's project as superficial and indicative of his "longing to escape . . . in[to] an idealised past" (Kilgour 17). However, in the context of antiquarian manuscript recovery, a context that the preface invokes at both its beginning and its end and a context that Walpole knew well, it is a surprising suggestion. Why can't William Marshal make his archival find make sense formally or ideologically? Why does Walpole ultimately resist representing a found text as historically or politically significant? What is at stake in such resistance?

Manuscript studies were well known to Walpole.[14] In her memoirs of her father, Charles Burney, Frances Burney notes that on a family visit to Walpole, he "favoured them with producing several, and opening some of his numerous repositories of hoarded manuscripts" (*Memoirs* 3.68). W. S. Lewis claims that Walpole "copied extracts from manuscripts . . . by the hour," and "his copies of the Harleian and other catalogues [were] heavily annotated with additional leaves bound in with notes and transcriptions" (*Horace Walpole's Library* 34). Walpole made two important purchases of manuscripts in the decade before he published *The Castle of Otranto*: the manuscripts of the antiquary George Vertue and of Sir Julius Caesar. Additionally, among Walpole's most valuable manuscripts was an original copy of the Charter of the Forest signed by Henry III: a rare reissue of the Magna Carta included in Blackstone's *Great Charter* that had been discovered at Hackney in 1743 and presented to him by his brother as a gift (Walpole, *Description* 52). Some manuscripts, as Burney reports, were kept in a secret strongbox, which was to be opened thirty years after Walpole's death (*Memoirs* 3.68). Others, Walpole kept in a specially designed glass closet next to the shelves where he stored his copies of antiquarian publications. According to Lewis, "this was the most intimate and personal section of the library" at Strawberry Hill: "In the Glass Closet and [on these shelves] were the books that he liked best" (*Horace Walpole's Library* 17).

Yet in his *Historic Doubts on the Life and Reign of King Richard III* (1768), Walpole's approach to manuscript sources and antiquarian methodologies is more ambivalent than we might expect from someone who "liked best" these kinds of materials. Walpole begins his *Historic Doubts* by claiming that "the generality of historians" have been "so incompetent for the province they have undertaken, that it is almost a question, whether, if the dead of past ages could revive, they would be able to reconnoitre [*sic*] the events of their own times" (i). Walpole notes that because "records" and "letters" have been destroyed by "wars, revolutions, factions, and other causes," antiquaries' claims to historical veracity are inevitably preposterous (vi). Walpole also argues that since the manuscripts that do exist are so few, so rudimentary, and so biased, historians "have thought it necessary to give a new dress to English history" (xiii). The lack of "authentic materials," he declares

> has obliged our later writers to leave the mass pretty much as they found it . . .
> It demands great industry and patience to wade into such abstruse stores as records and charters: and them being jejune and narrow in themselves, very acute criticism is necessary to strike light from their assistance . . . I doubt whether the whole stream of our historians, misled by their originals, have not falsified one reign in our annals in the grossest manner . . . It generally happens that the original evidence is wondrous slender, and that the number of writers have but copied one another; or, what is worse, have only added to the original, without any new authority (ix).

Walpole's *Historic Doubts* exemplifies his skepticism about the reliability of both medieval manuscripts and the antiquaries who would recover and examine them. Archival research, according to Walpole, is a precarious undertaking, characterized by "ignorance and misinterpretation." Many records are simply missing; and those few that do exist are "jejune," "narrow," or copied inaccurately from earlier sources. Read against statements such as these, the finder and editor of *The Castle of Otranto* emerges as an antiquary who is highly at risk of being both misled and misleading.

Pragmatic doubts about the reliability of archives and archiving antiquaries, however, did not constitute the sum total of Walpole's views on medieval manuscript recovery. In his *Catalogue of Royal and Noble Authors* (1758), Walpole shows that there was something more at stake in the archive than just the inevitability of historical inaccuracy: political faction. In the *Catalogue's* preface, Walpole adopts an antiquarian tone of objectivity, proclaiming that his catalogue is "written with the utmost impartiality towards all persons and parties: It would be unpardonable to be partial" (i). He also suggests that the antiquarian nature of his work—its focus on obscure details and its emphasis on domestic, rather than classical, history—will appeal only to the most curious and specialized of readers: "The Compiler of the following List flatters himself that He offers to the Public a present of some curiosity, though perhaps of no great value" (i). Walpole would seem, therefore, to be writing an unbiased revisionist account of England's earliest authors and positioning himself in alliance with the new science of history: capable of not only rising above Augustans' stereotypical aesthetic prejudices against a pre-Shakespearean literary tradition but also of rising above political faction as well. The joke, however, is on antiquaries and their sympathetic readers.

The *Catalogue* slyly satirizes the hypocrisy of antiquaries who present their politically biased judgments in objective language. For example, the first entry begins with brief discussions of Richard I, Henry I, and Edward I. None of these kings should be included in the *Catalogue*, Walpole cheekily asserts, because none were meritorious authors. Walpole pokes fun at Thomas Rymer's attempt to make Richard I into a "soft lute-loving Hero of poesy" (4). He also argues that although Bishop Tanner has newly discovered letters with literary pretensions written by Henry I, Henry I's works are hardly admirable if one "consider[s] the state of litterature [*sic*] in that age" (1). Similarly, he takes issue with Bishop Tanner's discovery of a Latin poem in the "Herald's Office" as proof that Edward I was a poet, "as one never heard of his having the least turn to Poetry." Walpole finds that this found "melody of a dying monarch is about as authentic as . . . the title of *Gloriosi*" (4). These examples demonstrate not only Walpole's familiarity with the archives and antiquaries' discoveries in them but also his conviction that antiquaries' findings were dubious recoveries that said more about their agendas than about actual history.

If we read the faux editor of *Otranto* as the kind of antiquary Walpole satirized in the *Catalogue*, his interpretations of his found text become farcical

confusions—fallacious attempts to make an insubstantial, potentially fraudu-
lent archival find more meaningful than it really is. But we must also take into
account the view that Walpole implicitly espouses in the *Catalogue* that antiquaries' archival "discoveries" are driven by royalist politics, as evidenced by
his consistent attacks on the literary productions attributed to kings. Walpole
frequently worried that antiquaries were secret Jacobites. For example, when
describing to William Bentley in 1753 a tour of Gothic buildings, Walpole
"promise[s]" that his "love of abbeys shall not make [him] . . . grow a Jacobite
like the rest of [his] antiquarian predecessors" (*Correspondence* 35.146). Walpole's conviction that antiquaries were in the tank for extreme royalist agendas can also be seen in his *Catalogue,* where he turns the antiquaries' rhetoric
of objectivity on its head by couching his findings in a politicized discourse
of freedom: "This freedom of discussion . . . every man ought to be at liberty
to exercise. The greatest Men certainly may be mistaken; so may even the
judgment of the ages, which often takes opinions upon trust. No authority . . .
is too great to be called in question; and however venerable Monarchy may
be in a state, no man ever wished to see the government of Letters under any
form but that of a Republic" (vi-vii).

Although Walpole appears here to be characterizing his liberated interpretations of neglected early literary texts, the *Catalogue*'s systematic critique
of antiquarian works that celebrated the literary achievements of monarchs
reveals Walpole's Whig agenda and satirical bite. The political implications
of Walpole's *Catalogue* were all too clear to one of his readers. The anonymously published *Remarks on Mr. Walpole's Catalogue of Royal and Noble
Authors* (1759) is a rancorous work that spends one-third of its time accus-
ing Walpole of harboring regicidal desires, another third righting his representations of the monarchy, and another third debating the natural rights of
kings and queens. The author declares that "the indecent manner in which
[Walpole] treats so many of the crowned heads and nobles of the kingdom,
without any apparent necessity for it, is very unbecoming the character of a
true Englishman, or *real gentleman*" (1). The author concludes that Walpole
and his friends are decided "enemies . . . to the monarchical government"
(35–36). *The Castle of Otranto*, I suggest, is a similar text with a similar political agenda.

Otranto's Bloody Records

Traditionally, *Otranto* has been read as a naive celebration of medieval history: the product of Walpole's antiquarian desire to immerse himself in the

past and resurrect an old-world order for his and his readers' pleasure. That he produced the "first Gothic novel" has largely been taken as an accident of Walpole's tastes in collectibles.[15] Characterizations of the work as a dreamy escape to bygone ages often go hand in hand with readings of *Otranto's* political agenda. For example, David Richter contends that the story reflects Walpole's desire to return to a time "when the old order [was] unquestioned and unquestionable: where monarchs [were] absolute and despots need not even profess enlightenment" (70). Similarly, John Stevenson sees *Otranto's* "central issue" as one of "legitimacy" (94), and although Stevenson reads the text as an ambivalent response to the monarchy, he nonetheless detects in *Otranto* an "operative political ideology" that "is strongly tinted with a belief in a quasi-divine kingship" (102).[16] Readings such as these, however, do not take into account evidence of Walpole's actual political position. Walpole was so far from endorsing an "old order" "where monarchs [were] absolute" that he claimed to have slept between a copy of the Magna Carta and a copy of the death warrant for Charles I (*Correspondence* 9.197).

Even scholars who take Walpole's Whig sympathies seriously have found it difficult to see a clear political point to *The Castle of Otranto.* Ever since Thomas Macaulay condemned Walpole in 1834 as a "bundle of inconsistent whims and affectations," and a man for whom "serious business was a trifle," and "trifles . . . serious business," critics have agreed that *Otranto* functions as either an escape from politics or merely an expression of the "amusement" Walpole took in political faction (1.260–261). James Watt argues, for example, that although *Otranto* "opposes notions of liberty, associated with Britain's ancient 'gothic' constitution, with notions of despotism, associated with the corrupt tyranny of Britain's contemporary government," these political valences are the inevitable result of the fact that Walpole was the son of Robert Walpole; they do not, in other words, reflect a meaningful agenda. Watt finds it "hard" to "translate" any of [Walpole's] works into an overt intervention in the field of politics, or to claim that the facade can be stripped away to reveal a hidden essence or truth about Walpole and his agenda. Walpole remained, in Macaulay's terms, "the most eccentric, the most artificial, the most fastidious, [and] the most capricious of men" (Watt 24).

Walpole's own descriptions of the composition of *Otranto* admittedly encourage interpretations of the work as a confused dream or a literary experiment with romance without obvious political purpose. In a letter written to William Cole in 1765, Walpole offers the most extensive account of the writing of *Otranto.* He claims that a dream featuring a disembodied and giant armored hand inspired the tale. After the dream, Walpole reports, he "sat down and began to write, without knowing in the least what [he] intended to say or relate . . . and [he] was very glad to think of anything other than politics" (*Correspondence* 1.88). Additionally, in the preface to the second edition, in which Walpole acknowledges his authorship and explains his ruse, he claims to have merely undertaken a literary experiment designed to combine the wild, improbable adventures of "ancient romance[s]" with the realism of the contemporary novel.[17]

Robert Miles suggests, however, that the preface to the second edition of *Otranto* may be, in fact, a "smokescreen" and a "diversionary tactic" designed to "deflect attention away" from the work's political overtones (107). Likewise, Toni Wein finds that "Walpole's thoroughly politicized upbringing militates against the notion that he viewed literature as an idealized aesthetic pursuit divorced from more materialistic ambitions, as is urged by those who see *Otranto* as a retreat from politics" (53).[18] For Wein, the second edition's added subtitle, "a Gothic story," suggests that the text hearkened not necessarily to the architectural aesthetics Walpole celebrated at Strawberry Hill, but rather to the Gothic politics he approved of, especially as they manifested themselves in the Magna Carta.

Nonetheless, Walpole's systematic allusions to persons who played a role in the medieval political conflicts over the constitution have never been thoroughly examined, and they suggest that *Otranto* is, in fact, explicitly engaged with historical figures and political events. Although scholars have explored Walpole's references to medieval Sicily, which include links between important figures in the Hohenstaufen dynasty and character names in *Otranto*, few have been able to make sense of these allusions.[19] Since the plot ultimately has little in common with medieval Sicilian conflicts, Walpole would seem either to have drawn unconsciously from histories he might have been reading or used Sicilian historical figures arbitrarily and without clear purpose. *Otranto*'s allusions to Sicilian history have stumped scholars, I believe, because they are less about actual events in Sicily and more about the effects of those events on England's political history.

Most eighteenth-century accounts of the Hohenstaufen conflicts were buried in histories of the reign of Henry III (1216–1272).[20] As these histories report, around 1255 Pope Alexander IV asked Henry to supply troops and money to defeat Manfred of Sicily. Henry did not send troops, but he did send money, and in order to raise the funds for such a venture, Henry had to call a meeting of the council of barons, as dictated by the Magna Carta. The council overwhelmingly disapproved of the plan. According to Tobias Smollett, when Henry "demanded a powerful supply to carry on the conquest of Sicily," he "could not have touched . . . a more discordant string" with the barons (*Complete History* 1.518). They refused his request, took the opportunity to list various grievances they had with the government, and declared their intent to enact substantial reforms. When they later met the king with their troops at Oxford to work out the details of those reforms, they presented him with a document known in the eighteenth century as the Statutes of Oxford; its first act required the king to "confirm the Great Charter which he had often sworn to do, without any effect" (Robinson 259). Ultimately, Henry III's involvement in the Sicilian affair set off a chain of events that "effected a political and constitutional revolution" (Treharne and Sanders 1). The barons forced Henry to reaffirm his commitment to the tenets of the Magna Carta; they informed the Pope that they would not support the war in Sicily; they exiled Henry III's closest advisors; and they took control of the government. At the end of it all, "the King reigned, but the Council ruled" (Treharne and Sanders 346).

Henry III's dispute with the barons was understood in the eighteenth century as, in many ways, generational; that is to say, it was read as an extension of the discord that had resulted in the signing of the Magna Carta by Henry's father, King John.[21] In *The Castle of Otranto*, Walpole obliquely invites readers to imagine these events and their consequences by casting Manfred as both Henry III and King John, kings who were represented in the eighteenth century as tyrants whose claims to the throne were weak and who would do anything to protect their ill-gotten interests. Smollett's description of Henry III as "capricious, proud, insolent, and arbitrary; arrogant in prosperity, and abject in adversity; profuse, rapacious, and choleric" could easily describe Manfred, as could his description of John as "contemptible," "proud, imperious, sudden, rash, cruel, vindictive, perfidious," "libidinous and inconstant, abject in adversity, and overbearing in success" (*Complete History* 549 and 454).[22]

Other aspects of *Otranto* suggest that Walpole had the political conflicts of King John and Henry III in mind. The figure of William Marshal, the presumed finder, editor, and translator of *Otranto*—and a pseudonym that has consistently eluded critical explanation—aligns with two other notable historical figures from the reigns of John and Henry III: William Marshal the Elder and William Marshal the Younger. Marshal the Elder played a part in the issuance of the Magna Carta, and the Younger helped broker the Statues of Oxford. Both men were well known in the eighteenth century as barons who deftly mitigated tyranny and supported English liberties—ironically, often by serving astutely in the kings' courts.[23]

Even minor characters in the tale find antecedents in these political conflicts. Isabella, the young woman relentlessly pursued by Manfred, conforms in many ways to King John's second wife, also named Isabella, who was twenty years his junior and whom he married by force. Likewise, Don Ricardo, Manfred's regicidal ancestor, appears to be an allusion to Richard I. In *Otranto*, Don Ricardo is responsible for poisoning Alfonso in order to claim his title—a narrative that hyperbolically reimagines Richard I's betrayal of his father Henry II. By tracing the history of Henry II, we also find two other names from the work in the records of English history: Matilda and Alfred. Matilda was the daughter of Henry I and a descendent of Alfred the Great. Upon the death of Henry I, Matilda was disinherited by Henry's nephew, King Stephen. Henry II was Matilda's son, and his accession to the throne in 1154 was perceived as a rightful restoration of an older lineage, a sign of the return of a limited monarchy that the Empress Matilda embodied by being a descendent of Alfred the Great, the Old English king prized as the ultimate progenitor of a limited, parliament-friendly monarchy.[24] The latter's name phonologically resonates with the tale's supernatural "Alfonso the Good." Like King John and Henry's breaches of the Magna Carta and Statutes of Oxford, respectively, Don Ricardo's poisoning of Alfonso and Manfred's murder of Matilda would be symbolic murders of the rights guaranteed by Old English forms of government—rights that the supernatural return of Alfonso the Good restores.

These references all combine to suggest that Walpole had in mind the conflicts over the constitution that typified the political climate of twelfth- and thirteenth-century England and that would go on to preoccupy the collecting activities of antiquaries like Cotton. Although the protagonist, Theodore, does not appear to have a clear medieval antecedent as other characters do, he likely alludes to an analogous though more contemporary political event: the attempt by Theodore von Neuhoff to free Corsica from Genoese rule in the 1730s and 40s. When Theodore's coup failed and he came to England seeking support, he found himself in debtor's prison in London, where he garnered the sympathy of Horace Walpole. Walpole raised money to procure Theodore's release and, upon his death, arranged to have a monument erected for him at Saint Anne, Soho. Much like the Theodore of *Otranto*, Theodore von Neuhoff was understood as a king who had "attained [his] Dignities by Dint of personal Merit," rather than "from the most illustrious ancestors" (*History of Theodore I* 1). He was also represented as a champion of liberties, as a man who "having no other Support than the Love his Subjects, could never have it in his Power to oppress them" (*History of Theodore I* 38).[25]

These histories of Sicily, Corsica, and England all share a common theme. They were understood as contests between tyrannical authority and freedom. The allusions to Sicilian history, to contemporary events in Corsica, and especially, to medieval English political history should be read as coded defenses of the kinds of anti-monarchical sentiments symbolized by the Magna Carta and its various incarnations—like Walpole's copy of the Charter of the Forest. Taken together, these allusions suggest that *Otranto* may be less about the movement of aristocratic property between generations, as the standard reading of its restoration of Theodore's ownership of Otranto submits, and more about the transmission of "ancient liberties" throughout the ages. Consequently, Theodore, who begins the story as a common peasant but ends it as the owner of Otranto, represents a restoration of the rights of the commonwealth guaranteed by the Magna Carta.[26] Theodore's love for Matilda, and the discovery of his legitimate descent from Alfonso the Good, emerge as symbolic connections to the Gothic liberties that despotic tyrants like Manfred would disavow.

The context of antiquarian manuscript studies makes this reading plausible because so many archival recoveries were driven by the desire to unearth medieval precedents for the Magna Carta or, alternately—much to Walpole's chagrin—documents that contradicted it. As suggested earlier, Walpole was concerned that too many antiquaries were driven by Jacobite sympathies, and that their archival "discoveries" tended to glorify monarchs rather than constitutions. At the time that Walpole was writing *The Castle of Otranto*, he was intensely concerned with the current use value of the constitution. As Wein observes, *Otranto* was written against the backdrop of political debates about the limited power of the monarchy that surrounded the controversial figure, John Wilkes (50).

These debates repeatedly invoked medieval legal precedents and the documents that preserved them.[27] In 1763, Wilkes published a series of pamphlets attacking the king and his advisors; as a result, the king issued a set of general warrants for Wilkes and his publishers, under which Wilkes and forty-eight others were arrested. Wilkes argued that the arrests were illegal because the Magna Carta protected the public against general warrants and guaranteed parliamentary members—such as Wilkes—the freedom to speak out against the king. By the summer of 1764, the scandal had escalated when the government, unable to convict Wilkes on the basis of his published political pamphlets, instead used a pornographic poem discovered during the arrests to convict Wilkes of obscene and seditious libel. Wilkes and his supporters continued to be outraged at the government's blatant disregard for "old English liberties"—a disregard now made manifest by the state's unwarranted discovery of a new document (Colley 105). Walpole was familiar with these debates and their repeated invocations of documents like the Magna Carta, and he was offended by them as both a Whig and an antiquary. Thirty years later, Walpole was still upset about what he perceived to be the abuse of the archive in the Wilkes trials. In "Sketch of a History Written in a Method Entirely New" (1783), an unpublished satirical experiment, Walpole mocks the antiquary Phillip Carteret Webb, whom Walpole describes as "a most villainous tool and agent in any iniquity" (*Correspondence* 1.277). Webb had used his historical expertise and access to the archives to draw up the warrant for Wilkes and buttress it with legal precedent.

In the "Sketch," after describing how the court accused Wilkes of "Treason!" Walpole writes that Lord Egremont and Lord Halifax agreed to do "whatever" the court "bid" them to do to prosecute the case, and "Mr. Wood & Carteret Webb" agreed to do "more" than they were "bid" by Egremont and Halifax ("Sketch" 6). Webb and Wood were both on site for the seizure of Wilkes's papers. When the legality of the warrants was questioned, Webb published, anonymously, his *Copies Taken from the Records of the Court of King's Bench* (1763): an antiquarian work that claimed merely to transcribe manuscripts that recorded the conditions for and historical practices of issuing warrants. The *Copies*, however, was an obviously partisan publication designed to justify the legal proceedings against Wilkes by appealing to a dubious and selective legal history and archive. Webb was eventually tried for perjury and accused of bribing one of Wilkes's associates.

Walpole, in his role as member of the House of Commons, supported Wilkes. He advised his nephew, Henry Seymour Conway, to do the same. As a result of this support, Conway lost his place in the king's court and an interdict was placed on Strawberry Hill. Walpole discusses these events primarily in his correspondence with George Montagu, the MP for Northampton, from 1763 to 1765. These letters, written around the time of *Otranto's* composition, reveal the distress Walpole experienced throughout the Wilkes controversy. At first, he is delighted by the threat to the Tories that Wilkes poses. In November of 1763, Walpole relates the recent political developments to Montagu, chastising Montagu for staying in the country as "London was never so entertaining" as it was in the midst of the Wilkes scandal: "Now is not this better than feeding one's birds [or] poring one's eyes out over old histories?" Walpole asks (*Correspondence* 10.110). Walpole does not write to Montagu again, however, for two months. By then, Wilkes had been convicted, and Walpole was decidedly less pleased with the situation: "It is an age, I own, since I wrote to you; but, except politics, what was there to send you? And for politics, the present are too contemptible *to be recorded*" (*Correspondence* 10.113, emphasis added).

Montagu was similarly distressed, writing to Walpole that he whispered "daily orisons . . . with [his] . . . Magna Charta in [his] hand" (*Correspondence* 10.141). Montagu's prayers and the piece of paper he held were in vain, since by April of 1764, Conway had been formally dismissed and constraints had been placed on Walpole's estate. In a letter to Montagu in early 1765, Walpole melodramatically laments that he hasn't died from a severe cold he's come down with because, if he had, the newspapers could have romantically attributed his death "to the long day in the House of Commons [debating the question of General Warrants]"; he would have "perished with our liberties" (*Correspondence* 10.147). For Walpole, the final nail in the coffin of his constitutional ideals came in May of the same year. Walpole writes that a recently passed regency bill has anointed "four kings" of England, some of them, troublingly, Whigs, who ought to know better than to take on kingly powers for themselves.[28] Montagu is worried as well. He replies that he plans to stay in the countryside, away from the political disputes. There, he might yet salvage "a hat of liberty on the shore, or a scrap of the Magna Charta . . . and save [them] from the flames" (*Correspondence* 10.158). Walpole replies, declaring that he now intends to give up politics. This decision causes him to reflect, surprisingly, on *The Castle of Otranto*. He admits that he wrote it "in the midst of grave nonsense and foolish councils of war," and he is now no longer "likely to disturb [himself] with the divisions of the Court" (*Correspondence* 10.154).

This is a telling and unexamined reference to *Otranto* that calls into question Walpole's suggestion to Cole that the story was written as a way to think about anything other than politics. In this letter, Walpole suggests exactly the opposite: that it was written "in the midst of" political conflict. Even though it is Montagu and not Walpole who consistently references the Magna Carta and the liberties it was supposed to protect in these letters, it is clear that Walpole was a sympathetic audience for such concerns.[29] Similarly, *The Castle of Otranto* approvingly invokes the Gothic liberties established and preserved in medieval documents like the Magna Carta while it also laments the failure of textual artifacts to ensure the transmission to future ages of the rights that they established. In the final chapter, Matilda dies at the hands of Manfred. Walpole rushes to the conclusion, as the ghost of Alfonso the Good finally materializes to throw the castle into ruins and solve the mystery. "'Behold in Theodore the true heir of Alfonso!'" declares the ghost before he rises up to the sky "in a blaze of glory" (195). Manfred's wife is the first to speak, and she proclaims that although she does not know how or why Theodore should be Otranto's rightful heir, she is convinced that he must be. Her plea to Manfred that they remove themselves to a convent in an effort to forestall any more supernatural acts of wrath prompts Manfred to confess the true history. His grandfather, Don Ricardo, had been Alfonso's disloyal chamberlain. Don Ricardo poisoned Alfonso and concocted a "fictitious will" that made himself the heir to Alfonso's estate (196). Beset by a storm on his way home and haunted by his guilt, Don Ricardo made a vow to erect churches in honor of St. Nicholas to atone for his crimes. His sacrifice, Manfred reports, was accepted upon one condition: "Ricardo's posterity should reign in Otranto until the rightful owner should be grown too large to inhabit the castle, and as long as issue male from Ricardo's loins should remain to enjoy it" (197). Jerome completes the history: before he was poisoned, Alfonso had quietly married a woman named Victoria. She bore him a daughter and that daughter married Jerome; Theodore is their son and, therefore, the grandson of Alfonso and the true heir to Otranto.

This climactic unraveling of two generations of history is delivered in under six hundred words, but it is crowded with references to paper artifacts: Manfred prefaces his confession by hoping that it will serve as "a bloody record" warning "future tyrants" about the ramifications of their tyranny; his confession reveals that his claims to Otranto are based on a forged document that has been treated as real for two generations; the friar, Jerome, offers to show Manfred an "authentic writing" that proves Theodore is Alfonso's grandson (195–199). The climactic scene of *The Castle of Otranto* invokes, therefore, a fake and a real textual artifact, and it attempts to establish *Otranto* itself as a meaningful textual artifact for future generations. At the same time, however, *Otranto* renders each of these paper artifacts powerless. The supernatural events and Manfred's confession replace Don Ricardo's "fictitious will" and right its misrepresentations. And when Jerome offers to produce an "authentic writing," Manfred interrupts him and dismisses the document: "It needs not," he shouts, "the horrors of these days, the vision we have but now seen, all corroborate thy evidence beyond a thousand parchments" (199).

Finally, Manfred's wish that the story be recorded so that it may function as a cautionary tale is inevitably undermined both by Marshal's contradictory preface and by the fact that the story itself is, of course, not a found text but a literary experiment.

For Silver, *Otranto's* systematic invalidation of texts in the conclusion is part and parcel of Walpole's antiquarian preference for things over documents and his conviction that the "shock, astonishment, surprise, or even 'horror' that antiquities inspire is the proof of their veracity"; the ghost of Alfonso the Good, then, in all his material glory, represents for Silver an impulse to create a "counter-history" that challenges the teleologies of the Enlightenment's narrative historiography ("Visiting" 561–562). Ruth Mack observes something similar, noting that *Otranto's* insistence on not only objects but also their "objectness" posits an "ontological" view of historical representation. That is to say, objects for Walpole promise to elide the "ordinary logic of representation" that we might use to characterize texts ("Horace Walpole" 378). Rather than point toward historical origins—or the "meaning" both spatially and temporally "behind" the text—the ubiquitous objects in the story create a "lateral" notion of history that emphasizes their "material heft" rather than the kind of allegorical significance one might traditionally ascribe to a text ("Horace Walpole" 378).

Both Silver and Mack make excellent points, but eighteenth-century antiquaries, including Walpole, thought of manuscripts as objects. Manuscripts were archived together alongside antiquities, including in Cotton's own library as well as in the British Museum, as noted earlier. In *The Castle of Otranto*, the texts invoked at its conclusion are as material as the objects depicted elsewhere in the tale. Manfred wants his story to function as a "bloody record"—a text marked powerfully by signs of the physical body, like the suit of armor. When Jerome offers to produce his "authentic writing," Manfred reimagines it as not one but "a thousand" parchments—a hyperbole that parallels the massiveness of Alfonso's ghostly body. The materiality of these texts is further enhanced by the preface to *Otranto*: William Marshal not only describes the hypothetical manuscript's visual-material features and temporally as well as spatially maps its history, much as an antiquary would for an object, but also invites readers to find the supposedly real manuscript on which the story is based.

The fact that Walpole consistently invalidates manuscript evidence is not a sign that Walpole prefers the material to the textual. Rather, *Otranto* emphasizes the ways that the archival buildup of the seventeenth century had the unfortunate effect of proving that even the most material kinds of texts could still be lost, ignored, misinterpreted, and forged. Walpole renders a "thousand parchments" into meaningless "evidence," and "bloody records" do not, in fact, prevent future tyrannies. For Walpole, the Wilkes controversy had made this regrettable state of affairs painfully clear. To read the final materialization of Alfonso as indicative of the triumph of not only truth and history but the truth of material history is to ignore the effects of his materiality. Alfonso ruins the castle and leaves Theodore to end the story by proclaiming that he will "forever indulge the melancholy that had taken possession of his soul" (200). For Walpole, as for Theodore, manuscripts did not function as they should have—as causal guarantors that ancient rights and liberties would persist as effects for future generations.

Consequently, *The Castle of Otranto* takes little refuge in the archival materials to which it so constantly alludes even as it appears to find the spirit of that matter as irrefutable as the giant, ghostly, armored Alfonso. Instead, Walpole insists that manuscript-artifacts, subject as they are to creative manipulation by faction, ought to be read as fictions. For someone like Walpole, who saw medieval manuscripts as evidentiary strongholds against tyranny, the abuse of such sources for the benefit of absolutism had poisoned the water in the well of the archive, as it were. The final events of *Otranto* throw the preface's invitation to find an authentic manuscript—and its promise that such a source will make the story an even more entertaining literary experience—into ironic relief. The political allusions that saturate *Otranto* made it prudent for Walpole to represent it as a work of fiction rather than as a political roman à clef. At the same time, by encouraging readers to treat manuscript-artifacts not as reliable historical documents but as entertaining fictions, Walpole could exploit the very archival practices that he critiqued. If partisan hacks would make manuscripts into propagandistic fictions, then Walpole would appropriate the dubious political use values of old, found documents by conditioning his readers to see such artifacts for what he felt they really were: political romances. In so doing, Walpole enters his own text into the archive as one political romance among all the others.

Following in the footsteps of Ian Watt, historians of the novel have taken an avid interest in what it is, exactly, about novels that make them seem so real. For Watt, of course, it is their formal realism: their investments in depicting everyday experiences with immediacy in settings where a clockwork universe determines the probable conditions of social relations. Accordingly, histories of formal realism tend to juxtapose the eighteenth-century novel against the earlier romance. Fever-pitched and charmed, romances' characters and plots defy belief. Critics such as Leonard Davis, Paul Hunter, and Michael McKeon have suggested that the shifts in historiography that went hand in hand with developments in the new science leveraged romance's claims to *vraisemblance* against themselves. No longer able to prop up their unbelievable plots or characters in vaguely historical settings or shade in their allegories with pretensions to the roman à clef, romance writers lost out to both historians and novelists in the eighteenth century. Novelists claimed gritty surface details for themselves in the service of verisimilitude, and historians dug down deep to stake their claims to empirical evidence. While documentary sources became one of historiography's cornerstones, the trope of the found manuscript —which romances had formerly invoked as well as parodied—became one of novelists' favorite gambits (Davis 177).[30] Realist fictions' pretensions to being found manuscripts allowed them to capture a share of both romances' popularity and histories' credibility.

Artifacts were one way in which genres of romance, and the quality of *vraisemblance* they displayed, remained in circulation. On the one hand, artifacts preserved romances by gesturing to the wonders and curiosities and relics with which romances had formerly comingled in the closets of their avid readers. In this regard, artifacts also perpetuated the critiques of romance that emerged in the Enlightenment; in the satires reviewed in chapter 1, for example, antiquaries were frequently charged with harboring outmoded romantic sensibilities when it came both to collecting and interpreting their favorite objects. Walpole agreed with the satirists. On the other hand, however, artifacts allowed facts and fancies to mingle more amicably together than they could in either the period's realist fictions or its histories. Walpole understood the political perils that could attend artifacts' romances; he also, however, appreciated the ways in which the romances that lingered and proliferated in the artifacts' gaps not only heightened the objects' appeal but also offered opportunities for critiquing, revising, and disseminating new interpretations of the past. The popularity of the found manuscript trope in realist as well as Gothic fictions suggests that Walpole was onto something. Manuscripts' fallibilities persisted as aesthetic boons. Fictional appeals to documentary evidence borrowed the artifacts' compelling and confounding material qualities in order to pique readers' imaginations; Walpole shows that doing so could also productively pique readers' suspicions.

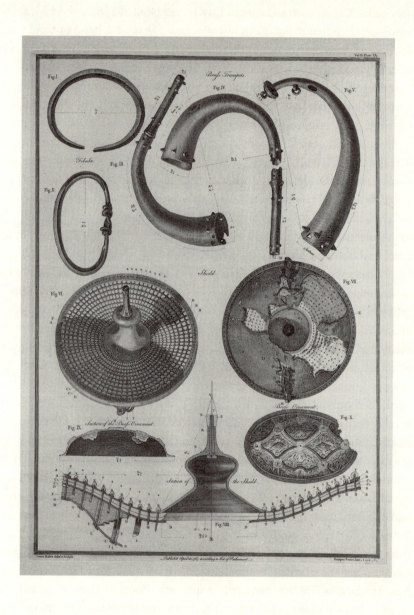

Brass Trumpets

Fibulæ

Fig.I.

Fig.II.

Fig.III.

Fig.IV.

Fig.V.

Shield

Fig.VI.

Fig.VII.

Brass Ornament.

Fig.IX. Section of the Brass Ornament.

Fig.X.

Section of the Shield.

Fig.VIII.

James Basire delin.et Sculpsit.   Publish'd April 22. 1763. according to Act of Parliament.   Antiquar. Societ. Auct.: Lond.

CHAPTER FIVE

Weapons: A Wilderness of Arms

C hapter 4 focused on the suspicions that trailed old manuscripts throughout the long eighteenth century. That chapter suggested that Horace Walpole presented *The Castle of Otranto* as a found text in order to critique the corruption of manuscript evidence and to encourage his own readers to engage in suspicious readings of archival discoveries. *The Castle of Otranto* notoriously features another type of artifact that was popularly collected and hotly debated in the period: weapons. Alfonso's impossibly giant helmet sets *Otranto*'s plot into motion by mysteriously falling out of the sky and crushing Manfred's son. Throughout the story, Alfonso's suit of armor appears piecemeal, accelerating the action, piecing the plot together, and haunting the characters. Walpole claimed, in fact, that he composed *Otranto* after a nightmarish vision in which the weapon-artifacts he had collected at Strawberry Hill grew outsized while he slept. Alfonso's suit of armor and the weapons in *Otranto* gloss Walpole's critique of manuscript evidence. The archives, for Walpole, had been weaponized, and they remained locked in a battle that seemed like it would never end.

This chapter focuses on the weapons that littered England's cultural landscape in the long eighteenth century—especially those that were piled up in the armories of the Tower of London. Like Don Saltero's, the Tower's armories were one of London's most popular tourist attractions. Visitors could tour them by invitation as early as 1498, and they could pay for the pleasure as early as 1599. When Frederick the Duke of Württemberg saw them in 1592, however, they were underwhelming: "full of dust" and in the "greatest disorder" (quoted in Benchley, 19). Charles II tasked his gunsmith, Joseph Harris—about whom little is now known—with the rearrangement of the Tower's stores of arms and armor (Parnell 57). Today, more than two million tourists trek to see the Tower's installations of weapons annually; the Line of Kings is touted as a must-see extravaganza; and the armories continue to boast of being the "oldest museum in the country" (Blackmore 1.vii). Visitors to the Tower in the eighteenth century experienced its weapon-artifacts as vibrant objects, but they were hardly entertained by their close encounter with the weapons' agencies. The Tower's weapons appeared simultaneously lively and deathly, beautiful and terrifying, artificial and natural, ordered and chaotic. Like the other artifacts examined so far, weapons could lead their societies of friends and enemies alike into speculations that tracked a past that receded at untimely moments. Weapon-artifacts especially provoked people to conjecture about the state of nature, including the ways in which it had, or should have, swayed the organization of government.[1]

This chapter begins with thick descriptions of a popular tour guide to the Tower's armories and two reports from its interior, one by Ned Ward and another by Samuel Molyneux. The vibrancy of old, obsolete weapons goaded both Ward and Molyneux into states of suspicion: over human nature, over the legitimacies of governments past and present, over what was historical fact and what was propagandistic fiction, and over objects' agencies. I next turn to consider Jonathan Swift's *Tale of a Tub* and Tobias Smollett's *Sir Launcelot Greaves*. Swift and Smollett were familiar with the Tower's collection of arms and armor; both depicted weapons as a means of critiquing the ways in which violence had begot violence while both also imagined how their own texts might function as weapons.[2] The idea that the past or its objects might be said to determine present conditions or behaviors proved to be intriguing as well as vexing for both writers. On the one hand, they imagined their own texts as weapons, triggered by previous attacks and firing at will. On the other, questions about the nature of weapons' vibrancy inspired both writers to reflect on the battle between the ancients and the moderns and to question their aesthetic investments in imitation as well as invention. Swift and Smollett attempted—through the form and the content of their satires—to mitigate the ways that literary imitations threatened to become unwilled repetitions of violence and literary inventions threatened to unleash uncontrollable effects into the public sphere.

Fear and Loathing in the Tower of London

Thirteen years before he joined his brother-in-law, Edward Cave, at *The Gentleman's Magazine*, David Henry capitalized on antiquarianism's popularity by publishing tour guides for St. Paul's Cathedral, Westminster Abbey, and the Tower of London. Henry's guide to the Tower describes the famous menagerie and the Jewel House but devotes more pages to the Tower's armories: four rooms stuffed with weapon-artifacts. The Small Armory featured bewildering arrangements of swords, shields, pistols, pikes, and helmets; the grand storehouse displayed a collection of cannons; the spoils seized at the defeat of the Spanish Armada were housed in a third room. The experience culminated in the Horse Armory, which featured life-size wooden effigies of England's monarchs lined up from the present to the past, dressed in their suits of armor, and set upon fake horses. The armories were rearranged in 1826 by the antiquary Samuel Meyrick, who was outraged at the historical fictions the Tower's armories propagated.[3] Before that, though, Henry's *Historical Description of the Tower of London and Its Curiosities* (1753) went through more than twenty editions. Its many editions indicate that few changes were made to the Tower's collections during the 1700s, and they speak to the overwhelming popularity of the Tower's collections of arms and armor.

Visitors to the armories of the Tower of London described them as unlike anything else to be seen.[4] In Samuel Richardson's instructional *Letters Written to and for Particular Friends* (1741), the Tower's armories provide the quintessential example of what a country tourist in London should write home about in order to provide a virtual experience for the whole family. Richardson's "young Lady in Town" dutifully reports on the Tower, about which her family had "heard so much talk" (212). Its armories were, in fact, the very first thing she visited (212), and she was not disappointed. They were a "fine Sight"; everything was "bright and shining" and arranged into "such beautiful Order" (213). She was, in a word, "delighted" (212). In Frances Burney's *Evelina*, the Tower is such a tourist attraction that the buffoon, Branghton, is shocked to learn that Evelina hasn't seen it herself. After an exasperating conversational roundabout on London's "public places" (during which Evelina demonstrates her naivete about the city), Branghton finally resorts to asking her (2.106), "[H]ow do you like the Tower of London?" This too, alas, Evelina has regrettably never seen. "Goodness," he shouts, "not seen the Tower! . . . You might as well not have come to London for aught I see, for you've been no where" (2.106).

Henry prepared his guide to the Tower because its collection of weapons had grown so vast as to overwhelm the tourists. Henry suggests that visitors to the Tower experienced the same kind of confusion and chaos as many of the visitors to Don Saltero's coffeehouse, discussed in chapter 2, also reported. As Henry described it, the Tower's tourists had started to complain that "the Mind, being crouded [*sic*] with too many Objects at once" could no longer "distinguish, amidst so great a Variety, what [was] worthy to be dwelt upon, and what [was] not" (iii). Not only were visitors overcome by the sheer number of weapons on display; they were also—like William Hutton had been at the British Museum—reportedly frustrated by the "[h]urry" with which they were "conducted by their Guides from one Thing to another" (iii). Henry designed his "little book" first and foremost to accompany the tourist interested in wandering around on her own (iv). With Henry's *Description* in hand, she could "direct" her own "Choice" of "Objects" and "compar[e]" Henry's "historical Facts" with the "Stories of the Guide" (iv). Designed as a self-guided tour of the Tower, Henry's *Description* offers the most thorough account of the armories as they existed in the eighteenth century.[5]

On the first story of the White Tower, there were two rooms of interest to the tourist looking for weapons: a "small Armory for the Sea-Service, having various Sorts of Arms very curiously laid up in it for more than 10,000 Seamen," and another with "Closets and Presses in Abundance, all filled with warlike Tools and Instruments of Death without Number" (7). The second and third stories above this room were similarly stuffed: one "filled principally with Arms," and another with "Arms and Armourers Tools" (7). There were also "Models of the new-invented Engines of Destruction" (7). On the top floor, a large "Cistern or Reservoir" sat unexpectedly heavy with water from the Thames; deep below, in the vaults, a store of saltpeter smoldered.

These, however, were not the main attractions. Roughly two-thirds the length of a football field and a little bit wider, the "grand Store House" to the north of the White Tower was a relatively new construction, begun by James II and finished by William I, who liked to dine amid its storehouse of weapons, waited on by white-gloved servants (9). To the south was another armory that housed the "Spoils of the Invincible Armada," one of the Tower's premier attractions (24). There, the "reliques" of "this memorable Victory, so glorious for our country," were on grotesque display. These included sharp pikes, gilded lances, Spanish ranseurs, a "curious" "Pistol in a shield," "ten Pieces of pretty little Canon," and the banner carried by the Spanish into battle—all purportedly captured by the British. There was an additional focus on Spanish "Engines of Torture": poison-tipped swords, cleverly engineered bullets described as "Spike-shot, Star-shot, Chain-shot, and link-shot" (33–34). There was a halberd studded with nails in "double gilt" gold, and a "Battle-Ax, so contrived as to strike four Holes in Man's Skull at once," never mind that it had "besides a Pistol in its Handle" (34).

Here, too, were other weapons not obviously related to the defeat of the Spanish Armada: the "Danish and Saxon clubs" wielded by the English against the Norman invaders, remarkable not only because they were more than 750 years old, "perhaps [the] Curiousties of the greatest Antiquity of any in the Tower," but also because they were "*Women's Weapons*" (32). The axe that beheaded Anne Boleyn lurked nearby, and beside that, Henry VIII's walking stick, embedded with "three Match-Lock Pistols" (33–34). As if recognizing that the touring reader might now feel downright assaulted by the spectacle, Henry concludes by mentioning a beautiful shield, contrived "in the most curious Workmanship" and depicting the "Labours of Hercules and other expressive Allegories" (36). The shield was captured at the Battle of the Armada, but it was dated to the year 1376, "near 100 Years before the Art of Printing was known in England" (36). A thing of old beauty and virtue.

Henry next walks his reader through the "Small Armoury," which, along with the Line of Kings, was the highlight of the Tower tour. The Small Armory was a "Wilderness of Arms," containing weapons polished until they were "bright shining" (36). There were enough weapons, Henry claims, to arm eighty thousand men at a "Moment's Warning" (37). What follows, however, suggests that the weapons were not quite so ready-to-hand as Henry claimed. All the weapons had been arranged into stunning sculptural installations. Columns and pyramids and a pair of folding gates were built out of pikes and pistols. There were also two organs: one made of blunderbusses, and another, "ten ranges high," made of more than two thousand pistols. Weapons were arranged into the shape of "Half-moons and Fans," "Furbelows and Flounces," the "waves of the Sea," the "rising Sun," and the "Star and Garter, Thistle, Rose and Crown," all "ornamented with "Pistols &c. and very elegant enriched with Birds and other Creatures" (37–39).

Figures of Hydra, Medusa, and Jupiter were there, too. Hydra's seven heads were "combined by Links of Pistols" (37). Medusa was surrounded by "three regular Ellipses of Pistols, with Snakes represented as stinging her" (38). Jupiter rode his chariot under a "rainbow" of "bayonets" (37–39). There was also the backbone of a whale skeleton made out of carbines (38). The Small Armory likewise housed the weapons confiscated after the failed Assassination Plot of 1696 and the Jacobite Rebellion of 1715, as well as the Swords of Justice and Mercy carried by the Old Pretender that same year. The pièce de résistance of the tour, however, was the Line of Kings in the Horse Armory: a series of painted wooden effigies representing England's monarchs, each sitting atop a life-size wooden horse, arranged in reverse chronological order. The mannequins were touted as "perfect Representation[s] of those illustrious Kings and Heroes of our own Nation" (44).[6]

Richardson's fictional letter writer "delighted" in such scenes, but not everyone enjoyed seeing the Tower's armories. Ned Ward was decidedly not delighted by his tour. He was disturbed.[7] Having heard "wonderful Tales and Tidings" about the Tower's history as well as "sundry reports" of its "amazing Objects [and] Enticing Rarities," Ward decided to go to the Tower with a friend for an irreverent gander. He showed up already skeptical, ill-disposed toward the Tower's political iconography, and eager to expose its hypocrisies. He immediately apprehends the Tower's guard of "Lazy Red-Coats" that "[loiter] about, like so many *City Bull-Dogs* at the *Poultry-Compter*" (5). At the front door, he stops to look at a "strange sort of Picture" that depicts a strange sort of "Creature" (5). When his companion asks what the picture represents, Ward declares it to be the face of the "seventh son of the seventh son"—an iron maiden, we might say, of the devil. It is, of course, the head of a lion, and it marks the Tower as a Royal Palace. Stare at it too long, though, and Ward promises it will "do you a Mischief" (6).

Ward gets only more irate as he continues on the tour. Even more than the menagerie, the mint, or the Jewel Room, the armory had been hawked to "General Applause" by those "Magnifying Mouths" of the "Boobily Bumpkins" shilling the thrills of the Tower. Ward was therefore "particularly desirous of obliging [his] Curiosity with this Martial Entertainment" (9). He enters the armories as suspiciously, however, as he did the Tower's gates. Small Amory is a misnomer, he snorts. They should call it what it is: an "*Arsenal*" (9). Ward sniffs out controversy right away among its artificial arrangements of weapons, "bright as a Good housewife's *Spits* and *Pewter* in the *Christmas-Holidays*" (10).

Here is neither astonishment nor delight, but chagrin—not only at the bric-a-brac shined up with spit, but at the political gall of it all. Piqued by one of the organs made of "fire arms," Ward's companion declares it "a kind of an Allegorical Emblem of a Wolf in Sheep's Clothing; for these Engines of Destruction, never plaid [*sic*] on to any purpose but in Wars, whose harsh and threatening sounds Proclaim nothing but Wounds, Death, Discord, and Desolation" (10). "[T]o have their Mischiveous [*sic*] Applications Disguise'd under the Form and Figure of a *Musical Instrument*," he continues, is an outrage. An organ should "breath[e] for nothing but Peace, Innocence, Delight, and Harmony" (10). This one in the Tower, though, is a "Devil [in] a Canonical Robe" (10).

Bypassing the storehouse, the Armada room, and the train of artillery, Ward goes straight to the Horse Armory, his blood pressure rising. The warders there were "Smutty Interpreter[s] of this Raree-Show" that "glitter[ed]" with "Superficial Heroes" (12). The "Monumental Shells of our Deceas'd Princes"—those "Princely-Scare-crowes," "empty Iron-sides," and "Men of Metal," all "mounted on Wooden Horses"—were "only by the Industry of common Hands shin'd Bright in Memory" (12). The warder described for the tourists each suit of armor and added "some short Memorandums of History" that was hardly pure history: some of it was "True," Ward admitted, but much of it was "False," and the warder resorted to "Invention when he wanted in Memory" (12).

Ward entered the exhibit at the Line of Kings irate, but the longer he stayed there, the more he "sunk into Death's Subteranean [*sic*] Territories" (12). The Line of Kings was a depressing spectacle of how "the *Just* and *Wicked*, by the Impartial Skeleton, are equally respected" (12). Neither could Ward, "without concern, behold *Tyrants* and *Martyrs*, *Conquerors* and *Cowards*, *Lawful Princes* and *Usurpers*, shine equally bright by the Skill of an *Armorer*, in the Eyes of the Common People" (12). Had the Tower shown its "Warlike Ornaments" in their true light, "stain'd" with "spots of Injur'd Blood," it would have been a valuable historical magazine, he thought, because it would have preserved "for Posterity those Cruelties which ought never to be forgotten" (12). Did Ward and his companion want to "see the Crowns or no," the warder asked as they exited the room? No, they most certainly did not.

Samuel Molyneux—who was the son of William Molyneux, a friend to George Berkeley, a fan of Addison, and very much disliked by Swift, who found Molyneux's Whiggish sympathies distasteful—visited the Tower of London as well in 1712. He toured the Tower as one of many antiquarian collections to be seen in the vicinity of London. He went there after having seen a performance of Addison's *Cato*, a play he thought would "be able to Spirit up the World into a new Sense of Roman Magnanimity & Love for their country" (131). Wary about the current state of political affairs but emboldened by Addison's *Cato*, Molyneux entered the Tower on a high note. The "Artillery, Standards and Colours taken" by his hero, the Duke of Marlborough, at the Battle of Blenheim were the first things he saw, and he saw them with pleasure and pride (45). What followed was sublime. There were the guns and cannons that could shoot three and seven and nine and thirty shots at a time! There was the Small Armory "beautifully . . . cover'd with Swords, Pistolls [*sic*], Carbines and Bayonetts [*sic*]" all arranged into "figures so exactly" that "nothing [could] be imagin'd more curious" (45).

Molyneux, however, starts to feel claustrophobic. There was only a small avenue to walk through the display, a "Space of 8 or 9 feet," and the "room," he said, was "a little dark" (45). This physical discomfort soon segues into mental discomfort, and Molyneux begins to have an experience very much like Ward's. Despite the Small Armory's magnificence, he cannot, as a "man of good nature & benevolence to mankind," bring himself to walk down its narrow aisle and take "Pleasure in this Repository of Death & Destruction" (45). Molyneux grants that "such Provisions" of weapons might be necessary, especially if England's enemies are bent on "Violence," "Wickedness," and "Rapine," but even this bellicose sentiment begins to feel empty (45). Who could see the Tower's "furniture of War, of Pain & Torture" and still be committed to "Happyness," or the "Virtues of Peace and Tranquility," or even one's "Fellow Creatures" (45), he wondered? Molyneux experiences the weapons in the Tower as disturbingly agential—not lively, but deathly.

Molyneux pauses to reflect on his reading of classical history, noting that he had long startled at the "Trojan Horse and its Bowells of Death"—a poignant observation in an armory with weapons designed to look like art and objects of nature. Ultimately, Molyneux leaves the armory with "Impressions of Horror," burdened by "Reflections of Regret and Concern" (45). The Horse Armory and the spoils from the Spanish Armada strike Molyneux as merely "Ornamental," full of forgettable and "useless" "Curiositys" (46). May all the armories soon be as useless, he muses. Unlike Ward, Molyneux continues the tour to the Jewel Room. In the wake of his walk through the armories, he decides that the Crown Jewels must be fakes.

The Weapons of the Ancients and the Moderns

The Tower of London might have housed the largest collection of weapon-artifacts in the long eighteenth century, but it was hardly the only one of its kind. Eager spectators could take in spectacles of arms and armor in other collections both public and private. Don Saltero's, for example, featured weapons, and displays similar to those at the Tower were also installed at the museums run by William Bullock, Thomas Gwenapp, Thomas Greene, and Ashton Lever.[8] Patterned arrangements of arms and freestanding suits of armor were likewise exhibited in aristocratic homes such as Walpole's Strawberry Hill and Sir Walter Scott's Abbotsford.[9]

Arms and armor were everywhere. Paper dolls could be dressed in a knightly costume; dictionaries of heraldry made the art and science of designed arms accessible to a rising middle class; didactic children's works, polemics, and sermons readily deployed weapons and armor as metaphors; the

Hanoverians used an armored challenger conspicuously in their coronation ceremonies; military conquests were celebrated with public extravaganzas.[10] The din of war pulsed throughout eighteenth-century British culture, and its drumbeat rattled far and wide. England was at almost constant war in the long eighteenth century, and in these conflicts, new technologies of war were readily deployed. A vast body of work has already documented the effects of the early modern military revolutions in terms of both military history and weapons technology.[11] In reconstructing complex battles, military strategies, and developments in weapons' technologies, however, military historians have often overlooked the lingering presence and function of obsolete arms and armor in eighteenth-century British culture. Attuned to their own past, writers like Swift keenly felt and lamented the modern state of war. Swift, especially, recognized that the weapons of the past haunted the modern's regimes of innovation.

In what follows, I read Swift's *Tale of a Tub* as a report from the battlefields of Grub Street. The *Tale* expresses Swift's concerns with the bellicose sensibilities that the Tower roused—and Swift had seen the beauties and horrors of the Tower's armories for himself on a sightseeing jaunt through London with his young nieces (*Journal* 1.123). At the same time, *A Tale of a Tub* also considers the violence that the new scientific materialisms had activated by staging a battle between the ancients and the moderns. Critics, in fact, have homed in on Swift's distaste for the so-called moderns' gunpowder, expressed in a particularly piquant passage in *Gulliver's Travels* (1726). For these critics, Swift's representation of gunpowder encapsulates his critique of the Whigs' abuses of power, which included the alliances they brokered with the new science and their support for a standing army.[12] Swift is never quite so direct about obsolete weapons as he is about gunpowder. Yet his preoccupation in the *Tale* with a number of conceptual minefields—the state of nature and the moderns' materialisms, both of which were implicated, as Swift might describe it, in the moderns' "histori-theo-physi-logical" debates about causality—indicates that he not only thought about the philosophical, ethical, and political implications of the Enlightenment's arms race, but that he also used weapons both modern and ancient to think analogically about his satirical preference for impersonation and the material text that such impersonation produced.

Swift offers one way, therefore, of understanding how the discomfiting experiences of nature and artifice, and history and fiction, among the Tower's weapon-artifacts could also characterize discursive representations of weaponry. Terry Castle has argued that Swift's *Tale* is, at its "most profound level," a meditation on the "written artifact as a radically unstable object" (34).[13] I suggest that the *Tale*'s engagement with weapons as artifacts activates this instability. The *Tale* expresses Swift's conviction that investing objects like weapons with historical and political agency is maddening and dangerous, while it also illustrates Swift's experimentation with imagining his own satire as a weapon responding to assaults that the moderns had launched: on the ancients, on the church, on the Tories, on William Temple, and on reason itself. Part of the point of the *Tale*, therefore, is to extend the moderns' ideas about history and matter to their logical limits in order to break their deterministic investments in the state of nature as a state of war.

Swift's eagerness to send up and drag down the moderns' origin stories is evident throughout the *Tale*, which is everywhere preoccupied with prefatory and appended textual apparatuses read out of order if read at all. In the ironic dedication to William Somers, the hack yokes this textual state of disorder to war. He notably praises Somers's martial exploits only to introduce the *Tale* itself as a diversionary tactic designed to forestall a breakout of violence during a time of peace, which the hack represents as long, but which the reader will recognize as having just begun (17, 20).[14] The hack describes the *Tale* as a tactical "borrow[ing]" of the "Weapons" from Hobbes's *Leviathan*, yet he attempts to recast those weapons as diverting toys. The *Tale*, he promises, will wear down the "Force" and "Edge" that characterizes the kinds of "formidable Enquir[ies]" asked by modern wits in the form of published "Pamphlets"—"Offensive Weapons"—designed to prick holes into (rather than paper over) the "weak sides" of "Religion and Government" (25).[15] The hack deigns to wear the mantle of the lesser hero, who would save the day by tossing the *Tale* out for the enquirers to play with instead—in the same way that sailors toss a tub to distract a whale from attacking a ship. But the hack, we must remember, is a modern, and the *Tale* he tells is one of those very same pamphlets he purports to combat: an offensive weapon laying siege to the church and to the state.

The whale skeleton made out of carbines at the Tower of London offers an analogical coordinate from material culture that epitomizes what the hack claims to have in mind for the *Tale*: a leviathan of weaponry that has been transformed into a diverting spectacle appreciated for its elaborate contrivances. However, Swift continually requires the moderns to stick to their guns as a long-winded way of illustrating how their theories of matter are incom-

patible with the histories the moderns claim those schemas reveal and produce. That is to say, the moderns claim for themselves a system of teleologi-
cal progress in which their ideas are the superior effects of the object-action
chains that preceded them. The hack famously makes this case later in the
Tale by ventriloquizing Burnet's claim in his *Sacred Theory of the Earth* (1684)
that the moderns may be said to be even more ancient than the ancients
because they have at their disposal both the learning of the ancients and the
knowledge gained by recent science.[16]

Swift finds such a statement to be ridiculous (one example of the ways
in which moderns temporally confuse the relationships between causes and
effects). More importantly, he also finds it to be incompatible with the moderns' own thing theories. In their embrace of Hobbes's mechanism as history, the moderns have not only set up a false system whereby the ancients
are more violent and less technologically sophisticated than themselves; the
moderns have also constrained—in ways they either do not realize or conveniently forget—their own accomplishments as the determined, unwilled
effects of a ferocious, primitive past. Despite the hack's claim, therefore, that
he lacks his contemporaries' satirical skills and that the *Tale* puts his wit to
work in the service of panegyric, Swift makes it impossible for the hack to
escape the topsy-turvy world of violence that he inhabits. To return to the
analogy between the *Tale* and the whale skeleton made out of carbines in the
Tower, the moderns would insist that they can turn carbines into an artificial
whale skeleton remarkable for its display of artistry and inventiveness, the
whole testifying to an ostensible state of aesthetic pacification in which the
savagery of nature and humans alike has been tamed by an Enlightened present.[17] Swift recoils at the unnaturalness of such a design—the ways in which
it is disturbing because it inverts a neoclassical order, conjuring a grotesque
nature out of (and after) artifice. He spends most of his energy in the *Tale*,
however, pointing out that the moderns' philosophical schemas mean that a
whale cannot be made into something other than a whale, or a carbine into
something other than a carbine.

In the prefatory "epistle" to "Posterity," the hack belies the moderns' conviction that the state of nature is an inescapable state of perpetual war by depicting Time itself as an armed entity. Time, the hack worries, will "s[i]nk"
the moderns' publications into "the Abyss of Things" and "annihilate[e]"
their work. According to the hack, Time wields a "large and terrible Scythe,"
and has "*Nails* and *Teeth*" that are long, strong, sharp, and hard; even Time's

"Breath" is poisonous (21). The hack pleads for Posterity to "disarm" Time of its primitive, "furious engines" and halt Time's "Methods of Tyranny and Destruction," while he also fears that Time's killing machine lacks a kill switch. No "mortal Ink and Paper of this Generation," the hack worries, can "make a suitable Resistance" (21). Meanwhile, readers will detect throughout the *Tale* the material marks of Time's effects: gaps in the text itself that testify to the work's ongoing state of disintegration and to Time's deadly aim.

The hack's representation of Time, as well as the subsequent gaps that appear in the manuscript, are familiar tropes from the long eighteenth century. The comedy hinges on the implication that the moderns the hack represents are, at best, naive. They are incapable of understanding what their reliance on Hobbesian notions, especially about the state of nature as a state of war and matter as so many particles colliding, hath wrought. At worst, the moderns are hypocrites. Notably, gaps in the manuscript occur when the hack reaches a limit in his philosophy or when he would be forced to make implicit controversies explicit—they are not, then, necessarily the effects of Time. Within the hack's system, though, the gaps must appear as the inevitable and violent work of Time. Yet the reader will recognize by the time she encounters the *Battel of the Books*, if not before, that the moderns are the ones armed to the teeth and bent on "Tyranny and Destruction" (30). The moderns have set their sights on the ancients and turned their own literary productions into furious engines aimed at a past that they want to reinvent in order to suit their own destructive, tyrannical impulses. Swift insists that the moderns' textual productions must suffer the same fate.[18]

In the *Battel* itself, the moderns are caught in the closed loops of their own causal confusions as they fight to acquire the weapons their inventions have supposedly rendered obsolete. The most striking instance of this occurs when the moderns regroup after an initial loss. Bentley—his deformities magnified by the armor designed to hide them—stalks up to a council of his compatriots. Among them is Scaliger, another modern cut from the same cloth as Bentley and therefore primed to insult; he declares that all the poetry Bentley has read has made him dull, and all the "Arts of civilizing" have made him "rude"; moreover, all of Bentley's "Learning" has made him "*more* Barbarous," and his "study of Humanity, *more* Inhuman" (261). Scaliger goes on to agree, however, to Bentley's rules of engagement: Bentley can take the weapons of any of the ancients he defeats in battle. Readers are likely to recognize that Bentley will hardly wield those weapons any better than Dryden will wear Virgil's suit of armor, while they can also appreciate that Bentley's telos will take him back to the very origins he has misconstrued.[19] That the *Battel of the Books* appears between the *Tale* and the *Mechanical Operation of the Spirit*—in the middle and at the center of a text, like a Cartesian vortex—also makes manifest Swift's concerns with the moderns' confounding narratives of origins and causalities.

From the center of the *Tale*, then, the *Battel* sucks the moderns down into their untimely logics. Poetry makes the moderns dull; learning makes them barbarous; their study of humanity makes them more inhumane. Concordantly, the hack's panegyrics are sleights, his fantastical allegories tell true stories, and his jokes are self-inflicted wounds. The hack's pretensions to rising above the fray, figured consistently in the *Tale* in images of air, height, and projectiles, are heavy and fat-bottomed, like the moderns who attempt to scale Parnassus (38–39). Swift offers another quick, explosive example of how the moderns' view of history and matter means that destructive objects, be they weapons or texts, cannot be transformed into other than what they are and, therefore, what the moderns also claim they were in the past. The hack spares few compliments for the ancients, but damning with faint praise, he grudgingly gives Homer credit for inventing gunpowder (84). The moderns' defeat in the *Battel*, despite the inventive weaponry wielded by the moderns Descartes, Gassendi, and Hobbes—arrows that pierce beyond the "atmosphere" and return as "meteors," cannonballs that turn into stars, alchemical "stink-pots," and bullets that soundlessly kill—is foreshadowed and set up as an ironically predetermined effect of Homer's invention. The moderns will be outwitted by the ancients not just because Swift likes the ancients' poetry and politics better than he likes the moderns' poetry and politics, but because the moderns' system demands as much.

Swift goes on to gloss the hack's anachronism of Homerian gunpowder with a discussion of the moderns' forgetfulness. The moderns have no need of memory, the hack maintains, because memory is an "Employment of the Mind upon things past," and the moderns "deal entirely with *Invention*, and strike all Things out of themselves, or at least, by Collision from each other" (88). But this schema, whereby invention occurs via things themselves violently colliding together, short-circuits the moderns' claims for their intellectual acts of will. It also reintroduces the historical record they would like to forget back into the mix. This point is made explicit in an additional text designed for the *Tale* that appeared in the 1720 edition of Swift's *Miscellaneous*

Works: "A Digression on the Nature Usefulness & Necessity of Wars & Quarrels." A précis of Hobbes's *Leviathan*, the "Digression" establishes the "State of War" as a "universal" "inclination" and the true origin or "foundation" of "Grandeur and Heroism" (*Tale* 265). "War, Famine, & Pestilence" are posited as the "cures for corruptions," rather than as either their causes or their effects, and the hack announces that he plans to write a panegyric on each of them that will accompany an additional panegyric on mankind (265). Such a worldview corrupts any claims the hack might make on behalf of his work or the moderns' progress.

As Irvin Ehrenpreis explains, the *Tale* stands as a "willful rejection" of "limited monarchy, classical literary standards, and rational judgment," but only so that Swift may better illustrate how such a rejection "leads to corruptions in government, religion, and learning" (1.202).[20] Swift holds the moderns to their aberrant "histori-theo-physi-logical" systems with the fastidiousness of a Tory, which is to say that his commitments to the letter of the law and the law avant la lettre divulge his own investments in a structural ordering that privileges constancy and continuity, precedent and tradition, and a model of progress premised on repetition. But he does not present a counterargument as content.[21] F. R. Leavis describes Swift's refusal to offer to the reader a system that might be endorsed in opposition to the moderns as "instrumental irony." In Swift's writing, Leavis observes, "the positive appears only negatively—a kind of skeletal presence, rigid enough, but without life or body: a necessary pre-condition, as it were, of directed negation" (83). "Image, action or blow" issue forth repeatedly from Swift's prose, and his instrumentalism "is purely destructive" and "a matter of surprise and negation" (83–85). Swift's readers experience the *Tale* as a "continuous and unpredictable . . . attack, which turns this way and that, comes now from one quarter and now from another" (88). "Swift's poetic juxtapositions," Leavis continues, are "destructive in intention" and they are at their best and "most successful" when they are disconcerting—when they are "spoiling, reducing, and destroying" (92–93). Leavis's diction throughout his analysis of Swift is telling. Swift's style is one of surprise and attack, punctuated by blows. Leavis senses the ways that Swift's form must reluctantly be appreciated for its material heft. Swift's instrumental irony was itself an iron instrument of violence.

Swift's conceptualization of his writing as weapon is part and parcel, then, of how the *Tale* has been uneasily appreciated for its aesthetic accomplishments. Few like what the work implies about Swift's political convictions—

generally accepted to be nasty, brutish endorsements of blunt authoritarianism but with little conviction that even an iron rule could forge a peaceful state—but most agree that Swift's style remains disconcertingly compelling.[22] Fast-paced and quick-witted, going too far for too long and in many directions all at once, Swift's prose lays siege to the reader, who has little recourse but to wave a white flag of surrender. That's partly the point. In the "Apology" appended to the later edition, Swift suggests that the work was, in fact, successful insofar as all the attacks it inspired were reduced to so many "dirt pellets" thrown at an impenetrable structure or futile attempts at hand-to-hand combat. Swift had sent the moderns back to their state of nature so that they could start all over again.[23]

Knight-Errantry and Errant Knights

While Swift waged his battles with the moderns and the moderns waged their battles with the ancients, an old, iron shield in the collection of the antiquary and naturalist Dr. John Woodward waited patiently. The elaborately engraved shield depicted with vivacity, variety, and force what Woodward believed to be Brennus's attack on Rome in 390 BC. Plutarch and Livy had retold the tale of Brennus's battle with admirable flair, and Livy cited it as the source for the aphorism, "woe to the conquered." Livy and Plutarch, of course, described the event centuries after the fact, but Woodward was not deterred by threats of anachronism. If anything, the shield was even more important if it had been present for a historical event that had to wait for hundreds of years to be recorded second- or third-hand.

Woodward had acquired his shield sometime before 1699. By 1707, he had become convinced, thanks to his correspondence with a number of antiquaries, historians, and scientists, that it constituted a remarkable discovery. Woodward's shield became an object of speculation and debate just a little too late to have attracted Swift's attention when the *Tale* was first drafted and published, but controversy over the shield had reached a fever pitch by the time another satire bearing Swift's stamp came into print. Pope admitted that Woodward and his shield inspired the scene in the *Memoirs of Martinus Scriblerus* in which Cornelius plans to use his shield as a cradle for the newborn Martin.[24] Joseph Levine has admirably told the story of Dr. Woodward's shield both as its own tale and as a piece of the larger battle between the ancients and moderns, situating it as a critical episode in the history of ideas.

Based on Swift's jaundiced characterization of modern antiquaries in the

Tale, it's hardly surprising that Woodward attracted the ire of the Scribleri-ans, standing as an example of "all that was wrong in the new science and the new history" (Levine, *Woodward* 4). Cornelius's distress at the sight of his own shield spit-shined into a newborn object in the *Memoirs* represents the increasing conviction of many of Woodward's associates: the shield was far more modern than it was ancient. Woodward's shield, however, tells another equally interesting story about the ways in which the methodologies that al-ternately goaded and resolved questions about the shield's provenance trans-formed ancient arms and armor from weapons into art objects. The *querelle* over Woodward's shield exemplifies another instance of how artifacts' histor-ical value could be subsumed into aesthetic value. Woodward's shield, in the end, was not what Woodward had thought it was. Befitting an object that so profoundly engaged the moderns who, as Swift saw it, waged war over science and history on Grub Street, the shield turned out, in the end, to be a relatively recent production, a historical fiction. While Woodward remained invested in the shield's deep history, those who disagreed with his dating found op-portunities to celebrate the shield as an aesthetically rich, if not exactly an an-cient, artifactual find. Even if the shield was not as old as Woodward thought it to be, in other words, it proved to be an important object for understand-ing metalwork, engraving, and iconography, and it persisted as an admirable specimen of workmanship.

The flurry with which the shield's matter, texture, imagery, and display of skill were debated unmoored the shield from its historical significance as a Roman artifact and as a defensive weapon, even as that debate was ostensibly waged in the service of determining the shield's real history. The shield came to signify, therefore, both antiquaries' fallibility as well as the eventual, hard-won successes of their methods. Although Woodward was in error, the anti-quarian sensibilities for which he was satirized triumphed in correctly dating and identifying the shield after all. The debate over Woodward's shield con-sequently laid the groundwork for scholarship on ancient arms and armor, which by the beginning of the nineteenth century constituted a subspecial-ization within antiquarian studies. By studying the shield in relationship to other objects, including other shields, tools, images, and texts, antiquaries flattened—not just reversed or inverted, as Swift maintained—the causal trajectories of weapons' forms and functions. In other words, antiquarian investigations into artifacts like Dr. Woodward's shield generated lateral re-lationships between objects based on shape, matter, quotation, and image, as well as in terms of genealogies of developments in technologies and arts.

Such histories did not necessarily depend upon the historian's chronological arrangement of big "bow-wow" individuals or events into order. Artifacts' referentiality shifted as a result. Direct through lines linking discrete objects to specific persons, places, or times were hatched, smudged, and shaded into networks of aesthetic associations.

Swift's attention to the imitative surface textures of his satirical form illustrates what he believed to be the futility of trying to produce backstories for artifacts; such attention, however, also reveals how those who had been keeping camp with the ancients started to be persuaded, if somewhat opportunistically, by the moderns. Pope's translations and commentaries on Homer offer representative examples of the moderns' encroaching influence. Pope reluctantly agreed with the moderns about one thing: the ancients had been more warlike than their admirers would like to admit. In a letter to Madame Dacier regarding her devout insistence on the ancients' superiority, Pope largely agreed with her position, but he allowed that the moderns had, perhaps, bested the ancients insofar as the moderns have given up "the custom of putting whole nations to the sword" (quoted in Levine, *Battle* 221). Despite such an admission, though, Pope also seized an opportunity to appropriate the moderns' object-oriented way of doing history in the service of re-apprising Homer's technical, aesthetic achievements. Pope's commentaries on Homer cast Homer as a painterly poet. His appeal to Homer's visual imagination also soothed the problem of Homer's depictions of war. Pope celebrates Homer's battles for their extensive use of technicolor variety, and he praises Homer's depiction of Achilles's shield for its display of formal unity. While modern critics condemned Homer for the rank fictionality of the mythical scenes and objects he depicted, Pope used the moderns' emphasis on objects' visual, material qualities and the speculations about states of nature that were premised on those qualities to argue two things.

Pope contends that Homer was writing as a historian, depicting scenes that preceded his lifetime by at least two centuries. Therefore, Homer could have represented worldviews with which he disagreed and in order to critique them. Anachronisms and inconsistencies hardly sullied the imaginative ingenuity or moral impulse of an attempt to represent a past that Homer himself had never experienced. Secondly and similarly, Pope suggested that Homer's representations of patently unbelievable—because nonexistent—objects were more viable than they might seem. The shield of Achilles, in particular, could be visualized despite its obviously fictional qualities, and once visualized, it could be shown both to conform to a certain sense of unified *scala naturae* and also to have anticipated the state of the martial and metallurgic arts not as they were when Homer was writing, but as they would eventually be. Throughout both essays, Pope turns to weapons not to elucidate the historical customs of the ancients at war, but rather to exemplify Homer's aesthetic genius.

In the same way that those writing in defense of the ancients could be compelled by the moderns, the moderns remained invested in the ancients—not least because the moderns' claims to superiority were staked on the genuine care and devotion with which they studied the ancients in the first place. Consequently, Pope's tactical recasting of Homer's descriptions of battles and weaponry into aesthetic tours de force licensed, in ways the ancients must have surely come to regret, reappraisals of the Gothic past based on what Swift might have frustratingly described as a similitude of style. If the moderns could not be said to have exceeded the ancients, then perhaps they might at least be said to have joined their ranks, especially once ancients like Homer had been modernized. This was the tack adopted by Richard Hurd in his *Letters on Chivalry and Romance* (1767), a representative, pre-Romantic attempt to drag medieval history out from the ancients' shadow and into their light.

Hurd attempts to salvage a time and a culture that his Augustan contemporaries had deemed "barbarous" (1). He is primarily concerned to establish the merits of romance, but to do so, he begins by defending and explaining the rise of Gothic chivalry. Hardly the "absurd and freakish institution" (10) the Augustans thought it to be, chivalry was "the natural and even sober effect" of feudalism (10). The "prodigious number of petty tyrannies" that emerged from the "feudal constitution" of the Middle Ages, each ensconced in its own castle fortress, produced "in a good degree, a state of war," Hurd acknowledges (8). And this state of war, in turn, generated a "distinct military order" defined by its "passion for arms" (11). Taken to its extreme, the state of war and the passion for arms produced over time a highly ritualized relationship to violence and a highly refined sense of justice, both born of necessity.

Hurd relies often enough on evidence from "old romances," especially Edmund Spenser's *The Faerie Queene* (1590–1596), for his defense of the "rise and genius of chivalry" (23–24), but his claims about chivalry's origins are established by way of analogy. Hurd observes a "remarkable correspondency [*sic*] between the manners of the old heroic times as painted by their great romancer, Homer" and "knight-errantry" (26).[25] Because the "same causes ever produce the same effects," Hurd continues, the "*civil* condition" of ancient

Greece and medieval Europe gave parallel if asynchronous birth to similar poetic modes (37–38). Consequently, Hurd emphasizes the "particularity of description" that attends both Homer's and Gothic romancers' representations of "battles, wounds, deaths"—particularities that especially include "minute" details of "arms" and martial "accoutrements" (27). This particularity arises from real material historical conditions, but Homer and Gothic romancers alike transform their historical realities into aestheticized representations that are purposefully designed for the moral benefit of future readers. For example, both Homer's *Iliad* and *Odyssey*, Hurd concludes, "express in the liveliest manner, and were intended to expose, the capital mischiefs and inconveniences arising from the *political state* of old Greece" (43). Along these lines, the *Iliad* takes as its primary concern micro-factional infighting, while the *Odyssey* examines how prime political movers act when no sovereign is present to restrain them. Hence, Homer's epics feature characters who are "*[d]aring* to madness" and "*[b]urning* with zeal" in the service of "deliver[ing] the *oppressed*" and "exalting their honor" (23). Hurd asks (43): "[C]an any thing more exactly resemble the condition of the *feudal times*?" He thinks not.

Like Pope, Hurd addresses Homer's perceived failures to achieve an Aristotelian standard of unity. He proceeds, then, to reassess the aesthetic merits of both Homer and Gothic romances based on what Hurd would term a "unity of design" rather than a unity of "action" (67). Homer's poetic difficulties, according to Hurd, resulted from his need to elucidate heroic qualities in the context of a plot managed chronologically and unfurling around a single event: a formal hiccup that holds Homer back, literally, in time. In contrast, Gothic romancers were freer to explore a unity of design, depicting a "number of related actions" featuring different characters, settings, and events—a rich "variety," in which each element works in the service of a "common purpose" (66). Gothic romancers' representations of time and causality could, consequently, be fancifully manipulated in the service of creating an interlaced poetic exploration of morality and faith, following different adventures and different characters at will—like the intertwining sculptural designs that decorate Gothic buildings. The freeing form of romances thus anticipates an encroaching freedom in the Gothic polity, but one delivered by the consolidation of power into a sovereign.

Hurd specifically appreciates the ways that Gothic romancers' commitments to design over action release them from the exigencies of historical accuracy and representational believability. Homer should have been so lucky, Hurd thinks, because the Gothic romancers could revel in the realization that "*poetical* truth is . . . almost as severe a thing as *historical*" truth (94). Hurd goes on to appeal to the maxim that "they, who deceive, are honester [*sic*] than they who do not deceive; and they, who are deceived, wiser than they who are not deceived" as proof positive that romances have more power to shape learning through imagination than history or real experience (103). By this point, Hurd has moved as far away from the material objects of history as he has from historical facts. Nevertheless, he has licensed the modern critic to rearrange the incongruities of the Gothic past until it resembles a coherent whole, replete with a laudable moral schema true to nature, if not, necessarily, to history. As Hurd explains, virtue can be excavated by the critic from chivalric romances if the critic understands that since the romances themselves are produced in and by states of war, virtue is to be understood as an "*essential*," but "not *principal*," component of Gothic productions.

When Smollett published his *Sir Launcelot Greaves* just a few years prior to Hurd's *Letters on Chivalry and Romance*, he anticipated this way of celebrating knight-errantry and felt uneasy about its political implications. Whereas Swift, whom Smollett admired and whose Tory allegiances Smollett shared, spins the *Tale* as one long experiment in thinking about weapons' actions, Smollett experiments with thinking about their design. *Sir Launcelot Greaves* sets ancient chivalry loose in modern England as a way of testing whether a passion for Gothic arms could exceed the historical conditions of discord and war that determined their production and use value. Greaves wears a suit of armor laden with chivalric history but unburdened by historical particulars, and his armor instigates the mini-plots of his early adventures in romance while serving as a foil for the structure of Smollett's serial satire. *Sir Launcelot Greaves* offers a representative example, then, of the ways that artifacts like Greaves's suit of armor had been hollowed out of their histories so that they could be appreciated for their designs and essence. But Smollett also suspects the uses to which such a critical schema could be put by modern politicians and their pen-wielding hacks.

Smollett's suspicions about the virtues of knight-errantry are apparent from the opening of *Sir Launcelot Greaves*. Donned in his suit of armor, Greaves bumbles into action amid a bunch of lowly pots and pans. The novel begins with an extended description of its main characters, each poised in situ in the kitchen of the Black Lion Inn. While a fire crackles in the background, the characters are stationed like so many automata waiting to be wound up among the kitchen's clean red brickwork, its "Windsor chairs," and the "shining plates of pewter and copper sauce-pans nicely scoured" that gleam in the "cheerful sea-coal" firelight (3). The pots and pans are livelier than any of the characters there assembled. This initial setup invokes a magic lantern show and is characteristic of Smollett's visual style, but these specific "shining," "dazz[ling]" pots and pans also foreshadow the entrance of Greaves, who bursts through the door dripping wet and "armed cap-a-pie" in his black-lacquered suit of armor (12).

Throughout the novel, readers are reminded of this scene when various characters describe Greaves's suit of armor as so many pots and lids patched together, or when those who catch the contagion of his knight-errantry transform actual kitchenware into their own quixotic costumes.[26] Objects are more than just decor in *Greaves*. Like the pots and pans in the opening scene, Greaves's suit of armor presages, determines, and comments on the actions of characters. Smollett repeatedly invites his readers to consider objects' essential qualities and the nature of their influence. Is a suit of armor fundamentally different than a kettle, and can a suit of armor escape its principal function as an object of war in order to serve as an essential aesthetic object? Greaves's costume consistently provokes unwilled imbroglios that demean rather than elevate his character. His knight-errantry breeds violence and madness. Comical though Greaves's costumed adventures may be, Smollett suggests that the function and form of Greaves's armor cannot be divorced from the historical contexts that determined its purpose.

Even in the extended opening scene, the characters in the kitchen inn get so frustrated at the digressive manner with which the lawyer Tom Clarke narrates Greaves's and his armor's backstory that they snatch up those gleaming pots and pans as would-be weapons while "discord" "clap[s] her sooty wings in expectation of battle" (30). The characters never resort to blows, but they hover on the precipice of a "denunciation of war" while they learn about Greaves's past. Greaves's armor not only seems to make warmongering contagious, erasing in the process his own sad history of benevolence; it also blinds Greaves to the historical conditions of the present. When Greaves first enters the inn, he encounters what will turn out to be his most persistent enemy: the cynic Ferret.[27] Ferret questions why Greaves appears as a "man cased in armour, such as hath been for above a whole century disused in this and every other country of Europe" (15). In response, Greaves launches into a hackneyed defense of chivalry, claiming that his aims are to "honour and assert the efforts of virtue; to combat vice in all her forms, redress injuries, chastise oppression, protect the helpless and forlorn, relieve the indignant, exert [his] best efforts in the cause of innocence and beauty, and dedicate [his] talents, such as they are, to the service of [his] country" (15).

Ferret is quick to condemn Greaves's knight-errantry. "What," he exclaims (15), "you set up for a modern Don Quixote?" On the contrary, Greaves attests. Greaves is no Don Quixote because he "see[s] and distinguish[es] objects as they are discerned and described by other men" (15). Greaves proclaims that he does not mistake a "windmill for a giant," nor "a public house for castle" (15). Instead, he bases his "reason without prejudice" on the "objects" as others see them, and his "perpetual war" is launched against "none but the foes of virtue and decorum" (15). Ferret takes the opportunity that Greaves has given him here to apply Greaves's own logic to his suit of armor and explains that people will presume that Greaves, dressed as he is, "rid[es] in affray of the peace" (16). Greaves takes another run here at a long, defensive harangue. Where some rabble-rousers "ride with blunderbusses, some with pistols, some with swords, according to their various inclinations," Greaves simply "wear[s] the armour of [his] forefathers" in defensive anticipation of the affronts he is likely to receive in the service of both the letter and the spirit of the law, sometimes even in excess of the law (16). Ferret seizes on Greaves's equivocations, suggesting that once weapons are involved, there is little distinction to be made between virtue and vice, defense and offense, patriotic duty and treason, perception and intention.

Having already purposefully misunderstood Greaves's "perpetual war" on injustice and oppression as a gloss on the long-running Seven Years' War, Ferret next lets loose his full vitriol on the current state of the nation, suggesting that Greaves's rhetoric parallels that used to support the continuation of the conflict. All the fighting, according to Ferret, has resulted in nothing but "shews of triumph and shadows of conquest" (17). Meanwhile, the standing army now "eat[s] up their fellow subjects," "mercenaries" are paid to fight "their own quarrels" among themselves, the "militia" are all "petty thieves," and the members of parliament "pillage the nation under colour of law, [to] enrich themselves" (17). Greaves is outraged. The war is both "just and necessary," he avows, and the suspicion that it has been conducted for profit has been one sown by Grub Street's propagandists. Grub Street's "domestic traitors," he continues, "are doubly the objects of detestation; first, in perverting the truth; and, secondly, in propagating falsehood" (18). The worst of these propagandists, Greaves goes on, is an "old, rancorous, incorrigible instrument of sedition" (18). Should Greaves ever meet him, "notwithstanding the maxims of forbearance" he has sworn, he would be "impel[ed] to some act of violence" and would "crush him like an ungrateful viper" (18).

This propagandist Greaves has in mind is none other than Ferret, who is standing right in front of him. Greaves does not perceive things as they really are. The next two-thirds of Smollett's plot follow the comic misadventures that arise from the ironic truths of Ferret's observations. Greaves's suit of armor will, in fact, constitute a series of affrays to the peace, and Greaves will find that his chivalric ideals are of little service to the nation. In one of his adventures, Greaves meets a rabble of soldiers back from the war. When one of the soldiers sees Greaves's armor, he starts (47): "Damn my eyes, who have we got here? old King Stephen from the horse armoury, in the tower?" The soldier's appeal to the Tower is a lofty one, and so the insult that follows is a real low blow. On second look, the soldier sneers, rattling his modern saber: the armor is just a "pewter pisspot" and a "lacquer'd potlid" (47). Greaves becomes embroiled in a brawl too quickly to offer much of a response, but we might expect Greaves to take real umbrage at someone who would degrade not only his own suit of armor but the august effigies of kings. Yet what's curious here and easily overlooked about Smollett's quick allusion to the Tower is the fact that King Stephen was not one of the sixteen kings displayed in the Line of Kings. This reference to a suit of armor that doesn't exist is partly a send-up of the corporal's ignorance, but it is also a moment in which the narrative points out that Greaves's aesthetic valorization of his suit of armor has threatened to compromise its status as a historical referent and reasonable agent. Smollett was not a fan, either, of King Stephen, whom he represented in his *History* as not only a tyrant with a penchant for bloodshed but also an appalling hypocrite.[28]

Readers have been stumped by what appear to be the mismanaged plot lines of *Sir Launcelot Greaves* as it proceeds serially but haphazardly from conflict to conflict, only to give way in the final third of the novel to a marriage plot.[29] Consequently, *Greaves* has been regarded as a largely failed experiment in combining the picaresque and romance with satire. For critics, *Greaves*'s few merits arise from Smollett's use of serialization in the first place as well as his adaptations of Fielding's popular metafictional style and Cervantes's *Don Quixote* in the service of an occasional satirical jab at the ministry. *Greaves*'s politics have proven as fraught as its form, however, for Smollett did not share his protagonist's convictions about the justness of the Seven Years' War. Smollett agreed with Ferret.

If we pay attention, however, to Greaves's suit of armor, the structure of Smollett's work proves more coherent than it may at first seem, and its politics also become a little clearer. *Greaves*'s segmented, serialized adventures clank and grind together like so many pieces of armor attempting to assemble into something complete, natural, timeless, and rational. The longer Greaves persists in his costumed knight-errantry, though, the closer he gets to Bedlam. While Greaves's armor leads him into conflict after conflict, Ferret the propagandist capers in schemes that increasingly exploit superstitions and incredulities. First, Ferret stages a ghost sighting; then he shills medical quackeries; and finally, he brings the novel to its climax in a session of occult fortune-telling. As Ferret's schemes become increasingly far-fetched (and increasingly dependent on a variety of props), Greaves sheds his armor and eventually goes home in the denouement to a retiring life of marital bliss and local philanthropy. The two plots that precede Greaves's marriage plot—his adventures in knight-errantry and Ferret's adventures in gimmicks—intersect and comment on each other. Greaves's appreciation for his armor's design, the ways in which its materiality represents a historical idea turned ideal without recourse to context, is not the antithesis to Ferret's factious plotting. Greaves's armor and Ferret's schemes are twinned counterparts.

By establishing a relationship between Greaves's armor and Ferret's plots, Smollett anticipates what the object-oriented ontologist Graham Harman describes as our contemporary tendency to "undermine" and "overmine" objects. Harman uses the term "undermining" to characterize the critical dissolution of objects "downward" into "a set of subatomic particles" (199). Harman aligns undermining with new criticism; new critics read texts as if they were elemental entities entirely unto themselves, impervious to cultural contexts, unchangeable and unchanging (199). While new critics undermine their objects of study by presuming they exist as unchangeable and unchanging entities, new historicists overmine them by dissolving texts into the ether of context and rendering them into constructions: "relational *effects* of hostile others and disciplinary power" (Harman 193, emphasis added). In contrast to undermining or overmining, object-oriented ontologists adopt what Harman describes as a "medieval" view of objects: the "reality" of an object exists both "over and above its matter" and "under and beneath its apprehension by the mind" (199). As Timothy Morton puts it: "We don't need to think of objects being pushed around by processes or particles or others' perceptions of them. They can do just fine on their own" ("Defense of Poetry" 213).

Smollett implies that the acts of undermining and overmining objects are related rather than distinct ways of understanding objects, and he illustrates the ways artifacts like Greaves's armor are particularly ripe for reduction and exaggeration. Smollett likewise detects that the kind of object-oriented middle ground proposed by object-oriented ontologists—in which objects may be said to "do just fine on their own"—actually tends to produce the acts of overmining and undermining with which object-oriented ontologists take issue. A quick example illustrates the point. While Greaves lies in bed under the spell of a feverish nightmare and the main characters in the inn hover on the brink of battle over Tom Clarke's digressive history of Greaves's past, a servant polishes Greaves's sword until it "sh[i]ne[s] as bright as the shield of Achilles" (31). There are ironic layers in this simile: a servant has been the one to finalize Greaves's transformation into an august Homeric hero, and Greaves's offensive weapon has been conflated with a weapon of defense. The chain of associations does not stop, however, at the ancient past made present in the servant's allusive shining. Greaves's sword is now also as bright, the narrator explains, as the "emblem" the luminaries who lead the "*Beef-stake Club*" wear on ribbons tied around their necks (31).[30]

In his conflation of Greaves's swordshine with Achilles's shield and then with the Beefstakes' emblem, Smollett capitalizes on his characters' investments in metal objects' as both mysteriously elemental and immune to the exigencies of perception prescribed by specific historical contexts. Smollett gestures, in other words, to the conviction that the sword's qualities are "over and above its matter and under and beneath its apprehension by the mind." From such a position, the sword is assumed to act autonomously in the preservation and circulation of heroic, patriotic sentiments as supposedly unassailable as the metal in which they ostensibly inhere. In order to become more like Achilles's shield, however, Greaves's sword has been undermined by the shining: a form of excavation that nonetheless depends upon the conceptual dissolution of the sword down into its metallic elements so that its timeless past can be dispersed. As a result, however, the sword also becomes metonymically available to assemble with the Beefstakes' contemporary emblem, where it will handily function as a "relational effect" of ideological power. One might say that Greaves's appreciation for the unity of his armor's design undermines it, leaving it liable to be overmined in the service of a renewed unity of action. Greaves's sword, in short, does not do just fine on its own.

Like Swift, Smollett worried that investing objects like weapons with agencies divested people of responsibility, and so Smollett must also confront the difficulty of writing an imitative work that aimed to express suspicions about the effects of imitation. Writing in *The Briton*, his periodical mouthpiece for the Bute ministry, Smollett began his first issue with a claim that could almost have been spoken by Greaves himself. The point of *The Briton* is "not to alarm, but appease; not to puzzle, but to explain; not to inflame, but to allay" (*Briton* 241). *The Briton* provoked John Wilkes to issue his controversial *North Briton*, and Smollett quickly realized that he had become embroiled in a battle of the books:

> Fired with honest indignation at the shameless emissaries of a rancorous faction . . . I seized the pen in order to vindicate the honor of my P[rin]ce, which had been so invidiously aspersed, and to justify the conduct of a ministry which had been irreproachable. I no sooner brandished my weapon, like a political knight-errant . . . than the caitiff crew exalted their throats with redoubled clamour; the monsters, the giants, and the dwarfs of falsehood, malice and misrepresentation (*Briton* 265).

The unintended but inevitable consequences of wielding the pen-as-weapon, "like a political knight-errant," parallel Smollett's growing alarm over the probable effects of England's "success" so far in the Seven Years' War. The nation has been "elevated," Smollett warns, to a "pitch of enthusiasm"; a "rage of conquest" now pervades and will "prove one of the greatest obstacles to peace. This is the more dangerous, as it is unlimited; one conquest will suggest another . . . until we are weakened, exhausted, and unable to proceed" (*Briton* 267). While Swift's *Tale* rides this out, Smollett's *Greaves* imagines what it would be like to lay one's weapons—and one's pen—down, and so Greaves takes off his armor and slips into a marriage plot.

Although Swift and Smollett remain compelled by the obvious truth that weapons are things that "do things," they were also suspicious about a metaphysics that would lend weapons a secret life of their own as well as a politics that would find purchase in such a theory of things. Like the other artifacts I have examined so far, weapons preserved the political crises that erupted in the seventeenth century. They could appear to be vital or mechanical pieces of matter, which meant they could also supply historical matters of fact for a range of ideological claims. Swift and Smollett both realized that old weapons, whether they were considered to be vital or mechanical, threatened to compromise the Enlightenment's commitments to reasoned progress by preserving and extending histories of violence. For Swift and Smollett, weapons offered them opportunities to critique political states of affairs and to experiment with the forms as well as the functions of their satires. Both writers considered whether their texts were weapons, too—and whether they could be otherwise.

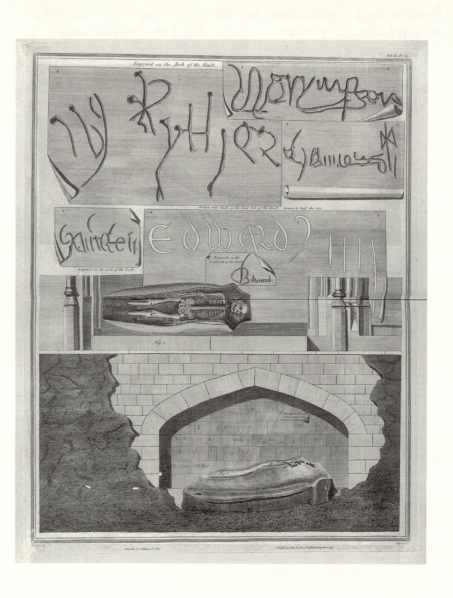

Engraved on the Arch of the Vault.

Written with Chalk on the East end of the Vault.   Drawn to half the size

Engraved on the arch of the Vault.

Engraved on the South side of the Vault.

Fig. 2.

Fig. 1.

Sculptelle Ara Antiquar London   Published according to Act of Parliament 1796

CHAPTER SIX

Grave Goods: The Kings' Four Bodies

P revious chapters have argued that throughout the long eighteenth century artifacts preserved old conflicts over England's political history. Chapter 2, on the ten thousand gimcracks at Don Saltero's, found that the artifacts on display reminded the coffeehouse's customers of relics—and of the sovereigns who exploited them in order to assert their own claims to divine right. Chapter 3 considered the period's fervor for coin collecting. Antiquaries believed that coins were the most durable, reliable, and intimate artifacts from the past, but kings as well as their rivals recognized that such a belief made coins especially effective as a species of propaganda. Chapter 4 explored how the crises of state in the seventeenth century kindled a search for manuscript evidence that promised to establish legal precedents for organizing modern governments. Many discovered, however, that manuscripts were missing or misleading, and some intrepid manuscript hunters forged what they could not find. Chapter 5, on weapons, examined the relationships between old, obsolete technologies of war and eighteenth-century debates about the degrees to which the past as well as its objects determined the conditions of the present. Throughout all of these chapters, I have argued that artifacts were "vibrant," in the new materialist Jane Bennett's phrasing—but not always in ways that were worth celebrating.

To use Bruno Latour's terminology, artifacts were supposed to be "intermediaries" of facts. More often, however, they proved to be "mediators" of interpretations that simultaneously registered and propagated states of suspicion about what was fact and what was fiction. Artifacts' vexed materiality, their fragmented qualities, made them especially adept as mediators of forms and stylistic techniques in the period's texts. Chapter 1, for example, suggested that the most popularly collected artifacts—coins, manuscripts, weapons, and grave goods—were popular because they were controversial remnants of the problems posed by the king's two bodies. These objects' vibrancy inhered not only in their capacity to manifest or symbolize divine right but also in their ability to expose divine right as either a necessary or a merely convenient fiction. Although the revolutionary idea that objects might be vital aspired to disassemble and redistribute the rights of sovereigns in the seventeenth century, such an idea yet left old coins, manuscripts, and weapons free to preserve and propagate vestiges of sovereign power.

At the end of the eighteenth century, in the midst of another revolution of state, vitalist ideas once again promised to disseminate power more equally among a state's citizens by investing all matter with agency. This chapter returns to the problem of sovereign power by recovering the history of four exhumations of royal corpses that antiquaries undertook between 1774 and 1813. Edward I's body was exhumed in 1774, Edward IV's in 1789, John's in 1797, and finally none other than Charles I's body was raised in 1813. Intrigued but wary as they examined kings' corpses, the antiquaries who exhumed sovereign bodies attempted to avert the controversies over both political philosophy and history that, as previous chapters have shown, continued to haunt their studies of artifacts. Despite the antiquaries' best efforts, however, the four kings' bodies would not rest easy in their graves. Edmund Burke, for one, was especially eager to stitch the body of the sovereign back together and breathe new life, like Victor Frankenstein, into the corpse of an absolutist state. Byron's textual engagement with the exhumation of Charles I, an occasional poem titled "Windsor Poetics," and Shelley's "Defense of Poetry" and "Ozymandias," likewise addressed the liveliness of the matter that lurked in the graves of England's sovereigns. This chapter shows that although Shelley and Byron were initially compelled by a vital theory of matter that made dust, bones, and tombs lively, both poets later came to realize that imbuing all matter with agency meant that a tyrant's body might come back to life again. Consequently, they reimagined Romanticism's forms of poetic fragmentation as a means of textually borrowing as well as supplanting artifacts' vibrancies.

Embalming Sovereignty

In the four exhumations of English monarchs conducted between 1774 and 1813, antiquaries attempted to encounter these sovereign bodies as pure matter, even dead matter.[1] They were eager to characterize their exhumations as acts of scientific historiography. The antiquaries' attempts to confine their studies of the kings' bodies to the physical and temporal spaces of the grave were not, however, always successful.[2] Beginning in 1770, Daines Barrington "expressed his ardent wishes" to inspect the body of Edward I, and he began a serious campaign, both to the members of the Society of Antiquaries and to John Thomas, then Dean of Westminster, to acquire permission to open and inspect Edward I's tomb in Edward the Confessor's Chapel of Westminster (Ayloffe 377). Barrington seems to have been entirely earnest in his hope simply to solve a somewhat perplexing historical mystery by bringing up the body. In his *Ancient Funerall Monuments* (1631), the early antiquary John Weever had noticed that there existed a series of warrants issued during the reigns of Edward III, Richard II, and Henry IV that made curious provisions for the extended care of Edward I's body long after his death. Specifically, these warrants indicated that Edward I had requested that his heart be sent to the Holy Land (along with one hundred and forty knights) and that his body accompany the army until Scotland fell to her English conquerors. The warrants issued during Edward III's reign and after, unusual in the context of provisions made for other deceased English monarchs, seemed to broker a post-mortem compromise. Edward I's heart and body remained in his tomb, but Weever believed that extra measures of preservation were applied to Edward I's corpse annually: a compromise. Antiquaries had since debated the nature of these preservation methods. One theory maintained that Edward I's body had been wrapped every year in a fresh cerecloth (a type of waxed linen). The other maintained that the body itself had been annually subject to a direct application of fresh wax.

Barrington wanted to exhume the body, therefore, to determine if unusual measures had been taken to preserve Edward I's corpse and, if they had, what exactly those measures entailed: a matter of merely settling a curious historical dispute carried on between a few specialists rather than answering the kinds of far more high-stakes questions that had characterized the antiquaries' research on manuscripts, for example. After four years of asking, Barrington was granted his request, and Edward I's tomb was opened on May 2, 1774 (Ayloffe 378). Other members of the Society of Antiquaries were there to witness the event, and they included Joseph Banks (who arrived late to the event), Richard Gough, and Joseph Ayloffe, who wrote the official report published both separately and in the Society's journal, *Archaeologia*. William Blake was also purportedly present at the exhumation to produce the visual documentation (Keynes 23).

Ayloffe's account of the opening of Edward I's tomb provides us with an opportunity to witness antiquaries at their ostensible best: as mere observers, careful to eschew politics in the name of scientific history, eager to refrain from intervening in the causal histories or future trajectories of the artifacts they excavated. In the case of their exhumation of Edward I, they appear to have been eager to let the corpse of a king speak as an artifact for itself, but also careful to ensure that the body didn't say anything that would be of much relevance outside the tomb. Ayloffe frames his account with a defense of the antiquaries' careful methodology. He begins by asserting that the entire affair was "extremely delicate," characterized by "natural politeness," and undertaken with "every imaginable precaution for preventing any injury being done, either to the sarcophagus, or its royal contents" (378). Again, in the conclusion, Ayloffe insists that they took "every possible precaution that no damage might be done either to the royal body, or its sarcophagus" (413). "[T]he corpse," he continues, "did not receive the least violation of injury; neither was it despoiled of any of its vestments, regalia, or ornaments. On the contrary, all things were suffered to remain in the same condition, situation, and place, wherein they were found" (413).

The antiquaries appear overly eager, perhaps, to insist that their approach to the king's body was "extremely delicate" (Ayloffe 378). They remained acutely "vigilan[t]" in two regards: in ensuring, first, that the corpse "did not receive the least violation or injury" and, second, that it was not "despoiled of any of its vestments, regalia, or ornaments" (Ayloffe 413). The antiquaries were careful, in other words, to confirm that they were neither reverent royalists on the hunt for relics, nor irreverent revolutionaries with a penchant for iconoclasm. Consequently, the antiquaries assumed a curiously suspended relationship to the corpse itself, a relationship characterized in terms of both temporal and spatial orientations. "All things were suffered," Ayloffe claims, "to remain in the same condition, situation, and place wherein they were found," a statement that simultaneously explains the antiquaries' actions as inert and imposes a similar kind of stasis onto the artifacts in the tomb (431).

Ayloffe's use of the term "precaution," in both the introduction and the conclusion, characterizes the antiquaries' method and, implicitly, their relationship to the matter of the corpse itself: their commitment to remaining, in a sense, pre-causal.[3] The antiquaries' commitment to political precaution directs the moves they make as they exhume the corpse, reported by Ayloffe without regard for narrative order. His report oscillates between distance and proximity, depth and surface, wholes and parts, the past and the present. At times, the report appears to organize itself in terms of space, only to switch to an organization defined by object, and then to one defined by chronology.

They seem to have begun their examination at the face. They note that a red sudarium, "much perished" and with a "cobweb-like feel" covered Edward I's face; they conclude that the sudarium's trifold form was "probably in imitation of the napkin wherewith our Saviour is said to have wiped his face when led to his crucifixion" (318). This, Ayloffe quickly glosses by reference to the anecdotes and practices propagated by "the Romish church," lest readers either conflate Edward I with Christ or suspect that the antiquaries were doing so (381). The antiquaries proceed to peel back the sudarium, but Ayloffe's write-up moves suddenly from describing the face of the corpse to describing the body as a whole. Gesturing back to the purpose of the exhumation in the first place, Ayloffe notes that the wax cloth under the sudarium, the cerecloth, appeared to have been wrapped around the body with special care; Edward's "fingers and thumbs" were each encased in "a separate and distinct envelope" of cerecloth (381).

Returning to the face, Ayloffe notes that the cerecloth was fitted so tightly that the antiquaries concluded that Edward I was beardless at the time of his embalmment, that he had a "very conspicuous" "dip" "between the chin and upper lip," that his lips were "prominent," his nose "short, as if shrunk," and his nostrils "visible," an homage to the antiquaries' numismatic and physiognomic interests. Briefly, Ayloffe mentions that they discovered that "some globular substance, possibly the fleshy part of the eye-balls, was movable in their sockets under the envelope," implicitly emphasizing here again that although they were bold enough to prod Edward I's flesh, they were not so bold as to remove the cerecloth. Below the face and around the neck, they discovered a "quantity of black dust"; they smelled it and touched it, but they could not conclude whether it was "flesh" or "spices" (381).

Throughout, Ayloffe's report maintains an empiricist tenor, marked especially by the passive voice that creeps in once the tomb is opened: "The corpse was discovered . . . almost entire, notwithstanding the length of time it had been entombed," for example (381). As if aware that even this kind of disinterested, detailed description of the corpse's physical state may invite speculation on the essential nature of the king's body (in an unusual degree, simultaneously, of both perfect preservation and black dust), Ayloffe moves quickly to direct his readers' attention down the body, to the hands, where the "joints of the middle finger of the right hand" were discovered to be "loose; but those of the left hand were quite perfect" (382). Ayloffe has taken his readers, once inside the coffin, from surface to depth (the folded sudarium to the face of the corpse) and from top to middle (the face to the hands). Given our proximity in these passages to the body itself, the ordering of Ayloffe's report is counterintuitive. He describes the body first and its habiliments second: the rich, red silk damask tunic decorated with "quatrefoils, of philligree-work, in metal gilt with gold" and "ornamented with five pieces of beautiful transparent glass" "coloured" to mimic rubies, amethysts, and sapphires, and surrounded by "an immense quantity of very small white beads"—an image of aesthetic relief and workmanship that contrasts the grotesque realities of the corpse (382).

The question of the essence of the matter of the king's body, divine and causal, or inert and passive, is continually skirted by Ayloffe's report of the exhumation. Every time his description threatens to linger too long on the decayed body, Ayloffe redirects his readers' attention. He takes them up or down the body, vertically or horizontally inside the coffin, or from part to whole and vice versa; he peripatetically returns to questions raised earlier in the report or redirects readers outward into arcane historical contexts and sources. Even Edward I's clothing and monarchical insignia threaten to become sites where too much attention to material detail may signal an undue veneration for the trappings of royalty. After lavishing consideration on the richness of Edward's tunic, mantle, and the gold cloth that covers his legs, Ayloffe inserts the detail that Edward I's crown is but a "fillet of tin" and "evidently of inferior workmanship" (384).

The other symbol of monarchy, the royal ring, was notably missing from the tomb, according to Ayloffe, a detail that will become surprisingly important later. Ascribing agency to this iconic symbol that he resists ascribing to the body itself, Ayloffe hypothesizes that the ring had "slipped off from the finger, and buried itself in some part of the robes"; he reports, even, that the antiquaries resisted "disturb[ing]" the robes "in order to search for it" (385). The ring that cannot be found, an object that descends deeper into the tomb either of its own volition or simply because a finger that wears it decays, invokes the inertness of the king's body. Discrete material particulars prove capable of action, but only within the confined spaces of the grave and the semantic map of specialized antiquarian inquiry. Possible agents in this entombed network—the sovereign body, the king's crown, the royal ring—are foreclosed from producing narratives that may be subject to interpretations that have bearing on political history. In the drawing attributed to Blake that illustrates the exhumation, Edward I appears as a piece of expressionless statuary: a mute effigy in a cold light made bright by a plain ink wash. The clinical white space of the page isolates the king's body in its coffin. The print that was published alongside Ayloffe's account charts the basic arc of the antiquaries' exhumation, from concealment to exposure, but also resists interpreting or even illustrating the findings that defined the original purpose of their investigation. The inclusion of four objects from the coffin at the bottom of the print, just above a key to the image's scale, proves spatially disorienting: the contents of the tomb are depicted outside but below the tomb itself.

Ayloffe's report reassembles the parts of the king's body and declares the whole to be relatively unremarkable. There is little about the state of Edward I's body that may be considered singular. He is not taller than a man might be expected to be; his "royal vestments, accompanied with the ensigns of regality" are not "on any account, to be considered as a peculiar mark of respect paid to him . . . but as being done merely in conformity to usual and antient custom" (387). Nor, to answer the question that drove the exhumation in the first place, were unusual measures taken to preserve his corpse. Certainly, measures—perhaps even extraordinary measures—to embalm the corpse of Edward I might have been taken at the time of his death, Ayloffe suggests, but these were taken only out of necessity in order to ensure that the body remained acceptably fresh-looking during the relatively long time it remained on display after the death. The debated warrants, the antiquaries find, were likely designed to purchase wax to make candles, which were to be lit in the memory of Edward I each year around the time of his death.

Nothing about Edward I's body is "extraordinary" (413). A mass of material details accumulates in this, the first scientific exhumation of a king undertaken in nearly a century and the first exhumation of an English king ever by a disinterested group of would-be scientists, but they conclude only that wax candles never mentioned in a historical record might once have been lit annually in honor of a king whose dying wishes were paid "little or no regard" (396). The antiquaries close the tomb, use a "strong cement of terrace" to "[fasten] down" the lid, and with the dean, they "retired from the chapel" (413). If Edward I's body is vital here, it is vital as a mere point of fact in a tightly circumscribed field of historical inquiry. George III requested a copy of Ayloffe's report, although why he wanted it or what he planned to do with the knowledge it provided are unclear; at best, it may have offered up a curious but unlikely model for preserving his own body.

Reanimating the Body

Fifteen years after the exhumation of Edward I, in 1789 the antiquaries stumbled upon an opportunity to exhume another royal corpse. Edward IV's body was accidentally discovered in the course of architect Henry Emlyn's renovations at Windsor Castle for George III. The third volume of *Vetusta Monumenta* (1796) contained an account of the discovery, along with an illustration drawn by Emlyn on site and then later etched by James Basire for publication (the frontispiece to this chapter). Emlyn's description of this exhumation is far briefer than that prepared for the exhumation of Edward I in 1774, even though it is made up of short reports by three different witnesses: Emlyn, James Douglas (the Dean of Windsor and Bishop of Carlisle), and James Lind, a physician-in-ordinary. The antiquaries also took two physical specimens in 1789—a lock of Edward IV's hair and a vial of liquid—which were archived by the Society.[4]

The vial of liquid generated the most interesting of the three eyewitness testimonies: Lind's chemical analysis. In 1789 the antiquaries present at the opening of Edward IV's tomb appear confident enough in their own purposes and reputations to disturb the body in a way that the antiquaries who exhumed Edward I in 1774 did not. In the case of Lind's report, especially, the king's body is treated as pure chemical matter. As molecules, the king's body would seem to be in its most volatile state, capable of invisible transformations and recombinations. Lind's chemical analysis of the king's body, however, sealed itself in a veritable air-pump against the political history of a king whose character was famously still enlivened by Shakespeare's most notorious villain.[5]

Lind's experiments on the vial of liquid were designed to determine whether it was an embalming substance or organic matter generated by the body's putrefaction. Lind begins by making basic observations of the liquid: "very much like that of walnut-pickle," "dark-brown in colour," and "dense" with a "quantity of matter, principally consisting of very small particles of a woody substance" (Emlyn 2). When the vial is shaken, the particles swirl. When left to sit, the particles sink to the bottom. Lind notes that the liquid is "inodorous" and, surprisingly, that it is also "tasteless, excepting a small degree of roughness or astringency" (Emlyn 2). It resembles "water which has remained some time in a rotten wooden vessel" (Emlyn 2). Lind evaporates portions of the liquid, first to remove the particles, and then again once the liquid has been separated from its matter. After this double-evaporation process, Lind next burns some of the "residuum" from the second evaporation, noting that it "produced a smell rather agreeable, but by no means like that of animal matter" and that the ensuing ashes "had a saline taste" (Emlyn 2). This would seem "to indicate a small impregnation of nitrous salt," and so next, Lind soaks "bibulous paper" in the liquid, and observes that it burns faster than paper not soaked in the liquid but slower than paper soaked in a solution more saturated with "nitre" (Emlyn 2–3).

In order to determine how salty the solution really must be, Lind concludes his experiments by diluting the liquid in a mixture of "acctated [*sic*] lead, nitrated silver, and salited [*sic*] terra ponderosa"; no change in the liquid was observed, and so Lind concludes that "no saline matter containing marine or vitriolic acid was to be found in it" (Emlyn 3). Thus, Lind arrives at the somewhat obvious conclusion. The fluid at the bottom of the tomb "was produced by the dissolution of the body itself" (Emlyn 3). Looping back to his scientific method that began with a sensual inspection of the liquid, Lind delivers the finale by musing that it "must not be wondered that this fluid was found without any particular taste or smell" because, like "wines, which, after a long period of years, become in great measure, if not entirely, tasteless and inodorous," the "putrid fermentation" of the liquid has now long since "been accomplished" and "all the solid parts, which had any taste or smell, must have been decomposed and deposited" (Emlyn 3).

Here, then, is the king's body in a surprising range of states, even when reduced to mechanical matter. If in 1774, "all things were suffered to remain in the same condition, situation, and place, wherein they were found," the very essence of Edward IV's decayed body was subject to experiments in 1789 that appeared capable of altering its fundamental physical form: from liquid to solid to evaporated substance, separated and dissolved, chemically combined, and finally, ingested by the historically minded chemist like wine. And yet all these alterations are undertaken in order to insist on the unchangeability of the matter itself, which remains not only tasteless and odorless, but definitively dead. At the conclusion of Lind's experiments, the king's body is the spiritless sign of a monarch's putrefaction—the same essential substance as it was before the experiments began. Hardly what either the vitalists or the mechanists once had in mind.

This is an antiquarian science of the body that understands history as pure time and space, rather than as event or action. It eschews allegory and symbolism, in ways that even Ayloffe's careful account did not quite accomplish. The absence of references to rituals that might have explained, for example, the state of Edward IV's body or the grave goods buried with him, becomes especially notable alongside the absence of reference to historical work already extant in the antiquaries' textual network, including Ayloffe's report of 1774. Emlyn, Douglas, and Lind must have been aware of this report, and the fact that they do not engage it is significant. What insight, for example, might the preservation of Edward IV's body have offered into the questions that preoccupied antiquaries just over a decade and a half earlier? What might the body reveal about historical practices of embalmment? Or the rituals of royal burial? Even these questions seem, in the context of the exhumation of 1789, to invoke a network of associations from which the antiquaries had further retreated. The matter of the king's body turns out to be just matter. Its parts begin and end suspended in perfect molecular equivalence and stasis. Lind's chemical experiments were timely but also unusually leaden given the important role chemistry not only played in the period's theories of matter but also its political controversies. As Richard C. Sha explains, chemistry was constantly interrogated for its political implications throughout the Romantic period.[6] Public debates about vitalism and its politics transpired in the well-known context of scientific lectures by John Hunter, John Abernathy, William Lawrence, and John Thelwall, as well as in the chemical experiments and speculations advanced by Thomas Beddoes, Joseph Priestley, John Dalton, and Humphry Davy.

Trained as a surgeon and specializing in exotic fevers, Lind was called to the tomb as a friend of Joseph Banks, who was also present at this exhumation, and because he was a physician-in-ordinary to the royal family in Windsor. Given Lind's method and personal connections, we might expect to catch a glimpse of chemistry's political controversies here on the eve of the French Revolution. But in Lind's sepulchral laboratory, we get little more than pickle juice. This is especially surprising given Hogg's description of Lind in his *Life of Percy Bysshe Shelley* (1858). Shelley had met the elderly Lind when he was at Eton, and he soon saw Lind as a father figure. According to Hogg, their friendship was cemented when Lind intervened to keep Shelley's own father from sending him to Bedlam in the throes of a violent fever, which Lind treated as a physician (1.32). More importantly, Hogg attributes Shelley's earliest interest in vitalism to none other than Lind, with whom, moreover, Hogg claims Shelley shared a radical political sensibility. Shelley, Hogg writes, "used to go to tea with the meek and benevolent physician at Eton; and after tea they used to curse King George the Third" (1.140). These curses, Hogg claims, were of a "peculiar character, differing much from ordinary execrations" (1.140). They contained an element of blasphemy, operating "demoniacally, by devoting their object to the evil spirits and infernal gods" (1.140–141).

Hogg goes on to explain that "Shelley had a decided inclination for magic, demonology, incantations, raising the dead, evoking spirits and devils, seeing ghosts, and chatting familiarly with apparitions," and "it is probable that he picked up, or improved, these medieval fancies" at Lind's tea table (1.141). There is little other evidence to confirm that Lind was the radical that Hogg makes him out to be.[7] Lind's analysis of the vial of liquid taken from Edward IV lent itself readily to two opposing interpretations. Either Lind enjoyed a moment of reverential communion with divine sovereignty, or he indulged in a sacrilegious disregard for the same. The Society of Antiquaries preserved the vial of liquid and the lock of hair, but both stagnated in the Society's collection. Lind's report went largely unnoticed by the public, despite Hogg's claim that Lind was himself a radical who had cast Shelley in his polemical mold.

Lind's chemical experimentation, however, seems to have set the stage for the exhumation of Edward I to be enlivened fifteen years after it had occurred. In 1790, John Wolcot, a poet better known by his pseudonym, "Peter Pindar," published his satirical *A Rowland for an Oliver*. *A Rowland* pretended to be by John Nichols, the antiquary and then-editor of *The Gentleman's Magazine*; Wolcot published *A Rowland* under Nichols's pseudonym, Sylvanus Urban, and framed it as a response to Peter Pindar—a clever, if dizzying, double disguise on Wolcot's part. In the preface to *A Rowland*, Wolcot included an unsavory anecdote about the antiquaries' 1774 exhumation of Edward I to launch an attack on Richard Gough, by then the Society of Antiquaries' most well-known member. The narrator facetiously credits Gough with having convinced him that antiquarianism was more than "the idle production of a couple of fellows that want to make a fortune by a history of cob-walls, old chamber pots, and rusty nails" (6). Gough's "zeal for the promotion of antiquarian knowledge could not be better proved," the narrator goes on to claim, "than by his running the risk of being well trounced for borrowing one of king Edward's fingers, as he lay exposed, a few years since, in Westminster Abbey" (6). In Wolcot's anecdote, the antiquaries exhumed the bodies of kings in order to collect the "pickle" preserving the body, and Ayloffe's emphases on the hands and fingers of Edward I appear, retrospectively, suspicious. Wolcot reports that Gough was now rumored to have slipped the finger of Edward I "gently into his pocket" (6).

The narrator goes on to explain that Gough was caught in the act by the Bishop of Rochester, another witness to the exhumation. The "hawk-eyed" Bishop insisted that Gough "be searched"; the finger was found, and Gough was "forced" to put it back (6). At first, the narrator of *A Rowland* adopts the tone of a disappointed antiquary. The Bishop "unluckily saw the deed," and the return of the stolen finger was a "disgrace of the science" (6). Yet the unsavory political implications of Gough's eagerness for an artifact from the king's grave become suddenly acute when the narrator flippantly quips: "Such was the intrepidity of my antiquarian friend, that he would have attempted the head, instead of a pitiful finger, as he had on a large watchman's coat for the purpose" (6–7). Wolcot also includes one final, telling detail. Joseph Banks reportedly also rushed to the exhumation with a "gallon jug" in order to collect the embalming fluid, but now, no fluid was to be had. The narrator says it was a shame, too, because Banks planned to make a "sauce" with the "precious liquor" and to serve it up at his "Attic entertainments in Soho-square" (7).

The report that Gough had tried to snatch a finger from Edward I's tomb in 1774 became legendary. It was reprinted separately as "Peter Pindar's Character of an Antiquarian" in the periodical *Walker's Hibernian Magazine* in October 1790. The antiquary Francis Grose included it in his collection *The Olio* two years later, in 1792. Twenty-three years after that—now more than forty years since the 1774 exhumation—William Combe reinvigorated the story once again in an inset piece in the second volume of his *Dance of Death* (1815–1816), which was illustrated by Thomas Rowlandson. In "Death and the Antiquaries," Combe writes that antiquaries have the dubious distinction of exploring "those curious parts of Science, / Which have been known but long forgot, / And would in dark oblivion rot, / Did not their ever anxious eyes / Pierce into all obscurities, / And thus unveil them once again / For modern Learning to explain" (2.271). This kind of research, Combe claims, is arduous. Antiquaries trek to the top of mountains, spelunk into caves, and clamber over Gothic ruins. "Sometimes," Combe coos conspiratorially, "[t]hey love to poke among the dead," and they "crave . . . to invade the grave" (2.272).

The anecdote about Gough appears here in Combe's text once again, "repeat[ing]" "in verse" what was "writ in prose" earlier by Wolcot and Grose. The personified figure of Death watches over the antiquaries as they pursue their exhumation of Edward I's "lifeless form" (2.272). Death reminds the antiquaries that they can look and listen, but they cannot touch. "I'll strike that curious fellow dumb," Death mutters, "if he purloins a Royal thumb," and a "fatal dart his breast shall sting, / If he slips off a royal ring" (2.273–274). Having invoked the rumor about Gough's handiwork, Combe demurs from the gossip, concluding that Death's "alarm / For any meditated harm" was "false" (2.274). "[N]ot a ring or rag was stole / But all untouch'd, and safe and whole" (2.274). Combe insists that the body of the king was "return'd / To his dark house and re-inur'd; / There in DEATH's mansion to remain, / Nor e'er to be disturb'd again"—that is, "Till the great globe itself shall shake; / Till the trump sounds and bids him wake" (2.274).

Why should the exhumation of Edward I in 1774 become controversial only after 1790 and continue to scandalize readers for the following four decades? Of course, it is possible—although there is no clear evidence to confirm it—that Gough really did try to pinch a finger from Edward I's tomb and that the story took more than a decade to come to light. As Lind's chemistry at the tomb of Edward IV in 1789 indicates, however, the exhumation may have been reanimated by the radical sciences of vitalism.[8] Peter Pindar's suggestion that the antiquaries were as eager for a head as for a finger bearing the royal ring in 1774, and the ensuing renegotiations of this image by Grose and Combe, could be understood, therefore, as a timely reflection on the heightened political stakes of vitalism after 1789.

In his *Reflections on the Revolutions of France* (1790), Edmund Burke seized an opportunity to appropriate the radical sciences of vitalism for his conservative political philosophy. Although Burke's preference for celebrating historical precedent over natural rights has frequently been recognized, it has rarely been examined within the contexts of the Romantics' theories of matter, which is particularly strange given Burke's emphasis throughout his *Reflections* on the matter of the historical dead.[9] For Burke, the dead are lively, and they guarantee the sovereign's right to rule. The liveliness of the dead extends to artifacts: the "durable records of all our acts" (71). Artifacts—such as the manuscript of the Magna Carta, coins, and the remnants of war—enshrine reasonable, influential, and imitable political precedents. They do not, however, enshrine fundamental or even natural rights. Burke's historiography is therefore curiously royalist, but not mechanical. Burke writes, for example, that "[t]he science of constructing a commonwealth, or renovating it, or reforming it, is, like every other experimental science, not to be taught *a priori*" (61). Burke describes the vitalisms of revolutionary sympathizers as misguided "metaphysic sophistry" (21) and "political metaphysics" (58). Their vitalism, he attests, sacrifices "real" for "theor[etical] rights" (58). Burke maintains that, in contrast, his theory of government vests people with real rights. They have, for example, the right to "live" by the "rule" of "law" and to enjoy "the fruits of their industry"; people also "have a right to the acquisitions of their parents; to the nourishment and improvement of their offspring; to instruction in life; and to consolation in death" (59).

For Burke all these real and lively rights are subsumed under the "convention" of the "law" which can be revealed only by the material objects that document legal and historical precedents (59). Burke emphasizes the materiality as well as the agency of precedents in his reference to "parents," "offspring," and "consolation in death" (33). "The idea of inheritance," he claims, "furnishes a sure principle of conservation, and a sure principle of transmission," curiously "without at all excluding a principle of improvement" (33). Burke is therefore able to maintain the theoretical force of matter's vital causality while insisting that it be grounded not in a priori natural rights but in the rights established and guaranteed by precedents, which are preserved and detectable only through artifacts.

Central to this neat parsing of a posteriori rights is Burke's conceptualization of "property": "working after the pattern of nature, we receive, we hold, we transmit our government and our privileges, in the same manner in which we enjoy and transmit our property and our lives" (33). Burke insists on kinship and property as privileged metaphors for the perennial security of civil society, and beneath that insistence lurks the conviction that artifacts vitally preserve and transmit political structures.[10] According to Burke, the French revolutionaries, along with their English sympathizers, have misunderstood the function of revolution by treating it as a tabula rasa or moment of origin: a cause unrelated to previous effects. The French Revolution has the dubious distinction, for example, of being singular: "the most astonishing thing that has hitherto happened in the world," Burke's sly way of satirizing the revolutionaries' ideas about vital causalities (10).

Of course, the revolutionaries and their sympathizers did not see things this way. Burke's interlocutor, Richard Price, believed that a revolution should entail a *return* to the causal agencies of natural rights—rights that had been corrupted subsequently and constrained by governments. Price and others therefore argued that the Revolution of 1688 had reestablished the legal precedent for the kind of government that they also had in mind: a government that granted the people the right to elect sovereigns, depose them if necessary, and reframe the organization of state according to the will of the people (Burke 16).[11] In order to illustrate the weaknesses in his opponents' arguments in both theoretical and historical terms, Burke excavates and rewrites the history of 1688. He begins by declaring that the members of the Constitutional Society and the Revolutionary Society have in mind a different revolution than the one that they say they do. "These gentlemen," he declares, "in all their reasonings on the Revolution of 1688, have [in mind] a revolution which happened in England about forty years before" (16). Price and his sympathizers are thinking, in other words, of the execution of Charles I in 1649 (16).

Later, Burke lobs a rhetorical question on the same theme: "Do these theorists mean to imitate some of their predecessors, who dragged the bodies of our antient [*sic*] sovereigns out of the quiet of their tombs" (23)? Indeed they do, Burke scoffs, and he goes on to insist that by desecrating the grave of government, the revolutionaries negate the very idea of vitality that underwrites their political philosophy. According to Burke, if the revolutionaries would adhere to the precedents of 1688, then they would find that the very vitalisms they claim to honor demand that they return to the past, not attempt to destroy it. In 1688, Burke says, the reformers of the government "regenerated the deficient part of the old constitution through the parts which were not impaired" (22). Reformers, in other words "kept" some "old parts" of the government "exactly as they were" because these parts would lead them to discover and to recover the other parts that "might be suited to them" (22). The reformers "acted by the ancient organized states in the shape of their old organization," whereas the misguided revolutionaries before 1649 had acted "by the organic *moleculae* of a disbanded people" (22). Government, Burke concludes, ought to be "a permanent body composed of transitory parts; wherein . . . the whole, at one time, is never old, or middle-aged, or young, but in a condition of unchangeable constancy, moves on through the varied tenour of perpetual decay, fall, renovation, and progression" (34). Government "is never wholly new" and "never wholly obsolete" (34).

As a representation of government, Burke's extended metaphor is designed to be a lively, coyly vitalist one that can compete with the vitalisms of the revolutionaries he condemned. Burke's state, for example, is enshrined as a "relation in blood," and we "[cherish]" it with "warmth" at "our hearths, our sepulchres, and our altars" (34). Burke describes his vision of government—consisting of "old parts exactly as they were" that remain lively in the present—as a "philosophical allegory" (34). He does not, he promises, indulge in "the superstition of antiquarians" (34). As John Barrell's *Imagining the King's Death* so thoroughly documents, Burke's detractors readily recognized that his vision of government entailed setting vitalism's radical possibilities to counterpurposes. They felt that Burke had cynically applied vitalist principles to the artifacts of the state in order to magically vest absolutist governments with enduring liveliness. Returning to Wolcot, then, we can now see the stakes of his condemnation of the antiquaries for swiping a finger from the tomb of Edward II. Burke argued that a royal finger and a royal ring preserved the vitality of sovereign power, even when the king's head had been cut off.

Exhuming Tyrants

While Edward I's finger threatened to reanimate the sovereign body and Lind's vital chemistry swirled around in a vial, another member of the Society of Antiquaries, Valentine Green, exhumed the body of one of England's most controversial monarchs—King John—in 1797. As with Edward I, the Society once again undertook an exhumation to settle a minor historical controversy. King John's body was buried in the Lady Chapel at Worcester Cathedral. Originally, the body was placed in a tomb in the Lady Chapel between the monuments of Oswald and Wulfstan. During the Reformation, the effigy of King John on the monument that marked his grave was moved to another monument, newly erected to commemorate him. Various historians debated whether the body had been moved along with the effigy. Some believed that the body remained in its original tomb; others did not. Green was in the former camp. When Arthur Onslow, Dean of Worcester, began planning to renovate the Cathedral, Green convinced him that they should open the tomb to confirm, once and for all, that the body of King John was not there. This discovery, Green promised, would allow Onslow to finalize his plan to move King John's Reformation-era monument back to the Lady Chapel—thus reuniting the monument with the body.

Before Green commenced with describing the findings in Worcester, he insisted—like Ayloffe—on the propriety of the antiquaries' activities. Their work was opportunistically undertaken in the course of renovation, he reassures his reader. Besides, the monument hindered approaches to the altar during church services. The exhumation was not the result of "caprices of modern reformation"; nor were the antiquaries interested in the "unnecessary and indecent disturbances of" a royal body (3). After all, they were looking for a body that they believed was not even there. The antiquaries began their investigation by removing the effigy from the top of the monument, then the lid of the monument, and finally the "rubbish" of bricks and stones inside the tomb that revealed wooden boards covering a coffin (3). Much to Green's surprise, the body of King John was in fact there. Immediately, the Dean and a local surgeon were called to the site.

The report that follows from Green is far more rhetorically ordered than those of either of the two previous exhumations. It is, however, tellingly inverted, beginning at the body itself and moving upward to the garments and concluding with a description of the coffin: an order that begins at the end of the antiquaries' actual exhumation, since observations about the corpse could be made only after peeling back the clothes, which, in turn, could only be done after opening the coffin. Green's description of King John's body lingers on the details of decay that Ayloffe flirted with but ultimately redirected. Lind's work for the 1789 exhumation appears to have set a precedent for this one in 1797. Specialized, medical terminology features prominently in Green's account of King John's body. Green notes, for example, that King John's skull was unusually positioned: "the foramen magnum, the opening through which the spinal marrow passes down the vertebrae, [was] turned upwards" (3). The king's head, in other words, was detached and upside down.

Although the antiquaries didn't pull back the sudarium or other habiliments to inspect King John's body directly, they observed it with as much anatomical precision as they could without disturbing the corpse. "The lower part of the os frontis," for example, was so "much perished, as to have become nearly of an even surface with the bottoms of the sockets of the eyes" (3). The passive "was much perished" describes, essentially, the king's forehead, now in a state of decay and sloping downward over the eyes; King John's upper and lower jawbones were in similar states of decay. Both were separated from the skull, and the upper jaw was displaced "near the right elbow" (4). The antiquaries paid particular attention to four teeth still extant in this jaw, "in very good preservation, and free from caries [sic]" (4). No teeth were present in the lower jaw, although the "coronoid processes" and "condyles" were both "very perfect" (4).

Moving down the body, they saw that the placement of both the right and left "ulna[s]" mirrored the placement of the arms on the effigy; they remarked that they could not see the rib cage and pelvis, although "part of the tibia of the right leg" was visible. The right leg, like the arms, was in the same position as the sculpted effigy on the tomb's lid, but the "knee of this limb appeared to be contracted"—forced into an unnatural position, the antiquaries surmised, by "other bones or fragments having fallen under it" (4). King John's toes, however, were in remarkably "good preservation"; "two or three" of his toenails, even, "were still visible" (4). "On the whole," Green writes, most of the bones of King John "appeared to have lain as they might naturally have done in their quiescent progress through the various stages of decay and dissolution" (4).

One other detail remains: a "vast quantity of the dry skins of maggots were dispersed over the body" (4). "[T]hese," Green reports, "are supposed to have been produced by some part of [the body] having gone into putrefaction (a circumstance imagined sometimes to have happened notwithstanding the precaution of embalming) previous to its removal, and the maggots having remained undisturbed, were upon the present discovery, seen in such great numbers" (4). Or maybe, the maggots came from King John's burial clothes, which were made out of leather, and "produced" as a result of its "natural putrefaction" (4).

The maggots enhance Green's empiricist image of the "quiescent progress" of the body moving mechanically forward through its natural process of putrefaction (4). His comment on natural decomposition also serves as an apologia for the antiquaries' exhumation method. In Green's methodical report, anatomy occupies a prominence of place that it did not in the exhumations of Edward I and Edward IV. At the end of his report, Green comes the closest he will get to drawing a larger philosophical or political point—and this about antiquaries' methodology rather than about the king's body. "In the course of this curious and interesting investigation," Green writes, "we have witnessed a no less curious result" (7). This "result" is the realization that antiquarianism was a valuable science: history for history's sake. "Happily," Green cheers, the antiquaries' investigation into King John's body has "closed the lips of conjecture" and "placed an ancient fact, beyond the reach of future doubt" (7). The antiquaries weren't, however, very successful at closing up lips and putting the past to rest. They kept King John's tomb open for one day so that the "royal remains" could be viewed "by some thousands of spectators, who crouded [sic] to the cathedral to see it" (7). The tomb had to be closed up suddenly when the "multitude" became "impatien[t]," even "ungovernable" (7).

When the antiquaries undertook the exhumation of Charles I in 1813, they did so in secrecy, wary not only of the mobs that had been whipped up in the seventeenth century but also of the sentimental fever that had come to characterize Romantic historiography.[12] Cromwell's and Charles I's ghosts haunted the Romantic theater.[13] Cromwell's skull circulated as a desirable collectible.[14] Objects associated with the life and execution of Charles I were also on prominent, if questionable, display in private and public collections.[15] The final resting place of Charles I's body was, however, unknown until 1813. In 1649, Cromwell's men feared that if they buried Charles I in Westminster, his grave would become a site of pilgrimage. They hastily buried his body in Windsor Castle because there it would be less accessible by the multitudes of relic-worshiping royalists should they discover the site of the body's burial.

After the Restoration and in the midst of the posthumous execution of regicides like Cromwell, Charles II planned to exhume Charles I and reinter him in Westminster. According to Clarendon, those few who had been present at Charles I's funeral could no longer find the body in Windsor's wreckage after the English Civil Wars.[16] In the course of renovating Windsor for the purposes of building a mausoleum for George III in the spring of 1813, workers accidentally poked a hole in the wall of the vault containing Henry VIII. Inside, they saw the two coffins that they expected to see (those of Henry VIII and Jane Seymour) and a surprising third. This third coffin was "covered with a black velvet pall" of the kind that had supposedly covered the coffin of Charles I. The Prince Regent granted permission for the coffin to be opened, and he personally attended the exhumation that occurred on April 1, 1813. Sir Henry Halford, the physician-extraordinary to George III and a fellow of both the Royal College of Physicians and the Society of Antiquaries, wrote and published the official report of their findings.

Halford begins his report by summarizing the relevant passages from those historians who had previously written about the burial of Charles I. He also included excerpts from these as appendixes. These historical accounts help verify the identification of the body, which the antiquaries confirm by comparing the corpse's face to a portrait of Charles I by Van Dyke (7). Halford next describes Charles I's cerecloth, presumably in a gesture to the ostensible purposes of earlier exhumations of royal bodies. In the case of Charles I, however, the antiquaries removed the cerecloth even though a "quantity of unctuous or greasy matter, mixed with resin" was "melted" between its folds; only "with great difficulty" could it be "detach[ed]" from the body (7). Eventually, "the whole face was disengaged from its covering" (8). Like Lind's report and especially Green's, Halford's description emphasizes the physical state of Charles I's body: "The complextion [*sic*] of the skin was dark and discoloured. The forehead and temples had lost little or nothing of their muscular substance; the cartilage of the nose was gone; but the left eye, in the first moment of exposure, was open and full, though it vanished almost immediately . . . [M]any of the teeth remained; and the left ear . . . was found entire" (8).

As was the case with the other exhumations, the artifact of Charles I's body was livelier than Halford's cool rhetoric would imply. "When the head" of Charles I "had been entirely disengaged" from the cerecloth, "it was found to be loose" (8). And then, "without any difficulty," the head "was taken up and held to view" (8). No indication is given by Halford as to who would have been so bold as to lift the head, but the image of a group of men, including the Prince Regent, holding Charles I's severed head aloft is an arresting one. Halford notes that the head was "quite wet" (8). The antiquaries, in fact, used a piece of paper and a piece of linen to soak up a sample of the liquid. Halford concludes, based on the color the liquid "gave to writing-paper, and to a white handkerchief," that it was, undoubtedly, Charles I's blood (8).

The scene is a ghastly one. The wet, severed head of Charles I is suspended above his body, 164 years after his execution, his blood inking parchment and linen. Halford's account presses on in gruesome detail. The "tendons and ligaments of the neck were of considerable substance and firmness" (9). The hair "was thick," black, and short—Charles I's famously luxe locks had been cut off before his head. The antiquaries' study of Charles I's body concludes with a grisly inspection of the very site where the executioner's ax fell. There, "the muscles of the neck had evidently retracted themselves" and "the fourth cervical vertebra was found to be cut through its substance" (9). The bone was "perfectly smooth and even, an appearance which could have been produced only by a heavy blow, inflicted with a very sharp instrument" (9). We are not encouraged to shed, with Hume, another tear over Charles I's untimely fate, and neither are we moved with the spirit of justice. As Halford writes, the fourth cervical vertebra is simply "the last proof" used to "identify King Charles I" (9). Having arrived at the identity of the corpse, "the coffin was soldered up again, and the vault closed" (10).

But not quite. Just as Edward I's exhumation became controversial some years after its historical moment, the exhumation of Charles I would also become controversial in 1874, thirty years after Halford's death. In that year, James F. Clarke gossiped in a published memoir that Halford had "purloin[ed] that portion of one of the cervical vertebrae which had been cut through by the axe" (352). Halford kept the bone of Charles I's neck "as a curiosity," and he would reportedly "pass it round the table after dinner for the examination of the guests" (352). Clarke said that "this slice of bone is still preserved in Sir Henry's family" (352).

The rumor was true. Halford had taken part of the fourth cervical vertebra that bore the mark of the ax, along with a lock of hair, a snippet of beard, and a tooth from the body of Charles I. [17] He commissioned a special-made box for the items, and left these to his son, who would eventually decide to return them. According to C. E. Newman, Halford's son was less concerned for his family's public reputation than he was anxious that he and his brother were childless. Their family estate—along with the objects his father had gathered from Charles I's exhumation—could, he worried, be sold to anyone. Halford's son returned the objects to the Prince of Wales in 1888. He was reportedly both surprised and heartbroken when he was welcomed at court with icy chagrin. The box was ritualistically lowered into the tomb at Windsor later that year in a solemn, private ceremony, placed upon the coffin where it supposedly remains today, still wrapped in Halford's handkerchief.

Vital Poetics

The tooth, hair, and neck bone taken from Charles I's tomb did not attract controversy until sixty-one years after they had been acquired, but a poem occasioned by the exhumation suggests that at least one person immediately felt discomfited by the specter of vitality that suddenly appeared in Charles I's grave: Lord George Gordon Byron's "Windsor Poetics." When he first wrote the poem, Byron appears to have been gleefully scandalized by the exhumation. As the poem traveled between manuscript and print copies, however, it lost some of its verve, and the revolutionary prospects of the vitalism it originally embraced started to unravel. Emendations to the poem, in fact, illustrate a variety of attempts by Byron and his readers to wrestle with the problem of whether Charles I's body was vital.[18]

Byron hastily scribbled a draft of "Windsor Poetics" sometime in the first week of April 1813—before Halford's account was made public. Byron had heard about the exhumation in a gossipy letter from Lady Melbourne.[19] At a dinner party that Lady Melbourne attended, the Prince Regent entertained his guests with the details of the discovery of Charles I's body. He even "acted out the manner of [Charles I's] decapitation on the shoulders of one of the guests" (Marchand 1.386).[20] Byron sent a revised version of the poem he had drafted as a giddy postscript in his reply to Lady Melbourne. He encouraged her to share the poem, and the verse quickly circulated among London's bon ton. Corin Throsby goes so far as to claim that "due to the popularity of Byron and the unpopularity of the Prince Regent, ["Windsor Poetics"] seems to be one of the most circulated poems between 1814 and 1816" (238).

The poem was not published, however, until 1818, when it appeared in John Anthony Galignani's Paris edition of *English Bards and Scotch Reviewers*. There "Windsor Poetics" was titled "Lines, composed on the occasion of H. R. H. the P . . . e R—g—t. being seen standing betwixt the coffins of Henry 8th and Charles 1st, in the Royal vault at Windsor." The poem, as published, appears in its entirety below:

FAMED for contemptuous breach of sacred ties,
By headless Charles see heartless Henry lies;
Between them stands another Sceptered thing,

It moves, it reigns, in all but name—a King:
Charles to his People, Henry to his Wife,
—In him the double Tyrant starts to Life:
Justice and Death have mixed their dust in vain,
The Royal Vampyres start to breathe again;
How shall we trust to tombs?—since these disgorge
The blood and dust of both—to mould a G . . . ge.

This is one of many versions of the poem. It differs from manuscript drafts and revisions of the poem in Byron's hand, copies prepared by his acquaintances, the epistolary version he sent to Lady Melbourne, reproductions of the poem in various commonplace books, and even the version of the poem that appeared in the second Paris edition of *English Bards and Scotch Reviewers* that was issued in 1819. Revisions to the poem suggest that some lines were more philosophically and politically knotty than others. Throsby speculates that although it is true that Byron liked to tinker with his verse, it is also reasonable to expect that not only did the poem become inevitably corrupted as a result of being continually copied and circulated, but also that some of the changes were designed to "[make] the poem less of a pointed dig at the Prince Regent" (239).

Byron knew his poem was dangerously seditious and libelous. When he sent it to Lady Melbourne, he said outright that he "wish[ed]" that the Prince Regent "had exchanged heads" with Charles I, or even better: that the two had been "stitched together" (Byron, *Letters* 3.37). Stitched together, the heads of Charles I and the Prince Regent would make "an admirable Janus of a fool & a knave," Byron joked (*Letters* 3.37). Byron goes on to declare in a bout of dark satire that Charles I was the "greatest *king* (that is—villain) that ever lived" (*Letters* 3.37). Because he was about to skip the country, Byron had few qualms about encouraging Lady Melbourne to share his poem about the exhumation. "I suppose you will be *tender* or *afraid*" to circulate the poem, he writes, but he also adds: "you need not mind any *harm* it will do me" (*Letters* 3.38).

In 1814, Byron continued to be cavalier about "Windsor Poetics" when Thomas Moore informed him that it had been widely circulated. "I cannot conceive how [the poem] has got about,—but so it is," Byron pronounced. In hindsight, he felt that that his satirical verse was "too *farouche*," a little more vicious than necessary; it could have been more "playful" (*Letters* 4.80). Although he, personally, had few reservations about the political sensibilities the poem expressed, Byron did counsel Moore against publishing it. He recognized that it was so treasonous in spirit that it would be "downright actionable"; "to print it would be peril to the publisher" (*Letters* 4.80). What's interesting about "Windsor Poetics" isn't the treasonous jouissance it takes in representing Charles I and the Prince Regent but, rather, the ways in which it struggles to reconcile vitalism with the genealogical as well as historical lineages of monarchs. "Windsor Poetics" is as concerned with matter as it is with tyrants, and its versions illustrate how vitalism's key tenets risked revitalizing divine right as much as they promised to deliver a democratic revolution.

The poem's initial desire to see the Prince Regent as just another mechanical object stays remarkably consistent across the variants. Important aspects of lines 3–4, for example, remain essentially the same from the draft to the published versions to the epistolary and commonplace book copies. In these lines, the Prince Regent is just "another Sceptered *thing*" (emphasis added).[21] Line 4 consistently uses the impersonal pronoun "it" to denote the Prince Regent as a mere object. These lines also, however, come under considerable pressure given the many changes to the line that follows. Various verbs creep in to describe the actions the Prince Regent can take: "moves," "reigns," "breathes," and "lives."[22] The latter two options speak to slippages between mechanistic and vitalist views of the king's body.

The representations of Charles I and Henry VIII as vampires in the poem likewise exemplify another instance where Byron and readers appear to have kept trying to find the right word for describing how the matter of the king's body acted. In one draft, Byron assigned to "tombs" the power to awaken or "disgorge" their vampire kings. In another version, the vampire kings "spring to life again" on their own. In the version Byron sent to Lady Melbourne, "each" body "quits his vault again." In the first edition of the printed poem, both bodies "start to breathe again." In another version of the poem, they "wake." In still another, they comingle in an unholy assemblage to "join and rise again." In short, the word choices that aim to depict Charles I and Henry VIII's bodies as mere mechanical entities swerve constantly into vitalist terrain. Their corpses prove capable of springing, quitting, breathing, waking, joining, and rising.

The poem's fluctuating images of "blood," "dust," or "dirt" that mix to "mould" or "make" the Prince Regent into a tyrant sovereign similarly indicate how a vitalist's principles could look a lot like a royalist's fantasies. Blood, of course, conjured the idea of hereditary sovereignty while kings' bodies could also be imagined as being composed of a substance that was more than the sum of dust or dirt—something vested with a mysterious life of its own. Revisions to these terms suggest that Byron and his readers uneasily encountered the organicism of kings' graves and bodies. "Windsor Poetics" concludes, then, with lines that call into question vitalism's tenets. One version ends by asking, "How shall we trust . . . Death?" In another version, "how shall we trust . . . the grave?" In another, "the grave" becomes "tombs." Yet other versions of the poem's conclusion exclaim variously, "Ah! What *can* tombs avail," "What *then shall* tombs avail," "What *can new* tombs avail," and "What *now can* tombs avail?"

In "Windsor Poetics" Byron and his readers long for a theory of matter that will guarantee that history arcs forward into revolutions that will right the wrongs of sovereign tyrants, but they start to suspect that vitalist principles mean that the headless, heartless matter of tyrants will not rest easy in old kings' graves. Although there is no concrete evidence that Shelley read "Windsor Poetics," his "Defense of Poetry" (1821) suggests that he had also come to wonder about vitalism's viability for a radical, revolutionary politics. Amanda Jo Goldstein's reading of Shelley's final poem, *The Triumph of Life* (1822), suggests something similar. *The Triumph of Life*, Goldstein claims, frets over "how the vitalist approach to life might collaborate with power in more overtly historical and political modalities" ("Growing Old" 69). More specifically, Goldstein argues that Shelley recognized that "vital power"—which could be conceptualized as something either "added" to or "immanent" within matter—"risked collaboration with power of the imperial kind" ("Growing Old" 70).

Goldstein shares with other Shelley critics an interest in the "peculiar pretense at substance" and the "special materiality of language" that characterize Shelley's poetics ("Growing Old" 75). She concludes that Shelley's *Triumph of Life*, with its representations of age and atmospherics, aspires to be like the filmy husks that atoms shed in Book 4 of Lucretius's *De Rerum Natura*: soft, translucent, and productively suspended in dynamic processes of decay. Notably, Shelley took up his *Triumph of Life* just as he had decided to set down for good his attempted verse drama, "Charles the First."[23] Shelley never finished that historical play. Critics agree that Shelley was stymied when it came to plotting the events of the 1640s through to their final scene at the scaffold and deciding if he could join Hume in shedding a tear, in the end, for Charles I's fate.[24] In 1822, Shelley admitted that his attempt at "Charles the First" had faltered because he could not "seize the conception of the subject as a *whole*."[25]

Shelley's "Defense of Poetry" offers another example of his thinking about the matter of verse, but the "Defense" suggests that Shelley conceptualized poems as entities that could be more substantial than filmy Lucretian husks without needing to aspire to the quality of wholeness that he failed to achieve for "Charles the First." The "Defense" registered Shelley's interest in imagining how poetry could achieve something like particulate solidity as a means of ensuring not only a poem's historical viability but also its future political vibrancy. In short, Shelley's "Defense" indicates that he imagined poems as artifacts and how doing so might ensure that poems would be more vital than objects from the past, including those bodies of sovereign despots.

In the "Defense," Shelley distinguishes poetry from genres of history.[26] Genres of history are time-bound, place-bound, and object-bound: a "catalogue of detached facts which have no other bond of connection than time, place, circumstance, cause, and effect" (486). Even when rendered as a narrative or "story," history persists as a "certain combination of events which can never again recur" (486). Shelley here halts the new historiography's vitalist implications—not unlike the antiquaries working the graves of Edward I, Edward IV, John, and even Charles I, who were also eager to insist that the bodies of the sovereigns they exhumed persisted in states of inertness. Shelley does not reinvest such bodies with vitality, but he still tries to preserve vitalism's radical promise. He does so by reimagining language itself as a series of historical fragments. As Shelley explains, a sentence, a phrase, or a word in a written history may yet attain the status of poetry—if it can be detached from genre as well as temporal contexts in which they were first uttered. These pieces of language lie in wait for a future poet to come along and "reanimate" the "sleeping, the cold, the buried image of the past" (485–486).

Similarly, poems written in the moment of the present alternately release and renew their relationships to the historical conditions in which they are inevitably composed as well as to the objects that they inevitably depict. The poet translates the present into a history for the future while also making the objects that populate the present more durable by translating them into fragments of poetic diction. Shelley's quintessentially Romantic privileging of the poet's perception, therefore, does not entirely negate the objects that the poet encounters or represents.[27] Instead, poems embody the "relation, subsisting, first between existence and perception and secondly between perception and expression" (505). Perception remains central for Shelley, but he nevertheless insists on a relationship, however filmy it may be, between the "percipient" and the "things" that really "exist" (505). Shelley argues, therefore, that poetry is not just an "effect" of the "active powers of the mind" (506). Neither should his readers believe that poetry has "no necessary connection with consciousness or will" (506). Rather, poetry subsists as a unique and embodied mode of perception that draws on while remaining independent from both the poet's mind as well as the historical, material conditions in which the poem's composition occurs and to which it necessarily refers.

Entangled with objects, minds, and presence at the moment of their composition, poems remain susceptible to suspicious interference for Shelley. Poems can be buffeted by accidents, constrained by limited perspectives, and subject to censorship. Shelley argues that such conflicts make their way into the poems themselves as combinations of "exultation and horror, grief and pleasure, eternity and change" ("Defense" 505). For Shelley, however, a poem also drifts over time, shape-shifting until it "subdues to union . . . all irreconcilable things" (505). Shelley famously describes poetry's capacity to enact a transfer between object and perception, and between the past, present, and future as its "vitally metaphorical" quality (482). He also says that by transforming perception and experience into poems, poets become the "unacknowledged legislators of the world" (507).

Poems are more vital, therefore, than the objects that they represent or the contexts in which they emerge in Shelley's "Defense"; and, eventually, a poem's vibrancy will characterize it as an artifact in and for the future. Poems, Shelley declares, must be "reserved for future generations to contemplate" (486). By way of illustration, Shelley's "Ozymandias" may be read not only as a poem that depicts an artifact but also as an artifact in its own right and, as such, the poem qualifies the vitalisms that threatened to reanimate the dead bodies of sovereign tyrants in Byron's "Windsor Poetics." "Ozymandias" accrues its vibrancy from the fragmented and decaying monument to the "king of kings" that it famously depicts. The monument is poised somewhere between the categories of the empty sepulchral monument and a sculpture. Although the monument is a representation of the body of the long-dead sovereign it depicts, it neither contains the body of the king nor marks the spot where the king is buried. The sovereign power of Ozymandias, such as it is, persists metonymically in "trunkless legs" and a "half sunk" "shattered visage," dissipating into countless dry, sandy grains (64).

In this way, Shelley's poem does what he claims poems do in contrast to the genres of history; poems "make space and give time" ("Defense" 500). The poem's moral and political force inheres in the poem's imagery of a giant sculpture of a tyrant from the past whose stony body now crumbles as a colossal wreck in a lonely desert (64). The diction of "Windsor Poetics" is discomfortingly animated by the matter of the dead sovereigns that have been exhumed, but "Ozymandias" imagines a flatter scene: a wreckage of large parts, scattered and broken across the "boundless and bare," "lone and level sands" (64). Recognizing that such scenes of dispersal may still threaten to be vital vestiges of the sovereign body, Shelley adopts a strategy in which the artifact becomes the agent not of history, but of poetry.

"Ozymandias" achieves this by nesting descriptions of the monument in a series of reported speech acts and palpable silences.[28] "Ozymandias" consists of dialogue, transcription, and quotation that refer to while never directly identifying or locating the artifact that the poem depicts. The poet-speaker documents what was said sometime in the past by an unnamed "traveler from an antique land" (64). The traveler quotes from memory what he once read written on the monument's pedestal, which was, in turn, once upon a time transcribed by the sculptor and dictated by Ozymandias. Despite the immediacy of Ozymandias's first-person act of dictation, "My name is Ozymandias," and his imperative tone, "Look on my works," readers experience a fourth-hand report of the poem's moral instructing them to "despair" when they look on the works of kings (64).

The time delay created by the nesting of the poem's imperative moral enhances the irony of the monument's poetic inscription. History has transformed the brash imperative boast of Ozymandias to his artifact's future interpreters—"Look on my works, ye Mighty, and despair!"—into a different kind of lesson in despair. A king who ruled with "wrinkled lip" and "cold command" produced only "despair" and "nothing" else (64). Readers of the poem are invited to ponder the political as well as the moral lessons conveyed by Ozymandias's decaying monument not only despite but also because of the intention that characterized its original design (64). The final evocative lines of the poem juxtapose the immediacy of Ozymandias's ironically imperative speech with silent, empty space. Although the inscription on the monument is attributed to Ozymandias, the meaning of that inscription belongs to the sculptor and to the poet. The sculptor preserved the dark truth of Ozymandias's character; the poet preserves the effect of Ozymandias's sovereignty. The silent empty space with which the poem concludes erases the monument itself but preserves its vitality as poetry, and the poem as well as the poet replaces the artifact as a record for the future of a vibrancy that promises to be more enduring and politically powerful than that of the king's own body.[29]

The Artifactual Form

Where did all those small, broken, rusty, dirty, moldy artifacts that once fascinated, vexed, and frustrated so many people go? Today, we rarely come into contact with the bric-a-brac that piled up in England during the long eighteenth century. When we do, the objects have already been cleaned up and identified. Their historical, cultural, or financial value has usually been settled: "Now recognized as authentic, Mr. Walton's nickel is expected to fetch $2 million to $5 million"; "a pair of scholars are announcing a surprising discovery: a previously unknown early handwritten parchment of the Declaration, buried in a provincial archive in Britain"; the "iron blade of an ornate dagger buried in Egypt with King Tutankhamen probably came from a fallen meteorite, researchers have determined"; the "bones buried under a parking lot belonged to Richard III."[1]

These headlines suggest that our contemporary representations of artifacts reflect how the objects failed to do what they were supposed to do in the long eighteenth century: to "speak" or "give evidence for themselves," as John Aubrey once put it. Artifacts are now presumed to be objects that cannot speak for themselves. They languish as indistinguishable, interchangeable items until they are spoken for—either by the experts who claim them as their objects of study, or by the individuals who claim them as their personal property. However, the history of artifacts should encourage us to think about artifacts differently: as fragmented objects that lead us to believe that we can complete their shapes, reconstruct their histories, and determine their meanings—but that always keep us guessing and second-guessing about what they are, what they mean, and why they matter. As Aubrey also explained, the parts of artifacts that persist "keep" us from "being lost" while we undertake the task of interpreting them; yet the parts that are missing still "leave us Room to guess" (*Miscellanies* [1714], 24). By leaving us with room to guess, artifacts turned out to be incapable of telling the whole truth and nothing but the truth: of acting dependably and independently—in other words, as the agents of facts.

This book has suggested, for example, that old coins could be prized for their hard durability as well as for their soft ductility. Accordingly, they could be celebrated for their power to preserve historical facts and to impress noble virtues into the memories of their present collectors—or used as devices for circulating falsehoods and factional propaganda among the public. Similarly, manuscripts seemed to determine the conditions of the present by establishing the legal precedents that the English government should either honor or reject; they also, however, were vulnerable to destruction, misinterpretation, and forgery. Likewise, obsolete weapons could be taken as evidence that the worst of human nature endured throughout the ages and was inescapable, or they could be touted as unfortunate but necessary tools for effecting social and political change. Finally, the grave goods found in the tombs of monarchs might confirm that the past had finally been put to rest; but they might also raise the specter of an everlasting spirit—for better or worse.

These competing interpretations of artifacts returned again and again to both historical and philosophical conflicts over sovereignty. As objects, artifacts seemed capable of providing objective answers to questions over who as well as what had the power to initiate, control, and take action. Instead, however, artifacts exposed how claims about the nature of matter's sovereignty often belied their interpreters' biases regarding the nature of government and vice versa. Rather than resolve the conflicts they were called upon to settle, artifacts kept those conflicts going—for a while, at least. The prologue explains that my study began with Latour's directive to "follow the actors," because Aubrey's declaration that old things could "speak" or "give evidence for themselves" seemed like an early iteration of Latour's claim that objects are actants: things that have the power to do things (*Reassembling* 12). Artifacts did not do the things that they were supposed to do, but they did do things, and so it was surprising to realize that the old coins, manuscripts, weapons, and grave goods that compelled and confounded so many people in the long eighteenth century rarely appeared in either studies of material culture or in the "Latourian litanies" that have become a stylistic staple of recent writing about the nature of objects.[2]

Latourian litanies tend to lavish their attention on two types of objects: everyday objects and technological inventions. In so doing, the litanies aim to redress the disciplinary conventions that studies of material cultures have established. In material culture studies, "people make" objects that, in turn, "make people": the most-considered objects are items like the clothes that people wear, the goods that they purchase and exchange, or the sentimental tokens that they treasure (Miller, *Materiality* 38). Objects give rise to "cultural biographies" and "social histories" that challenge the idea that the world of objects is an "impersonal machine" (Miller, *Materiality* 34, 48).[3] Objects become personalized in such studies that illustrate how people's "desire and demand" determine objects' "value in specific social situations" (Appadurai 4).[4] The new materialists who have been influenced by Latour's work turn to everyday objects and technological inventions in order to insist that objects should not be subsumed to the category of items made by or for people. The new materialists focus on everyday objects that are ready-to-hand in order to illustrate that such objects are not so ready-to-hand as they may seem. Likewise, the new materialists emphasize the ways in which technological innovations thwart—rather than satisfy—our "desire and demand."

Studies of material culture are more likely to focus on old things than work in the new materialisms, but artifacts rarely make the cut in either field. As Bill Brown might have put it in his "Thing Theory," artifacts are neither material culture's objects nor new materialisms' things. We tend to examine objects , Brown writes, for what they may "disclose about history, society, nature, or culture—above all, what they disclose about *us*," but we only "glimpse" things, which have distinct lives of their own (4). To be sure, people were interested in what artifacts disclosed about "history, society, nature, or culture" in the long eighteenth century, but they were also interested in the artifacts themselves: in the believable as well as unbelievable stories that *they* seemed to tell on their own about the strange worlds they inhabited where the warp and weft of time and matter contracted into hard facts only to break apart again into fragmented figments. On the rare occasions when old objects appear in the new materialisms, they usually illustrate the shortcomings of previous scientific and philosophical projects that failed sufficiently to heed objects' agencies. Robert Boyle's air-pump is one such object that now stands as a classic example, and it exemplifies the new materialisms' preferences—as the name itself suggests—for the new or inventive, even when considering the old or the obsolete.[5] In the pages of material culture studies and the new materialisms alike, there is hardly a cankered coin, charred manuscript, rusty weapon, or moldering bone to be found. Instead there are gifts or global capital, postage stamps or digital networks, ceremonial swords or drones, relics or DNA.[6]

Latour's description of the conditions in which a researcher is most likely to catch a nonhuman actor exerting its agency suggests why artifacts in particular have not always fared well in either material culture studies or in the new materialisms. According to Latour, an object's agency can best be de-

tected at the moment the object is invented, when it has been sufficiently distanced from its "users" by time or space, when an accident occurs, when an
object has "receded into the background for good," or when it has been taken
up by a "fiction," "counterfactual history," or "thought experiment" (*Reassembling* 81–82). Artifacts dwell in all these conditional states, except for one.
Artifacts are sufficiently distanced from their users both in time and space as
the things buried in and by the past; they enter into the present pocked with
signs of this distance. Their survival is an accident of time, their discovery
often equally accidental. They do not have obvious use functions in the present. You are unlikely to try to buy milk with an ancient coin, use a medieval
manuscript for completing your math homework, bring a rusty sword to a
gunfight, or repurpose anything you find in a king's grave. Throughout this
study, artifacts have been taken up repeatedly by fictions as well as histories,
and I have suggested that artifacts are, by their very nature, invitations to indulge in thought experiments about the past. At the site of "invention," however, artifacts pose real difficulty. Artifacts are pointedly not the scientific,
technological, or engineering innovations with which so much of the work in
the field of the history of science influenced by Latour's actor-network-theory
is rightly concerned; nor are they good candidates for the kind of inventive
self-fashioning that interests those working in material culture studies.

Artifacts became important objects of study precisely for this reason. Many
in the long eighteenth century well knew how eager some politicians and historians were to invent and reinvent the past. The material fact of the artifact itself, its agency as a nonhuman object, was supposed to halt invention.
The antiquary Humphrey Wanley made this point explicitly. He well knew
that England had recently lived through "great Quarrels." He maintained that
such quarrels had resulted because "persons" were "inexperience[d]" with
England's "Antiquities and ancient Constitution." The old objects that were
left over from the past were therefore the best means, he declared, "whereby
ma[n]y *innovations* and troublesome Debates may be prevented" (quoted in
Sweet 35, emphasis added). At some point in their pasts, of course, artifacts
must have been inventions. But artifacts were not considered to be inventions in the long eighteenth century if by that term we mean something like
"an instrument, an art, etc. originated by the ingenuity of some person, and
previously unknown; an original contrivance or device."[7] To read artifacts
as things contrived by an ingenuous person risked turning them back into
objects that were made by and for people, with potentially disastrous consequences. Holding fast to the idea that artifacts were neither invented things

nor the inventors of history, people in the long eighteenth century followed the artifacts, as Latour suggests an actor-network-theorist should—until they confronted artifacts' failure to perform reliably as the agents of matters of fact. Then, artifacts did start to seem like inventions.

Like Latour, those who followed artifacts in the long eighteenth century also stumbled into controversies—not just controversies over which specific matters of fact the artifacts really evinced, but also the controversial realization that when artifacts were presumed to speak for themselves, what they said sounded a lot like propaganda. Artifacts' propensity to sound like propagandists explains why they've gone missing from studies of material cultures as well as the new materialisms. In material culture studies, artifacts' propensity to talk the most about political histories and philosophies throughout the long eighteenth century would go on to make them unlikely case studies for assessing the relationships between individual subjects and the things they made that made them. The case of the missing artifacts in the new materialisms is more complicated. Latour's actor-network-theory builds on his earlier *We Have Never Been Modern*, which famously claims that the Enlightenment falsely "purified" the relationships between humans and objects by relegating them to separate spheres. Objects, Latour argues, were divested of their capacity for agency and action when Enlightenment scientists and philosophers relegated objects to the status of the stuff that humans perceive, use, control, and understand. Latour's account of the Enlightenment's preference for minds over matter has been taken for granted in the new materialisms. In these contexts, structural inequalities inhere in the privileging of human perception and will over the agency that nonhuman objects possess.

The new materialists claim that a critical method that adopts the premise that objects have agency entails a productive decentering of the human subject. Such a decentering, they explain, will divulge new opportunities for resisting political inequalities and thereby introduce more progressive forms of democracy for humans and nonhumans alike. Samantha Coole and Diana Frost's introduction to the edited collection, *New Materialisms* (tellingly subtitled *Ontology, Agency, and Politics*), offers a representative example of how, as Timothy Morton puts it, objects' agency is "vital and contested political terrain" (*Hyperobjects* 20). Coole and Frost insist that acknowledging objects' agency entails a "radical reappraisal of the contours of the subject, a reassessment of the possibility and texture of ethics, an examination of new domains of power and unfamiliar frames for imagining justice, and an exploration of the sources, quality, and dimensions of agency" (37). The new materialisms, they write, are both "profoundly philosophical and also insistently politically engaged," and their oft-cited edited collection bespeaks the tendency of work that falls under the aegis of the new materialisms to be especially salient for feminists, environmental activists, and critics concerned with topics such as bioethics, biopolitics, and the geopolitical and socioeconomic effects of global capital (37).[8]

The Latourian litany that introduces Bonnie Honig's *Public Things* similarly exemplifies the political imperatives of the new materialisms. "Public things," she writes, "include universities, local, state, and national parks, prisons, schools, roads and other transportation systems, the military, governments, electricity and power sources, including hydropower, gas, and oil pipelines, and nuclear plants, airwaves, radio and television broadcast networks, libraries, airport security, and more" (4). Public things, Honig clarifies, "furnish the world of democratic life. They do not take care of our *needs* only. They constitute us, complement us, limit us, thwart us, and interpellate us into democratic citizenship" (5). When a public thing works as well as when it "crumbles," it heightens our awareness of the "civic contests that surround [it] and us" (6). Why aren't artifacts considered to be "vital and contested political terrain" or "public things"? Why don't they enter into conversations about "new domains of power and unfamiliar frames for imagining justice"? After all, the political stakes of what artifacts said or evinced beginning in the seventeenth century were almost unimaginably high. Artifacts had the power to make the case for or against regicide and revolution, for or against what constituted treason, for or against democracy.

But that is what proved to be the problem with artifacts. Artifacts were agents of competing political histories as well as philosophies.[9] Artifacts were not easily assembled into the service of political agendas—even those agendas that we admire and long to see enacted the most—because they were once assembled into the service of multiple and competing political agendas. Eighteenth-century antiquaries and their publics anticipated Langdon Winner's question: "Do artifacts have politics?" And their emphatic answer was: no. Artifacts *were* political insofar as they were called upon to convey matters of fact about political history and philosophy.[10] The facts that artifacts evinced were therefore political but, like the artifacts themselves, they were not presumed to be partisan. That is to say, although artifacts had the power to act as political agents, they enjoyed such power precisely because they were not thought to be inventive or invested in the matters of fact that they revealed. Nor were artifacts presumed to be invested in the consequences of their revelations. And yet, one could not escape the sense that something about this way of understanding artifacts was not quite right, especially when a single artifact seemed to deliver content that validated the principles of opposing factions. Artifacts could not be depended upon as the reliable agents of political history or philosophy if they were willing to tell everyone what they wanted to hear.

The old coins, manuscripts, weapons, and grave goods that fascinated and frustrated so many people in the long eighteenth century were eventually discarded, then, for the same reason that they inspired so much thinking, research, and writing in the first place: because artifacts' fragmented materiality engendered interpretations that were always subject to suspicion and critique. The suspicions and critiques that artifacts stoked, however, should make them more rather than less important for those who study objects today. The history of artifacts can give those who scrutinize and theorize objects new criteria they might use not only to identify objects that are in need of more consideration but also to group previously unassociated objects together and reassess or predict their functions. Additionally, artifacts invite us to revise what we know about the history and likely outcomes of our attempts to interpret what objects are and what they mean. In particular, the history of artifacts draws our attention to the political stakes—including the successes and the failures—of turning to objects in the hopes they will explain natural as well as cultural phenomena.

People who cared about artifacts in the long eighteenth century also cared about politics. They felt that artifacts could provide hard evidence of the practices as well as the ideas that characterized the best and the worst forms of government. In the end, however, artifacts did not act reliably as the agents of political histories or philosophies. They did not disclose indisputable facts about power's origins, distribution, or its previous forms of organization. Neither, then, could artifacts guarantee that future forms of government would be related to those that came before it. Claims about political histories or philosophies that were premised on the evidence offered by artifacts, therefore, appeared to remain compromised by the investments of the individuals who interpreted the artifacts throughout the long eighteenth century. Although the history of artifacts shows that focusing our attention on objects does not necessarily produce more politically progressive worldviews or practices, that history does establish artifacts as objects that have the ability to act—but artifacts lead us to look to the texts that they afford in order to assess their influence.

Artifacts became important objects of study in the seventeenth century when they were called upon to speak and give evidence for themselves about matters of fact, especially with regard to political history and philosophy in the midst of a crisis over how England's government should be organized. Throughout the long eighteenth century, artifacts continued to speak about these subjects to those who longed for more democracy as well as to those who longed to restore the sovereign's absolute right to rule. I have suggested that artifacts' states of fragmentation afforded the production of competing interpretations and that, as a result, artifacts and their interpretations roused suspicions and critiques. Artifacts were simultaneously too material and too political—yet not material or political enough, which is why they no longer capture the kind of popular or critical attention they previously enjoyed.

At the same time, however, I have maintained that the history of artifacts confirms that they are things that do things. By simultaneously requiring that speculations be provided to fill in the object's gaps while grounding those speculations in the observable matter that still endured in the object, artifacts were adept at getting people interested in interpreting them.[11] As fragmented objects caught in the medias res of change, artifacts were, for a while at least, well positioned to enter into discursive networks where debates about matters of fact flourished. Throughout the long eighteenth century, artifacts' states of fragmentation made them amenable to being reduced to elemental particulars as well as dissolved into social constructions; their states of fragmentation could also refer their interpreters either backward in time to the object's point of origin or forward into the present and possible futures. It may be useful, however, to think of artifacts as stiff "quasi-objects": more hard than soft. Latour, who borrows the term "quasi-objects" from Michel Serres, explains that quasi-objects occupy a middle ground between the organic objects of nature and the things that people conceive, make, and control. As Latour puts it, quasi-objects are "much more social, much more fabricated, much more collective than the 'hard' parts of nature," while they are also "much more real, nonhuman and objective than those shapeless screens on which society—for unknown reasons—needed to be 'projected'" (*Modern* 53).

Thinking of artifacts as stiff quasi-objects allows us to account for the ways that they traveled between what we might describe as their fact networks and their art networks (before they fell through the cracks). In their fact networks, artifacts were valued primarily for their "hard" materiality: as nonhuman objects vested with the power to relay information about not only the past but also about themselves as pieces of matter. In their fact networks, artifacts yielded historical, philosophical, and scientific content. Artifacts' states of fragmentation, however, meant that the content that was still missing from the objects either needed to be accounted for or supplied. Reconstructions of artifacts' missing content inevitably veered into imaginative guesswork, and so artifacts entered into their art networks. In their art networks, artifacts did not, however, soften so much as become "shapeless screens." Artifacts continued to be assessed for their ability to relay content in their art networks; they might yield *some* matters of fact, after all. Moreover, the imaginative guesswork that artifacts provoked in the first place—and the suspicions they raised as a result—confirmed that they were, in many ways, agential as nonhuman objects. Acknowledging artifacts to be stiff quasi-objects foregrounds their status as real things in possession of distinct material properties that made them both compelling and confounding throughout the long eighteenth century.

Incapable, however, of settling firmly in their fact networks, artifacts produced discursive debate, and in their art networks, the content that the artifacts failed to deliver in the fact networks became translated into form. In other words, the fact finding and guesswork provoked by artifacts' states of fragmentation generated texts that referred to real artifacts as well as texts that attempted to reproduce aspects of the artifacts' materiality. Textual engagements with artifacts rarely mitigated the artifacts' controversies by disavowing artifacts' agencies outright. Instead, they incorporated aspects of the artifacts' materialities. Like the artifacts themselves, the texts that resulted were especially ripe for interrogation into their truth-claims, their ideological motivations, and their authors', readers', and critics' commitments to objects as agents without intent. In this way, artifacts had effects on the structures, meanings, and readings of many of the texts produced in the long eighteenth century, and readers learned not only to dig deeper for and into artifacts but also to bring that digging to bear on textual interpretations and representations of objects.

The works I have examined in this study may be said, therefore, to chart the emergence of an "artifactual form." They show that the artifactual form can acclimatize in poetry as well as prose, in fiction as well as nonfiction. They likewise suggest that the artifactual form is a liminal aesthetic mode, emerging historically between the Augustans and the Romantics, encompassing both simultaneously, and preserving them in an ongoing state of tension and interchange. The artifactual form is compelling as an aesthetic mode because it stages contradictions and provokes its readers to interact with the text as if it were an artifact in need of completion and interpretation. The artifactual form leads us not only to rediscover artifacts that might benefit from more critical scrutiny but also to identify more clearly the structures, commitments, and likely impacts of the texts that engage with the artifacts. An artifactual form also reshapes our understanding of literary history by inviting us to reevaluate the significance of once-popular but now little-read texts, especially those that do not conform to conventional genre distinctions. It also invites us to reread well-known texts to reconsider their structural and representational investments. As fragments, artifacts are objects that mean one thing and then another and yet another. The artifactual form borrows features from the artifact, indexing the fraught relationships between objects and their representations, causes and effects, facts and ideologies.

Despite its iteration in disparate genres and its tendency to register as well as produce conflicting interpretations, the artifactual form has several distinct features. The artifactual form can make a text seem as if it is depicting or referring to a real artifact. In most cases, texts that depict or refer to an actual artifact are good candidates for assessing whether or not their form might be artifactual. Obviously, texts that are factual frequently refer to extant objects, and those texts may describe these objects as artifacts—but the artifactual form is more often deployed as a means of engaging with those objects whose states of fragmentation forestall or prevent people from piecing together the object's complete shape or full history. An artifactual form appears just as frequently, therefore, in texts that we would describe as literary rather than historical, and it often appears in nonfictional texts when a degree of intractable uncertainty attends a represented object. When a text purports to depict or refer to an artifact, it usually signals an attempt to introduce the text into the networks where an artifact is prioritized for what it can convey with regard to matters of fact. Consequently, the appearance of a supposedly real artifact in a nonfictional or a literary work often indicates the text's interest in addressing questions that artifacts themselves were once called upon to answer: questions about history, philosophy, or politics that cannot be answered solely by recourse to subjective, individual experience. In this way, the artifactual form can introduce nonfictional elements into works of literature, join disparate genres of texts together through allusions, and serve as a means for expressing the larger historical, political, or philosophical stakes of the text.

An artifactual form indicates a preference, implicit or explicit, for mimesis, imitation, or unity with the artifact(s) that the text represents. This preference has long been taken as a hallmark of neoclassical aesthetics. In the artifactual form, depictions of artifacts aspire to be commensurate with the objects themselves; representation aims to be like the mirror instead of the lamp, in M. H. Abrams's well-known formulation. These texts adopt stylistic strategies that declare that their loyalties lie not with their authors or their readers but with the artifacts that purportedly exist in an a priori relationship to their representation. Sometimes, the visual arrangements of a text indicate its attempt to mirror the artifacts it represents. Poems shaped like the objects that they meditate upon are an obvious example. Texts that emphasize rich descriptions of objects' shapes, textures, colors, and arrangements or that tackle questions of authenticity also typify this aspect of the artifactual form. Often, however, a text's investments in mimesis, imitation, or unity can be detected in its metafictional gambits, conceptual conceits, or in its experiments with genre, plot, character, or setting. Histories arranged into strict chronological order, satires keyed to real events or persons, plays in which action unfolds in real time, narratives that take special interest in settings, criticism that adopts the terms and tenor of the objects it critiques, and even avant-garde representations of objects are all examples of the means by which a text can appear to be conjoined with the artifacts it purports to represent.

An artifactual form demonstrates a yearning for the ideas that representations of the artifact aim to convey to inhere in and emerge from—either in part or in their entirety—the object itself. That is to say, an artifactual form mitigates the agency of its author, text, or medium by appearing as the effect of the a priori object that the text represents. In its yearning for an artifact to determine the nature and effects of its representation, an artifactual form tends to make use of the techniques of realism that would achieve believability via plots driven by mechanistic relationships between so-called natural causes and effects. Such plots appear to be preestablished (by, for example, history) or readily verifiable because they conform to conventions or expectations. The techniques whereby the agency of the artifact that a text represents precedes and exceeds that of the author, text, or medium need not, however, always be relegated to those techniques we associated with realism. The presence of a third-person narrator that privileges description or adopts a passive relationship, usually grammatically expressed, to events, characters, settings, and concepts often strives to render the text as the effect of the artifact it represents. So too, however, might a first-person narrative attempt to emphasize a lively artifact's agency over that of the person who encountered it. In such works, the author may strive to appear as the artifact's intermediary. An artifactual form can be detected, therefore, in the presence of a point of view or points of view construed as other than that of the text's author. The recent trend of object biographies as well as the eighteenth-century popular genre of the it-narrative are examples of such points of view. The techniques these works use in order to situate meaning as before or outside of the text and as somewhere other than in the exclusive hands of the author or the reader are, however, broadly applicable.

So much, we might say, for the fact-half of an artifactual form. An artifactual form, however, is characterized by *appearance*, *preference*, and *yearning*. Texts that adopt an artifactual form might *not* refer to a real artifact. And even if a text does refer to a real artifact, it never perfectly achieves imitation, mimesis, or unity with the artifact it represents. Neither does an artifactual form succeed in relegating the agency of the author, text, or medium to the artifact that the text represents. In its need to resort to stylistic artifice in order to reproduce the facts in artifacts, an artifactual form registers a particularly profound rupture between the signified and the signifier. This rupture, however, is not the crisis of representation with which deconstruction has made us so familiar—a crisis located within and constructed by the structure of language. Rather, it is a crisis over the failure of objects like artifacts to initiate textual representations that are commensurate with the objects themselves.

Artifactual forms, therefore, express frustrations that range from discomfort and irritation to tragic grief and comic outrage when the following possibilities must be confronted: either an artifact has failed to transmit all that it can materially or conceptually, its interlocutors have failed to perceive accurately all that the artifact has materially or conceptually transmitted, or the mirroring medium in which such transmissions have been recorded is inadequate to the task at hand. In other words, artifactual forms are representations that acknowledge their own insufficiencies as such. They may take special pains to establish authenticity at the level of description or narration, or they may experiment with styles and technologies of representation. In the process, however, an artifactual form questions the inherent representability of objects, but it takes comfort, sometimes cold and sometimes warm, in the agencies, however imperfect, that inhere in the representation itself. Consequently, artifactual forms exhibit properties similar to those of the artifact. The artifactual form's investments in representation as unmediated reproduction correspond to the matter that remains in the artifact while its affective dissonances register a confrontation with the part of the artifact that is still missing and cannot be definitively known. Like artifacts, artifactual forms can often be minor or recovered works that are of interest, perhaps, only to the (post)modern antiquary, but they may also be well-known works remarkable for their singularity. More importantly, however, artifactual forms are fragmented, but not necessarily in the ways we have come to understand the Romantic form of the fragment. The text itself need not be a fragment, per se, but the artifactual form's relationships to the objects it represents exist in states of incompleteness, erosion, or decay.

Pragmatically, texts that adopt an artifactual form can be difficult to comprehend and appreciate outside of their moments of origin, even if the work in question is finished or complete. Their allusions to historical contexts are usually extensive, specific, and fraught. Over the course of a text's duration, therefore, it becomes both necessary and increasingly difficult to reestablish its networks of influences, references, and allusions. This means that texts that feature aspects of an artifactual form usually call for historicist readings that explore a given work's relationships to historical contexts and other works—either those by the same author, those in the same genre, or those composed in the same historical period. The text itself is therefore encountered by the reader as a piece of a whole or as part of a sequence, like an artifact. And like an artifact, the work may be judged as either the mechanistic consequence of these other works or as the vital agent of their disruption. This is a process that also invokes the artifact's unique temporal displacement. An artifactual form's disunity with the moment of its present encounter invites the reconstruction of an earlier state in which the text's interpretations were, presumably, more intuitive.

Yet, like an artifact, the fragmentation and temporal displacement of the artifactual form engender modes of uncertainty that produce suspicion and critique. On the one hand, an artifactual form asks its readers to undertake a search for originals outside of and before the text that can only, at best, be imperfectly recovered. On the other hand, an artifactual form insists on the text's own proliferating modes of agency, both to inaugurate the digging in the first place and to shape the perceptions, interpretations, and consequences of the discoveries such digging will dust up. After all, an artifactual form has already internally registered how the objects outside of and before the text are not themselves the guarantors that we would have them be. The artifactual form conditions a hermeneutics of suspicion not least, then, by performing such a hermeneutics in the first place. The artifactual form generates multiplying, competing interpretations, which return readers to the text. As they question the text's relationships to its supposed origins and to that which it represents, readers generate yet more readings, each as unresolvable as the last and the first.

The texts that emerge around artifacts are a heady but puzzling mix of dull facts and vibrant fictions, history, and romance. Such disparate states of believability heighten the work's affect or *schein*. Artifacts taught us how to dig for more—how to read with suspicion by keeping an eye out for a text's origins or real-world referents as well as for its ideological investments and by arming ourselves with evidence to critique both the claims of the text itself and those made by its other readers. In the long eighteenth century, the artifactual form, like the study of artifacts themselves, responded both to the crises over sovereignty that erupted in the seventeenth-century state and the negotiation of those crises in a media culture saturated by the thrills as well as the perils of fiction. These contexts suggest that the artifactual form emerges when we become acutely anxious over our own and others' ability to perceive and to represent reliably our shared cultural conditions as they disintegrate into a fundamental break with history. Artifacts show us what's at stake when we claim that objects are speaking or giving evidence for themselves. The artifactual form may be particularly responsive, therefore, to political crises and cultural paradigm shifts in which diametrically opposed worldviews become irreconcilable: those moments when two intractable factions appear to be using the same piece of evidence for competing claims, like reading the same book but discovering different stories therein. For these reasons, artifacts and the kinds of texts that they inspire are likely due for a comeback.

Notes

Prologue

1. John Britton first described Aubrey as an "archaeologist" in his *Memoir of John Aubrey, F.R.S.*, 3. See also Parry's "Earliest Antiquaries" (39) and Burl's *John Aubrey & Stone Circles*. For more on Aubrey, see Hunter, *John Aubrey and the Realm of Learning*; Williams, *The Antiquary*; Bennett, *John Aubrey: Brief Lives*.

2. Jones, *The Most Notable Antiquity of Great Britain*. For more on prehistoric monuments and antiquarianism, see Piggot, *Ancient Britons and the Antiquarian Imagination*; Smiles, *The Image of Antiquity*; Haycock, *William Stukeley*; Hill, *Stonehenge*.

3. John Leland is usually credited as the first official antiquary. Legend has it that Henry VIII tasked Leland with searching in the libraries of the recently dispersed for rare manuscripts and conferred on Leland the title of "antiquarius" as an acknowledgment of his admirable work. Leland was one of the few people before Aubrey to have noticed Avebury. He included a brief description of the site in his manuscript notebooks, later published by Thomas Hearne as *The Itinerary of John Leland the Antiquary*; see Burl's *Prehistoric Avebury* (37–45).

4. See also Phillips, "Reconsiderations on History and Antiquarianism"; and Miller, ed., *Momigliano and Antiquarianism*.

5. For more on antiquarianism and art history, see Myrone and Peltz, eds., *Producing the Past*; Smiles, *Eye Witness*; Arnold and Bending, eds., *Tracing Architecture*; and Hanson, *The English Virtuoso*. For more on the impact of antiquarianism on literary history and style, see Ferris, *The Achievement of Literary Authority*; Zimmerman, *History and the Novel in the British 18th Century*; Trumpener, *Bardic Nationalism*; Phillips, *Society and Sentiment*; Lynch, *The Age of Elizabeth in the Age of Johnson*; Mack, *Literary Historicity*; Goode, *Sentimental Masculinity and the Rise of History, 1790–1890*; Gallagher, *Historical Literatures*.

6. In addition to Sweet's and Heringman's work on antiquarianism, discussed above, see also Douglas, *English Scholars, 1660–1730*; Mendyck, *"Speculum Britanniae"*; Parry, *The Trophies of Time*; Harmsen, *Antiquarianism in the Augustan Age*; Woolf, *The Social Circulation of the Past*; Pearce, ed., *Visions of Antiquity* and the companion exhibition catalogue: Stark et al., eds., *Making History*; Vine, *In Defiance of Time*; Kalter, *Modern Antiques*; and Schnapp, ed., *World Antiquarianism*. For earlier influential studies of antiquarianism that remain ambivalent about its intellectual merits, see the work of Piggott, including his *Ruins in a Landscape* and *Ancient Britons*. The definitive history of the Society of Antiquaries remains Evans, *A History of the Society of Antiquaries*.

7. Macaulay's *Pleasure of Ruins* remains a classic study on the popularity of ruins in the period; see also Andrews, *The Search for the Picturesque*; Janowitz, *England's Ruins*; Woodward, *In Ruins*; and Dillon, *Ruin Lust*. On sentimental objects, see Festa, *Sentimental Figures of Empire in Eighteenth-Century Britain and France*; Park, *The Self and It*; Lamb, *The Things Things Say*; and Blackwell, ed., *The Secret Life of Things*. The scholarship on the rise of the museum and the history of collecting is vast. Some representative examples include Miller, *That Noble Cabinet*; Impey and MacGregor, eds., *The Origins of Museums*; Pomian, *Collectors and Curiosities*; Pearce, *On Collecting*; Bennett, *The Birth of the Museum*.

8. On commodities, see especially Festa; and Lamb, *The Things Things Say*; see also Mui and Mui, *Shops and Shopkeeping in Eighteenth-Century England*; McKendrick, Brewer, and Plumb, *The Birth of A Consumer Society*; Brewer and Porter, eds., *Consumption and the World of Goods*; Bermingham and Brewer, eds., *The Consumption of Culture 1600–1800*; Berg, *Luxury and Pleasure in Eighteenth-Century Britain*; Wall, *The Prose of Things*. On global commodities, see especially Roach, "The Global Parasol"; and Jenkins, *A Taste for China*. On fashion, specifically, see Batchelor, *Dress, Distress and Desire*; Smith, *Women, Work and Clothes in the Eighteenth-Century Novel*; and Campbell, *Historical Style*.

9. The desirability and everyday familiarity of these objects, qualities I discuss below, distinguish them from the kinds of abject waste that Gee discusses in her *Making Waste*.

10. See, for example, Bill Brown's influential "Thing Theory."

11. I discuss the period's materialisms at length in chapter 1, but the account of the debates over matter that occurred throughout the long eighteenth century is especially indebted to Toulmin and Goodfield, *The Architecture of Matter*, 173–306; Yolton, *Thinking Matter*; Rogers, *The Matter of Revolution*; Thomson, *Bodies of Thought*, 201–228; and Mitchell, *Experimental Life*.

12. As exemplified by O'Gorman's *The Long Eighteenth Century*, "the long eighteenth century" denotes the years between, roughly, the Glorious Revolution of 1688 and the Reform Act of 1832. I share O'Gorman's interest in the confluence of the cultural and the political signaled by the phrase as well as his wariness of histories that render the period as a "great patriotic drama, or as a continuing story of national success" (6).

13. See, especially, Pocock, *The Ancient Constitution and the Feudal Law*; Fussner, *The Historical Revolution*; Kramnick, *Bolingbroke and His Circle*; and Smith, *The Gothic Bequest*.

14. Consider Hayden White's famous claim that "the historian speaks for [facts], speaks on their behalf, and fashions the fragments of the past into a whole" (*Tropics* 125).

15. The scholarship on fragmentation has tended to focus on the importance of fragments for the Romantics and on that which is missing from the fragments themselves. See, for example, Levinson, *The Romantic Fragment Poem*; Harries, *The Unfinished Manner*; Regier, *Fracture and Fragmentation in British Romanticism*.

16. This way of graphing the artifact adapts George Kubler's insights about the "shape of time" that typifies the life cycles of art objects. Kubler positions art objects on a timescale in between that of tools and fashions. According to Kubler, tools "have extremely long durations," and fashions occur in quick bursts (38–39). The long duration of tools and the short durations of fashions make it almost impossible to document changes in both types of objects. In contrast, Kubler identifies the life cycle of an art object as one characterized by "principal inventions"—the creation of an "important work of art"—and an "entire system of replicas, reproductions, copies, reductions, transfers, and derivations" that follows in its wake (39). As Kubler examines how art objects transform over time, he pauses to ask "whether artifacts do not possess a specific sort of duration, occupying time differently" (83). The representations of artifacts that proliferated in England during the long eighteenth century suggests that they do.

17. In addition to Daston and Park's study of wonders, see also Greenblatt, *Marvelous Possessions*; Burns, *An Age of Wonders*; and Kareem, *Eighteenth-Century Fiction and the Reinvention of Wonder*.

18. By the middle of the eighteenth century, Samuel Johnson would notably define both curiosity and wonder as states of mind before defining them as objects. Curiosity is first and foremost "inquisitiveness; inclination to enquiry" (1.542); wonder is first and foremost "admiration; astonishment; amazement" (2.1183). For more on curiosities, see n. 7 (above); Swann, *Curiosities and Texts*; MacGregor, *Curiosity and the Enlightenment*.

19. Walpole was writing to Lady Ossory, who was then in Northamptonshire, from his home on Arlington Street in London: a distance of around eighty miles.

20. See also Kareem's discussion of wondering at versus wondering about—which she describes as the "interplay between" the "marvel and the curiosity"—in her *Eighteenth-Century Fiction and the Reinvention of Wonder*, 8–9.

21. See also Heringman and Lake, "Introduction: Romantic Antiquarianism"; Lake, "Antiquarianism as a Vital Historiography for the Twenty-First Century." Silver in *Metaphors of Mind* and Heringman in *Sciences of Antiquity* also find Latour's methodology to be provocative for similar reasons—but Heringman also finds Latour's conceptualization of agency to be problematic (6).

22. I share Steven Pincus's conviction that Whiggish accounts of the Enlightenment's political history overstate the period's peaceable civility. See Pincus's *1688*.

23. See Bennett's *Vibrant Matter*.

24. Bill Brown established that objects are items that we examine in order to discover what they "disclose about history, society, nature, or culture—above all, what they disclose about *us*," but things are entities that we can only "glimpse" and that have distinct lives of their own (4).

25. For more on neoclassicism and ancient antiquities, see Hicks, *Neoclassical History and English Culture*; Barkan, *Unearthing the Past*; Coltman, *Fabricating the Antique*; Redford, *Dilettanti*; Kelly, *The Society of Dilettanti*; Bignamini, *Digging and Dealing in Eighteenth-Century Rome*; Sachs, *Romantic Antiquity*.

26. See, especially, Coole and Frost's "Introduction," in *New Materialisms*. Recent theoretical work on objects falls under the aegis of "the new materialism," "thing theory," "speculative realism," and "object-oriented ontology." I go on to describe this work primarily as "new materialist" throughout this volume in order to emphasize the ways in which the theorists working in all these fields foreground their departure from the "old materialisms" of Enlightenment philosophy. Manuel DeLanda and Rosi Braidotti are both credited with inventing the terms "neo-" and "new materialism." See Dolphijn and van der Tuin, eds., *New Materialism*, 13–18, for a history of the term and its implications.

27. See Festa; Park; Lamb, *The Things Things Say*; Blackwell, ed.; and Wall. Additionally, see Deutsch, "Oranges, Anecdote and the Nature of Things"; Macpherson, *Harm's Way*; Kramnick, *Actions and Objects from Hobbes to Richardson*; Calè and Craciun, "The Disorder of Things"; Lupton, *Knowing Books*; Pasanek, *Metaphors of Mind*; Silver, *The Mind Is a Collection*; Zuroski and Yonan, "A Dialogue as Introduction." My ideas about artifacts' materiality are especially indebted to Lupton's, Pasanek's, and Silver's studies. For a recent and extended consideration of how Latour's findings do and do not apply to the eighteenth century, specifically, see Lupton, Silver, and Sneed, "Introduction: Latour and Eighteenth-Century Studies," and the other essays in the special issue on Latour and eighteenth-century studies that their essay introduces.

28. See also Cole, "The Call of Things."

29. See also Pittock, *Material Culture and Sedition, 1688–1760*; and Guthrie, *The Material Culture of the Jacobites*.

Chapter 1 · Leaving Room to Guess

1. "artefact | artifact, n. and adj." *OED* Online, June 2018.

2. See, especially, Digby's experiments with "sympathetic powder" discussed in Hedrick, "Romancing the Salve"; Lobis, *The Virtue of Sympathy*.

3. For more on satirical treatments of antiquaries, see Bending, "The True Rust of the Barons' Wars" and "Every Man Is Naturally an Antiquarian." See also Levine, *Dr. Woodward's Shield*, 114–129; Hill, "Antiquaries in the Age of Romanticism," 9–34; and Brown, *The Hobby-Horsical Antiquary*.

4. "[S]everal attempts," in fact, were made to combine the Society of Antiquaries and the Royal Society (Gough, "Introduction" xxxviii). See also Heringman, *Sciences of Antiquity*;

Sweet, *Antiquaries*, 87–89; Evans, *History of the Society of Antiquaries*, 94–95. See also Hunter, "The Royal Society and the Origins of British Archaeology"; Shapiro, *A Culture of Fact*, 34–62.

5. See, especially, Pasanek's *Metaphors of Mind* and Silver's *The Mind Is a Collection*. This volume owes a great deal to these books as well as their authors. See also Steedman, *Dust*; McLaughlin, *Dirt*; Schwartz, *Worm Work*; Waldman, *Rust*; Lacquer, *The Work of the Dead*; Müller, *White Magic*; Kramnick, *Paper Minds*.

6. Those who followed in Aubrey's footsteps kept his studies of stones and other objects in the public's consciousness by referencing his papers at Oxford, where they have remained preserved since Aubrey's death, accumulating the marginalia of his devotees. See the prologue for more on Aubrey.

7. Aubrey's own political allegiances are difficult to recover. His description of the meeting of Parliament on November 3, 1640, as a day "so direfully fatal to England" suggests a certain amount of distaste for the rising tide of republicanism, while his cordial relationship to Charles II likewise would indicate Aubrey felt some sympathy for the royalist cause. Aubrey's histories of Wiltshire and Surrey similarly bemoan the destruction to England's antiquities that occurred in the Civil Wars, and Aubrey was also Thomas Hobbes's friend and biographer. Yet Aubrey was also reportedly a member of a republican club so radical that it attracted the ire of even Cromwell's cronies. Aubrey's early nineteenth-century biographer, the antiquary John Britton, maintained that Aubrey's "loyalty to the House of Stuart was no doubt sincere; but it is displayed rather by invectives against the tyranny of the Puritans than by any expressions or regard for their ill-fated but misguided victims—Charles the First—or his profligate successor" (78). See also Williams, *The Antiquary*, 10–25.

8. Aubrey is referring here to Bacon's definition of antiquities as "*tanquam Tabulata Naufragii*." See Bacon, *The Advancement of Learning*, Book II, sec. 2:3, 90.

9. "oestrum | estrum, n." *OED* Online, January 2018.

10. See also: Bloch, *The Royal Touch*; Sharpe, *Rebranding Rule*; Woolrych, *Britain in Revolution*.

11. See n. 11 in the prologue; for more readings of theories of matter in the long eighteenth century, see also Reill, *Vitalizing Nature in the Enlightenment*; Festa, *Sentimental Figures*; Thompson and Meeker, "Empiricism, Substance, Narrative: An Introduction"; Drury, "Haywood's Thinking Machines"; Nowka, "Taking Coins and Thinking Smoke-Jacks"; Park, *The Self and It*; Macpherson, *Harm's Way*; Kramnick, *Actions and Objects*; Lamb, *The Things Things Say*; Packham, *Eighteenth-Century Vitalism*; Weiss-Smith, *Empiricist Devotions*; Thompson, *Fictional Matter*.

12. Rogers finds that the most ardent vitalists "retreat[ed] from [vitalism's] broadest social and political implications" after the execution of Charles I, and is careful to point out that the vitalists William Harvey and Margaret Cavendish were royalists (16).

13. Rogers likewise observes that Locke's philosophy was more indebted to vitalist thinking than we have tended to recognize; after Locke, vitalism remained in conceptual circulation as the "general scheme of individual agency and decentralized organization" (12).

14. See also DeGabriele, *Sovereign Power and the Enlightenment*; Hammond, *The Making of Restoration Poetry*, 107–138, and "The King's Two Bodies"; Boulton, *Arbitrary Power*; Poole, *The Politics of Regicide in England, 1760–1850*, 1–24; Barrell, *Imagining the King's Death*, 1–48; Kahn, *Wayward Contracts*, 279–284, and *Future of Illusion*, 55–82; and Santer, *The Royal Remains*, 3–88.

15. See O'Gorman, *The Long Eighteenth Century*.

16. Pincus documents a rift that emerged between the ways "Establishment" and "Opposition" Whigs described the revolution of 1688 after the trial of Henry Sacheverell in 1710.

Establishment Whigs represented 1688 as the infamously bloodless revolution that it has since been known as and attested to it as a "restoration of the ancient constitution" (18). Opposition Whigs insisted that the event was "transformative and chronologically open-ended" (21). Pincus argues that the Revolution of 1688 was "the first modern revolution," notable not least because Opposition Whigs understood it to entail a fundamental break with history. His careful parsing, however, of the ways in which the history of the revolution itself was contested—especially at its centenary celebration and in the contexts of the French Revolution—has shaped my sense of how central the period's understanding about the past and the history of sovereignty, Parliamentary sovereignty, and the sovereignty of the people were for defining the modern, eighteenth-century state. See Pincus, *1688*. See also Jacob, *The Newtonians and the English Revolution, 1689–1720,* and *The Radical Enlightenment*; Greaves, *Deliver Us From Evil*; Dickinson, *The Politics of the People in Eighteenth-Century Britain*; Rogers, *The Matter of Revolution*; Israel, *Radical Enlightenment,* and *A Revolution of the Mind*.

17. See also Silver, 1–20.

18. For more on causality, see Flew et al., *Agency and Necessity*; Clatterbaugh, *The Causation Debate in Modern Philosophy, 1637–1739*; Ott, *Causation and the Laws of Nature in Early Modern Philosophy*; Allen and Stoneham, eds., *Causation and Modern Philosophy*; and, especially, Kramnick, *Actions and Objects*.

19. Somner's research would notably fall victim to political faction, too. Nicholas Battely's preface to the 1703 edition of the *Antiquities* notes that Somner "collected the Antiquities of Canterbury in a time of Peace," but in the year that the work was first published (1640) "a dismal Storm did arise" when the Parliament indicted the Archbishop of Canterbury, William Laud, for high treason. "[A]fterwards," Battely writes, "the Madness of the People did rage, and prevail beyond resistance" (Somner *Antiquities* [1703] 5). At Canterbury Cathedral, the historical objects that interested Somner were smashed in a fit of iconoclastic rebellion: "the Inscriptions, Figures, and Coats of Arms, engraven upon Brass were torn off from the ancient Monuments; and whatever there was of beauty or decency" was destroyed (Somner *Antiquities* [1703] 5). "During those distractions of our Church and State," Somner's research proved "so disagreeable to then prevailing Powers, as that the best Fate which the Book or its Author could at that time expect was to lie hid, and to be sheltered under the Security of not being regarded" (*Antiquities* [1703] 5). For more on the relationships between iconoclasm and materialisms old and new, see Bruno Latour, *Iconoclash*; and Drury, "Twilight of the Virgin Idols."

20. The dispute between Edward Coke and John Cowell over Cowell's *The Interpreter* (1607) is perhaps the most characteristic earliest example of how antiquarian research could reach a fever pitch in the midst of conflicts between the crown and Parliament. Cowell's *The Interpreter* is one of the first legal dictionaries and is based extensively on historical documents; the definitions for "Subsidy," "King," "Parliament," and "Prerogative" were called into question by Coke for stoking royalist sympathies. All copies of Cowell's *Interpreter* were ordered to be burned in 1610, and Cowell was briefly imprisoned. Yet some copies survived, and Cowell's *Interpreter* alongside Coke's works enjoyed a posthumous publication history, although some of the contentious terms and their definitions were alternately excised from and reintroduced into the dictionary. The antiquary White Kennett prepared a new edition of Cowell's dictionary in 1701. Kennett related the *Interpreter's* history of controversy in his preface to the work, claiming in Cowell's defense that "it was infinitely hard to speak of Prerogative, Property, Government, Laws, and mutual Rights, with that caution and regard, as not to make some to murmur, and others to insult; especially where Parties and their Passions were even then prevailing" (Cowell iv). Kennett's edition promised that Cowell's "heap" of words would be "serviceable to the Antiquary, to the Historian, to the Lawyer" as well as "to any Scholar, nay to every English Reader"—a listing that demonstrates the proximity antiquaries

and lawyers continued to have in eighteenth-century readerships. See Cowell, *The Interpreter;* White, *The Interpreter of Words and Terms;* Hicks, *Men and Books Famous in the Law*, 49–54.

21. See Evans, 14–32, for a more extensive account of the activities of antiquaries during the reigns of the Stuarts. The classic account of conflicts over precedent remains Pocock, *The Ancient Constitution and the Feudal Law.*

22. See also Pittock, *Material Culture and Sedition, 1688–1760;* and Guthrie, *The Material Culture of the Jacobites.*

23. For more on maggots in the eighteenth century, see Hunter, *Before Novels*, 13–16; Schwartz, *Worm Work;* for waste and putrefaction, see especially Gee, *Making Waste.*

24. See especially MacDougall, *Racial Myth in English History.* See Smiles's *Eye Witness;* and Sweet, *Antiquaries*, especially 8–24, for more on antiquaries' methods, including conflicts therein. On seventeenth- and eighteenth-century historians' anxieties about the appropriation of their research for dubious political purposes, see Shapiro, *A Culture of Fact*, 34–62, and *Probability and Certainty in Seventeenth-Century England*, 119–162. For more on the trouble with facts generally in the long eighteenth century, see Poovey, *A History of the Modern Fact*, 1–22. See also Law, *The Rhetoric of Empiricism;* and Daston, "Historical Epistemology."

25. As Sweet puts it, artifacts "provided the basis for the construction of the national past and it was the growth of interest in national history that was the crucial factor in bringing antiquarianism out of the gentleman's study and before the broader public at large" (349).

26. As Ralph Cudworth explained in his *True Intellectual System* (1678), there were more than two ways to understand the nature of matter. There was the "*Hylopathian or Anaximandrian*" version, generally linked to Artistotle, in which "Dead and Stupid" matter was the basis for all things, including "*Qualities and Forms*, Generable and Corruptible"; there was the "*Atomical or Democritical*" version which was similar, but concluded that atoms in motion produced "*Figures*"; there was the "*Cosmoplastick*" version of matter which "supposes on *Plastick* and *Methodical* but *Senseless Nature*, to preside over the whole Corporeal Universe"; finally, there was the "*Hylozoick or Stratonical*" version, in which "all matter" was presumed to be "*Living* and *Energetick*," but nevertheless "devoid of all *Animality, Sense* and *Consciousness*" (1.134–135). Cudworth, notably hostile to the vitalists, neglects to include their fifth option: that all matter was presumed to be "living and energetick" *and* in possessions of some notion of "sense" or "consciousness." When Samuel Johnson set out to define "matter" in his *Dictionary*, he required eleven entries to get the job done, identifying it variously as "body; substance extended," "that of which anything is composed," a "subject; thing treated," "the whole," a "cause of disturbance," a "space or quantity nearly computed"; and a "thing; object; that which has some particular relation, or is subject to particular consideration" (2.118–119).

27. See also Jonathan Lamb's essay, in which he traces Latour's interest in restoring to objects the "rights of real and effective representation." Lamb, "Bruno Latour, Michel Serres, and Fictions of the Enlightenment," 184.

28. See n. 25 in the prologue. See also Coole and Frost, "Introduction."

29. As Andrew Cole pithily points out: "People have been using, thinking, and writing about things for . . . let's just say for a long time" ("Call of Things" 106). Additionally, see Curtius's suggestion that "medieval forms of life subsist till about 1750," in Curtius, *European Literature and the Latin Middle Ages*, 583–586.

30. See also Eisenstein *The Printing Press as an Agent of Change*, 186–257; and McKeon, *The Origins of the English Novel, 1600–1740*, 39–64.

31. The phrase is usually attributed to William Blackstone, but it was readily in use throughout the period. See Blackstone, *Commentaries on the Laws of England*, i.281.

32. See also Bender, "Enlightenment Fiction and the Scientific Hypothesis."

Chapter 2 · Ten Thousand Gimcracks

1. See, for example, the following representative list of items recorded in the forty-eighth edition of *A Catalogue of the Rarities to be Seen at Don Saltero's Coffee-House* (1795), all of which were in Glass Case No. I: "A piece of Q. Catharine's skin" (item no. 7); "A curious sword set with polished steel" (item no. 24); "The reverse of Oliver Cromwell's medal, by Dassier, in plaister, gilt" (item no. 53); "A pack of historical cards" (item no. 74).

2. The origin of Salter's collection in Sloane's cabinet was repeated throughout the accounts of Don Saltero's listed below. For a brief comparison between the objects in Sloan's collection and Saltero's, see King, "Ethnographic Collections." A man known only as Vice Admiral Munden, of whom I can find no record, reportedly also donated a spate of objects that he acquired on various trips to Spain. Several publications, along with the benefactor list appended to the many editions of Saltero's catalogue, point toward Saltero's establishment as a growing repository of gratis donations. For example, the *Philosophia Britannia* notes that Maurice Wheeler's invention of a clock in which its parts work by virtue of "descend[ing] along an inclined plane" and which was described in No. 161 of the *Philosophical Transactions* was now a donated item on display at Saltero's (Martin 1.137). Thomas Pennant similarly reports that his grandfather donated a log shaped like a hog (13). William Henry Pyne gestures toward the extravagance of Salter's acquisitive practices; Salter apparently went to great lengths to acquire the carved head of "Funny Joe," "a humourist, a half-witted fellow, who, in the [early 1700s]" smoked his pipe as he rode on top of the "carts which conveyed the criminals from Newgate to Tyburn." Salter offered to trade "any ten articles in his museum," a "half ounce phial [*sic*] of the universal-deluge-water, and a petrified wig" for the artifact, but to no avail ([Pyne], *Wine and Walnuts* 1.244).

3. One copycat venture set up shop as a bun-house across the street. There, customers could inspect "mementos of domestic events, in the first half of the last century," "portraits," a "bottle conjurer," a "model of a British soldier," and some "grotto works" (*Mirror of Literature* 3.297 and 6.302). The other copycat exhibition was Adams's at the Swan in Kingston Road. Adams's display of five hundred objects purported to include "Adam's eldest daughter's hat," "sir Walter Raleigh's tobacco-pipe," an "engine to shell green pease with," and "the very comb that Abraham combed his son Isaac [*sic*] and Jacob's head with" (*Miscellaneous and Whimsical Lucubrations* 73).

4. See Knight, ed., *London*, 4.316; Cunningham, *A Handbook for London*, 1.266; Timbs, *Club Life of London*, 2.44–48; Bryan, *Chelsea in the Olden and Present Times*, 108–112; Walford, *Old and New London*, 5.61–64; Smith, *Historical and Literary Curiosities*, not paginated; Niven, ed., *Selections from the British Apollo*, 74–81; MacMichael, "Don Saltero's Tavern, Chelsea," 110–111; and Rigby and Rigby, *Lock, Stock, and Barrel*, 244.

5. In addition to Hutton's report, other diaries and correspondences describe a visit to Don Saltero's. See Caulfield, *Portraits, Memoirs, and Characters*, 1.135; Curwen, *Journal and Letters*, 347; Franklin, *Works of the Late Doctor Benjamin Franklin*, 1.128; Hunter, *The Works of John Hunter, F.R.S.*, 1.89; Thoresby, *Diary of Ralph Thoresby*, 2.376; and von Uffenbach, *London in 1710*, 161.

6. For more about the Native American artifacts on display at Saltero's, see Bickham, "'A Conviction of the Reality of Things.'" For a postcolonial reading of Saltero's, see Todd, "Your Humble Servant Shows Himself."

7. See Altick, *The Shows of London*, 18–19.

8. My list here and elsewhere, unless noted otherwise, is drawn from the first edition of *A Catalogue of the Rarities to be Seen at Don Saltero's Coffee-House* (1729), not paginated.

9. On collections of natural history specimens, see Daston and Park, *Wonders and the Order of Nature: 1150–1750*; Miller and Reill, eds., *Visions of Empire*; Jenkins, *Vases and Volcanos*; Poliquin, *The Breathless Zoo*.

10. See, for example, Grose, *Military Antiquities*, plates XXIX and XXX in vol. 2, depicting a "shirt of chain mail, in the collection of curiosities at Don Saltero's coffee-house, Chelsea," and "a cuirass, said to have belonged to King Henry VIII. It consists of small laminae of metal fixed on leather, which yield to any motion of the body by sliding over each other— The original is at Don Saltero's coffee-house." The antiquary Samuel Meyrick questioned the authenticity of the cuirass in his "Observations on the Body Armour Anciently Worn in England," 131.

11. Chalmers, in his 1822 edition of *The Tatler*, identifies this coffin as the likely object that Steele had in mind, but describes it in the following manner: "a coffin containing the body or relics of a Spanish saint, who had wrought miracles, which had fallen some how or other into [Vice Admiral Munden's] hands. This coffin, or rather carved and gilded chest, which long graced a corner of the Museum at Saltero's Coffee-house, was sent from Japan, with the bones of a friar in it, to reconcile a king of Portugal, but was snapped up by an English captain, and deposited in this treasure of curiosity" (1.303). Chalmers cites the *Censor* (1717) vol. 1, no. 21, as a gloss on this source, but I can find no mention of the coffin or Saltero's in this issue of the *Censor*.

12. See Guthrie, *The Material Culture of the Jacobites*; and Pittock, *Material Culture and Sedition*.

13. See also Baldwin, "Toads and Plague."

14. Burnet also explores this claim in his letter to Robert Boyle on the catacombs at Rome and Naples. See *Some Letters Containing an Account of what Seem'd Most Remarkable*, 204.

15. This list is taken from the forty-eighth edition of the catalogue. See *A Catalogue of the Rarities to be Seen at Don Saltero's Coffee-House* (1795), unpaginated.

16. See also Orr, *Treason and the State*, 61–100.

17. For more on Quixotism, see Hammond, "Mid-Century English Quixotism and the Defence of the Novel," which contains a helpful overview of how various histories of the novel have addressed quixotism and the influence of Cervantes.

18. References to Don Saltero's can also be found in the following: the anonymous *Justice Triumphant*, 42; Smythies, *The History of Lucy Wellers*, 1.71; Canning, "On the Tragedy of Elvira," 89; Hays, *Epistle to C. Churchill*, 5; the anonymous *The Younger Brother, A Tale*, 1.22; Cumberland, *The Fashionable Lover*, 26; Stevens, *Songs, Comic, and Satyrical*, 3 (which purported to be based on a manuscript found at Saltero's); Anstey, *The Priest Dissected*, 23; *The Adventures of a Hackney Coach*, 2.66; Wolcot, *Peter's Prophecy*, 41, and *The Royal Tour, and Weymouth Amusements*, 70; O'Keefe, *Lie of a Day*, 5–6; Hall, "The Follower of the Family," 157; Whitehead, *Richard Savage*, 2.145; and Thomson, *The White Mask*, 1.136, 1.166. Saltero's also came under brief satirical political scrutiny in *The Instructive Library*, a work attributed to Jonathan Swift, which invents the titles of various political pamphlets. In this work, "*Don Saltero Barberoso*, at Chelsea" is given creative credit for authoring the non-extant title "*Nicknackatoriana* . . . Theological Discourses . . . Most Humbly Dedicated to the F[ellow]s of the R[oyal] S[ociety]" (8). Finally, in *Marriage A-La-Mode . . . Being an Explanation of the Six Prints Lately Published by the Ingenious Mr. Hogarth* (1746), the description of the third plate of Hogarth's series contains a tantalizing reference to Saltero's, linking the coffeehouse with the interior depicted in Plate 3 of Hogarth's series. After listing the items in the plate, including "Pots and Plaisters," "Two Skeleton's," and a "strange Collection / Of Instruments made for Injection," the narrator concludes that they are all "things as queer as / The *Chelsea*-Medley at Saltero's" (21).

19. See Black, *The English Press in the Eighteenth Century*; Spector, *Political Controversy*; Weber, *Paper Bullets*; Raymond, *The Invention of the Newspaper*, and *Pamphlets and Pamphleteering in Early Modern Britain*; Harris, *Politics and the Rise of the Press*; Barker, *Newspapers, Politics and English Society, 1695–1855*; see also Seidel, "Narrative News."

20. "magazine, n." *OED* Online, June 2018.

21. See also Davis, *Factual Fictions*, 42–84; Seidel, "Narrative News"; Hunter, *Before Novels*, 167–194; McKeon, *Origins*, 46–50.

22. See Ketcham, *Transparent* Designs.

23. See also Silver, *The Mind Is a Collection*, 49–61.

24. For an excellent account of how textual representations of Saltero's objects rely extensively on antithesis, see Benedict, "Saying Things," 705.

25. See also Hunter, *Before Novels*, 127–128.

Chapter 3 · Coins

1. Throughout this chapter, I use the terms "coins" and "medals" interchangeably, but I prefer to use "coin" as a way of emphasizing the transactional nature of the artifacts as hybrid objects that required interpreters to complete them. Although "coin" denotes currency and "medal" denotes coins that were struck for commemorative purposes, D. R. Woolf notes that both were "spoken of in the same breath by [early] collectors, who were wont to confuse the two" (236). In the eighteenth century, considerable debate occurred over whether medals could function as coins, and proposals were floated for minting medals as currency, yet the terms were still used interchangeably. The antiquary David Jennings defined medals this way for the novice collector: "By Medals we understand, in general, such Pieces in the form of Coin, as were either the Current Money of the Ancients; or struck on particular occasions, and designed to preserve to posterity the portrait of some Great Person, or the memory of some Illustrious Action" (1). In "Addison on the History of a Shilling" (1710), the shilling, which begins its life in the mint of Elizabeth I, is circulated in the eighteenth century "as a Medal" and as a "coin" (186). Sweet describes coins as the "commonest relics of antiquity" (13), and Woolf claims that coins "were by far the most frequently discovered and most vendible of all antiquarian objects" (232). See also Haskell, *History and Its Images*, 1–25; Cunnally, "Ancient Coins as Gifts and Tokens of Friendship during the Renaissance"; Valenze, *The Social Life of Money in the English Past*.

2. Helen Thompson makes a similar claim in her *Fictional Matter*, arguing "against a 'realist' regime of transparently apprehended and transparently rendered facts, both in science and fiction" (1). Thompson finds that the discourse and practice of chemistry, specifically—with its deep concerns over matter—"define[d] empirical understanding" in ways that did "not segregate worldly things from imperceptible causes"; rather, "micromatter" was conceptualized as agential and productive, specifically, of "sensory knowledge" that troubled empirical science's investments in and appeals to truths and facts (2).

3. As these passages suggest, Evelyn is primarily interested in medals rather than coins. Nevertheless, he recognizes that the line between the two proves difficult to draw, not least because medals could be exchanged as money for goods (9).

4. For a more recent account of medals as mnemonic devices in ancient Rome, see Onians, *Classical Art and the Cultures of Greece and Rome* (200–202).

5. See also Yates, *The Art of Memory*.

6. The emphasis on memorization in the study of history was prominent enough for Bolingbroke to criticize those "who, having few ideas to vend of their own growth," study history in order to "store their minds with crude unruminated facts and sentences; and hope to supply, by bare memory, the want of imagination and judgment" (5); see Bolingbroke, *Letters on the Study of History*.

7. Diedre Lynch draws a direct connection between Granger's project and Locke's "incite[ment] [to] readers to design their own personal histories" (*Economy* 34). For Lynch, the cognitive "activity" of Locke's readers "is to be understood in tandem with the conscientiously modern practices of early-eighteenth-century gentlemen and ladies who filled up

their libraries and curio cabinets with collections of coins, medals, and paintings or—when compiling 'grangerized' *Biographical Histories of England* became the rage—assembled series of engraved portrait 'heads' " (34). See Lynch, *The Economy of Character*.

8. See Richards, *The Early History of Banking in England*, especially pages 139–153, for an account of how Newton, Locke, and Somers tried to solve the nation's coinage problem. See also Murphy, *The Origins of English Financial Markets*, 1–9 and 66–88; and Deng, *Coinage and State Formation in Early Modern English Literature*, 88–102.

9. In William Blackstone's historical account of the laws of England, the practice of alter- ing coins figured in a list of three crimes of high treason instituted during the reign of Mary (1553–1558); the first of these related to being a "papist," the second was the "falsifying [of] the coin or other royal signatures," and the last was attempting to guarantee "the protestant succession" (4.87). Blackwell notes that the law was originally designed only to address the corruptions of coins minted in gold or silver—corruptions that were problematic because they compromised the material value of the coin. These laws, however, could not "restrain the evil practices of coiners and false moneyers" (4.88). Clipping and counterfeiting them came to be considered as a direct offense to the sovereign, a "breach of allegiance" that "infring[ed] on the king's prerogative" because the counterfeiter had become a pretender, taking on for them- selves the "attributes of the sovereign, to whom alone it belongs to set the value and determi- nation of coin . . . [W]hoever falsifies this is an offender against the state" (4.88).

10. See Guthrie, 13–18, 23–25, and 34–36.

11. See also Werrett, "Healing the Nation's Wounds."

12. See Knoppers, *Constructing Cromwell*, 56–62; and Nightingale, "Thomas Rawlins, and the Honorary Medals of the Commonwealth."

13. See Evans, 71; and Nichols, *Literary Anecdotes of the Eighteenth Century*, 6.157n.

14. Vertue was Catholic, and although he published a few images that were likely to appeal to Jacobite collectors, he did so anonymously; see Alexander, "George Vertue as Engraver," 211. Elsewhere, I've argued that Vertue's engraving of Stuart medals—the frontispiece for this chapter—treats the question of Jacobite sympathies with marked ambivalence and caution; see Lake, "Plate 1.55," online.

15. See Pasanek, 58–60; and also Silver, 226–230. Deidre Lynch similarly recognizes the period's use of coin metaphors as indexes of character, finding that an early modern homiletic tradition that represented individuals as pieces of metal continued to influence theories of character well into the eighteenth century (*Economy* 35).

16. J. G. A. Pocock's claim that Locke was notable among his contemporaries for his sheer lack of apparent interest in history is relevant here. See Pocock, *Virtue, Commerce, and History*, 237. See also Glat, "John Locke's Historical Sense"; and Seliger, *The Liberal Politics of John Locke*, 230–239.

17. Boyle also developed an instrument for determining whether coins were counterfeit. See his "An Essay-Instrument, Wherewith to Examine if COIN be Adulterate or Counterfeit," in *The Philosophical Works of the Honourable Robert Boyle*, 2.372–374.

18. See Johnson, "The Money=Blood Metaphor, 1300–1800," 122. J. G. A. Pocock further explores Hobbes's affinity for antiquarianism. See Pocock, *Politics, Language, and Time*, 260–261.

19. Notably, Beattie rejects the materialist implications of Locke's cognitive model, railing against those "antient and modern" thinkers who would subscribe to the notion that "every thing perceived by us, whether a thought of the mind, or an external object . . . makes upon the brain a certain impression" and that, consequently, impressions "can only be made by that, which has solidity, magnitude, and figure" (1.10–11). What, then, Beattie cheekily asks (1.11), is the "weight of a sound," or may the shape of a "toothache" be said to be "triangular, or circular, or of a square form?" For Beattie, these queries "prove the absurdity" of theories

like Locke's that insist on cognitive impressions that bear clear material relationships to their external source objects. Beattie doesn't, however, provide an alternative model.

20. Regrettably, *The Medall* is one of Dryden's least-considered works, but my study of it has been informed by the following: Sutherland, "Dryden's Use of Popular Imagery in 'The Medal'"; Golden, "A Numismatic View of Dryden's *The Medal*"; Maurer, "The Design of Dryden's *The Medall*"; Reverand, "Patterns of Imagery and Metaphor in Dryden's 'The Medall'"; Zwicker, *Politics and Language in Dryden's Poetry*, 49–55; Brown, "The Ideology of Restoration Poetic Form"; Gardiner, "Dryden's 'The Medall' and the Principle of Continuous Transmission of Laws"; Harth, *Pen for a Party*, 161–205; Hammond, *Restoration*, 139–167; Kingsley, "Dryden and the Consumption of History"; and Pasanek, 57–58 and 63–64.

21. Barbara Benedict concludes that Addison "undoubtedly" read Evelyn's treatise. See Benedict, "The Moral in the Material," 66.

22. See Gallagher, *Nobody's Story*.

23. Philander laughs at antiquaries who use their senses to gauge the age of a coin by its metal:

> I have seen an Antiquary like an old Coin, among other tryals [*sic*], to distinguish the age of it by its Taste. I remember when I laught [*sic*] at him for it, he told me with a great deal of vehemence, there was much difference between the relish of ancient and modern brass, as between an apple and a turnep [*sic*]. It is a pity, says Eugenius, but they found out the Smell too of an ancient Medal. They would then be able to judge of it by all the senses. The Touch, I have heard, gives almost as good evidence as the Sight, and the Ringing of a Medal is, I know, a very common experiment (145).

24. See Mikhail Bakhtin's classic essay, "Forms of Time and of the Chronotope in the Novel" (1937).

25. For more on *Chrysal* and coin narrators, see Lynch, *Economy*, 95–99; Lamb, *Things*, 201–228; Lupton, *Knowing Books*, 53–65; Douglas, "Britannia's Rule and the It-Narrator"; Flint, "Speaking Objects"; Bellamy, "It-Narrators and Circulation"; Festa, *Sentimental Figures of Empire in Eighteenth-Century Britain and France*, 112–132; Nowka, "Talking Coins and Thinking Smoke-Jacks."

26. Johnstone, like Dryden, notably draws out Clayton's conviction that spirit and agency were yoked to proportion and quantity. See *Chrysal*, 22.

Chapter 4 · Manuscripts

1. See Kiernan, *Beowulf and the Beowulf Manuscript*.

2. This chapter is deeply indebted to Christina Lupton's excellent *Knowing Books*, especially her chapter titled "The Theory of Paper" (70–94).

3. See Robertson, *Legitimate Histories*; Leerssen, "Literary Historicism"; and Russett, *Fictions and Fakes*.

4. See also Sharpe, *Sir Robert Cotton, 1586–1631*, 36, 162–163.

5. See Turner, *Magna Carta*, 145–182.

6. See Sweet, *Antiquaries*, 38–48 and 196.

7. Pine's engraving of the "Great Charter" (1733) is in the British Museum (1861,0513.331).

8. See Sloan and Burnett, eds., *Enlightenment*, for a discussion of the museum's earliest policies and procedures.

9. McKeon also discusses these two cases as examples of naive versus extreme skepticism (*Origins* 50).

10. According to Woolf, although the collection of medieval documents had been popular in the early modern period, interest in medieval documents had waned in the wake of the Civil War, which had "wreaked havoc on particular repositories of records" (157). Woolf notes

that "the centralized recording of historical manuscripts . . . began informally among the re-vived Society of Antiquaries" around 1720 when members of the society agreed to "catalogue all the materials on English history in their custody" (156). David McKitterick suggests that a resurgence of interest in manuscripts resulted from a new influx of materials when private libraries were dispersed and then consolidated between 1700 and 1750. See McKitterick, "Bibliography, Bibliophily, and the Organization of Knowledge," 39. See also Ramsay, "'The Manuscripts Flew About Like Butterflies.'"

    11. See, especially, Baines, *The House of Forgery in Eighteenth-Century Britain*; and Russet, *Fictions and Fakes*.

    12. Walpole did this successfully enough that several readers, including William Mason, Thomas Gray, and John Langhorne, the reviewer for the *Monthly Review*, believed the work to be an authentic archival find. Walpole was well positioned to adopt the tone of the antiquary: he was a member of the Society of Antiquaries until 1772 and a trustee of Sir Hans Sloane's es-tate (and was therefore on the board of the British Museum). Walpole was also known for his collection of antiquities and his own antiquarian research and publications, discussed more below. For a comprehensive review of Walpole's antiquarian activities, see Lewis, "Horace Walpole, Antiquary."

    13. For a compelling examination of the ways antiquaries' aesthetic shortcomings made them particularly vulnerable to being duped by frauds, see Baines, 151–156. Walpole frequently disparaged antiquaries in his letters, especially after 1772, when he resigned from the Society of Antiquaries. As early as the mid-1760s, however, Walpole appears to have been dissatisfied with his antiquarian peers, remarking in a letter to the antiquary William Cole in 1770 that he had "dropped" his "attendance" at the society's meetings "four or five years ago from being sick of their ignorance and stupidity" (*Correspondence* 1.206). For other examples of Walpole's contempt for antiquaries and their research, see *Correspondence*, 1.218–219, 1.265, and 11.358.

    14. Walpole's extensive knowledge of archival sources and antiquaries' manuscript discov-eries is evident throughout his *Catalogue of Royal and Noble Authors*, discussed more below. Additionally, Walpole would base the main arguments of his *Historical Doubts* on archival evidence that was later shown to be something other than what he thought it was: a wardrobe list instead of a coronation roll.

    15. Kenneth Clarke was one of the first critics to place Walpole and his efforts at Straw-berry Hill at the helm of the eighteenth-century reevaluation of Gothic architecture (25–49). See also Bayer-Berenbaum, *The Gothic Imagination,* 47–71; Botting, *Gothic,* 32–38; and Watt, *Contesting the Gothic,* 14–19. Representing the *Castle of Otranto* as the first "Gothic novel" has been commonplace since the late eighteenth century. See Warburton, ed., *The Works of Alexander Pope, Esq.,* 4.166–167; Barbauld, *The British Novelists,* 22.i; and Scott, "Prefatory Memoir to Horace Walpole," in *Ballantyne's Novelists' Library,* 5.lx. Contemporary critical accounts have continued to represent Walpole's work as the "first" Gothic novel. See, for example, Varma, *The Gothic Flame,* 42; MacAndrew, *The Gothic Tradition in Fiction,* 6; Clery, "The Genesis of Gothic Fiction," 21; Richter, *The Progress of Romance,* 74.

    16. For example, despite identifying the historical setting as the "key characteristic" of the work and the genre it would instigate, Robert Hume claims that Walpole "show[ed] no serious interest in veracity of fact or atmosphere" (283). MacAndrew similarly concludes that the work's "relationship [to actual history] is tenuous at best, as the eighteenth century probably knew" (10). Mehrotra declares *Otranto* "a historical novel without the history" (21). Richter finds that Walpole's "standards of historical accuracy were not high, even for his own time" (70). Although Sabor has argued that Walpole was "a valuable historian," he suggests that Walpole was a better recorder of his own times than he was an antiquary (7). Similarly, even as Mack and Wall have recently asserted the need to take seriously Walpole's antiquarianism and the representations of material-historical objects in *The Castle of Otranto*, they have also

been reluctant to see *Otranto*'s obsession with artifacts as historically referential. For Wall, Walpole makes use of ridiculously oversized medieval objects in the story to critique the eighteenth century's commercialized obsession with things (118). For Mack, Walpole uses medieval objects to theorize the transition from the text-based histories of the Enlightenment to the artifact-based archaeologies of the nineteenth century. *Otranto*'s antiquarianism remains indefensibly "anachronistic" from the historian's perspective (Mack, "Horace Walpole" 370).

17. See, also Kiely, *The Romantic Novel in England*, 25–42.

18. Wein, however, concludes that Walpole was nevertheless a "devious man" and sees the work's politics as identity politics that blend idealized notions of the ancient aristocracy with eighteenth-century middle-class values (50).

19. Summers and Clery have identified the connections between the main character of Walpole's book, Manfred, and Manfred of Sicily, who was the "illegitimate son" of Frederick II, who declared himself king in 1258 by "exploit[ing] rumours of the death of [the legitimate grandson of Frederick II, Conrad]" (Clery, "Introduction" 116–117, n.5). Thus, three main characters bear the same names as Sicilian figures: Manfred, Conrad, and Frederick. *Otranto* has little else in common with Sicilian history, however. Wein has consequently read *Otranto* as a jumbled roman à clef that makes reference to a variety of politicians ranging from Henry VIII to Lord Bute, John Wilkes, and Walpole's cousin, Conway. According to Wein, Manfred is Lord Bute and Henry VIII; William Marshal is Bolingbroke; Theodore is Wilkes and Walpole's cousin; Alfonso the Good is Alfonso IV. John Samson similarly reads *Otranto* as a roman à clef of the Wilkes-Conway-Grenville controversy that ultimately works through Walpole's political and sexual ambivalences (*British Identities*, chapter 2). See also Samson, "Politics Gothicized."

20. This falls within the time period in which "William Marshal" surmises that the story was originally written. For eighteenth-century accounts of the Hohenstaufen conflicts and their effects on England, see Tyrrell, *The General History of England*, 3.281–290; Rymer, *Acta Regia*, 31–34; Baker, *A Chronicle of the Kings of England*, 84–87; Robinson, *A Compleat and Impartial History of England*, 258–261; Kimber, *The History of England*, 132–135; and Smollett, *A Complete History of England*, 1.517–570.

21. See, for example, Kimber, 133; Robinson, 259; and *The History of England Faithfully Extracted*, 164.

22. Smollett's description of these kings' characters is not unique. See, for example, Heckford, *Characters . . . of All the Kings and Queens of England*, 23; and Egerton, *A New History of England, in Verse*, 112–113.

23. Egerton praises William Marshal as a "noble earl, so good, so wise, so brave": "warm in freedom's, and his country's cause, / Confirms old charters, and enacts new laws; / Does the wide wounds of former errors heal, / And labours only for the public weal" (121). Smollett also praises "William Mareschal," who was famous for holding up the young Henry III to the barons who had rebelled against King John and saying (1.456), "Behold your king!" This phrase resonates with Alfonso's final confrontation with Manfred in *The Castle of Otranto* when, after Matilda has been murdered, he bursts through the castle walls and shouts (195), "Behold in Theodore the true heir of Alfonso!"

24. See Sweet for an examination of eighteenth-century celebrations of Alfred, which she describes as the "cult of King Alfred" (190–191, 198, 210, 215–217). Walpole owned a copy of Spellman's biography of Alfred (Hazen 1.lv).

25. Walpole owned a copy of *The History of Theodore I* and went to some trouble to send Horace Mann a copy (*Correspondence* 18.235, 18.249, 18.265, 18.292–294, 18.303, 18.318). Walpole was, however, dubious about Theodore's merits. He and Mann exchanged numerous letters about Theodore's plight, often gossiping about his insolent character and tawdry love affairs. When Theodore accused Mann of stealing money, Walpole finally confessed that he

was "done with countenancing kings" (*Correspondence* 20.374). But when Theodore died, Walpole's sympathies were rekindled. Writing to Mann in September of 1757, Walpole says that he "is putting up a stone in St. Ann's churchyard for . . . King Theodore; in short, his history is too remarkable to be let perish. Mr. Bentley says, that I am not only an antiquarian, but prepare materials for future antiquarians . . . I would have served him [Theodore], if a king, even in jail, could have been an honest man" (*Correspondence* 21.139–140). Furthermore, Walpole understood Theodore's cause as one of liberty, even though he felt that Theodore was, like all kings, a problematic leader for such a cause. In the same letter to Mann, Walpole writes, "Our papers say, that we are bustling about Corsica; I wish if we throw away our own liberty, that we may at least help others to theirs" (*Correspondence* 21.141).

26. In his biography of Walpole, Martin Kallich also discusses Walpole's celebration of the constitution and his conviction that the turn of events under the reign of George II and George III signaled an end to English liberty (42–56).

27. Linda Colley writes that "much of the public symbolism of [Wilkes's] movement was a celebration of Whig constitutionalism. . . . For example, a typical procession of Wilkite voters assembled at a tavern named after William of Orange, before setting out to vote for their hero, under banners of Magna Carta and the Bill of Rights." Colley goes on to argue that "[Wilkes] and his supporters were able to portray his personal dilemmas . . . as but a continuation of the Englishman's centuries-old struggle for liberty" (111). See also Sainsbury, *John Wilkes*, 231–232; and Cash, *John Wilkes*, 159–162. West shows that depictions of the Magna Carta were frequently included in visual representations of Wilkes (69, 73–74).

28. This parallels contemporary explanations of the ultimate failure of the barons' reform in the wake of the Sicilian affair; eighteenth-century historians agreed that the barons, especially the Earl of Leicester, wrested control away from Henry only to reinstate one of their own as king. Kimber, for example, explains that once the barons had control, the Earl of Leicester "exercis'd supreme Authority in the Name of the King . . . and made use of the Royal Name, for whatever he had a Mind to enforce" (134). See also Baker, 87; and Robinson, 261.

29. Throughout his correspondence, Walpole consistently celebrates the Magna Carta. See *Correspondence*, 15.31, 28.288, 29.351, 34.102, 34.173, and 42.402–404.

30. See also McKeon, *Origins*, 56; Zimmerman, *History and the Novel in the British 18th Century*; Rigney, *Imperfect Histories*; Lynch, *The Age of Elizabeth in the Age of Johnson*; Thompson and Meeker, "Empiricism, Substance, Narrative: An Introduction"; Mack, *Literary Historicity*; Gallagher, *Historical Literatures*; Thompson, *Fictional Matter*.

Chapter 5 · Weapons

1. See Mintz, *The Hunting of Leviathan*, 23–38; Pocock, *The Machiavellian Moment*, 333–360, 462–505, and *Barbarism and Religion*, 2.309–381, 3.276–324; Spadafora, *The Idea of Progress*; Rawls, *Political Philosophy*, 41–53 and 103–121; Bates, *States of War*, 63–79 and 102–108; and Engberg-Pedersen, *Empire of Chance*, 1–9.

2. Work in the history of science and technology as well as in the field of military history has long debated the topic of determinism, especially since Lynn White controversially proposed that feudalism occurred once the invention of the stirrup had made fighting on horseback easier (2–38); White's thesis was famously condemned by P. H. Sawyer and R. H. Hilton. See also Mumford, *Technics and Civilization*; Heilbroner, "Do Machines Make History?"; Winner, *Autonomous Technology*; McNeill, *The Pursuit of Power*; O'Connell, *Of Arms and Men*; Downing, *The Military Revolution and Political Change*; Marx and Smith, eds., *Does Technology Drive History?*; Rogers, ed., *The Military Revolution Debate*; Parker, *The Military Revolution*; and Wyatt, "Technological Determinism Is Dead; Long Live Technological Determinism." For how the new materialists respond to charges that theirs is a deterministic philosophy, specifically, see Bryant, 288–289; Morton, *Realist Magic*, 67–82; Dolphijn and van

der Tuin, 54–58 and 95–98; and Edwards, "The Materialism of Historical Materialism." On determinism in the long eighteenth century, specifically, see Drury, *Novel Machines*, 5–12.

3. For more on Meyrick, arguably the first specialist in arms and armor, see Lowe, *Sir Samuel Meyrick and Goodrich Court*. Prior to the publication of Meyrick's *Critical Inquiry* (1824), Strutt's *Horda Angel-Cynnan* and Grose's *Military Antiquities*, as well as his *Treatise on Ancient Armour*, sufficed as the standard antiquarian reference works.

4. Even Henry admitted that "a discerning Eye will discover a thousand Peculiarities in the Disposition of so vast a Variety of Arms, which no Description can reach" (40).

5. Henry's *Historical Description* was the most popular but by no means the only description of the Tower and its armories on offer. All these descriptions are fairly consistent both in terms of the list of items they highlight and in their brief, occasional confession that the Tower was an unnerving experience. See, for example, Bailey, *The Antiquities of London and Westminster*, 48–59; Boreman, *Curiosities in the Tower of London*, 2.19–118 (one of the earliest books for children, and charmingly miniature at only 2.5 x 1.8 inches big); *The Entertainer*, 2.158–161; *A Companion to Every Place of Curiosity and Entertainment*, 21–28; *A Brief Description of the Cities of London and Westminster*, 91–105; *The London Guide*, 26–29; *The Curiosities of London and Westminster Described*, 1.3–50. Blackmore's *The Armouries of the Tower of London* remains the standard scholarly history of the Tower's collection. See also Altick, 87–89.

6. As Henry explains, the kings on display were George I, William III, Charles II, Charles I, James I, Edward VI, Henry VIII, Henry VII, Edward V, Edward IV, Henry VI, Henry V, Henry IV, Edward III, Edward I, and—finally—William the Conqueror (see below). Meyrick was especially outraged by the Line of Kings because all the wrong suits of armor were on all the wrong kings. See also Mercer, "Samuel Meyrick, the Tower Storekeepers, and the Rearrangement of the Tower's Historic Collections of Arms and Armour, c. 1821–69."

7. Ward would go on to publish two critiques of the British armed forces: *The Wooden World Dissected* and *Mars Stript of His Armour*.

8. See Altick, 235–241 and 390–391.

9. For Strawberry Hill, see Pyhrr. For more on Sir Walter Scott's collection, see Maxwell-Scott, ed., *Catalogue of the Armour and Antiquities at Abbotsford*; for other grand displays of patterned arms and armor, see the illustration of guard rooms in Pyne's *The History of the Royal Residences*.

10. I am especially grateful to the Yale Center for British Art for letting me look at so many different and delicate representations of weapons in the long eighteenth century, including their copy of the paper doll, "The Protean Figure and Metamorphic Costumes" (GV1199 P7). Two souvenir panoramas of George IV's coronation in the collection (DA537.C67 and DA576.S68), along with George Nayler's commemorative bejeweled presentation copy of *The Coronation of George IV* (1824) (S260B), illustrate the Hanoverian's use of the challenger, a practice discontinued by Queen Victoria. See also Strong, *Coronation*, 365–375. Items in the Yale Center for British art that are notable for their illustrations of heraldry include an annotated copy of Mark Anthony Porny's *The Elements of Heraldry* (1765) (CR19 P6); *Heraldry in Miniature* (1788) (CR4801 H4); Barak Longmate's *Pocket Peerage* (1793) (CS421 L66); Thomas Willement's *Regal Heraldry* (1821), which has a letter of acknowledgment from the Society of Antiquaries pasted in (CR1620 W55); and an extra-illustrated copy of John Bernard Burke's *The General Armory of England, Scotland, and Ireland* (1842) (CR1719 B87). For an account of eighteenth-century antiquarian interests in heraldry, see Sweet, 38–48. Children's books that feature arms and armor prominently include *The Throne That Jack Built* (1820) (DA538 A1 T5) and Stacey Grimaldi's *A Suit of Armour for Youth* (1824) (N7740 G7). For examples of armor used metaphorically in polemics and sermons, see Mather, *The Armour of Christianity*; the anonymous *Antichrist's Armour-Bearer Disarm'd*; Erskine, *The Builder's Armour, or the Work and Warfare of Spiritual Builders*; Walsh, *The Whole Armour of God*; and the anonymous

Protestant Armour. For more on the public celebrations of military victories, see Doderer-Winkler's descriptive recovery of the celebrations for the Peace of Aix-La-Chapelle in 1748, *Magnificent Entertainments*, 7–19 and 216–217.

11. For discussions of eighteenth-century and Romantic British warfare, specifically, see Namier, *England in the Age of the American Revolution*; Chandler, *The Art of Warfare in the Age of Marlborough*; Brewer, *The Sinews of Power*; van Creveld, *Technology and War*, 81–152; Addington, *Patterns of War*, 112–143; Novak, "Warfare and Its Discontents"; Porter, *War and the Rise of the State*, 105–148; Cardwell, *Arts and Arms*; Bell, *The First Total War*; Favret, *War at a Distance*; and Richardson's articles, "Imagining Military Conflict" and "Atrocity in Mid Eighteenth-Century War Literature."

12. See Rawson, *Satire and Sentiment*, 29–97; Loar, *Political Magic*, 154–161.

13. See Probyn, "Haranguing upon Texts"; and Walsh, "Text, 'Text,' and Swift's 'A Tale of a Tub.'" My understanding of the *Tale* has also benefited from the insights offered in Paulson, *Theme and Structure in Swift's Tale of a Tub*; Levine, "The Design of *A Tale of a Tub*"; and Clark, *Form and Frenzy in Swift's Tale of a Tub*.

14. Whether the dedication was composed in 1697 or composed or revised in 1702 (a matter of some debate), the peace was short; either the hack is referring to the peace brokered after nine years of war with Spain in August 1697, at which point it had lasted less than a month at the time of ostensible composition, or he is referring to that peace in 1702, at which point it had hardly lasted as long as the the war itself. See *Tale*, 338 n.2.

15. See also Keiser, "Very Like a Whale"; and Scruggs, "Swift's Use of Lucretius in *A Tale of a Tub*."

16. See also Starkman, *Swift's Satire on Learning in A Tale of a Tub*; and, more recently, Lynall, *Swift and Science*, 50–88.

17. An essay authored by Steele for *The Spectator* makes this claim directly and links the moderns' interest in diversions with the inventions of the Royal Society:

> Among those Advantages which the Publick may reap from this Paper, it is not the least, that it draws Mens Minds off from the Bitterness of Party, and furnishes them with Subjects of Discourse that may be treated without Warmth or Passion. This is said to have been the First Design of those Gentlemen who set on Foot the Royal Society; and had then a very good Effect, as it turned many of the greatest Genius's of that Age to the Disquisition of natural Knowledge, who, had they engaged in Politicks with the same Parts and Application, might have set their Country in a Flame. The Air-Pump, the Barometer, the Quadrant, and the like Inventions, were thrown out to those busy Spirits, as Tubs and Barrels are to a Whale, that he may let the Ships sail on without Disturbance, while he diverts himself with those innocent Amusements (Addison et al., 2.519).

18. Swift's reasoning here also seems to belie an awareness of modern antiquarianism's disciplinary history; Hume makes the point more directly, observing that around the middle of the fifteenth century three things happened simultaneously that were, implicitly, related: "The study of antiquity became fashionable," "the art of printing" was invented, and the "invention of gunpowder changed the whole art of war." This was the birth of modernity for Hume, and this moment in the past is the one in which "each incident has a reference to our present manners and situation" (*History* 3.81).

19. See Weinbrot's claim in "He Will Kill Me Over and Over Again" that Swift is interested in "decline through innovation" (247). See also Weinbrot's *Menippean Satire*, 162–194.

20. See, for example, the competing Swift biographies by J. A. Downie, Ian Higgins, and F. P. Locke.

21. Notably, Temple had sketched a plan for a history of England that Swift thought to

take up but found he could not. Swift's engagement with history is addressed by Marshall in her *Swift and History*, but she only briefly considers the *Tale's* historical implications (98).

22. See, especially, Orwell's influential "Politics vs. Literature," and Said's "Swift's Tory Anarchy."

23. For more on the fraught attempts by the Society of Antiquaries to understand stone implements as either weapons or fossils, see Goodman's excellent, "Recovering the Vestiges of Primeval Europe." For more on the dawning significance of prehistory and deep time in the long eighteenth century, more generally, see Daniel, *The Idea of Prehistory*; Rudwick, *Bursting the Limits of Time*; and Heringman, *Sciences of Antiquity*, 216–220.

24. See Levine, *Woodward*, 238–254.

25. Hurd actually lifts this passage from the *Memoirs of the Academy of Inscriptions and Belles Lettres*. See Engell, "Romantische Poesie," 20.

26. See, especially, the outfit Captain Crowe adopts in Chapter XVI, which is made of "plates of tinned iron," a "potlid," and a "hop-pole" (129).

27. Critics generally agree that the character of Ferret satirizes John Shebbeare and his attacks on George II's ministry, attacks that had come to settle on the issues at play in controversies over the Seven Years' War; see: Rousseau and Hambridge, "On Ministers and Measures."

28. See Smollett's *History*, 1.31–47.

29. *Sir Launcelot Greaves* has not enjoyed the same critical attention as his more canonical works. See, however, Bloch, "Smollett's Quest for Form"; Rousseau, "Smollett and Politics"; Price, "Smollett and the Reader in *Sir Launcelot Greaves*"; Beasley, *Tobias Smollett, Novelist*, 184–226; Punday, "Satiric Method and the Reader in *Sir Launcelot Greaves*"; Douglas, *Uneasy Sensations*, 95–129; Skinner, *Constructions of Smollett*, 140–160; Folkenflik, "Tobias Smollett, Anthony Walker, and the First Illustrated Serial Novel in English."

30. Smollett is referring here to the Sublime Society of Beefstakes, a club that included members such as William Hogarth and John Wilkes, well known for its expressions of rank nationalism and Whig rabble-rousing. See *Greaves*, 213 n.6.

Chapter 6 · Grave Goods

1. Until recently, Christopher Scalia's "The Grave Scholarship of Antiquaries," was the single critical study of antiquaries' exhumations, and Scalia addresses only Valentine Green's exhumation of the body of King John. Thea Tomani has recently published a study titled *The Corpse as Text* in which she discusses the exhumation of King John (23–56) and Charles I (187–210), but not that of Edward I or Edward IV. Tomani's study is excellent, but it comes to a different conclusion than this chapter. Tomani finds that antiquaries "read" corpses as if they were "texts," but this volume finds that they tried to treat the kings' bodies as mere matter. Their publics, however, were very interested in whether the bodies could speak. On antiquaries' interest in sepulchral monuments more generally, see Sweet, 260–276.

2. Ayloffe reports on several accidental discoveries of royal corpses that had previously resulted in some observations, but on the whole Ayloffe implies that the antiquaries' work in 1774 was the first intentional, scientifically minded exhumation of a monarch.

3. The link between "causal" and "precaution" here is admittedly more associative than etymological; "causal" derives from the Latin *causa*; "caution" from the Latin *cavēre*. See "caution, n." *OED* Online, March 2017, and "causal, adj. and n." *OED* Online, March 2017.

4. According to Douglas, workers snipped the lock for themselves, but the antiquaries were quick to reacquire this specimen and store it along with the vial of liquid in the collections of the Society. Joseph Banks reportedly requested the collection of fluid at the exhumation in 1774, but there is no evidence that his wish was granted until the opportunity presented itself again in 1789 (discussed below). The Society of Antiquaries still has Edward

IV's lock of hair, but no trace of the vial of liquid remains. I am grateful to the Society for their assistance with my inquiries.

5. See Latour, *We Have Never Been Modern*, 17–43; and Shapin and Schaffer, *Leviathan and the Air-Pump* 80–109.

6. See Sha, "The Motion behind Romantic Emotion." See also Kuhn, *The Structure of Scientific Revolutions*, 40–82 and 118–142; Golinski, *Science as Public Culture*; and Mitchell, *Experimental Life*, 43–73.

7. A more recent biographer of Lind maintains that he was devoted to George III. See Cooper and Wallis, "Lind, James."

8. See Barrell and also Roe, *The Politics of Nature*; Wharam, *The Treason Trials, 1794*; Jones, *Radical Sensibility*; Gatrell, *The Hanging Tree*; Epstein, *Radical Expression*; Morris, *The British Monarchy and the French Revolution*; Poole, *The Politics of Regicide in England 1760–1850*; Ruston, *Shelley and Vitality*, 24–73; Barrell and Mee, "Introduction" to their *Trials for Treason and Sedition, 1792–1794*; Solomonescu, *John Thelwall and the Materialist Imagination*, 13–33.

9. Recent critical treatments of Burke have primarily concerned themselves with Burke's status and influence as a conservative political theorist. Few have considered Burke's representations of objects and the political implications of those representations; and in this regard, the *Enquiry* into the sublime is the central, critical preoccupation. My thinking on Burke's representations of objects in the *Reflections* has been shaped primarily by Pappin, *The Metaphysics of Edmund Burke*. I have also benefited from consulting Canavan, *The Political Reason of Edmund Burke*; Chapman, *Edmund Burke: The Practical Imagination*; Wilkins, *The Problem of Burke's Political Philosophy*; Stanlis, *Edmund Burke*; Furniss, *Edmund Burke's Aesthetic Ideology*; and two recent edited collections: Blakemore, ed., *Burke and the French Revolution*; and Whale, ed., *Edmund Burke's Reflections on the Revolution in France*.

10. This is a prominent enough feature of Burke's argument that he will go on to assuage his readers' concern that he may privilege property over government and rights by declaring that

> SOCIETY is indeed a contract. Subordinate contracts for objects of mere occasional interest may be dissolved at pleasure—but the state ought not to be considered as nothing better than a partnership agreement in a trade of pepper and coffee, calico, or tobacco, or some other such low concern, to be taken up for a little temporary interest, and to be dissolved by the fancy of the parties. It is to be looked on with other reverence, because it is not a partnership in things subservient only to the gross animal existence of a temporary and perishable nature. It is a partnership in all science; a partnership in all art; a partnership in every virtue and in all perfection. As the ends of such a partnership cannot be obtained in many generations, it becomes a partnership not only between those who are living, but between those who are living, those who are dead, and those who are to be born (96).

11. Pincus documents the competing accounts of the Glorious Revolution that emerged throughout the eighteenth century and became especially significant at its centenary celebration and in the contexts of the French Revolution; see, especially, his discussion of Burke's and Price's debate (21–25).

12. Phillips's *Society and Sentiment* thoroughly traces what might be called the sentimentalization of Enlightenment historiography in the Romantic period. See also Rigney; and Bann's touchstone work, especially his *Romanticism and the Rise of History*. See also Goode, *Sentimental Masculinity and the Rise of History, 1790–1890*; Underwood, "Romantic Historicism and the Afterlife." On the sentimentality of Romantic deathways, see Schor, *Bearing the Dead*; Clymer, "Graved in Tropes"; Fuss, "Corpse Poem"; Westover, *Necromanticism*; Lutz,

Relics of Death in Victorian Literature and Culture; and Laqueur, *The Work of the Dead*. On Romantic antiquarianism's affective contours, specifically, see Siegel, "Response: Mere Antiquarianism."

13. See Johnstone and Nicholes, "Transitory Actions, Men Betrayed."

14. Fitzgibbon's *Cromwell's Head* is the most recent popular object biography of Cromwell's skull.

15. Popular objects associated with Charles I range from coins, his pearl earring, and the handkerchiefs dipped in blood at his scaffold, to pieces of the Royal Oak that hid Charles II from Parliamentary soldiers. See Pittock, 147–150; and Lacey, *The Cult of King Charles the Martyr*, 61–66.

16. Clarendon's claim was contradicted, however, by a report in Antony Wood's "Athenae Oxonienses," based on testimony from Sir Thomas Herbert, that the location of the king's body was, in fact, precisely known. Halford summarizes these claims in his report (6).

17. C. E. Newman claims that an account of the relics prepared for Halford's grandson maintains that these items were accidentally left out of the coffin when it was sealed and that George IV thought "it was not worth reopening the coffin, and handing them to Halford, said: 'These things are more in your line than mine, you had better keep them' " (222). Newman's source is here unidentified, but he claims that Halford had a fondness for Charles I and cites one source as describing "Sir Henry's special interest in the martyred king," an interest also reflected in Halford's estate at Wistow near Leicester, where Charles I had reportedly left his saddle when changing horses in the course of his attempted escape from Parliamentary soldiers (222).

18. For canonical treatments of Romantic theories of matter, see Abrams, *The Mirror and the Lamp* and *Natural Supernaturalism*, 147–198, 409–463; for more recent studies, see Gigante, *Life: Organic Form and Romanticism*; Richardson, *British Romanticism and the Science of the Mind*; Mitchell, *Experimental Life*; Oerlemans, *Romanticism and the Materiality of Nature*; Ean Gottlieb, *Romantic Realities*; Goldstein, *Sweet Science*.

19. Notably, Halford was Byron's ex-mother-in-law's personal physician, and William Michael Rossetti claimed that Halford had personally recommended John Polidori's services to Byron. For more details, see Harson, "A Clarification concerning John Polidori, Lord Byron's Physician."

20. For more on "Windsor Poetics," including a newly discovered draft in Byron's hand, see Stauffer, "Sorting Byron's 'Windsor Poetics' "; see also Tatchell, "Byron's 'Windsor Poetics' "; Throsby, "Byron, Commonplacing and Early Fan Culture." Some—but not all—versions of the poem are included in *Byron: The Complete Poetical Works*, 3.86–87, 3.424–425. Bits of the poem's composition and circulation history are also discussed in Byron's *Letters and Journals*, 3.37–38; 4.79–81.

21. The only copy of the poem that does not reproduce this phrasing is the 1816 copy that Tatchell identifies in James St. Aubyn's commonplace book; "wretched" replaces "sceptered," but the use of the impersonal pronoun remains (5).

22. For a discussion of Byron's thoughts on the period's materialisms as evidenced by *Don Juan* (1819), see Chandler, " 'Man Fell with Apples' " and *England in 1819*, 350–388.

23. Dana Van Kooy reads Bryon's "Windsor Poetics" and Shelley's "Charles the First" as two works that speak to one another, although there's no evidence that Shelley read Byron's verse. See Van Kooy, *Shelley's Radical Stages*, 106–127.

24. Ruston doesn't discuss "Charles the First" but notes as part of her larger project of unpacking Shelley's relationship to the vitalist debates of 1814–1819 that Shelley was intrigued as well as unsettled by the vitalists' perceptions of drama as the genre "best calculated to excite compassion" (109).

25. See Johnstone and Nicholes ; Crook, "Caluminated Republicans and the Hero of Shel-

ley's 'Charles the First'"; Cox, "Dramatist"; Simpson, *Closet Performances*, 306–307; Scrivener, *Radical Shelley*, 297–314; Woodings, "'A Devil of a Nut to Crack'"; Cameron, "Shelley's Use of Source Material in 'Charles the First'"; Wright, "Shelley's Failure in Charles I"; White, "Shelley's 'Charles the First.'"

26. See, also Kucich, "Eternity and the Ruins of Time"; Chandler, *England in* 1819, 483–524; Roberts, *Shelley and the Chaos of History*; Hamilton, *Metaromanticism*; White, *Romantic Returns*, 101–164; Haley, *Living Forms*, 35–58; Sachs, *Romantic Antiquity*, 146–178.

27. See Mitchell, "Romanticism and the Life of Things"; Peer, ed., *Romanticism and the Object*; Calè and Craciun, "The Disorder of Things"; Jacobus, *Romantic Things*. This is also the crux of the debate about Romantic ideology. See, especially, Mellor, *English Romantic Irony*; McGann, *The Romantic Ideology*; Levinson, *Wordsworth's Great Period Poems*.

28. My reading of "Ozymandias" is indebted to Freedman, "Postponement and Perspectives in Shelley's 'Ozymandias.'" Although "Ozymandias" features prominently in critical accounts of the Romantic fragment, it is often sidelined in recent discussions of Romanticism, objects, and material cultures. Exceptions include Haley, 194–218; Gidal, *Poetic Exhibitions*, 225–229; and Janowitz, "Shelley's Monument to Ozymandias."

29. On the preservation of Shelley's bodily remains, see Hunt, "Account of the Death and Cremation of Percy Bysshe Shelley"; Trelawny, *Recollections of The Last Days of Shelley and Byron*, 134–153; Wheatley, "'Attracted by the Body'"; Lee, *Virginia Woolf's Nose*, 5–36; Pascoe, *Hummingbird Cabinet*, 2–4.

Afterword

1. See Matthew Healey, "Once-Maligned Coin"; Jennifer Schuessler, "New Parchment Declaration of Independence"; Declan Walsh, "King Tut's Dagger"; John F. Burns, "Bones under Parking Lot."

2. On "Latourian litanies," see Bogost, *Alien Phenomenology*, 38–56; Ngai, "Network Aesthetics"; Cole, "Those Obscure Objects of Desire."

3. See also Olsen, *In Defense of Things*, 21–39.

4. In his "Thing Theory," Brown similarly suggests that material culture studies depended upon "turning away from the problem of matter" that preoccupies scientists (6).

5. Latour's study of the failed personal rapid transportation system, Aramis, makes this point explicitly. Objects become obsolete when they no longer appear to adapt to, anticipate, or inaugurate changing sociocultural conditions or networks. For more on the air-pump, see Shapin and Schaffer's *Leviathan and the Air-Pump*, which is notably central to Latour's *We Have Never Been Modern*. See also Schaffer, "The Show That Never Ends"; and Daston, "The Coming into Being of Scientific Objects."

6. Lupton, Silver, and Sneed also address the ways in which Latour's work is "relatively resistant to historical narrative" (166). See Lupton, Silver, and Sneed, "Introduction: Latour and Eighteenth-Century Studies." The titles in Bloomsbury's Object Lesson series offer good examples of the presentism of recent object-oriented studies.

7. "invention, n." *OED* Online, December 2016.

8. See the discussion of Bennett's *Vibrant Matter* in chapter 1.

9. See also McKeon, "Cultural Crisis and Dialectical Method."

10. See Winner, "Do Artifacts Have Politics?"

11. See Ngai's discussion of the "interesting" in *Our Aesthetic Categories*.

Works Cited

Abrams, M. H. *The Mirror and the Lamp: Romantic Theory and the Critical Tradition* (1953). Oxford: Oxford UP, 1971.

———. *Natural Supernaturalism: Tradition and Revolution in Romantic Literature*. London: Norton, 1971.

An Act for the Better Settling and Preserving the Library . . . Called Cotton House . . . for the Benefit of the Publick. London, 1701.

Addington, Larry H. *The Patterns of War through the Eighteenth Century*. Bloomington: Indiana UP, 1990. 112–143.

Addison, Joseph. "Addison on the History of a Shilling." *The Commerce of Everyday Life: Selections from* The Tatler *and* The Spectator, edited by Erin Mackie, 183–187. New York: Bedford / St. Martin's, 1998.

———. *Dialogues upon the Usefulness of Ancient Medals*. London, 1726.

Addison, Joseph, et al. *The Spectator*. Edited by Donald F. Bond. 5 vols. Oxford: Clarendon Press, 1965.

The Adventures of a Hackney Coach. 2 vols. London, 1781.

Ædes Strawberrianae . . . The Sale Catalogue of the Collection . . . at Strawberry Hill. London, 1842.

Akenside, Mark. *Pleasures of the Imagination*. London, 1744.

———. "The Virtuoso." *Gentleman's Magazine* 7, no. 4 (1737): 244–245.

Alexander, David. "George Vertue as Engraver." *The Volume of the Walpole Society* 70 (2008): 207–517.

Allen, Keith, and Tom Stoneham, eds. *Causation and Modern Philosophy*. London: Routledge, 2010.

Altick, Richard. *The Shows of London*. Cambridge: Harvard UP, 1978.

Alvarez, David. " 'Poetical Cash': Joseph Addison, Antiquarianism, and Aesthetic Value." *Eighteenth-Century Studies* 38, no. 3 (2005): 509–531.

Andrews, Malcolm. *The Search for the Picturesque: Landscape Aesthetics and Tourism in Britain, 1760–1800*. Stanford: Stanford UP, 1989.

The Annual Register, or a View of the History, Politics, and Literature for the Year 1802. London, 1803.

Anstey, Christopher. *The Priest Dissected: A Poem*. Bath, 1774.

The Antichrist's Armour-Bearer Disarm'd. Edinburgh, 1733.

Appadurai, Arjun, ed. *The Social Life of Things*. Cambridge: Cambridge UP, 1988.

Arnold, Dana, and Stephen Bending, eds. *Tracing Architecture: The Aesthetics of Antiquarianism*. Oxford: Blackwell, 2003.

Arnold, Ken. *Cabinets for the Curious: Looking Back at Early English Museums*. Aldershot: Ashgate, 2006.

Aubrey, John. *Brief Lives*. Edited by Richard Barber. London: Boydell and Brewer, 2004.

———. *Miscellanies*. London, 1696.

———. *Miscellanies* (1696). London, 1714.

———. *Monumenta Britannica* (c. 1665–1693). Edited by J. Fowles and R. Legg. 3 vols. Boston: Little, Brown, 1981.

Austen, Jane. *Northanger Abbey* (1818). Edited by R. W. Chapman. Oxford: Oxford UP, 1933.

Ayloffe, Joseph. "An Account of the Body of King Edward the First, as It Appeared on Opening His Tomb in the Year 1774." *Archaeologia* 3 (1775): 367–413.

Bacon, Francis. *The Advancement of Learning* (1605). Edited by William A. Wright. Oxford: Clarendon Press, 1891.

Bailey, Nathan. *The Antiquities of London and Westminster.* London, 1722.

Baines, Paul. *The House of Forgery in Eighteenth-Century England.* Aldershot: Ashgate, 1999.

Baker, Henry. *Of Microscopes.* 2nd ed. 2 vols. London, 1785.

Baker, Richard. *A Chronicle of the Kings of England.* London, 1730.

Bakhtin, Mikhail. "Forms of Time and of the Chronotope in the Novel." In *The Dialogic Imagination*, edited by Michael Holquist and translated by Michael Holquist and Caryl Emerson, 84–258. Austin: U of Texas P, 1981.

Baldwin, Martha. "Toads and Plague: Amulet Therapy in Seventeenth-Century Medicine." *Bulletin of the History of Medicine* 67 (1993): 227–247.

Bann, Stephen. *Romanticism and the Rise of History.* New York: Twayne, 1995.

Barad, Karen. *Meeting the Universe Halfway: Quantum Physics and the Entanglement of Matter and Meaning.* Durham: Duke UP, 2007.

Barbauld, Anna Laetitia. *The British Novelists.* 50 vols. London, 1820.

Barkan, Leonard. *Unearthing the Past: Archaeology and Aesthetics in the Making of Renaissance Culture.* New Haven: Yale UP, 2001.

Barker, Hannah. *Newspapers, Politics and English Society, 1695–1855.* London: Routledge, 1999.

Barrell, John. *Imagining the King's Death: Figurative Treason, Fantasies of Regicide, 1793–1796.* Oxford: Oxford UP, 2000.

Barrell, John, and Jon Mee. "Introduction." *Trials for Treason and Sedition, 1792–1794.* Edited by John Barrell and Jon Mee. 8 vols. London: Pickering and Chatto, 2006–2007.

Barthes, Roland. *Mythologies* (1957). Translated by Richard Howard and Annette Lavers. New York: Farrar, Straus and Giroux, 2013.

Batchelor, Jennie. *Dress, Distress and Desire: Clothing and the Female Body in Eighteenth-Century Literature.* London: Palgrave Macmillan, 2005.

Bates, David. *States of War.* New York: Columbia UP, 2012.

Baudrillard, Jean. *The Ecstasy of Communication* (1987). Translated by Bernard Schütze and Caroline Schütze. New York: Semiotext(e), 1988. 88–89.

———. *The System of Objects* (1968). London: Verso, 1996.

Bayer-Berenbaum, Linda. *The Gothic Imagination: Expansion in Gothic Literature and Art.* Rutherford: Fairleigh Dickinson UP, 1982.

Beasley, Jerry C. *Tobias Smollett, Novelist.* Athens: U of Georgia P, 1998.

Beattie, James. *Dissertations Moral and Critical.* 2 vols. Dublin, 1783.

Beckett, William. *Free and Impartial Enquiry into the Antiquity and Efficacy of Touching for the Cure of the King's Evil.* London, 1722.

Bell, David A. *The First Total War: Napoleon's Europe and the Birth of Warfare as We Know It.* New York: Mariner, 2007.

Bellamy, Liz. "It-Narrators and Circulation: Defining a Subgenre." In *The Secret Life of Things*, edited by Mark Blackwell, 117–146. Lewisburg: Bucknell UP, 2006.

Benchley, William. *England as Seen by Foreigners in the Days of Elizabeth and James the First.* London, 1865.

Bender, John. "Enlightenment Fictions and the Scientific Hypothesis." *Representations* 61 (1998): 6–28.

Bending, Stephen. "Every Man Is Naturally an Antiquarian: Francis Grose and Polite Antiquities." *Art History* 25, no. 4 (2002): 520–530.

———. "The True Rust of the Barons' Wars: Gardens, Ruins, and the National Landscape."

In *Producing the Past: Aspects of Antiquarian Culture and Practice, 1650–1850*, edited by Martin Myrone and Lucy Peltz, 83–93. Aldershot: Ashgate, 1999.

Benedict, Barbara. *Curiosity: A Cultural History of Early Modern Inquiry*. Chicago: U of Chicago P, 2002.

———. "The Moral in the Material: Numismatics and Identity in Evelyn, Addison, and Pope." In *Queen Anne and the Arts*, edited by Cedric D. Reverend, 65–84. Lewisburg: Bucknell UP, 2015.

———. "Saying Things: Collecting Conflicts in Eighteenth-Century Object Literatures." *Literature Compass* 3/4 (2006): 689–719.

Benjamin, Walter. *Selected Writings*. Edited by Howard Eiland et al. Cambridge: Harvard UP, 2004–2006.

Bennett, Jane. *Vibrant Matter: A Political Ecology of Things*. Durham: Duke UP, 2010.

Bennett, Kate. *John Aubrey: Brief Lives with an Apparatus for the Lives of Our English Mathematical Writers*. 2 vols. Oxford: Oxford UP, 2018.

Bennett, Tony. *The Birth of the Museum: History, Theory, Politics*. London: Routledge, 1995.

Berg, Maxine. *Luxury and Pleasure in Eighteenth-Century Britain*. Oxford: Oxford UP, 2005.

Bermingham, Ann, and John Brewer, eds. *The Consumption of Culture 1600–1800: Image, Object, Text*. London: Routledge, 1995.

Bickham, Troy. "'A Conviction of the Reality of Things': Material Culture, North American Indians and Empire in Eighteenth-Century Britain." *Eighteenth-Century Studies* 39, no. 1 (2005): 29–47.

Bignamini, Ilaria. *Digging and Dealing in Eighteenth-Century Rome*. New Haven: Yale UP, 2010.

Black, Jeremy. *The English Press in the Eighteenth Century*. Philadelphia: U of Pennsylvania P, 1987.

Blackmore, Howard L. *The Armouries of the Tower of London*. 2 vols. London: HMSO, 1976.

Blackstone, William. *Commentaries on the Laws of England*. 4 vols. London, 1765–1769.

———. *The Great Charter and Charter of the Forest*. London, 1759.

Blackwell, Mark, ed. *The Secret Life of Things: Animals, Objects and It-Narratives in Eighteenth-Century England*. Lewisburg: Bucknell UP, 2014.

Blakemore, Steven, ed. *Burke and the French Revolution*. Athens: U of Georgia P, 1992.

Bloch, Marc. *The Royal Touch: Sacred Monarchy and Scrofula in England and France* (1961). Translated by J. E. Anderson. London: Routledge, 2015.

Bloch, Tuvia. "Smollett's Quest for Form." *Modern Philology* 65, no. 2 (1967): 103–113.

Blunt, Reginald. *In Cheyne Walk and Thereabout: Containing Short Accounts of Some Ingenious People and Famous Places*. London: Mills & Boon, 1914.

Bogost, Ian. *Alien Phenomenology, Or, What It's Like to Be a Thing*. Minneapolis: U of Minnesota P, 2012.

Bolingbroke, Henry St. John, Viscount. *Letters on the Study of History* (1735). London, 1752.

Bond, Donald F., ed. *The Spectator*. 5 vols. Oxford: Clarendon Press, 1965.

———., ed. *The Tatler*. 3 vols. Oxford: Clarendon Press, 1987.

Bordieu, Pierre. *Outline of a Theory of Practice*. Translated by Richard Nice. Cambridge: Cambridge UP, 1977.

Boreman, Thomas. *Curiosities in the Tower of London*. 2 vols. London, 1741.

Borlase, William. *Antiquities Historical and Monumental of the County of Cornwall*. 2nd ed. London, 1769.

Botting, Fred. *Gothic*. New York: Routledge, 1996.

Boulton, James T. *Arbitrary Power: An Enlightenment Obsession*. Nottingham: U of Nottingham P, 1967.

Boyle, Robert. *A Free Enquiry into the Vulgarly Received Notion of Nature* (1685). Edited by Edward B. Davis and Michael Hunter. Cambridge: Cambridge UP, 1996.

———. *The Philosophical Works of the Honourable Robert Boyle.* 3 vols. London, 1725.

———. *The Works of . . . Robert Boyle.* 6 vols. London, 1772.

Brewer, John. *The Sinews of Power: War, Money and the English State, 1688–1783.* Cambridge: Harvard UP, 1988.

Brewer, John, and Roy Porter, eds. *Consumption and the World of Goods.* London: Routledge, 1993.

The British Apollo, Or Curious Amusements for the Ingenious. London, 1708.

Britton, John. *Memoir of John Aubrey, F.R.S.* London: Wiltshire Topographical Society, 1845.

Brown, Bill. "Thing Theory." *Critical Inquiry* 28, no. 1 (2001): 1–22.

Brown, Iain Gordon. *The Hobby-Horsical Antiquary: A Scottish Character, 1640–1838.* Edinburgh: National Library of Scotland, 1980.

Brown, Laura. *Fables of Modernity: Literature and Culture in the Eighteenth Century.* Ithaca: Cornell UP, 2001.

———. "The Ideology of Restoration Poetic Form." *PMLA* 96, no. 3 (1982): 395–407.

Bryan, George. *Chelsea in the Olden and Present Times.* London, 1869.

Bryant, Levi. *The Democracy of Objects.* Ann Arbor: Open Humanities P, 2011.

Burke, Edmund. *Reflections on the Revolution in France* (1790). Edited by L. G. Mitchell. Oxford: Oxford UP, 1993.

Burke, John, and John Bernard Burke. *A General Armory of England, Scotland, and Ireland.* London, 1842.

Burl, Aubrey. *John Aubrey & Stone Circles: Britain's First Archaeologist, from Avebury to Stonehenge.* Stroud: Amberley, 2010.

———. *Prehistoric Avebury.* 2nd ed. New Haven: Yale UP.

Burnet, Gilbert. *An Exposition of the Thirty-Nine Articles of the Church of England.* London, 1699.

———. *Some Letters Containing an Account of What Seem'd Most Remarkable.* Amsterdam, 1687.

Burney, Frances. *Evelina; Or, a Young Lady's Entrance into the World.* 3 vols. London, 1779.

———. *Memoirs of Dr. Burney.* 3 vols. London, 1832.

Burns, John F. "Bones under Parking Lot Belonged to Richard III," *New York Times*, February 4, 2013.

Burns, William E. *An Age of Wonders: Prodigies, Politics, and Providence in England, 1658–1727.* Manchester: Manchester UP, 2002.

Butler, Samuel. *Characters and Passages from Notebooks,* Edited by A. R. Waller. Cambridge: Cambridge UP, 1908.

Butterfield, Herbert. *The Whig Interpretation of History.* London: G. Bell, 1931.

Byron, Lord George Gordon. *Letters and Journals.* Edited by Leslie A. Marchand. 13 vols. London: John Murray, 1974–1994.

———. "Windsor Poetics." In *The Complete Poetical Works*, edited by Jerome McGann, 3.86 and 3.424–425. 7 vols. Oxford: Clarendon Press, 1980–1993.

Calè, Luisa, and Adriana Craciun. "The Disorder of Things." *Eighteenth-Century Studies* 45, no. 1 (2011): 1–13.

Cameron, Kenneth Neill. "Shelley's Use of Source Material in 'Charles the First.'" *Modern Language Quarterly* 6 (1945): 197–210.

Campbell, Timothy. *Historical Style: Fashion and the New Mode of History, 1740–1830.* Philadelphia: U of Pennsylvania P, 2016.

Canavan, Francis. *The Political Reason of Edmund Burke.* Durham: Duke UP, 1960.

Canning, George. "On the Tragedy of Elvira." In *Poems.* London, 1767.

Cardwell, M. John. *Arts and Arms: Literature, Politics and Patriotism during the Seven Years War*. Manchester: Manchester UP, 2004.

Carley, James P. "The Manuscript Remains of John Leland, 'The King's Antiquary.'" *Text: Transactions for the Society for Textual Scholarship* 2 (1985): 112–120.

Carruthers, Mary. *The Book of Memory: A Study of Memory in Medieval Culture*. Cambridge: Cambridge UP, 1990.

Cash, Arthur. *John Wilkes: The Scandalous Father of Civil Liberty*. New Haven: Yale UP, 2006.

Castle, Terry. "Why the Houyhnhnms Don't Write: Swift, Satire and the Fear of the Text." *Essays in Literature* 7 (1980): 31–44.

A Catalogue of the Rarities to Be Seen at Don Saltero's Coffee-House. London, 1729.

A Catalogue of the Rarities to Be Seen at Don Saltero's Coffee-House. London, 1795.

Caulfield, James. *Portraits, Memoirs, and Characters, of Remarkable Persons*. 4 vols. London, 1819.

Certeau, Michel de. *The Practice of Everyday Life*. Translated by Steven Rendall. Berkeley: U of California P, 1984.

Chalmers, Alexander, ed. *The Tatler; A New Edition*. 4 vols. London, 1822.

Chandler, David. *The Art of Warfare in the Age of Marlborough* (1976). New York: Spellmount, 1997.

Chandler, James. *England in 1819: The Politics of Literary Culture and the Case of Romantic Historicism*. Chicago: U of Chicago P, 1998.

———. "'Man Fell with Apples': The Moral Mechanics of Don Juan." In *Rereading Byron*, edited by Alice Levine and Robert N. Keane, 67–86. London: Routledge, 1993.

Chapman, Gerald W. *Edmund Burke: The Practical Imagination*. Cambridge: Harvard UP, 1967.

Clark, John R. *Form and Frenzy in Swift's Tale of a Tub*. Ithaca: Cornell UP, 1970.

Clarke, James F. *Autobiographical Recollections of the Medical Profession*. London, 1874.

Clarke, Kenneth. *The Gothic Revival; An Essay in the History of Taste*. New York: Scribner's, 1929.

Clatterbaugh, Kenneth. *The Causation Debate in Modern Philosophy, 1637–1739*. London: Routledge, 1998.

Clerke, A. M. "Molyneux, Samuel (1689–1728)." Revised by Anita McConnell. In *Oxford Dictionary of National Biography*, edited by H. C. G. Matthew and Brian Harrison. Oxford: Oxford UP, 2004. Online ed., edited by David Cannadine, 2004 (accessed May 2, 2015).

Clery, E. J. "The Genesis of Gothic Fiction." In *The Cambridge Companion to Gothic Fiction*, edited by Jerrold E. Hogle, 21–40. Cambridge: Cambridge UP, 1995.

———. "Introduction." In *The Castle of Otranto*, edited by W. S. Lewis. Oxford: Oxford UP, 1996.

Clymer, Lorna. "Graved in Tropes: The Figural Logic of Epitaphs and Elegies in Blair, Gray, Cowper, and Wordsworth." *ELH* 62, no. 2 (1995): 347–386.

Cole, Andrew. "The Call of Things: A Critique of Object-Oriented Ontologies." *Minnesota Review* 80 (2013): 106–118.

———. "Those Obscure Objects of Desire." *Artforum* 53, no. 10 (Summer 2015): 318–322.

Colley, Linda. *Britons: Forging the Nation 1707–1837*. New Haven: Yale UP, 1992.

Collingwood, R. G. *The Idea of History* (1946). Edited by Jan van der Dussen. Oxford: Oxford UP, 1994.

Coltman, Viccy. *Fabricating the Antique: Neoclassicism in Britain, 1760–1800*. Chicago: U of Chicago P, 2006.

Combe, William. *The English Dance of Death*. 2 vols. London, 1815–1816.

A Companion to Every Place of Curiosity and Entertainment. London, 1767.

A Concise Epitome of the History of England . . . Designed for the Amusement and Information of Youth. London, 1800.

Coole, Diana, and Samantha Frost. "Introduction." In *New Materialisms: Ontology, Agency, and Politics*, edited by Diana Coole and Samantha Frost, 1–46. Durham: Duke UP, 2010.

Cooper, Thompson, and Patrick Wallis. "Lind, James (1736–1812), physician." In *Oxford Dictionary of National Biography*, accessed June 5, 2019. ref:odnb-9780198614128-e-16670.

Cowell, John. *The Interpreter, Or, Booke Containing the Signification of Words* [1607], edited by Kennett White. London, 1701.

Cowen, Brian. *The Social Life of Coffee: The Emergence of the British Coffeehouse*. New Haven: Yale UP, 2005.

Cox, Jeffrey N. "Dramatist." In *The Cambridge Companion to Shelley*, edited by Timothy Morton, 65–84. Cambridge: Cambridge UP, 2006.

Crook, Nora. "Caluminated Republicans and the Hero of Shelley's 'Charles the First.'" *Keats-Shelley Journal* 56 (2007): 155–172.

Cudworth, Ralph. *True Intellectual System of the Universe*. 2 vols. London, 1678.

Cumberland, Richard. *The Fashionable Lover: A Comedy*. London, 1772.

Cunnally, John. "Ancient Coins as Gifts and Tokens of Friendship during the Renaissance." *Journal of the History of Collections* 6, no. 2 (1994): 129–143.

Cunningham, Peter. *A Handbook for London: Past and Present*. 2 vols. London, 1849.

The Curiosities of London and Westminster Described. 2 vols. London, 1786.

Curtius, Ernst Robert. *European Literature and the Latin Middle Ages* (1953). Princeton: Princeton UP, 2013.

Curwen, Samuel. *Journal and Letters of the Late Samuel Curwen*. Edited by George Atkinson Ward. New York, 1842.

Daniel, Glyn. *The Idea of Prehistory*. London: C. A. Watts, 1962.

Daston, Lorraine. "The Coming into Being of Scientific Objects." In *Biographies of Scientific Objects*, edited by Lorraine Daston, 1–13. Chicago: U of Chicago P, 1999.

———. "Historical Epistemology." In *Questions of Evidence: Proof, Practice, and Persuasion across the Disciplines*, edited by James K. Chandler, Arnold Ira Davidson, and Harry D. Harootunian, 282–289. Chicago: U of Chicago P, 1994.

Daston, Lorraine, and Katherine Park. *Wonders and the Order of Nature: 1150–1750*. New York: Zone Books, 1998.

Davis, Leonard. *Factual Fictions: The Origins of the English Novel* (1983). Philadelphia: U of Pennsylvania P, 1996.

DeGabriele, Peter. *Sovereign Power and the Enlightenment: Eighteenth-Century Literature and the Problem of the Political*. Lewisburg: Bucknell UP, 2015.

de Man, Paul. "The Rhetoric of Temporality" (1969). In *Blindness and Insight: Essays in the Rhetoric of Contemporary Criticism*, 2nd ed., 187–228. London: Routledge, 1983.

Deng, Stephen. *Coinage and State Formation in Early Modern English Literature*. New York: Palgrave Macmillan, 2011.

Deutsch, Helen. "Oranges, Anecdote and the Nature of Things." *Substance* 38, no. 1 (2009): 31–55.

Dickinson, H. T. *The Politics of the People in Eighteenth-Century Britain*. London: Palgrave Macmillan, 1994.

Digby, Kenelm, Sir. *Two Treatises in the One of Which the Nature of Bodies, in the Other, the Nature of Mans Soule Is Looked into in Way of Discovery of the Immortality of Reasonable Soules*. Paris, 1644.

Dillon, Brian. *Ruin Lust*. London: Tate, 2014.

Doderer-Winkler, Melanie. *Magnificent Entertainments: Temporary Architecture for Georgian Festivals*. New Haven: Yale UP, 2013.

Dolphijn, Rick, and Iris van der Tuin, eds. *New Materialism: Interviews & Cartographies*. Ann Arbor: Open Humanities P, 2012.

Douglas, Aileen. "Britannia's Rule and the It-Narrator." *Eighteenth-Century Fiction* 6, no. 1 (1993): 70–89.

———. *Uneasy Sensations: Smollett and the Body*. Chicago: U of Chicago P, 1995.

Douglas, D. C. *English Scholars, 1660–1730*. London: Cape, 1939.

Downie, J. A. *Jonathan Swift: Political Writer*. London: Routledge, 1984.

Downing, Brian A. *The Military Revolution and Political Change*. Princeton: Princeton UP, 1993.

Drury, Joseph. "Haywood's Thinking Machines." *Eighteenth-Century Fiction* 21, no. 2 (2008): 201–228.

———. *Novel Machines: Technology and Narrative in Enlightenment Britain*. Oxford: Oxford UP, 2018.

———. "Twilight of the Virgin Idols: Iconoclash in the *The Monk*." *Eighteenth-Century Theory and Interpretation* 57, no. 2 (2016): 217–233.

Dryden, John. *The Medall* (1682). In *The Works of John Dryden*, edited by H. T. Swedenburg. 20 vols. Berkeley: U of California P, 1956–1990.

Earle, John. *Micro-Cosmographie, Or, A Peece of the World Discovered*. London, 1628.

Edgeworth, Maria. *Practical Education*. 2 vols. London, 1798.

Edwards, Jason. "The Materialism of Historical Materialism." In *New Materialisms: Ontology, Agency, and Politics*, edited by Diana Coole and Samantha Frost, 281–298. Durham: Duke UP, 2010.

Egerton, Charles. *A New History of England, in Verse*. London, 1780.

Ehrenpreis, Irvin. *Swift: The Man, His Works, and the Age*. 3 vols. Cambridge: Harvard UP, 1962–1983.

Eisenstein, Elizabeth. *The Printing Press as an Agent of Change* (1979). Cambridge: Cambridge UP, 1997.

Ellis, Aytoun. *The Penny Universities: A History of the Coffee-Houses*. London: Secker and Warburg, 1956.

Ellis, Markman. *The History of Gothic Fiction*. Edinburgh: Edinburgh UP, 2000.

Emlyn, Henry, et al. "The Vault, Body, and Monument of Edward IV." *Vetusta Monumenta* 3 (1796): vii, viii, 1–4.

Engberg-Pedersen, Anders. *Empire of Chance: The Napoleonic Wars and the Disorder of Things*. Cambridge: Harvard UP, 2015.

Engell, James. "Romantische Poesie: Richard Hurd and Friedrich Schlegel." In *Cultural Interactions in the Romantic Age: Critical Essays in Comparative Literature*, edited by Gregory Maertz, 13–29. Albany: State U of New York P, 1998.

The Entertainer; Containing a Great Variety of Instructive Entertainment. 2 vols. London, 1766.

Epstein, James A. *Radical Expression: Political Language, Ritual and Symbol in England, 1790–1850*. Oxford: Oxford UP, 1994.

Erskine, Ralph. *The Builder's Armour, or the Work and Warfare of Spiritual Builders*. Edinburgh, 1743.

Erskine-Hill, Howard. *Poetry of Opposition and Revolution: Dryden to Wordsworth*. Oxford: Clarendon Press, 1996.

Evans, Joan. *A History of the Society of Antiquaries*. Oxford: Oxford UP, 1956.

Evelyn, John. *Numismata: A Discourse of Medals, Ancient and Modern*. London, 1697.

Favret, Mary A. *War at a Distance: Romanticism and the Making of Modern Wartime*. Princeton: Princeton UP, 2009.

Felski, Rita. *The Limits of Critique*. Chicago: U of Chicago P, 2015.

Ferris, Ina. *The Achievement of Literary Authority: Gender, History, and the Waverley Novels*. Ithaca: Cornell UP, 1991.

Festa, Lynn. *Sentimental Figures of Empire in Eighteenth-Century Britain and France.* Baltimore: Johns Hopkins UP, 2006.

Fielding, Sarah. *The Adventures of David Simple.* 2 vols. London, 1744.

Fitzgibbon, Jonathan. *Cromwell's Head.* Kew: The National Archives, 2008.

Flew, Antony, et al. *Agency and Necessity.* London: Blackwell, 1987.

Flint, Christopher. "Speaking Objects: The Circulation of Stories in Eighteenth-Century Prose Fiction." *PMLA* 113, no. 2 (1998): 212–226.

Folkenflik, Robert. "Tobias Smollett, Anthony Walker, and the First Illustrated Serial Novel in English." *Eighteenth-Century Fiction* 14, no. 3/4 (2002): 507–532.

Foote, Samuel. *The Nabob.* London, 1772.

———. *Taste.* London, 1752.

Franklin, Benjamin. *Works of the Late Doctor Benjamin Franklin.* Edited by Henry Stueber. 2 vols. London, 1793.

Freedman, William. "Postponement and Perspectives in Shelley's 'Ozymandias.'" *Studies in Romanticism* 25, no. 6 (1986): 63–73.

Furniss, Tom. *Edmund Burke's Aesthetic Ideology.* Cambridge: Cambridge UP, 1993.

Fuss, Diana. "Corpse Poem." *Critical Inquiry* 30, no. 1 (2003): 1–30.

Fussner, Frank Smith. *The Historical Revolution: English Historical Writing and Thought, 1580–1640* (1962). London: Routledge, 2010.

Gale, Samuel. *Account of Some Antiquities at Glastonbury.* London, 1784.

Gallagher, Catherine. *Nobody's Story: The Vanishing Acts of Women in the Marketplace, 1670–1820.* Berkeley: U of California P, 1994.

Gallagher, Noel. *Historical Literatures: Writing about the Past in England, 1660–1740.* Manchester: Manchester UP, 2012.

Gardiner, Anne. "Dryden's 'The Medall' and the Principle of Continuous Transmission of Laws." *Clio* 14, no. 1 (1984): 51–70.

Gatrell, V. A. C. *The Hanging Tree: Execution and the English People, 1770–1868.* Oxford: Oxford UP, 1994.

Gee, Sophie. *Making Waste: Leftovers and the Eighteenth-Century Imagination.* Princeton: Princeton UP, 2010.

Gell, Alfred. *Art and Agency: An Anthropological Theory.* Oxford: Clarendon Press, 1998.

Gibson, James J. *The Ecological Approach to Visual Perception.* Boston: Houghton Mifflin, 1979.

Gidal, Eric. *Poetic Exhibitions: Romantic Aesthetics and the Pleasures of the British Museum.* Lewisburg: Bucknell UP, 2001.

Gigante, Denise. *Life: Organic Form and Romanticism.* New Haven: Yale UP, 2009.

Ginzburg, Carlo. *Clues, Myths, and the Historical Method.* Baltimore: Johns Hopkins UP, 1990.

Glat, Mark. "John Locke's Historical Sense." *The Review of Politics* 43, no. 1 (1981): 3–21.

Golden, Samuel A. "A Numismatic View of Dryden's *The Medal.*" *Notes and Queries* 9 (1962): 383–384.

Goldstein, Amanda Jo. "Growing Old Together: Lucretian Materialism in Shelley's 'Poetry of Life.'" *Representations* 128, no. 1 (2014): 60–92.

———. *Sweet Science: Romantic Materialism and the New Logics of Life.* Chicago: U of Chicago P, 2017.

Golinski, Jan. *Science as Public Culture: Chemistry and Enlightenment in Britain, 1760–1820.* Cambridge: Cambridge UP, 1992.

Goode, Mike. *Sentimental Masculinity and the Rise of History, 1790–1890.* Cambridge: Cambridge UP, 2009.

Goodman, Matthew R. "Recovering the Vestiges of Primeval Europe: Archaeology and the

Significance of Stone Implements, 1750–1800." *Journal of the History of Ideas* 72, no. 1 (2011): 51–74.

Gottlieb, Evan. *Romantic Realities: Speculative Realism and British Romanticism*. Edinburgh: Edinburgh UP, 2016.

Gough, Richard. *Anecdotes of British Topography*. London, 1768.

———. "Introduction." *Archaeologia* 1 (1770): i–xliii.

Granger, James. *Biographical History of England*. 4 vols. London, 1769.

———. *Catalogue of Engraved British Portraits*. London, 1769–1774.

Gray, Thomas. *The Traveller's Companion* (1799). 2nd ed. London, 1800.

Greaves, Richard. *Deliver Us from Evil: The Radical Underground in Britain, 1660–1663*. Oxford: Oxford UP, 1986.

Green, Valentine. *An Account of the Discovery of the Body of King John*. London, 1797.

Greenblatt, Stephen. *Marvelous Possessions: The Wonder of the New World*. Chicago: U of Chicago P, 1991.

Grey, Richard. *Memoria Technia; Or a New Method of Artificial Memory*. London, 1730.

Grimaldi, Stacey. *A Suit of Armour for Youth*. London, 1824.

Grose, Francis. *Military Antiquities*. 2 vols. London, 1786–1788.

———. *The Olio*. London, 1792.

———. *A Treatise on Ancient Armour*. London, 1786.

Guthrie, Neil. *The Material Culture of the Jacobites*. Cambridge: Cambridge UP, 2014.

Haley, Bruce. *Living Forms: Romantics and the Monumental Figure*. Albany: State U of New York P, 2003.

Hall, Anna Maria. "The Follower of the Family." In *Stories of the Irish Peasantry*, 126–160. London, 1840.

Hamilton, Paul. *Metaromanticism: Aesthetics, Literature, Theory*. Chicago: U of Chicago P, 2003.

Hammond, Brean S. "Mid-Century English Quixotism and the Defence of the Novel." *Eighteenth-Century Fiction* 10, no. 3 (1998): 247–268.

Hammond, Paul. "The King's Two Bodies; Representations of Charles II." In *Culture, Politics and Society in Britain, 1660–1800*, edited by Jeremy Black and Jeremy Gregory, 13–48. Manchester: Manchester UP, 1991.

———. *The Making of Restoration Poetry*. Cambridge: Boydell & Brewer, 2006.

Hanson, Craig Ashley. *The English Virtuoso: Art, Medicine, and Antiquarianism in the Age of Empiricism*. Chicago: U of Chicago P, 2009.

Harman, Graham. "The Well-Wrought Broken Hammer: Object-Oriented Literary Criticism." *New Literary History* 43, no. 2 (2012): 183–203.

Harmsen, Theodor. *Antiquarianism in the Augustan Age: Thomas Hearne 1678–1735*. New York: Peter Lang, 2000.

Harries, Elizabeth Wanning. *The Unfinished Manner: Essays on the Fragment in the Later Eighteenth Century*. Charlottesville: U of Virginia P, 1994.

Harris, Bob. *Politics and the Rise of the Press: Britain and France, 1620–1800*. London: Routledge, 1996.

Harson, Robert R. "A Clarification concerning John Polidori, Lord Byron's Physician." *Keats-Shelley Journal* 21/22 (1972/1973): 38–40.

Harth, Phillip. *Pen for a Party: Dryden's Tory Propaganda in its Contexts*. Princeton: Princeton UP, 1993.

Haskell, Francis. *History and Its Images: Art and the Interpretation of the Past*. New Haven: Yale UP, 1993.

Haycock, David Alastair Boyd. *Dr. William Stukeley (1698–1765): Antiquarianism and Newtonianism in Eighteenth-Century England*. Woodbridge: Boydell Press, 2002.

Hayles, Katherine N. *How We Became Posthuman: Virtual Bodies in Cybernetics, Literature, and Informatics.* Chicago: U of Chicago P, 1999.

Hays, Daniel. *Epistle to C. Churchill.* London, 1761.

Hazen, Allen T., ed. *A Catalogue of Horace Walpole's Library.* 3 vols. New Haven: Yale UP, 1969.

Healey, Matthew. "Once-Maligned Coin Nears Its Big Payday," *New York Times,* April 13, 2013.

Hearne, Thomas. *A Collection of Curious Discourses, Written by Eminent Antiquaries.* Oxford, 1720.

———. *The Itinerary of John Leland the Antiquary.* 2nd ed. London, 1744–1745.

Heckford, William. *Characters . . . of All the Kings and Queens of England.* London, 1787.

Hedrick, Elizabeth. "Romancing the Salve: Sir Kenelm Digby and the Powder of Sympathy." *The British Journal for the History of Science* 41, no. 2 (2008): 161–185.

Heilbroner, Robert L. "Do Machines Make History?" *Technology and Culture* 7, no. 3 (1967): 335–345.

Henry, David. *An Historical Description of the Tower of London and Its Curiosities.* London, 1753.

Heringman, Noah. *Sciences of Antiquity: Romantic Antiquarianism, Natural History, and Knowledge Work.* Oxford: Oxford UP, 2013.

Heringman, Noah, and Crystal B. Lake. "Introduction: Romantic Antiquarianism." *Romantic Circles Praxis Series.* June 2014. https://www.rc.umd.edu/praxis/antiquarianism/index.html.

Hicks, Frederick Charles. *Men and Books Famous in the Law.* Rochester, NY: Lawyers Co-operative Publishing, 1921.

Hicks, Philip. *Neoclassical History and English Culture: From Clarendon to Hume.* New York: St. Martin's Press, 1996.

Higgins, Ian. *Swift's Politics: A Study in Disaffection.* Cambridge: Cambridge UP, 1994.

Hill, Rosemary. "Antiquaries in the Age of Romanticism." Dissertation, Queen Mary University of London, 2011.

———. *Stonehenge.* Cambridge: Harvard UP, 2013.

The History of England Faithfully Extracted. London, 1715.

History of Theodore I. London, 1743.

Hogg, Thomas Jefferson. *The Life of Percy Bysshe Shelley.* 2 vols. London, 1858.

Hopper, Samuel. *A Catalogue of the Manuscripts in the Cottonian Library.* London, 1777.

Houstoun, James. *Some New and Accurate Observations . . . of the Coast of Guinea.* London, 1725.

Hume, David. *An Enquiry concerning Human Understanding.* Edited by Tom L. Beauchamp. Oxford: Clarendon Press, 2000.

Hume, Robert. "Gothic versus Romantic: A Revaluation of the Gothic Novel." *PMLA* 84, no. 2 (1969): 282–290.

Hunt, Leigh. "Account of the Death and Cremation of Percy Bysshe Shelley" [1822]. Ashley MS 915. British Library, London.

Hunter, John. *The Works of John Hunter, F.R.S.* Edited by James G. Palmer. 5 vols. London, 1835–1837.

Hunter, J. Paul. *Before Novels: The Cultural Contexts of Eighteenth-Century English Fiction.* London: Norton, 1990.

Hunter, Michael. *John Aubrey and the Realm of Learning.* London: Duckworth, 1975.

———. "The Royal Society and the Origins of British Archaeology." *Antiquity* 65 (1971): 113–121, 187–192.

Hurd, Richard. *Letters on Chivalry and Romance.* London, 1767.

Hutton, William. *A Journey from Birmingham to London.* London, 1785.

Hyde, Edward, Earl of Clarendon. *History of the Rebellion and Civil Wars in England*. Oxford, 1702.

Impey, Oliver, and Arthur MacGregor, eds. *The Origins of Museums: The Cabinet of Curiosities in Sixteenth- and Seventeenth-Century Europe*. Oxford: Oxford UP, 1985.

An Index to the First Fifteen Volumes of Archaeologia. London, 1809.

Israel, Jonathan. *Radical Enlightenment: Philosophy and the Making of Modernity 1650–1750*. Oxford: Oxford UP, 2002.

———. *A Revolution of the Mind: Radical Enlightenment and the Intellectual Origins of Modern Democracy*. Princeton: Princeton UP, 2009.

Jacob, Margaret. *The Newtonians and the English Revolution, 1689–1720*. Ithaca: Cornell UP, 1976.

———. *The Radical Enlightenment: Pantheists, Freemasons and Republicans*. London: Allen & Unwin, 1981.

Jacobus, Mary. *Romantic Things: A Tree, A Rock, A Cloud*. Chicago: U of Chicago P, 2012.

Janowitz, Anne. *England's Ruins: Poetic Purpose and the National Landscape*. London: Blackwell, 1990.

———. "Shelley's Monument to Ozymandias." *Philological Quarterly* 63, no. 4 (1984): 477–491.

Jenkins, Ian. *Vases and Volcanos: Sir William Hamilton and His Collection*. London: British Museum, 1996.

Jennings, David. *An Introduction to the Knowledge of Medals*. London, 1764.

Johnson, Jerah. "The Money=Blood Metaphor, 1300–1800." *The Journal of Finance* 21, no. 1 (1966): 119–122.

Johnson, Samuel. *A Dictionary of the English Language*. 2 vols. London, 1755.

———. *The Lives of the English Poets; and a Criticism on Their Works*. 3 vols. London, 1779–1781.

Johnstone, Charles. *Chrysal, Or, the Adventures of a Guinea*. Edited by Kevin Bourque. 2 vols. Richmond, VA: Valancourt, 2011.

Johnstone, Kenneth, and Joseph Nicholes. "Transitory Actions, Men Betrayed: The French Revolution in Romantic Drama." *The Wordsworth Circle* 23, no. 2 (1992): 76–96.

Jones, Chris. *Radical Sensibility: Literature and Ideas in the 1790s*. London: Routledge, 1993.

Jones, Inigo. *The Most Notable Antiquity of Great Britain* (1655). London: Scolar Press, 1972.

Justice Triumphant: Or, the Organ in the Suds. A Farce. London, 1747.

Kahn, Victoria. *Future of Illusion: Political Theology and Early Modern Texts*. Chicago: U of Chicago P, 2014.

———. *Wayward Contracts: The Crisis of Political Obligation in England, 1640–1674*. Princeton: Princeton UP, 2004.

Kallich, Martin. *Horace Walpole*. New York: Twayne, 1971.

Kalter, Barrett. *Modern Antiques: The Material Past in England, 1660–1780*. Lewisburg: Bucknell UP, 2012.

Kames, Henry Home, Lord. *Introduction to the Art of Thinking*. Edinburgh, 1761.

Kantorowicz, Ernst. *The King's Two Bodies* (1957). Princeton: Princeton UP, 1997.

Kareem, Sarah Tindal. *Eighteenth-Century Fiction and the Reinvention of Wonder*. Oxford: Oxford UP, 2015.

Keiser, Jess. "Very Like a Whale: Metaphor and Materialism in Hobbes and Swift." *Modern Philology* 113, no. 2 (2015): 198–223.

Kelly, Jason M. *The Society of Dilettanti: Archaeology and Identity in the British Enlightenment*. New Haven: Yale UP, 2010.

Ketcham, Michael G. *Transparent Designs: Reading, Performance and Form in the* Spectator *Papers*. Athens: U of Georgia P, 1985.

Keynes, Geoffrey. *Blake Studies*. Oxford: Clarendon Press, 1971.

Keynes, Simon. "The Reconstruction of a Burnt Cottonian Manuscript: The Case of Cotton MS. Otho A.I." *The British Library Journal* 22, no. 2 (1996): 113–160.

Kiely, Robert. *The Romantic Novel in England*. Cambridge: Cambridge UP, 1972.

Kiernan, Kevin. *Beowulf and the Beowulf Manuscript*. Ann Arbor: U of Michigan P, 1996.

Kilgour, Maggie. *The Rise of the Gothic Novel*. New York: Routledge, 1995.

Kimber, Isaac. *The History of England*. London, 1746.

King, Edward. *A Speech Delivered by Edward King, Esq. President of the Society of Antiquaries of London*. London, 1784.

King, J. C. H. "Ethnographic Collections: Collecting in the Context of Sloane's Catalogue of 'Miscellanies.'" In *Sir Hans Sloane: Collector, Scientist, Antiquary, Founding Father of the British Museum*, edited by Arthur MacGregor, 228–244. London: British Museum, 1994.

Kingsley, Margery. "Dryden and the Consumption of History." In *Enchanted Ground*, edited by Jayne Lewis and Maximillian E. Novak, 31–51. Toronto: U of Toronto P, 2004.

Kliger, Samuel. *The Goths in England: A Study in Seventeenth and Eighteenth Century Thought*. Cambridge: Harvard UP, 1952.

Knight, Charles. *London*. 6 vols. London, 1841–1844.

Knoppers, Laura Lunger. *Constructing Cromwell: Ceremony, Portrait, and Print 1645–1661*. Cambridge: Cambridge UP, 2000.

Kramnick, Isaac A. *Bolingbroke and His Circle: The Politics of Nostalgia in the Age of Walpole* (1968). Ithaca: Cornell UP, 1992.

Kramnick, Jonathan. *Actions and Objects from Hobbes to Richardson*. Stanford: Stanford UP, 2010.

———. *Paper Minds: Literature and the Ecology of Consciousness*. Chicago: Chicago UP, 2018.

Kroll, Richard W. F. *The Material Word: Literate Culture in the Restoration and Early Eighteenth Century*. Baltimore: Johns Hopkins UP, 1991.

Kubler, George. *The Shape of Time: Remarks on the History of Things*. New Haven: Yale UP, 1962.

Kucich, Greg. "Eternity and the Ruins of Time: Shelley and the Construction of Cultural History." In *Shelley: Poet and Legislator of the World*, edited by Betty T. Bennett and Stuart Curran, 14–29. Baltimore: Johns Hopkins UP, 1996.

Kuhn, Thomas. *The Structure of Scientific Revolutions* (1962). Chicago: U of Chicago P, 2012.

Kuiken, Kir. *Imagined Sovereignties: Toward a New Political Romanticism*. New York: Fordham UP, 2014.

Lacey, Andrew. *The Cult of King Charles the Martyr*. London: Boydell Press, 2003.

Lacquer, Thomas. *The Work of the Dead: A Cultural History of Mortal Remains*. Princeton: Princeton UP, 2015.

Lake, Crystal B. "Antiquarianism as a Vital Historiography for the Twenty-First Century." *The Wordsworth Circle* 50, no. 4 (2019): 1–16.

———. "Plate 1.55: Stuart Medals." In *Vetusta Monumenta: Ancient Monuments, a Digital Edition*, edited by Noah Heringman and Crystal B. Lake, online. University of Missouri, 2019. https://scalar.missouri.edu/vm/vol1plate55-stuart-medals.

Lamb, Jonathan. "Bruno Latour, Michel Serres, and Fictions of the Enlightenment." *Eighteenth-Century Theory and Interpretation* 57, no. 2 (2016): 181–195.

———. *The Things Things Say*. Princeton: Princeton UP, 2011.

Lane, Margaret. *Samuel Johnson and His World*. New York: Harper and Row, 1975.

Langford, Paul. *A Polite and Commercial People*. Oxford: Oxford UP, 1989.

Latour, Bruno. *Aramis, or the Love of Technology* (1993). Translated by Catherine Porter. Cambridge: Harvard UP, 1996.

———. *Iconoclash*. Cambridge: MIT Press, 2002.

———. *Reassembling the Social: An Introduction to Actor-Network-Theory*. Oxford: Oxford UP, 2005.

―――. *We Have Never Been Modern*. Translated by Catherine Porter. Cambridge: Harvard UP, 1993.

Law, Jules Davis. *The Rhetoric of Empiricism: Language and Perception from Locke to I. A. Richards*. Ithaca: Cornell UP, 1993.

Leavis, F. R. "The Irony of Swift." In *Determinations: Critical Essays*, 79–108. London: Chatto & Windus, 1934.

Lee, Hermione. *Virginia Woolf's Nose: Essays on Biography*. Princeton: Princeton UP, 2005.

Leerssen, Joep. "Literary Historicism: Romanticism, Philologists, and the Presence of the Past." *Modern Language Quarterly* 65, no. 2 (2004): 221–243.

Leland, John. *The Itinerary of John Leland the Antiquary*. Edited by Thomas Hearne. 9 vols. Oxford, 1710.

Letters of the Ghost of Alfred . . . On the Occasion of the State Trials. London, 1798.

Levine, Caroline. *Forms: Whole, Rhythm, Hierarchy, Network*. Princeton: Princeton UP, 2015.

Levine, Jay Arnold. "The Design of *A Tale of a Tub* (with a Digression on a Mad Modern Critic)." *ELH* 33, no. 2 (1966): 198–227.

Levine, Joseph. *The Battle of the Books: History and Literature in the Augustan Age*. Ithaca: Cornell UP, 1994.

―――. *Dr. Woodward's Shield* (1977). Ithaca: Cornell UP, 1991.

Levinson, Marjorie. *The Romantic Fragment Poem: A Critique of Form*. Greensboro: U of North Carolina P, 1986.

―――. *Wordsworth's Great Period Poems*. Cambridge: Cambridge UP, 1986.

Lewis, W. S. "Horace Walpole, Antiquary." In *Essays Presented to Sir Lewis Namier*, edited by Richard Pares and A. J. P. Taylor, 178–203. London: Macmillan, 1956.

―――. *Horace Walpole's Library*. Cambridge: Cambridge UP, 1958.

Lillywhite, Bryant. *London Coffee-Houses*. London: Allen and Unwin, 1963.

Loar, Christopher. *Political Magic: British Fictions of Savagery and Sovereignty*. New York: Fordham UP, 2014.

Lobis, Seth. *The Virtue of Sympathy: Magic, Philosophy, and Literature in Seventeenth-Century England*. New Haven: Yale UP, 2015.

Locke, F. P. *Swift's Tory Politics*. London: Duckworth, 1983.

Locke, John. *An Essay concerning Human Understanding* (1698). Edited by Peter H. Nidditch. Oxford: Clarendon Press, 1975.

Longmate, Barak. *The Pocket Peerage of England, Scotland, and Ireland* (1790). 2nd ed. 2 vols. London, 1793.

The London Guide. London, 1782.

Lovejoy, A. O. *The Great Chain of Being* (1936). Cambridge: Harvard UP, 1964.

Lowe, Rosalind. *Sir Samuel Meyrick and Goodrich Court*. Little Logaston, UK: Logaston Press, 2003.

Lynall, George. *Swift and Science: The Satire, Politics, and Theology of Natural Knowledge, 1690–1730*. New York: Palgrave Macmillan, 2012.

Lupton, Christina. *Knowing Books: The Consciousness of Mediation in Eighteenth-Century Britain*. Philadelphia: U of Pennsylvania P, 2011.

Lupton, Christina, Sean Silver, and Adam Sneed. "Introduction: Latour and Eighteenth-Century Studies." *Eighteenth-Century Theory and Interpretation* 57, no. 2 (2016): 165–179.

Lutz, Deborah. *Relics of Death in Victorian Literature and Culture*. Cambridge: Cambridge UP, 2014.

Lynch, Deidre Shauna. *The Economy of Character: Novels, Market Culture, and the Business of Inner Meaning*. Chicago: U of Chicago P, 1998.

―――. "Novels in the World of Moving Goods." In *A Concise Companion to the Restoration and Eighteenth Century*, ed. Cynthia Wall, 212–243. Oxford: Blackwell, 2004.

Lynch, Jack. *The Age of Elizabeth in the Age of Johnson*. Cambridge: Cambridge UP, 2003.

MacAndrew, Elizabeth. *The Gothic Tradition in Fiction*. New York: Columbia UP, 1979.

Macaulay, Rose. *Pleasure of Ruins*. New York: Walker, 1953.

Macaulay, Thomas Babington. *Critical and Historical Essays, Contributed to the Edinburgh Review*. 3 vols. London, 1850.

MacDougall, Hugh A. *Racial Myth in English History: Trokans, Teutons, and Anglo-Saxons*. Hanover: UP of New England, 1982.

MacGregor, Arthur. *Curiosity and the Enlightenment: Collectors and Collections from the Sixteenth to Nineteenth Centuries*. New Haven: Yale UP, 2007.

——, ed. *Sir Hans Sloane, Collector, Scientist, Antiquary, Founding Father of the British Museum*. London: British Museum, 1994.

——, ed. *Tradescant's Rarities: Essays on the Foundation of the Ashmolean Museum, 1683, with a Catalogue of the Surviving Early Collections*. Oxford: Oxford UP, 1983.

Mack, Ruth. "Horace Walpole and the Objects of Literary History." *ELH* 75, no. 2 (2008): 367–387.

——. *Literary Historicity: Literature and Historical Experience in Eighteenth-Century Britain*. Stanford: Stanford UP, 2008.

MacMichael, J. Holden. "Don Saltero's Tavern, Chelsea." *Notes and Queries* 241 (1908): 110–111.

Macpherson, Sandra. *Harm's Way: Tragic Responsibility and the Novel Form*. Baltimore: Johns Hopkins UP, 2009.

Madox, Thomas. *Formulare Anglicanum, Or a Collection of Ancient Charters and Instruments*. London, 1702.

Malcolm, J. P., ed. *Letters between the Rev. James Granger . . . and Many of the Most Eminent Literary Men*. London, 1805.

Marchand, Leslie A. *Byron: A Biography*. 3 vols. New York: Knopf, 1957.

Marriage A-La-Mode . . . Being an Explanation of the Six Prints Lately Published by the Ingenious Mr. Hogarth. London, 1746.

Marshall, Ashley. *Swift and History: Politics and the English Past*. Cambridge: Cambridge UP, 2015.

Martin, Benjamin. *Philosophia Britannica*. 2 vols. London, 1747.

Marx, Leo, and Merritt Roe Smith, eds. *Does Technology Drive History? The Dilemma of Technological Determinism*. Cambridge: MIT Press, 1994.

Mather, Cotton. *The Armour of Christianity*. Boston, 1704.

Maurer, A. E. Wallace. "The Design of Dryden's *The Medall*," *Papers on Language and Literature* 2, no. 4 (1966): 293–304.

Maxwell-Scott, Mary, ed. *Catalogue of the Armour and Antiquities at Abbotsford*. Edinburgh, 1888.

McGann, Jerome. *The Romantic Ideology*. Chicago: U of Chicago P, 1983.

McKendrick, Neil, et al. *The Birth of a Consumer Society: The Commercialization of Eighteenth-Century England*. Bloomington: Indiana UP, 1982.

McKeon, Michael. "Cultural Crisis and Dialectical Method: Destabilizing Augustan Literature." In *The Profession of Eighteenth-Century Literature*, edited by Leo Damrosch, 42–61. Madison: U of Wisconsin P, 1992.

——. *The Origins of the English Novel, 1600–1740* (1987). Baltimore: Johns Hopkins UP, 2002.

McKitterick, David. "Bibliography, Bibliophily, and the Organization of Knowledge." In *The Foundations of Scholarship: Libraries and Collecting, 1650–1750*, edited by David McKitterick and David Vaisey, 29–64. Los Angeles: William Andrews Clark Memorial Library, 1992.

McLaughlin, Terence. *Dirt: A Social History*. London: Dorset Press, 2011.

McNeill, William H. *The Pursuit of Power: Technology, Armed Force, and Society since A.D. 1000*. Chicago: U of Chicago P, 1984.

Mehrotra, Kewal K. *Horace Walpole and the English Novel: A Study of the Influence of The Castle of Otranto, 1764–1820*. New York: Russell & Russell, 1970.

Mellor, Anne K. *English Romantic Irony*. Cambridge: Harvard UP, 1980.

Memoirs of the Extraordinary Life, Works, and Discoveries of Martinus Scriblerus. London, 1741.

Mendyck, Stan A. E. *"Speculum Britanniae": Regional Study, Antiquarianism and Science in Britain to 1700*. Toronto: Toronto UP, 1989.

Mercer, Malcolm. "Samuel Meyrick, the Tower Storekeepers, and the Rearrangement of the Tower's Historic Collections of Arms and Armour, c. 1821–69." *Arms & Armour* 10, no. 2 (2013): 114–127.

Meyrick, Samuel. "Observations on the Body Armour Anciently Worn in England." *Archaeologia* 19 (1818): 120–145.

Miles, Robert. *Gothic Writing, 1750–1820: A Genealogy*. London: Routledge, 1993.

Miller, Daniel, ed. *Materiality*. Durham: Duke UP, 2005.

Miller, David P., and Peter Hans Reill, eds. *Visions of Empire: Voyages, Botany, and Representations of Nature*. Cambridge: Cambridge UP, 1996.

Miller, Edward. *That Noble Cabinet: A History of the British Museum*. Columbus: Ohio State UP, 1974.

Miller, Peter, ed. *Momigliano and Antiquarianism: Foundations of the Modern Cultural Sciences*. Toronto: U of Toronto P, 2007.

Milton, John. *Complete Prose Works of John Milton*. Edited by Don M. Wolfe. 8 vols. New Haven: Yale UP, 1953–1982.

Mintz, Samuel I. *The Hunting of Leviathan* (1958). Cambridge: Cambridge UP, 1970.

The Mirror of Literature, Amusement, and Instruction. 38 vols. London, 1822–1841.

The Miscellaneous and Whimsical Lucubrations of Lancelot Poverty-Struck. London, 1758.

Miscellanies on Several Curious Subjects. London, 1714.

"Miscellanies upon Various Subjects." *Critical Review, Or Annals of Literature* 59 (1785): 309–310.

Mitchell, Robert. *Experimental Life: Vitalism in Romantic Science and Literature*. Baltimore: Johns Hopkins UP, 2013.

Mitchell, W. J. T. "Romanticism and the Life of Things: Fossils, Totems, and Images." *Critical Inquiry* 45, no. 1 (2001): 167–184.

Molyneaux, Samuel. *The London Letters of Samuel Molyneaux*. Edited by Ann Saunders. London: London Topographical Society, 2011.

Momigliano, Arnaldo. "Ancient History and the Antiquarian." *Journal of the Warburg and Courtauld Institutes* 13, no. 3/4 (1950): 185–315.

Morris, Marilyn. *The British Monarchy and the French Revolution*. New Haven: Yale UP, 1998.

Morton, Timothy. *Hyperobjects: Philosophy and Ecology after the End of the World*. Minneapolis: U of Minnesota P, 2013.

———. "An Object-Oriented Defense of Poetry." *New Literary History* 43, no. 2 (2012): 205–224.

Mui, Hoh-Chueng, and Lorna H. Mui. *Shops and Shopkeeping in Eighteenth-Century England*. Kingston: McGill-Queen's UP, 1989.

Müller, Lothar. *White Magic: The Age of Paper*. New York: Polity, 2016.

Mumford, Lewis. *Technics and Civilization*. New York: Harcourt Brace, 1934.

Murphy, Anne L. *The Origins of English Financial Markets*. Cambridge: Cambridge UP, 2009.

Murray, John Fisher. *Environs of London, Western Division*. Edinburgh, 1842.

Myrone, Martin, and Lucy Peltz, eds. *Producing the Past: Aspects of Antiquarian Culture and Practice, 1700–1850*. Aldershot: Ashgate, 1999.

Nadler, Steven M., ed. *Causation in Early Modern Philosophy*. University Park: Pennsylvania State UP, 1993.

Nalson, John. *An Impartial Collection of the Great Affairs of State.* 2 vols. London, 1682–1683.

Namier, Lewis. *England in the Age of the American Revolution* (1930). 2nd ed. London: Macmillan, 1961.

———. *The Structure of Politics at the Accession of George III.* London: Macmillan, 1929.

Nayler, George. *The Coronation of George IV.* 2 vols. London, 1824.

Newman, C. E. "The Fourth Cervical Vertebra of Charles I." *Journal of the Royal College of Physicians* 13, no. 4 (1979): 221–223.

Ngai, Sianne. *Our Aesthetic Categories: Zany, Cute, Interesting.* Cambridge: Harvard UP, 2012.

Nichols, John. *Literary Anecdotes of the Eighteenth Century.* 9 vols. London, 1812–1815.

Nicolson, William. *The English Historical Library.* London, 1696.

Nightingale, B. "Thomas Rawlins, and the Honorary Medals of the Commonwealth." *The Numismatic Chronicle and Journal of the Numismatic Society* 13 (1850): 129–133.

Niven, G. W., ed. *Selections from the British Apollo.* Paisley: A. Gardner, 1903.

Novak, Maximillian E. "Warfare and Its Discontents in Eighteenth-Century Fiction: Or, Why Eighteenth-Century Fiction Failed to Produce a *War and Peace.*" *Eighteenth-Century Fiction* 4, no. 3 (1992): 185–206.

Nowka, Scott. "Talking Coins and Thinking Smoke-Jacks: Satirizing Materialism in Gildon and Sterne." *Eighteenth-Century Fiction* 22, no. 2 (2009): 195–222.

O'Connell, Robert L. *Of Arms and Men: A History of War, Weapons, and Aggression.* Oxford: Oxford UP, 1990.

Oerlemans, Onno. *Romanticism and the Materiality of Nature.* Toronto: U of Toronto P, 2015.

O'Gorman, Frank. *The Long Eighteenth Century: British Political and Social History, 1688–1832* (1997). London: Bloomsbury, 2016.

O'Keefe, John. *Lie of a Day: A Comedy.* London, 1800.

Olsen, Bjørnar. *In Defense of Things: Archaeology and the Ontology of Objects.* London: Rowman & Littlefield, 2010.

Onians, John. *Classical Art and the Cultures of Greece and Rome.* New Haven: Yale UP, 2009.

Orr, D. Alan. *Treason and the State: Law, Politics, and Ideology in The English Civil War.* Cambridge: Cambridge UP, 2007.

Orwell, George. "Politics vs. Literature: An Examination of *Gulliver's Travels.*" *Polemic* 5 (1946): 45–53.

Ott, Walter. *Causation and the Laws of Nature in Early Modern Philosophy.* Oxford: Oxford UP, 1999.

Packham, Catherine. *Eighteenth-Century Vitalism: Bodies, Culture, Politics.* London: Palgrave Macmillan, 2012.

Pappin, Joseph L. *The Metaphysics of Edmund Burke.* New York: Fordham UP, 1993.

Park, Julie. *The Self and It: Novel Objects and Mimetic Subjects in Eighteenth-Century England.* Stanford: Stanford UP, 2009.

Parker, Geoffrey. *The Military Revolution: Military Innovation and the Rise of the West, 1500–1800.* Cambridge: Cambridge UP, 1996.

Parnell, Geoffrey. *The Tower of London: Past and Present* (1998). London: The History Press, 2009.

Parry, Graham. "Earliest Antiquaries." In *Making History,* edited by David Stark et al., 37–39. London: Society of Antiquaries, 2007.

———. "Mists of Time." In *Making History,* edited by David Stark et al., 17–19. London: Society of Antiquaries, 2007.

———. *The Trophies of Time: English Antiquarians of the Seventeenth Century.* Oxford: Oxford UP, 1995.

Pasanek, Brad. *Metaphors of Mind: An Eighteenth-Century Dictionary.* Baltimore: Johns Hopkins UP, 2015.

Pascoe, Judith: *The Hummingbird Cabinet: A Rare and Curious History of Romantic Collectors.* Ithaca: Cornell UP, 2005.

Paulson, Ronald. *Theme and Structure in Swift's Tale of a Tub.* New Haven: Yale UP, 1960.

Pearce, Susan. *On Collecting: An Investigation into Collecting in the European Tradition.* London: Routledge, 1995.

———, ed. *Visions of Antiquity: The Society of Antiquaries of London 1707–2007.* London: Society of Antiquaries, 2007

Peer, Larry, ed. *Romanticism and the Object.* London: Palgrave Macmillan, 2009.

Pennant, Thomas. *The History of the Parishes of Whiteford and Holywell.* London, 1796.

Phillips, Mark Salber. "Reconsiderations on History and Antiquarianism: Arnold Momigliano and the Historiography of Great Britain." *Journal of the History of Ideas* 57, no. 2 (1996): 297–316.

———. *Society and Sentiment: Genres of Historical Writing in Britain, 1740–1820.* Princeton: Princeton UP, 2000.

Piggott, Stuart. *Ancient Britons and the Antiquarian Imagination: Ideas from the Renaissance to the Regency.* London: Thames and Hudson, 1989.

———. *Ruins in a Landscape: Essays in Antiquarianism.* Edinburgh: Edinburgh UP, 1976.

Pincus, Steven. *1688: The First Modern Revolution.* New Haven: Yale UP, 2009.

Pine, John. "Great Charter" [1733]. Prints and Drawings: 1861,0518.331. British Museum, London.

Pinkerton, John. *An Essay on Medals.* London, 1784.

Piper, H. W. *The Active Universe: Pantheism and the Concept of Imagination in the English Romantic Poets.* London: Athlone Press, 1962.

Pittock, Murray. *Material Culture and Sedition, 1688–1760.* London: Palgrave Macmillan, 2013.

Pocock, J. G. A. *The Ancient Constitution and the Feudal Law* (1957). Cambridge: Cambridge UP, 1987.

———. *Barbarism and Religion.* 6 vols. Cambridge: Cambridge UP, 1999–2015.

———. *The Machiavellian Moment.* Princeton: Princeton UP, 1975.

———. *Politics, Language, and Time: Essays on Political Thought and History.* Chicago: U of Chicago P, 1972.

———. *Virtue, Commerce, and History: Essays on Political Thought, Chiefly Eighteenth Century.* Cambridge: Cambridge UP, 1985.

Pointer, John. *Britannia Romana, or Roman Antiquities in Britain.* Oxford, 1724.

Poliquin, Rachel. *The Breathless Zoo: Taxidermy and the Cultures of Longing.* Philadelphia: U of Pennsylvania P, 2012.

Pomian, Krzysztof. *Collectors and Curiosities: Paris and Venice, 1500–1800.* Translated by Elizabeth Wiles-Portier. Cambridge: Cambridge UP, 1990.

Poole, Steve. *The Politics of Regicide in England, 1760–1850.* Manchester: Manchester UP, 2000.

Poovey, Mary. *Genres of the Credit Economy.* Chicago: U of Chicago P, 2008.

———. *A History of the Modern Fact: Problems of Knowledge in the Sciences of Wealth and Society.* Chicago: U of Chicago P, 1998.

Pope, Alexander. *The Twickenham Edition of the Poems of Alexander Pope.* Edited by John Butt et al. 11 vols. New Haven: Yale UP, 1939–1969.

Porny, Mark Anthony (Antoine Pyron du Martre). *The Elements of Heraldry.* London, 1765.

Porter, Bruce D. *War and the Rise of the State: The Military Foundations of Modern Politics.* New York: Free Press, 1994.

"Preferments, Marriages, and Casualties." *Gentleman's Magazine* 1, no. 10 (1731): 451.

Prescott, Andrew. "'Their Present Miserable State of Cremation': The Restoration of the Cotton Library." In *Sir Robert Cotton as Collector: Essays on an Early Stuart Courtier and His Legacy,* edited by C. J. Wright, 391–454. London: British Library, 1997.

Price, John Vladimir. "Smollett and the Reader in *Sir Launcelot Greaves*." In *Smollett: Author of the First Distinction*, edited by Alan Bold, 193–208. London: Vision / Barnes and Noble, 1982.

Probyn, Clive. "Haranguing upon Texts: Swift and the Idea of the Book." In *Proceedings of the First Münster Symposium on Jonathan Swift*, edited by Herman J. Real and Heinz J. Vienken, 187–197. Munich: Wilhelm Fink Verlag, 1985.

"The Protean Figure and Metamorphic Costumes." London, 1811.

Protestant Armour: Or, the Church of England-Man's Defence. London, 1769.

Pulleyn, William. *The Etymological Compendium*. London, 1828.

Punday, Daniel. "Satiric Method and the Reader in *Sir Launcelot Greaves*." *Eighteenth-Century Fiction* 6, no. 2 (1994): 169–188.

Pyhrr, Stuart W. "The Strawberry Hill Armoury." In *Horace Walpole's Strawberry Hill*, edited by Michael Snodin, with Cynthia Roman, 221–233. New Haven: Yale UP, 2009.

[Pyne, William Henry]. *The History of the Royal Residences*. 3 vols. London, 1819.

———. *Wine and Walnuts, Or, After Dinner Chit-Chat*. 2 vols. London, 1824.

Ramsay, Nigel. " 'The Manuscripts Flew About Like Butterflies': the Break-Up of English Libraries in the Sixteenth Century." In *Lost Libraries*, edited by James Raven, 125–144. London: Palgrave Macmillan, 2004.

Rawls, John. *Lectures on the History of Political Philosophy* (2000). Cambridge: Harvard UP, 2008.

Rawson, Claude. *Satire and Sentiment, 1660–1830*. Cambridge: Cambridge UP, 1994.

Raymond, Joad. *The Invention of the Newspaper: English Newsbooks 1641–1649*. Oxford: Clarendon Press, 1996.

———. *Pamphlets and Pamphleteering in Early Modern Britain*. Cambridge: Cambridge UP, 2006.

Redford, Bruce. *Dilettanti: The Antic and the Antique in Eighteenth-Century England*. Los Angeles: J. Paul Getty Museum, 2008.

Regier, Alexander. *Fracture and Fragmentation in British Romanticism*. Cambridge: Cambridge UP, 2010.

Reill, Peter H. *Vitalizing Nature in the Enlightenment*. Berkeley: U of California P, 2005.

Remarks on Mr. Walpole's Catalogue of Royal and Noble Authors. London, 1759.

Reverand, Cedric D. "Patterns of Imagery and Metaphor in Dryden's 'The Medall.' " *The Yearbook of English Studies* 2 (1972): 123–134.

Richards, R. D. *The Early History of Banking in England* (1929). London: Routledge, 2012.

Richardson, Alan. *British Romanticism and the Science of the Mind*. Cambridge: Cambridge UP, 2001.

Richardson, John. "Atrocity in Mid Eighteenth-Century War Literature." *Eighteenth-Century Life* 33, no. 2 (2009): 92–114.

———. "Imagining Military Conflict during the Seven Years' War." *Studies in English Literature* 48, no. 3 (2008): 585–611.

Richardson, Samuel. *Letters Written to and for Particular Friends*. London, 1741.

Richter, David. *The Progress of Romance: Literary Historiography and the Gothic Novel*. Columbus: Ohio State UP, 1999.

Ricoeur, Paul. *Figuring the Sacred: Religion, Narrative, and Imagination*. Translated by David Pellauer. Minneapolis: Fortress Press, 1995.

Rigney, Ann. *Imperfect Histories: The Elusive Past and the Legacy of Romantic Historicism*. Ithaca: Cornell UP, 2001.

Rigby, Douglas, and Elizabeth Rigby. *Lock, Stock, and Barrel: The Story of Collecting*. New York: Lippincott, 1944.

Roach, Joseph. *Cities of the Dead: Circum-Atlantic Performance*. New York: Columbia UP, 1996.

———. "The Global Parasol: Accessorizing the Four Corners." In *The Global Eighteenth Century*, edited by Felicity A. Nussbaum, 93–106. Baltimore: Johns Hopkins UP, 2003.

Roberts, Hugh. *Shelley and the Chaos of History*. University Park: Pennsylvania State UP, 1997.

Robertson, Fiona. *Legitimate Histories: Scott, Gothic, and the Authorities of Fiction*. Oxford: Clarendon Press, 1994.

Robinson, James. *A Compleat and Impartial History of England*. London, 1739.

Roe, Nicholas. *The Politics of Nature: Wordsworth and Some Contemporaries* (1992). 2nd ed. London: Palgrave Macmillan, 2002.

Rogers, Clifford, ed. *The Military Revolution Debate: Readings on the Military Transformation of Early Modern Europe*. Boulder: Westview Press, 1995.

Rogers, John. *The Matter of Revolution: Science, Poetry, and Politics in the Age of Milton*. Ithaca: Cornell UP, 1996.

Rosenstein, Leon. *Antiques: The History of an Idea*. Ithaca: Cornell UP, 2008.

Rousseau, G. S. "Smollett and Politics: Originals for the Election Scene in *Sir Launcelot Greaves*." *English Language Notes* 14, no.1 (1976): 32–38.

Rousseau, G. S., and Roger A. Hambridge. "On Ministers and Measures: Smollett, Shebbeare, and the Portrait of Ferret in *Sir Launcelot Greaves*." *Etudes Anglaises* 32 (1979): 185–191.

Rudwick, Martin J. S. *Bursting the Limits of Time: The Reconstruction of Geohistory in the Age of Revolution*. Chicago: U of Chicago P, 2005.

Rushworth, John. *Historical Collections of Private Passages of State*. London, 1659.

Russett, Margaret. *Fictions and Fakes: Forging Romantic Authenticity, 1760–1845*. Cambridge: Cambridge UP, 2006.

Ruston, Sharon. *Shelley and Vitality*. London: Palgrave Macmillan, 2005.

Rymer, Thomas. *Acta Regia*. London, 1726–1727.

Sabor, Peter. "Horace Walpole as a Historian." *Eighteenth-Century Life* 11 (1987): 5–17.

Sachs, Jonathan. *Romantic Antiquity: Rome in the British Imagination, 1789–1832*. Oxford: Oxford UP, 2010.

Said, Edward. "Swift's Tory Anarchy." *Eighteenth-Century Studies* 3, no. 1 (1969): 48–66.

Sainsbury, John. *John Wilkes: The Lives of a Libertine*. Aldershot: Ashgate, 2006.

Samson, John. "Politics Gothicized: The Conway Incident and *The Castle of Otranto*." *Eighteenth-Century Life* 10 (1986): 145–158.

Santer, Eric L. *The Royal Remains: The People's Two Bodies and the Endgames of Sovereignty*. Chicago: U of Chicago P, 2011.

Sawyer, P. H., and R. H. Hilton. "Technical Determinism: The Stirrup and the Plough." *Past & Present* 24 (April 1963): 90–100.

Scalia, Christopher. "The Grave Scholarship of Antiquaries." *Literature Compass* 2, no. 1 (2005): online.

Schaffer, Simon. "The Show That Never Ends: Perpetual Motion in the Early Eighteenth Century." *The British Journal for the History of Science* 28, no. 2 (1995): 157–189.

Schmidt, Claudia M. *David Hume: Reason in History*. University Park: Pennsylvania State UP, 2003.

Schnapp, Alain, ed. *World Antiquarianism: Comparative Perspectives*. Los Angeles: J. Paul Getty Research Institute, 2013.

Schor, Esther. *Bearing the Dead: The British Culture of Mourning from the Enlightenment to Victoria*. Princeton: Princeton UP, 1994.

Schuessler, Jennifer. "A New Parchment Declaration of Independence Surfaces. Head-Scratching Ensues," *New York Times*, April 21, 2017.

Schwartz, Janelle A. *Worm Work: Recasting Romanticism*. Minneapolis: U of Minnesota P, 2012.

Scott, Sir Walter. *The Antiquary*. 3 vols. London, 1816.

———. *Ballantyne's Novelists' Library*. 10 vols. Edinburgh, 1823.

Scrivener, Michael Henry. *Radical Shelley: The Philosophical Anarchism and Utopian Thought of Percy Bysshe Shelley*. Princeton: Princeton UP, 1982.

Scruggs, Charles. "Swift's Use of Lucretius in *A Tale of a Tub*." *Texas Studies in Literature and Language* 15, no. 1 (1973): 39–49.

Scurr, Ruth. *John Aubrey: My Own Life*. London: Chatto & Windus, 2015.

Seidel, Michael. "Narrative News." *Eighteenth-Century Fiction* 10, no. 2 (1998): 125–150.

Seliger, Martin. *The Liberal Politics of John Locke*. New York: Praeger, 1969.

Sha, Richard C. "The Motion behind Romantic Emotion." In *Romanticism and the Emotions*, edited by Joel Faflak and Richard C. Sha, 19–47. Cambridge: Cambridge UP, 2014.

Shadwell, Thomas. *The Virtuoso*. London, 1676.

Shapin, Steven, and Simon Schaffer. *Leviathan and the Air-Pump: Hobbes, Boyle, and the Experimental Life* (2005). Princeton: Princeton UP, 2017.

Shapiro, Barbara J. *A Culture of Fact: England, 1550–1720* (2000). Ithaca: Cornell UP, 2003.

———. *Probability and Certainty in Seventeenth-Century England*. Princeton: Princeton UP, 1983.

Sharpe, Kevin. *Rebranding Rule: The Restoration and Revolution Monarchy, 1660–1714*. New Haven: Yale UP, 2013.

———. *Sir Robert Cotton, 1586–1631: History and Politics in Early Modern England*. Oxford: Clarendon Press, 1979.

Shelley, Percy Bysshe. "A Defense of Poetry." In *Shelley's Poetry and Prose*, edited by Donald H. Reiman and Sharon B. Powers, 478–509. New York: Norton, 1977.

———. "Ozymandias." In *Shelley's Poetry and Prose*, edited by Donald H. Reiman and Sharon B. Powers, 103. New York: Norton, 1977.

Siegel, Jonah. "Response: Mere Antiquarianism." In *Romantic Antiquarianism*, edited by Noah Heringman and Crystal B. Lake. *Romantic Circles Praxis* (February 2014): online.

Silver, Sean. *The Mind Is a Collection: Case Studies in Eighteenth-Century Thought*. Philadelphia: U of Pennsylvania P, 2015.

———. "Visiting Strawberry Hill: Horace Walpole's Gothic Historiography." *Eighteenth-Century Fiction* 21, no. 4 (2009): 535–564.

Simpson, Michael. *Closet Performances: Political Exhibition and Prohibition in the Dramas of Byron and Shelley*. Stanford: Stanford UP, 1998.

Siskin, Clifford, and William Warner. "This Is Enlightenment: An Invitation in the Form of an Argument." In *This Is Enlightenment*, edited by Clifford Siskin and William Warner, 1–6. Chicago: U of Chicago P, 2010.

Skinner, John. *Constructions of Smollett: A Study of Genre and Gender*. Newark: U of Delaware P, 1996.

Smiles, Sam. *Eye Witness: Artists and Visual Documentation in Britain, 1770–1830*. Aldershot: Ashgate, 2000.

———. *The Image of Antiquity: Ancient Britain and the Romantic Imagination*. New Haven: Yale UP, 1994.

Smith, Charles. *Historical and Literary Curiosities*. London, 1875.

Smith, Chloe Wigston. *Women, Work and Clothes in the Eighteenth-Century Novel*. Cambridge: Cambridge UP, 2013.

Smith, R. J. *The Gothic Bequest: Medieval Institutions in British Thought, 1688–1863*. Cambridge: Cambridge UP, 1999.

Smollett, Tobias. *The Adventures of Peregrine Pickle*. 3 vols. London, 1751.

——. *A Complete History of England.* 4 vols. London, 1757–1758.

——. *The History and Adventures of an Atom.* 2 vols. London, 1769.

——. *The Life and Adventures of Sir Launcelot Greaves* (1760). Edited by Robert Folkenflik and Barbara Laning Fitzpatrick. Athens: U of Georgia P, 2002.

——. *Poems, Plays, and "The Briton."* Edited by O. M. Brack Jr. and Byron Gassman. Athens: U of Georgia P, 2014.

Smythies, Susan. *The History of Lucy Wellers.* 2 vols. London, 1755.

Solomonescu, Yasmin. *John Thelwall and the Materialist Imagination.* London: Palgrave Macmillan, 2014.

Somner, William. *The Antiquities of Canterbury.* London, 1640.

——. *The Antiquities of Canterbury in Two Parts,* edited by Nicholas Battely. London, 1703.

——. *The Insecuritie of Princes.* London, 1648–1649.

Spadafora, David. *The Idea of Progress in Eighteenth-Century Britain.* New Haven: Yale UP, 1990.

Spanheim, Ezekiel. *Disputationes de Usu et Præstantia Numismatum Antiquorum.* Rome, 1664.

Spector, Robert. *Political Controversy: A Study in Eighteenth-Century Propaganda.* Westport, CT: Greenwood, 1992.

Sprat, Thomas. *The History of the Royal Society.* London, 1667.

Squirrell, Robert. *Observations Addressed to the Public in General on the Cow-Pox, Shewing That It Originates in Scrophula, the Evil.* London, 1805.

Stanlis, Peter J. *Edmund Burke: The Enlightenment and Revolution.* London, Transaction, 1991.

Stark, David, et al., eds. *Making History: Antiquaries in Britain, 1707–2007.* London: Royal Academy Books, 2007.

Starkman, Miriam K. *Swift's Satire on Learning in A Tale of a Tub.* Princeton: Princeton UP, 1950.

Stauffer, Andrew M. "Sorting Byron's 'Windsor Poetics.'" *Keats-Shelley Journal* 51 (2002): 30–34.

Steedman, Carolyn. *Dust: The Archive and Cultural History.* New Brunswick: Rutgers UP, 2004.

Steele, Richard, et al. *The Tatler.* Edited by Donald F. Bond. 3 vols. Oxford: Clarendon Press, 1987.

Stevens, George Alexander. *Songs, Comic, and Satyrical.* Oxford, 1772.

Stevenson, John Allen. *The British Novel, Defoe to Austen: A Critical History.* New York: Twayne, 1990.

Stewart, Susan. *On Longing: Narratives of the Miniature, the Gigantic, the Souvenir, the Collection* (1993). Durham: Duke UP, 2007.

Strong, Roy. *Coronation: A History of Kingship and the British Monarchy.* New York: Harper-Collins, 2005.

Strutt, Joseph. *Horda-Angel-Cynnan: The Manners and Customs, Arms and Habits of the Inhabitants of England.* 3 vols. London, 1774–1776.

Stukeley, William. *Itinerarium Curiosum: Or, An Account of the Antiquities, and Remarkable Curiosities in Nature or Art, Observed in Travels through Great Britain.* 2nd ed. 2 vols. London, 1776.

Sutherland, W. O. S. "Dryden's Use of Popular Imagery in 'The Medal.'" *The University of Texas Studies in English* 35 (1956): 123–134.

Swann, Marjorie. *Curiosities and Texts: The Culture of Collecting in Early Modern England.* Philadelphia: U of Pennsylvania P, 2001.

Sweet, Rosemary. *Antiquaries: The Discovery of the Past in Eighteenth-Century Britain.* London: Hambledon Continuum, 2006.

Swift, Jonathan. *The Cambridge Edition of the Works of Jonathan Swift.* 18 vols. Cambridge: Cambridge UP, 2008–2014.

———. *Journal to Stella*. Edited by Harold Williams. 2 vols. Oxford: Clarendon Press, 1948.

———. *A Tale of a Tub and Other Works* (1704). Edited by Marcus Walsh. Cambridge: Cambridge UP, 2010.

[Swift, Jonathan.] *The Instructive Library*. London, 1710.

Tamen, Miguel. *Friends of Interpretable Objects*. Cambridge: Harvard UP, 2004.

Tatchell, Molly. "Byron's 'Windsor Poetics.'" *Keats-Shelley Memorial Bulletin* 25 (1974): 4–5.

Terada, Rei. "Looking at the Stars Forever." *Studies in Romanticism* 50, no. 2 (2011): 275–309.

[Theobald, Lewis]. *The Censor*. 2nd ed. 3 vols. London, 1717.

Thompson, Helen. *Fictional Matter: Empiricism, Corpuscles, and the Novel*. Philadelphia: U of Pennsylvania P, 2016.

Thompson, Helen, and Natania Meeker. "Empiricism, Substance, Narrative: An Introduction." *The Eighteenth Century* 48, no. 3 (2007): 183–186.

Thomson, Ann. *Bodies of Thought: Science, Religion, and the Soul in the Early Enlightenment*. Oxford: Oxford UP, 2008.

Thomson, Katharine. *The White Mask*. 3 vols. London, 1844.

Thoresby, Ralph. *The Diary of Ralph Thoresby, F.R.S., 1677–1724*. Edited by Joseph Hunter. 2 vols. London, 1830.

The Throne That Jack Built. London, 1820.

Throsby, Corin. "Byron, Commonplacing and Early Fan Culture." In *Romanticism and Celebrity Culture, 1750–1850*, edited by Tom Mole, 227–244. Cambridge: Cambridge UP, 2009.

Timbs John. *Club Life of London*. 2 vols. London, 1866.

Todd, Angela. "Your Humble Servant Shows Himself: Don Saltero and Public Coffeehouse Space." *Journal of International Women's Studies* 6, no. 2 (2005): 118–135.

Tomani, Thea. *The Corpse as Text: Disinterment and Antiquarian Inquiry, 1700–1900*. London: Boydell and Brewer, 2017.

Toulmin, Stephen, and Jane Goodfield. *The Architecture of Matter*. Chicago: U of Chicago P, 1962.

Treharne, R. F., and I. J. Sanders, eds. *Documents of the Baronial Reform and Rebellion, 1258–1267*. Oxford: Clarendon Press, 1973.

Trelawny, Edward John. *Recollections of The Last Days of Shelley and Byron* (1858). Cambridge: Cambridge UP, 2011.

The Trial of Mrs. Harriet Errington, Wife of George Errington, Esq . . . for Committing Adultery. London, 1785.

Trumpener, Katie. *Bardic Nationalism: The Romantic Novel and the British Empire*. Princeton: Princeton UP, 1997.

Turner, Ralph V. *Magna Carta: Through the Ages*. London: Routledge, 2003.

Tyrrell, James. *The General History of England*. 5 vols. London, 1704.

Underwood, Ted. "Romantic Historicism and the Afterlife." *PMLA* 117, no. 2 (2002): 237–251.

Valenze, Deborah. *The Social Life of Money in the English Past*. Cambridge: Cambridge UP, 2006.

van Creveld, Martin. *Technology and War* (1989). New York: Free Press, 1991.

Van Kooy, Dana. *Performance and Cultural Memory in the Post-Napoleonic Era*. London: Routledge, 2016.

Vann, Richard T. "The Free Anglo-Saxons: A Historical Myth." *Journal of the History of Ideas* 19, no. 2 (1958): 259–272.

Varma, Devandra. *The Gothic Flame; Being a History of the Gothic Novel in England, Its Origins, Efflorescence, Disintegration, and Residuary Influences*. New York: Russell & Russell, 1966.

Vertue, George. *Medals, Coins, Great-Seals, Impressions from the Elaborate Works of Thomas Simon*. London, 1753.

Vine, Angus. *In Defiance of Time: Antiquarian Writing in Early Modern England.* Oxford: Oxford UP, 2010.

von Uffenbach, Zacharias Conrad. *London in 1710.* Edited and translated by H. Quarrell and Margaret Mare. London: Faber & Faber, 1934.

Waldman, Jonathan. *Rust: The Longest War.* New York: Simon and Schuster, 2015.

Walford, Edward, and Walter Thornbury. *Old and New London.* 6 vols. London, 1880.

Wall, Cynthia. *The Prose of Things: Transformations of Description in the Eighteenth Century.* Chicago: U of Chicago P, 2006.

Walpole, Horace. *The Castle of Otranto.* Twickenham, 1764.

———. *Catalogue of Royal and Noble Authors.* Twickenham, 1758.

———. *A Description of the Villa of Horace Walpole . . . at Strawberry Hill.* Twickenham, 1774.

———. *Historic Doubts on the Life and Reign of King Richard.* Twickenham, 1768.

———. "Sketch of a History Written in a Method Entirely New." Unpublished manuscript at Lewis Walpole Library, c. 1783.

———. *The Yale Edition of Horace Walpole's Correspondence.* Edited by W. S. Lewis. 48 vols. New Haven: Yale UP, 1937–1983.

Walsh, Declan. "King Tut's Dagger Made of 'Iron from the Sky,' Researchers Say," *New York Times,* June 6, 2016.

Walsh, Marcus. "Text, 'Text,' and Swift's 'A Tale of a Tub.'" *The Modern Language Review* 85, no. 2 (1990): 290–303.

Walsh, Thomas. *The Whole Armour of God.* London, 1759.

Warburton, William. *A Critical and Philosophical Enquiry into the Causes of Prodigies.* 2 vols. London, 1727.

———. *The Works of Alexander Pope, Esq* (1751). 9 vols. London, 1770.

Ward, Edward. *The London Spy Compleat.* London, 1703.

———. *Mars Strip of His Armour.* London, 1708.

———. *The Secret History of Clubs.* London, 1709.

———. *The Wooden World Dissected.* London, 1706.

Watt, James. *Contesting the Gothic: Fiction, Genre, and Cultural Conflict, 1764–1832.* Cambridge: Cambridge UP, 1999.

[Webb, Phillip Carteret.] *Copies Taken from the Records of the Court of King's Bench.* London, 1763.

Weber, Harold M. *Paper Bullets: Print and Kingship under Charles II.* Lexington: UP of Kentucky, 1996.

Weever, John. *Ancient Funerall Monuments.* London, 1631.

Wein, Toni. *British Identities, Heroic Nationalisms, and The Gothic Novel, 1762–1824.* London: Palgrave Macmillan, 2002.

Weinbrot, Howard. "'He Will Kill Me Over and Over Again': Intellectual Contexts of the Battle of the Books." In *Proceedings of the First Münster Symposium on Jonathan Swift,* edited by Herman J. Real and Heinz J. Vienken, 225–248. Munich: Wilhelm Fink Verlag, 1985.

———. *Menippean Satire Reconsidered: From Antiquity to the Eighteenth Century.* Baltimore: Johns Hopkins UP, 2005.

Weiss-Smith, Courtney. *Empiricist Devotions: Science, Religion, and Poetry in Early Eighteenth-Century England.* Charlottesville: U of Virginia P, 2016.

Wendeborn, Gebhard Friedrich August. *A View of England Towards the Close of the Eighteenth Century.* 2 vols. London, 1791.

Werrett, Simon. "Healing the Nation's Wounds: Royal Ritual and Experimental Philosophy in Restoration England." *History of Science* 33 (2000): 377–399.

West, Shearer. "Wilkes's Squint: Synecdochic Physiognomy and Political Identity in Eighteenth-Century Print Culture." *Eighteenth-Century Studies* 33, no. 1 (1999): 65–84.

Westover, Paul. *Necromanticism: Traveling to Meet the Dead, 1750–1860*. London: Palgrave Macmillan, 2012.

Whale, John C., ed. *Edmund Burke's Reflections on the Revolution in France: New Interdisciplinary Essays*. Manchester: Manchester UP, 2000.

[Whalley, Peter]. *Essay on the Manner of Writing History*. London, 1746.

Wharam, Alan. *The Treason Trials, 1794*. Leicester: Leicester UP, 1992.

Wheatley, Kim. "'Attracted by the Body': Accounts of Shelley's Cremation." *Keats-Shelley Journal* 49 (2000): 162–182.

White, Deborah Elise. *Romantic Returns: Superstition, Imagination, History*. Stanford: Stanford UP, 2000.

White, Hayden. *Metahistory: The Historical Imagination in Nineteenth-Century Europe*. Baltimore: Johns Hopkins UP, 1973.

———. *Tropics of Discourse: Essays in Cultural Criticism*. Baltimore: Johns Hopkins UP, 1978.

White, Kennett. *The Interpreter of Words and Terms*. London, 1701.

White, Lynn Townsend Jr. *Medieval Religion and Technology*. Berkeley: U of California P, 1978.

White, Newman I. "Shelley's 'Charles the First.'" *The Journal of English and Germanic Philology* 21, no. 3 (1922): 431–441.

Whitehead, Charles. *Richard Savage*. 3 vols. London, 1842.

Wilkes, John. *Encyclopaedia Londinensis*. 24 vols. London, 1810–1829.

Wilkins, Burleigh T. *The Problem of Burke's Political Philosophy*. Oxford: Clarendon Press, 1967.

Willement, Thomas. *Regal Heraldry; The Armorial Insignia of the Kings and Queens of England*. London, 1821.

Williams, Kelsey Jackson. *The Antiquary: John Aubrey's Historical Scholarship*. Oxford: Oxford UP, 2016.

Winner, Langdon. *Autonomous Technology: Technics-out-of-Control as a Theme in Political Thought*. Cambridge: MIT Press, 1977.

———. "Do Artifacts Have Politics?" *Daedalus* 109, no. 1 (1980): 121–136.

Wolcot, John [Peter Pindar]. "Peter Pindar's Character of an Antiquarian." *Walker's Hibernian Magazine, or Compendium of Entertaining Knowledge* 2 (October 1790): 310–312.

———. *Peter's Prophecy*. London, 1788.

———. *A Rowland for an Oliver*. London, 1790.

———. *The Royal Tour, and Weymouth Amusements*. London, 1795.

Woodings, R. B. "'A Devil of a Nut to Crack': Shelley's 'Charles the First.'" *Studia Neophilologica* 40, no. 1 (1968): 216–237.

Woodward, Christopher. *In Ruins*. New York: Pantheon, 2002.

Woolf, D. R. *The Social Circulation of the Past: English Historical Culture, 1500–1730*. Oxford: Oxford UP, 2005.

Woolrych, Austin. *Britain in Revolution, 1625–1660*. Oxford: Oxford UP, 2002.

Wright, C. J., ed. *Sir Robert Cotton as Collector*. London: British Library, 1977.

Wright, Walter F. "Shelley's Failure in Charles I." *ELH* 8, no. 1 (1941): 41–46.

Wyatt, Sally. "Technological Determinism Is Dead; Long Live Technological Determinism." In *Handbook of HTS Studies*, edited by Edward J. Hackett et al., 165–180. Cambridge: MIT Press, 2008.

Yates, Frances A. *The Art of Memory*. London: Routledge, 1966.

Yolton, John. *Thinking Matter: Materialism in Eighteenth-Century Britain*. Minneapolis: U of Minnesota P, 1984.

The Younger Brother, A Tale. 2 vols. London, 1770–1772.

Zimmerman, Everett. *History and the Novel in the British 18th Century*. Ithaca: Cornell UP, 1996.

Zuroski, Eugenia. *A Taste for China: English Subjectivity and the Prehistory of Orientalism.* Oxford: Oxford UP, 2013.

Zuroski, Eugenia, and Michael Yonan. "A Dialogue as Introduction." *Eighteenth-Century Fiction* 31, no. 2 (2019): 253–270.

Zwicker, Steven N. *Politics and Language in Dryden's Poetry: The Art of Disguise.* Princeton: Princeton UP, 1982.

Index

satire, 45, 97, 135; and Addison, 97, 98, 101, 103; on antiquarianism, 22, 24–27, 39–40; and artifactual form, 203; and Burke, 178; and Byron, 186; and Dryden, 80, 89, 92, 95; and Johnstone, 104; and manuscripts, 26, 119, 123; and Smollett, 138, 156, 159–60; and Swift, 138, 145, 146, 147, 153; and H. Walpole, 119, 123, 130, 135; and Woodward's shield, 151, 152

science, 34, 42, 48, 54, 55, 82, 167; and Don Saltero's, 52, 53, 63; and exhumations of kings, 166, 171, 172–73, 174, 177; and history, 52–53, 135; and Steele, 58; and Swift, 145, 147, 152; and Woodward, 152

scientists, 3, 26–27, 63, 79

Scott, Sir Walter, 105, 144; *The Antiquary*, 26

Scriblerians, 152

scrofula. *See* king(s), and royal touch

Serres, Michel, 200

Seven Years' War, 104, 158, 160, 162, 223n27

Seymour, Edward, 30

Shadwell, Thomas, 40; *The Virtuoso*, 24

Shaftesbury, Earl of, 88–89, 96, 101; medal of, 90–92, 93–94, 95, 106

Shakespeare, William, 172

Shebbeare, John, 223n27

Shelley, Percy Bysshe, 174, 175; "Charles the First," 188, 189; "Defense of Poetry," 15, 166, 188, 189–90; "Ozymandias," 15, 166, 190–91; *The Triumph of Life*, 188

Sicily, 126–27, 129

Sidney, Algernon, 39

Sloane, Sir Hans, 47, 116, 218n12

Smollett, Tobias, 15; *Complete History*, 127, 159; *Peregrine Pickle*, 66; *Sir Launcelot Greaves*, 66, 138, 156–62, 223n27

Society of Antiquaries, 25, 26, 38–39, 47, 166, 167, 175, 180, 183, 218n12, 223–24n4

Somers, William, 146

Somner, William: *Antiquities of Canterbury*, 35–38; *The Insecuritie of Princes*, 35–36

souvenirs, 7, 9–10, 11

sovereigns, 5, 22, 32–33, 59, 177, 189. *See also* king(s); monarchs

sovereignty, 14, 48, 191, 194, 206

Spectator, The, 13, 48–49, 63–64, 67, 69–75

speculative realism, 42, 209n26

Spenser, Edmund, *The Faerie Queene*, 154

spirit, 22, 35, 36–37, 49, 50, 54, 71, 105

Squirrell, Robert, 51

Statutes of Oxford, 127, 128

Steele, Richard, 64, 66, 67, 70, 73, 74, 214n11, 222n17; and Don Saltero's, 50–51, 53–54, 55, 58–59, 98

Stephen, 128, 159

Stonehenge, 1, 2

stone henges, 1–2, 3, 4, 80, 81

St. Paul's Cathedral, 138

Stuarts, 31, 112

supernaturalism, 28, 120, 128, 132. *See also* occult

superstition, 28, 31, 53, 55, 56, 71, 84, 120, 121, 160

suspicion, hermeneutics of, 22, 45, 46

Swift, Jonathan, 15, 50, 143, 153, 154, 222n18; "Apology," 151; *Battel of the Books*, 148–49; *Gulliver's Travels*, 145; *Journal*, 145; *Mechanical Operation of the Spirit*, 149; *Miscellaneous Works*, 149–50; *Tale of a Tub*, 138, 145–48, 149–52, 156, 162

Tanner, Bishop, 123

Tatler, The, 50, 58, 67, 73

Temple, William, 146

Thelwall, John, 174

Theobald, Lewis, 59

thing theory, 5, 42, 147, 195, 209n26

Thomas, John, 166

Tories, 58, 59, 70, 146, 150, 156

Tower of London, 15, 137–44, 145–46, 147, 159

truth, 12, 56, 193, 201; and Addison, 64; and Beckett, 56–57; and Burnet, 57; and coins, 14, 81, 84, 88, 110, 194; and Don Saltero's, 53, 64; and Dryden, 89; and Hurd, 156; and Johnstone, 80; and Rushworth, 116–17; and Shelley, 191; and Smollett, 159, 162; and Swift, 162; and H. Walpole, 125, 134; and Whalley, 63

tyranny, 32, 34, 125, 128, 129, 132, 134, 148, 187, 188. *See also* despotism; king(s)

Vertue, George, *Medals, Coins, Great-Seals, Impressions*, 85, 121

vibrancy, 12–13, 22, 50, 63, 81, 89

violence, 138, 145, 146, 147, 148, 150, 154, 157, 159, 162, 163. *See also* war

Virgil, 149

vitalism, 15, 33–35, 40, 49, 166; and Burke, 177–79; and Byron, 185, 187, 188; and Dryden, 90, 94–95; and Shelley, 174, 188, 189, 190; and Somner, 36, 37

Vitruvius, 2